35 Video Podcasting Careers & Businesses to Start

◆

Step-by-Step Guide for Home-Grown Broadcasters

Anne Hart

ASJA Press
New York Lincoln Shanghai

35 Video Podcasting Careers & Businesses to Start
Step-by-Step Guide for Home-Grown Broadcasters

Copyright © 2005 by Anne Hart

ASJA Press
an imprint of iUniverse, Inc.

iUniverse books may be ordered through booksellers or by contacting:

iUniverse
2021 Pine Lake Road, Suite 100
Lincoln, NE 68512
www.iuniverse.com
1-800-Authors (1-800-288-4677)

ISBN-13: 978-0-595-37882-1
ISBN-10: 0-595-37882-X

Printed in the United States of America

Contents

1

DESCRIPTION OF BUSINESS

Launching Your Career or Business in Video Podcasting

The Video Podcast Infomercial

Are you looking for a job in video podcasting? Then start by researching the newest trends—compressed video in small mobile players such as cell phones and iPod-like devices. Anyone with a digital video camcorder, microphone, computer and some technical savvy can launch an Internet video podcast show to inform, direct or enlighten. You can offer foresight, insight, or hindsight. Open a business or find a job delivering digital video recordings—usually free—as podcasts.

If you want to make money with video podcasting, offer to sell a sponsor's publicity and advertising on your video, or an author's creative works, interviews, or sermons. You can even show people how to fill out tax forms using a video podcast for instruction on most any subject people can learn independently.

People who subscribe to video podcasts usually want to view for free. You can charge for a course to train or teach a class by video lecture and/or demonstration, but what if you want an actual paid job in video podcasting? And can you make more money in video than in the older, audio MP3 file 'radio' podcasting?

Check out the RSSJobs Web site at: http://www.rssjobs.com/index.jsp?cid=10. Careers in video podcasting are beginning to bloom as seen by a variety of podcasting associations, news publications, and career information. Even job listings unrelated to podcasting are 'broadcast' by RSS feeds. You can create your own job in podcasting by showing others how to find passion in their careers and making motivational video podcasts, but what if you want to use video podcasting to actually get hired? Are there jobs in video podcasting yet? Or is the field still primarily for entrepreneurs on the Web?

Any job you'd get right now would be as a content producer for a large news corporation, as an online journalist, or in the technical end of setting up podcast tedhnology for larger corporations in information dissemination and news broadcasting or at colleges that offer courses online.

To get into the field, you might start with your own video podcasting Web site offering to help others find highly valued hard-to-find information or data so new the media hasn't seen it yet. Video podcasting is a font-loading ancillary like a newsletter-type trade journal particular to a specific industry. An example would be a video podcast on the latest news in XYZ widget manufacture on what deals the competition are signing or what's new in a specific industry. The difference between a slow, paper print industrial newsletter or trade journal and a video podcast is the speed the news is delivered, fresh from an RSS feed.

When you use RSS feeds to look for any type of job, you use an RSS Reader to make Web browsing less time consuming. An RSS feed researches every RSS capable site you want to read at one time. The feed gives you a list of everything on the site. The RSS feed also lets you know which items you've already read. Then it highlights the updated and new Web sites that you haven't seen.

Not only can you search for a job, but you can find a job, make a career, or open your own business writing, producing, and syndicating video podcasts. What's in it for you? And how can you compete with the huge news TV conglomerates already distributing free news video podcasts on the Web? Podcasting also is a global pulpit. Churches are using video podcasts.

Aren't the news organizations merging, downsizing, and employing fewer newsgathering personnel in favor of expanding news syndication channels? Video podcasts are not only for news and opinion. Compressed video files on Web sites that can be downloaded to mobile players such as video iPods and comparable devices are wonderful tools for learning and creative innovation. Video content finally has been democratized.

Podcasting, a term originally based on the name for Apple's portable media player and similar devices from its competition, allows customers to download audio and/or video segments for free to their computers and portable devices. The popularity of home-grown broadcasters is revolutionizing movie making. In a parallel information dissemination industry, print-on-demand publishing revolutionized the ability of freelance journalists to become published book authors.

Here are the steps you can follow to learn how to open a business producing short video segments that can play on viewers' mobile players or personal computers. These video segments can be how-to information, interviews with authors, courses, tutorials, religious sermons, life stories, animation/cartoons, games, plays, narrated, dramatized novels, science, travel, parenting skills, children's programming, music, dance, poetry, infomercials, reality TV, historical, news, opinions, health, nutrition, exotic, ancient, or traditional ethnic weddings, rites of passage celebrations, reviewing movies, books or other creative projects such as architecture, housing, or virtual reality, sports, competitions, job interviews, exercise, comedy, or financial advice.

Broadcast commentary or conduct interviews about business, politics, global trade, environmental science, organizational communications management, or anything that is popular culture, high-brow, ethnic traditions, folklore, comedy and humor. Research what topic is most in demand by niche audiences compared to what is requested by the general public.

Your video podcasts may be aimed at various age groups, children, adolescents, parents, honeymooners, young marrieds, middle-aged empty nesters, or mature adults and gerontologists. If you do your market research before you start, you'll find an audience or special interest group for your expertise or field of concentration.

Offer an alternative from the usual cooking shows seen on satellite TV, such as special diets or vegan cooking, or ethnic and holiday cooking not seen on TV, such as cooking without added trans-fats, salt or sugar, or cooking for metabolic syndrome. Or offer after-school tutoring or home-schooling with videos of trips to local museums. Perhaps you want to show video segments of what's it like to be old or how parents can solve problems with new babies or pet training. You're the expert in the topic. Videos can serve hobbies such as scrap booking and quilting or hiking local trails. Or show what's it like at work in different careers aimed at young people deciding on what college major to choose.

The popularity of home-based entrepreneurial broadcasting revolutionized the creative expression industry. Home-grown radio shows, called podcasts are saved as audio MP3 files and uploaded to the Web. Bandwidth-saving video compression software takes up far less space than the usual .mpeg or wmv. video files uploaded to the Web.

Following in the steps of the largest news conglomerates that feature online video news segments, home-grown audio broadcasting soon evolved into online, downloadable video. From school lectures, politics, and pet training to music, comedy, and life stories, video segments can be compressed and saved to small, mobile players such as video iPods.

News programs are among the most popular podcasts, but amateurs have changed podcasting into a global phenomenon. Video podcasts can help you learn a foreign language, plan travel, or entertain kids with movies or games in an auto's back seat while you drive.

What sells best to the general public in video podcasting is how-to information specific to very specialized niche areas. Examples would be how to knit a certain type of garment, how to home-school children in a specific subject, how to build a tool shed, dog house, or repair a broken toilet, sink, or other appliance.

If you think video podcasting will follow the type of entertainment that's on satellite TV stations, you're correct. The music videos, the talking-head lectures from distance learning universities, and the general fare that you see on TV and pay TV will be what will also be offered on video podcast. However, you'll see the niche, underground, and hidden markets as well.

What' you'll see on video podcasts are tutoring in high-school or middle-school subjects as well as university courses, weddings and funeral eulogies, pet training and house-sitting, numerology and astrology, psychic readers, the usual pornography videos, and religious programming. You'll also see more distance learning and home schooling alternatives, more travel and extreme telecommuting to one's job or business from anywhere on the globe with Internet access on the go.

Video content competes with the entire entertainment industry and schools. To sell your video content, you need to market your video clips as if they were self-published books competing with all the books on bookstore shelves. But even in the book industry, a little more than 55% of books are lined on the bookshelves.

The rest are sold in niche, hidden markets. Examples would be sports, gift, and specialty stores, book fairs, school librarians, and in specialty catalogues. School librarians buy contemporary controversies and issues in the news books and pamphlets that students use to research term papers.

Follow the market that school librarians buy from. Lead with video podcasts. Provide research and resources that help students organize their assignments, term papers, and debates. Follow the money and the markets used by self-published book authors that are successful in marketing their wares. Market your video podcasts—to niche audiences and markets by launching your content in the media.

Educators, preachers, advertisers, counselors, consultants, lawyers, doctors, dancers, artists, musicians, politicians, historians, librarians, movie producers, documentarians, life story videographers, chefs, knitters, crafters, dog trainers, house remodelers, contractors, strippers, pornographers, social scientists, radio talk show hosts, demographers, novelists, scientists, lecturers, travel agents, professional travelers, resort owners, publicists, public speakers, activists, infomercial producers, journalists, playwrights, parents, students, sales representatives, song writers, rappers, and poets (and anyone else with video content) have equal access to video podcast production and content creation.

The common denominator of what might sell as video podcast content and become a viable business is whether the content offers the audience what the specific audience wants to see. Some of the best markets are how-to videos that show people how to solve a problem and get results step-by-step so the viewers can follow.

Here's how to start a career, get a job, or open a variety of businesses in video podcasting. It's about putting up on the Internet's Web video content that anyone with a device such as a video iPod can download video content. If you want a job in video podcasting, you can work for the companies that make the equipment—hardware or software, or those who produce the video content. Or you can start your own business by putting your own video on your Web site. All you need is a camcorder, a computer, and a software program that edits your video so you can create a video podcast online.

Content is in demand now, that video podcasting is still in its infancy. So there's room to jump in at any age and from any niche.

You can still go the relatively "old fashioned" route for your latest music television productions (MTV) if you're a musician by looking at the content available through music stores online such as the iTunes Music Store. Or you can put your own content online for streaming video that's downloadable to devices such as iPods and its competition.

School lectures, foreign language learning, and anything that can be taught are ripe for video podcasting. You can open your own school and teach what you're expert in, without having to show your degrees and licenses, as long as a license or degree is not required for the subject you're teaching. An example would be on how to knit dog sweaters or how to publicize your book. You can interview authors and put up a speaker's panel that people can download on life experiences.

Examples of a video podcast movie would be *Crookz*, a video podcast (iTMS link) spoof of *Cops*, is offered at the iTunes Music Store. View what's out there, and then make your own movies, documentaries, or other video offerings.

What you need to start your own video podcasting production business is a Web camera called a 'webcam' and a digital video camera, called a "DV camera." Creating a video podcast is the first step in becoming a video producer on a neighborhood budget.

Podcast listening is not for music fans any more. Students want to see lectures in video. Older adults want to see their life stories on an iPod or other small, lightweight, mobile device. Children want to see video while they sit in the back seat of cars when on long vacation rides. Adults want to see automobile travel videos showing them where they are going.

So by democratizing video content on the Web with video podcasting enterprises and services, the whole movement of video production for all is following in the path of print on demand published authors. And you need to market your video podcasts much in the same way as print-on-demand published authors market their books to specialized, niche audiences and markets.

It's a revolution that you want to join, moving from print-on-demand text books whose content is not controlled by copyeditors from major publishing houses to public speakers whose content is not controlled by major news media conglomerates. Now we have video content producers whose visual imagery is not controlled.

This has all come about because there are far more book authors and video producers in the masses than there are room for the converging publishing houses and large video production corporations to allow every author or producer publication or dissemination. Now everyone potentially has a voice and video content that can be heard around the world.

Blogging isn't enough because many video blogs lack credibility in the mainstream media. Video podcasting now has become simple for non-technical people to publish creative projects online. With less people reading books, and more books being published by print-on-demand authors, the door is open for businesses to step in and offer what people want: visual learning.

Video offers those who want to learn by seeing, or see how hands-on learning is actually done. Text almost always moves to audio and then to video in a learning situation.

You're still competing with the entertainment industry just as computerized interactive learning modules of the 1996 era competed with textbook publishing. According to the Apple Insider article titled, *Apple Files For Podcasting Trademark*, September 14, 2005 posted at the Web site: http://www.appleinsider.com/article.php?id=1271om, Apple has applied for trademarks relating to the word iPodcast.

If you're starting a business or looking for a job or career in the world of video podcasting, you need to list as many forms of video entertainment, learning, and leisure that would make money as video podcasts. It helps if you can find celebrities to endorse your how-to, entertainment, or infomercial video podcast.

You can produce and upload video content for other entrepreneurs, including vendors at trade shows and expos. Let's look at how to product a typical 28 ½ minute video podcast informercial for a Web site, DVD, or CD used to market a product.

If you're going to make money working in the field of video podcasting, one of the most commercial ways related to schooling or training is the infomercial for a product. Although no audience would pay to watch an infomercial, your advertiser certainly will.

Your clients would be corporations, advertising agencies, publicists, book authors, doctors and other healthcare professionals in practice with advice to sell, and manufacturers as well as technical and business training schools. Here's how you begin to develop your video podcast infomercial.

The Video Podcast Infomercial

1. Produce Video and MP3 Pod-casts and DVDs: Internet Video Infomercials Solving Problems, Revealing Results & Showing People Benefits and Profits

2. Let the viewers follow your instructions step-by-step

3. Show Advantages

Keep everything you show in a video grouped in threes. People remember three items grouped together. Information given in threes impacts the memory and stays within the average attention span for watching a video segment.

Infomercial pod casting is do-it-yourself online radio, which can also be put on disks such as DVDs or CDs. You create video podcasts as well as backup MP3 audio files that people can download from CDs, DVDs, or their computers through your Web site. Pod casting also is about listening to your infomercials on iPods and other audio players. Making videos for podcasts as well as MP3 audio files are easier and cheaper to produce than recording videos. If you want to go the video route, choose an industrial-quality camcorder, not an amateur quality.

According to the October 18, 2005 article, *Creating a Video Podcast on Mac Os X,* Apple has added a tutorial at http://www.apple.com/quicktime/tutorials/videopodcasts.html to its site giving directions you easily can follow to create a video podcast using Mac OS X and QuickTime Pro. You'll learn how to use QuickTime 7 Pro to make an .m4v file that has H.264 video and AAC audio, compatible with iTunes and the latest iPods.

To produce professional-quality podcasts, you need an RSS feed. Check out the site at: http://www.masternewmedia.org/news/2005/03/22/where_to_find_the_right.htm. There are search engines and directories entirely devoted to the indexing of RSS feeds. Read eWeek at: http://www.eweek.com/. Build your own RSS feed for your Web site. Go to *Feed for All RSS Feed Creation Tool* at: http://www.feedforall.com/. Pay attention to the *FeedForAll* Web site if you want to learn how to create, edit, manage, and publish RSS feeds.

According to the site, RSS is the standard for content distribution and syndication. The reason you create an RSS feed is to keep visitors to your Web site informed of current material. New RSS feeds can be quickly and easily created with *FeedForAll*. Advanced features enable you to easily and rapidly create professional looking RSS feeds. Also, read the informative book titled, *Syndicating Web Sites with RSS Feeds for Dummies* by Ellen Finkelstein, ISBN: 0764588486, published 2005.

Learn about podcasting because you can build your business around your own podcasts. This is one more way to show people how to cut expenses. Your audio books also can be podcasted as MP3 audio files and narrated as video podcasts saved as Windows Media files or mpeg, or any other file extension commonly accepted by the audience for video podcasts. Where you find this information is in the numerous video podcasts magazines and e-zines on the Web. In your search engine use the key words "video podcasting how-to publications" and take your pick of this burgeoning information industry.

Another way to publish audio books as narrated video podcasts is to promote business clients by having dramatizations and public speakers or panels and interviews as video podcasts. Author interviews are a good way to start interviewing people on video or dramatizing documentaries from real life or life story applications. Streaming video and DVD multimedia also are other possibilities.

You can use podcasting to create travel or neighborhood walking and touring guides, talk about any subject, or show people by example how to cut expenses. It's about making your audio files mobile. People not only listen to current information at Web sites, but also can listen to advertising at trade shows. Podcast online or on disk infomercials and instruction on any subject, including how to start niche-market businesses.

Show others how to save money by shopping for shelf-pulls and overstocked items at hidden markets. Help your audience find little-known opportunities. Offer tips for making non-toxic cleaning products from basic household ingredients, spices, or natural scents.

Sure, you can record to CDs, DVDs, or your Web site, but podcasting is the current trend—broadcasting news from your Web site or downloading the audio MP3 file to an iPod or other audio device.

Downloading video via portable devices is here now. Podcasting in MP3 audio to Web sites is like 1940 radio compared to current high definition television. Video is as mobile as audio is mobile. People listen to talk or music podcasting and radio while driving, but view video podcasts when at school lectures, in libraries, while hiking, and when riding public in transportation. An example would be while taking a long overseas or cross-country flight.

Use podcasting for training sessions. Put travel guides in the podcasting formats so people can download the video MP4 and/or audio MP3 files as they walk through various neighborhoods. The podcast video promises mobility of viewing dramatizations and documentaries or listening to hundreds of songs or lectures, books, or training materials, even learning foreign languages saved in the MP3 file format and also podcasted from your Web site as news or easy listening. Anything that can be recorded in video can be viewed as a video podcast and used as instruction or entertainment. Combined, you get 'edutainment.'

Your next step is to develop direct mail copywriting on podcasts or DVDs to show people how to cut expenses. Infomercial producers can write or hire a freelancer to write infomercials sharing information with people on how to cut expenses and get higher quality goods from hidden markets such as shelf pulls and overstocked items or wholesale items that may be ordered by anyone.

Video podcasting infomercials are similar in production techniques to the "cable TV" and trade show-style infomercial. These 28 1/8 minute-in-length ads broadcast direct mail marketing programs and track TV-shopping audiences. Direct mail copywriting and producing for video telemarketing is one of the highest paying freelance writing available. The manufacturers of the product pay you to podcast the infomercial or produce it on a DVD.

Writers who specialize in writing direct mail copy for both print mail order and video infomercials headed for cable, Internet, or Satellite television can create thriving writing and production businesses catering to telemarketing and mail order corporate clients and copywriters. Another career track is to write in-house for firms who manage telemarketing.

For those who enjoy the music business, contact musicians, and open a business that sells their music to the movie industry. Another venue is medical marketing. Write reviews of audio books and videos online or for magazines.

You have a choice of either writing or producing an infomercial or doing both. An infomercial is a long commercial video, running to a half-hour in length, but usually precisely timed at 28 1/2 minutes. It's created to sell by telemarketing. The best infomercial producers use around 400 cuts with music. Many people are interviewed in the infomercial.

Infomercials wait for audience response. The viewer orders the product or service by phoning a toll-free number or sending money to an address flashed on the screen to order the product.

A demonstration video script that solicits audience response through telemarketing on cable stations, or a videobiography script for non-broadcast television personifies and proves a point. Read the book Response Television, by John Witek, Crain Books, Chicago, IL (1981), to get an idea of how response television works. Also read Television and Cable Contacts, Larimi Communications Associates, Ltd., 5 W. 37th St., New York, NY 10018 (212) 819-9310.

INCOME POTENTIAL:

Video producers of infomercials charge by the hour plus production expenses. The current fees vary with location and complexity of job required. Some producers charge $35 and up an hour plus expenses of production. Check the current rate in your area charged by your competition. Check the current rate in your area charged by your competition. Others create a budget with all expenses first, including cost of tape and crew's requirements, then add an hourly fee, plus the post-production editing and distribution expenses.

BEST LOCALE TO OPERATE THE BUSINESS:

Infomercials can be produced on-site at any location of a business. Being near your clients helps. Big centers for production of infomercials include Los Angeles, San Francisco, San Diego, New York, Chicago, and Orlando, Florida. San Francisco is the hub for multimedia and interactive infomercials, including the San Jose/Silicon Valley area for the software infomercials.

TRAINING REQUIRED:

It's best to take courses in video production or read books on how to produce infomercials before you begin. Join professional associations and volunteer. Attend trade shows for infomercial producers and watch a variety of infomercials. Study the number of cuts in popular infomercials.

GENERAL APTITUDE OR EXPERIENCE:

Creativity, imagination, and experience with a variety of sales and marketing alternatives are beneficial. You're always offering the benefits and advantages of a product. Therefore, sales and marketing training combined with video production experience or coursework is best. It will save you money if you can write your own scripts as well.

EQUIPMENT NEEDED:

You'll need your Internet or digital video camera attached to your PC and hooked into your Internet Service Provider, narrator, host, editing equipment or access to video editing services, your video crew, and a good sound stage or work area to tape the commercial. There should be an audience, and special effects to show the phone number and address where television viewers can phone or send in the order for the product. You'll need to hire operators who take the call on a 24-hour basis. Charge phone expenses to your client's budget.

You'll also need a computer to track your customers so you'll have a list of television viewers who shop after watching infomercials. Watch infomercials and note the special effects used.

OPERATING YOUR BUSINESS:

Escape doesn't work in a how-to infomercial. A viewer watching a tape on on how to buy real estate doesn't want to be swept away to a castle in a fantasy setting for long. It might work in an infomercial selling a general idea or theory that applies to many people in many jobs, such as how to get power and success in relationships or careers.

Infomercial scriptwriters don't resort to gimmicks. They give information for decision-making by presenting the points in as straightforward a manner as possible for intelligent decision-making. The questions of who, what, how, why, where, and when are answered as in an in-depth straight news article.

The viewers want to be well-informed before they spend their life-savings, their "blood money" on a cable television advertisement. They are wondering whether they can buy it cheaper in a store or at the swap meet as they dial the phone.

Will they be hit with a handling and shipping charge that raises the cost another ten dollars? The customer wonders what happens when they give their credit card number to a total stranger on a toll-free number across the country. Who else will have access to that credit card number?

Some beginning infomercial writers turn out scripts that use the techniques of a Hollywood filmmaker to make people watch. Instead, they should be writing to make people buy one brand over another. There's no correlation between a person liking an infomercial and being sold by it.

Use direct, tough commercials because they work. Hard hitting, informative infomercials and commercials sell a product where the customer is watching solely to get information. Soft-sell imagery doesn't work in infomercials like they do in 30-second commercials selling the imagery of the pleasure of eating a bar of chocolate.

Infomercials emphasize believability, clarity, and simplicity over creativity. Don't write confusion into a script by putting in too much dazzle, sensation, and entertainment that overpower the information and message. The emphasis is on helping the customer make a sensible purchase.

Small budgets often do better than big ones in the infomercial for cable T.V. production. TV's longest-running commercial which offers a record set of "150 Music Masterpieces" through mail order by phoning a toll-free number, was made in 1968 for only $5,000. It sold millions of dollars worth of records through mail order because of this one television advertisement.

There are a dozen types of infomercials. They include the following:

1) Product demonstration.

Scripts are used for trade show exhibition and continuous loop playing.

2) Testimonials.

Real people on tape add credibility for a product.

3) The pitchman.

A straight narrator delivers a sales pitch on the product to give vital information in the shortest period of time. This is a talking head short that should only be used for brief commercials or a scene in an infomercial of less than 10 seconds.

4) Slice-of-life.

This is a dramatization between two people and a product.

In an infomercial or training script, the dramatization is a container that can be used to portray true-life events to teach people how to make decisions or how and where to get information.

5) Socio-economic lifestyle.

The social class of the user is emphasized to show how the product fits into a certain economic class such as blue collar, yuppie, new parent, career woman climbing the ladder, or senior citizen retiree.

Examples are Grey Poupon, the upper-caste mustard selling to social climbers and Miller Beer dedicated to blue collar workers celebrating the idea of the working man and woman being rewarded for hard labor with a cold beer.

6) Animation.

Cartoon infomercials sell to children in school and at home. Adults become impatient watching a cartoon demonstration. Animation is expensive to produce for cable television. Use it only to sell to children or to sell supplies to professional animators in non-broadcast demonstration video tapes used to sell products through mail order or at an animator's trade show or exhibit.

7) Jingles.

Lyrics work in short commercials because they are remembered. A best-selling board game called '*Adverteasements*' makes players recall all the advertising jingles and trivia information from their past. Ask any person in the street to sing the jingle of an advertisement, and chances are he or she will remember the jingle.

8) The mini-feature film with visual effects.

(Case studies don't report that action set in fantasy 'scapes' sells more products.)

9) Humor.

In short commercials humor works well as in "Where's the beef?" In long infomercials, it distracts from the information. Some humor can be used to prove a point in a long commercial. Infomercials sell credibility. Humor distracts from believability.

10) Serial characters.

A fictional character who appears in print ads and short commercials, such as Mr. Whipple or the Pillsbury Doughboy is very effective.

In a longer commercial, viewers will soon tire of the fantasy character and change the channel. Infomercial viewers want to see real people's testimonials, people like themselves with whom they can identify. Keep the fictional character out of a true-story informational commercial. People want references. Give them references who testify why the product works so well.

11. Tell-me-why infomercials.

Give people reasons why the product works as it does and why they should buy it. Reason-why copy works better in print than in a short T.V. or radio commercial. However, in an infomercial for cable, obtaining "tell me why" information is the reason people watch in the first place. Viewers want the writer to go ahead. Make their day.

12. Feelings, Intuition, and Sensation.

Tug at my guilt-strings. Persuasive infomercials use feelings backed up by logical points that prove a point about a product. Move the viewer by writing genuine emotional copy. A dramatization showing a person shedding tears of joy that someone has telephoned long distance is persuasive. It makes viewers feel guilty they haven't called their mother in years. Infomercials emphasize demonstrations, testimonials, pitchpersons, and straight-sell formulas.

A little emotion within a dramatization can be very persuasive. Either it will sell the product or evoke guilt and anger in the viewer for not having lived up to expectations. The viewer could have conflicting feelings.

He may not want to call someone he dislikes because of having suffered emotional abuse in that person's presence. A whole slew of nasty or sentimental feelings totally unrelated to selling the product can be unleashed by one emotional scene in a commercial.

The emotional, "tug at my guilt-strings" 'approach' works when selling nostalgia. Emotion persuades people to make more telephone calls, or send more candy and flowers by wire.

Using the emotion strategy in infomercials works well for selling sentiment, communications products, craft and knitting machines, charm bracelets, products for the elderly, or greeting cards. Look at the success of the long-running AT&T commercial, "Reach Out and Touch Someone." Who doesn't remember that command to extravert?

To write an infomercial that sells, first find out the producer's budget. Then deliver a selling message within the budget and time limits. Turn the sound off. Can you still understand what is being sold? Sight and sound works together. Use sound only to explain what the picture is demonstrating.

Keep the pictures simple. Use words to make an impact, the fewer the words, the better. The more complex the graphics, the few the words are used to explain them. Computer graphics, special effects, and animation are expensive. The stand-up presenter and demonstrator cost much less.

Ninety words can be spoken in 60 seconds. Forty-five words can be crammed into 30 seconds. Many 30 and 60-second commercials contain far less words so the viewer can really get the information. Compare this to the print ad which usually runs 1,500 words in a 30–60 second read.

Sell every second the script is on the airwaves. The first four seconds of an infomercial are the same as the headlines of a print ad. The viewer takes four seconds to decide if he/she will sit through the rest of the infomercial or commercial.

Open the infomercial with a real-life situation. It must hook the viewer in those first four seconds. The music and visuals can add the background. The opening is called the cow-catcher. It's supposed to grab the viewer. After seven minutes, the average attention span wanes quickly.

Use motion to keep attention riveted. Show the syrup pouring, the machines working, the demonstrator moving. Let the viewer hear the whirr of the machine as it moves forward. The sound is more appetizing than the look.

Use titles superimposed over the picture to reinforce a sales point not covered in the narration. The address and phone of the company are always superimposed in addition to the narrator's spoken words. What if the viewers are deaf or blind, can they still read or hear the infomercial? Have titles superimposed on the info-mercial saying "Not available in stores," when applicable.

The market for Spanish language infomercials is skyrocketing in the South-west and in California and Mexico. Bilingual video scriptwriters are in demand. In some of the major cities such as Los Angeles and New York, infomercials in several foreign languages are broadcast on cable television's ethnic and foreign language programming stations or on radio.

Some video magazines to sell products are made in two languages, especially to reach the huge Hispanic market in California and the Southwest. Every infomer-cial repeats the product name and selling point several times. Most viewers aren't paying attention when the infomercial comes on. A repetitive script is necessary in this case. The product name and selling point is repeated at the beginning, middle, and end of the infomercial.

Viewers of infomercials get bored quickly if the presenter isn't somewhat dif-ferent. Use a child who looks five years old, for example, to sell a product emo-tionally. Have an adult present the points and logic behind the demonstration for credibility.

Show people using the product constantly throughout the infomercial. Prod-uct neglect is the primary reason why infomercials don't sell. Show people dem-onstrating, talking about, and applying the product to many different uses. Proven techniques in print ads also work in television infomercials, such as color reversals, black background with white letters superimposed over a photo, etc. In infomercials, viewers call or write to order the product.

Announce this at the beginning with something like, "Get your pencil and paper ready to take advantage of this one-time offer." Few people sit down in front of a T.V. set with a notepad. It's entertainment time.

The infomercial is an unwanted intrusion that angers a lot of people. Late night infomercials interrupt late night films. People may be grumpy at 3:00 a.m. or 5:00 a.m. when many infomercials are broadcast. Prime-time cable infomercials interrupt the entertainment. Give people a chance to get out of bed or away from the graveyard shift desk clerk slot and get paper and pencil.

Use a celebrity to do a voice-over or on-camera narration. Identify the celebrity by name and superimposed title. In local retail infomercials, give the directions or address of the store.

Short T.V. and radio commercial basic lengths run 10, 30,60, and 120 seconds. Infomercials run 5, and 30 minutes. The 30 minute length actually runs 28 1/2 minutes. Infomercial lengths stop short of 30 minutes or 5 minutes to allow for short commercials to be broadcast before and after the infomercial on cable T.V. stations.

The 10-second commercials identify a product to support another longer commercial. Sometimes two different product companies share one commercial—offering two different products.

Mail order advertisers use 2-minute infomercials on T.V. to be convincing, then follow up the campaign on cable T.V. with a longer infomercial to give more complete product demonstration. Cooking shows that demonstrate appliances such as food choppers are popular.

A short T.V. commercial sticks to one main sales point. Only in five to thirty-minute infomercials and in print brochures is there the time to cover all the points. So the only reason a person watches an infomercial or reads a lengthy sales brochure is to consider the most important points you want to emphasize.

The video script format for infomercials uses the two-column format. Video (visuals) is typed on the left. Audio (sound, music, speech, and special effects) is typed on the right.

The video directors are given in upper and lower case letters. The audio or speaking part is typed in capital letters so the narrator or actor can see the speaking parts stand out for easy reading or memorization.

The visuals show the product demonstration. The narration tells the viewers the unique features and benefits of the product. Don't tell how good it is, tell how it will benefit the viewer.

The ending makes the most impact. A play on words can lend humor to the script if it also lends credibility to the product and emphasizes how the customer will save money and get superior merchandise.

If something is more expensive on T.V. than it is when found in the store, sometimes the customer is persuaded by being told he's worth it. The emotional impact hits home by asking, "Don't you think I'm good enough to deserve this product?" It works particularly well on wives who know their husbands are very tight with money and affection.

The customer's attitude toward infomercials is "When someone starts to make money, someone else will appear to take it away." To combat this psychological attitude, infomercial producers focus on "target marketing." It's the idea of having different promotional videos aimed at various segments of the market.

Software sometimes labeled in artsy language, which simply said is "aiming." In a direct campaign, you target a specific audience of consumers or niche market that includes short news releases explaining the purpose and main pointers in the infomercial. The summary may *aim* an infomercial campaign at doctors by sending video tapes to *hospitals' training departments* and another infomercial campaign aimed at *lawyers*—for the same computer product. You look at what lawyers and doctors have in common—the need for training on software that does *specific tasks* that both lawyers and hospitals' training departments perform.

A writer of infomercial scripts uses numerous testimonials, endorsements, and product claims highlighted by music, hundreds of cuts to the product, to users of the product, to satisfied customers amidst a background of special lighting and entertainment to maintain the viewer's attention for the half-hour commercial.

The average adult's attention span for viewing a non-fiction video is only seven minutes. Cut this to five minutes for children's attention spans. Commercials often are inserted in TV programs after each ten-minute segment.

The quality of an infomercial writer's script can be carefully measured by audience tracking to see how many orders for the product come in at any time. A video demonstration tape or video magazine acts as a company brochure to sell a product requiring non-impulse buying. The customer still has to come into a store or send away for the product, such as real estate.

This is the age of product intelligence for video scriptwriters. Consumers demand real information. Information has turned the word 'sell' into a noun as in information becoming "real sell."

Infomercials on television advertising became popular when the cost of buying time on cable television became low. Advertisers can afford to run five minute to half-hour commercials on cable.

The video scriptwriter of infomercials needs to give complete information and a sales pitch at the same time. Interactive technologies allow viewers at home or corporate viewers at the office or plant to choose which segments of an infomercial they wish to see instead of flipping through a parts catalogue.

Corporate viewers now use their computer keyboards to order products seen on a video tape linked to their computer through desktop video devices. Desktop video enables viewers to interact with a personal computer at home or in the office and with a video cassette tape played on a home or office VCR player and send out orders through a computer modem to anyone's telephone number, usually, with a toll-free 800 number.

Consumers are hungry for information by which they make decisions. A video writer puts in information and leaves out the jingles and other frills seen on short T.V. broadcast commercials that imprint the brain and wring the emotions.

In one survey, 68 percent of viewers said that short commercials don't give any points about a product. They only create an image. An infomercial is designed to give important points. It's similar to a product demonstration tape script or an instructional video.

Information alone is not remembered. The viewer will always take images emotionally. A creative writer's tendency to achieve dramatic results by waiving the rules works in short commercials where style and form evoke more emotions than substance.

For example, a black background with white lettering where the white lettering is printed over or with a photo background imprints the brain. People remember a reversed color advertisement better than white background with black letters.

The success rates of infomercials that break the rules are unpredictable. Video copywriters use what works to obtain consistently high sales results. In any bookstore the how-to books dominate and appeal to the mass audience reader. People come in for straight information when they want to make decisions on what to buy or how to build it.

HOW TO WRITE THE SCRIPTS FOR THE VIDEOS YOU WILL PRODUCE:

Use symbolism and metaphor in your infomercial. A script can visualize the waves of the ocean, flow of a river, or waterfall, or ticking of a clock with the handles speeded up to show the passage of time or evolution of a species. A toy crane truck can recreate an accident to teach decision-making.

Use symbolism and metaphor on camera to re-create the events of your life as they flow, perhaps, by showing the flowing river near a client's hometown.

Symbolism creates new meanings in a script. The symbol must be recognizable by the audience and cross-cultural. What works in one culture may be taboo in another. Find out what the taboo colors are for the country the video will go to.

For example, in Saudi Arabia, red is a taboo color. Writing is never shown in red ink. In China certain shades of blue signify death. Exporters who featured blue dishes in China found the products didn't sell because of the shade. Color symbols are important if the tape is headed for export.

In video production, symbolism is used in corporate history videos to show the change of a company's product. It can also show someone age on camera or grow up from childhood. Metaphor compares a person to another object.

In an infomercial (to publicize someone's color consulting franchise whose logo is a rose), show the main character or proprietor to symbolize her logo. She is like a rose and is selling a product that is supposed to remind the viewer of everything a rose symbolizes. The product is like a rose. It's colorful,-sweet-scented, and blooming.

To symbolize this imagery in a video script, cut to the leading character's velvet, black hair and pouting, red lips. Then cut to a bouquet of dark, red rose. Go back to the character walking through her home dressed in the same shade of red to form a certain imagery of the soul of Spain or a wild, Irish rose.

Then a quick cut to her business, a color consulting firm, where she's matching the red shades of a lipstick to a client's best colors. Then cut to your logo stationery, a red rose. A final cut to a bouquet of red roses is placed in her arms as she welcomes her new baby home, named Rose. (The client may want the baby to turn into the business logo on camera.)

HOW DO ALL THESE CONTAINERS FIT TOGETHER TO PRODUCE AN INFOMERCIAL?

A video script's design is composed of all those containers, edited together, fitted side by side. The important points plus the container adds up to (or equals) the springboard.

A creative springboard is the sum total of each container and each point combined, edited together, fitted so that the whole video or film flows like one piece of cloth with no seams or hanging threads. Is the script sound-oriented for radio, or audio-text? A visually-oriented script with fewer words is filled with symbolism and metaphor instead of straight points. Which creative springboard does the producer define?

Time is budget. A sound-oriented or verbal script's purpose is to <u>persuade</u>, to inform, to warn, to close a sale, to obtain feedback, or to be remembered. A visually-oriented script is there to entertain, evoke emotions, and imprint the imagery on a viewer's brain which will be recalled later without thinking. It's subliminal.

Verbal-oriented video scripts offer information that enable viewers to make intelligent decisions about a product or service. Subliminals imbedded in an infomercial are never revealed verbally. Infomercials and information videos work on the left-hemisphere of the brain, the logical, analytical, decision-making side that seeks verbal information.

Visual-oriental scripts work on the right hemisphere of the brain that controls emotions and imagery. That's where subliminals are imbedded, and art forms evoke feelings.

One day a viewer daydreams about that candy bar shown on television next to the image of a beautiful woman in flowing chiffon making romantic gestures. Who can forget the decade-plus Nestle's chocolate bar lyric in the background that begins, "Dreams like this…"?

TARGET MARKET:

Writers who specialize in writing direct mail copy for print mail order and video infomercials headed for cable, Internet, or Satellite television can create thriving writing and production businesses catering to telemarketing and mail order corporate clients and copywriters. Another career track is to write in-house for firms who manage telemarketing.

For those who enjoy the music business, contact musicians, and open a business that sells their music to the movie industry. Another venue is medical marketing.

Video and audio tapes are sent by mail order along with print advertising copy and information to customers. Video newsletters may also be included. Direct mail order copywriters for video or print write advertisements, sales letters, and demonstration video scripts to obtain orders for products such as magazine subscriptions and insurance.

A company purchases computer-sorted mailing lists of people in certain geographical, income, professional, ethnic, or age groups. The demonstration tapes or video newsletters are sent to potential customers to motivate viewers to buy a product by direct mail order. An audience-tracking study is followed up to measure the effectiveness of the written copy or the video script. If many products sold through mail order, the writer is judged excellent. The writer's income goes up. The freelancer is now in demand by infomercial producers and direct mail order copy publishers.

Anyone watching an infomercial is an information seeker. A sales video, like a feature film, informs as well as sells escape. The reason to write a nonfiction video script is to create grounds for a decision from the viewer's end. A decision is made not only about a product or service, but about those who identify with the product or feel repelled by the tape.

The infomercial producers set their own guidelines to battle poor public perception of the long-form commercials. The National Infomercial Marketing Association (NIMA) requires members to produce programs based on truthful information in compliance with laws and regulations.

Guidelines cover crucial issues such as sponsorship identification, program production, product claim substantiation, testimonials and endorsements. See the former National Infomercial Marketing Association's guidelines for members. The former National Infomercial Marketing Association is now called the Electronic Retailing Association. The group's Web site is at: http://www.retailing.org/new_site/default.asp

Writers need to work into the script the ways in which customers can order and pay for the product. What prices are fair? Can the customer buy it cheaper in a discount chain? Then why would he order from cable T.V. and pay more? Is it sold in the stores? Are similar and competing products sold in stores, but this product is sold only on T.V.?

The writer must write copy to sell at the client's prices, sometimes knowing in advance that the customer can get it cheaper in the store than by ordering from T.V. Also, what warranties are on the product? What guarantees do the claims make on T.V.? What are the guidelines for refunds?

THE NATIONAL INFOMERCIAL MARKETING ASSOCIATION
(Now called the Electronic Retailing Association)

In the early 1990s, as a condition of the National Infomercial Marketing Association (NIMA) membership, guidelines on refunds, guarantees, warranties, and prices in their information publications for members stated that refunds, guarantees, warranties, and prices are required. Not all infomercial producers are or were members of NIMA. Not all clients of infomercial producers are or were members either.

Today, as a potential video podcaster, you'd look for a client with a product if you do not produce your own product or service that you want to promote through your video podcast. It's the client who makes the product, then hires an infomercial producer as an independent contractor or freelancer. The infomercial producer either hires a freelance infomercial video scriptwriter for the project or has staff writers working in-house. Some video producers specialize only in making infomercials and nothing else in a local area. As a video podcaster, you can make your own product and promote it in your podcast. An example would be an inspirational or motivational speech or sermon, news, or a course offered online.

Back in the early nineties, membership guidelines stated that among NIMA members, if a guideline is violated, a complaint is presented to a review board—two NIMA members and three consultants. If the board finds a violation, the program must be removed from the airwaves within 10 days.

Members in good standing can certify TV station and cable networks that each infomercial complies with the guidelines. NIMA provides telecasters with a list of members in good standing every six months. By codifying the conduct of infomercial producers, the infomercial industry can be lead out of a difficult period when many viewers' attitudes toward infomercials were low.

Regulations set by NIMA state in part that each video will be preceded and followed with a clear announcement that it's a paid advertisement. There must be sufficient product to meet the demand within 30 days. There must be reliable evidence for all claims. Testimonials from consumers have to be voluntary and from bona fide users of the product. The stated price of the product must disclose all additional costs, postage, and handling.

RELATED OPPORTUNITIES:

You can produce and/or write direct mail copy for advertising agencies, direct mail firms, and manufacturers. Also, sales videos or podcasting compressed video files, MP4, or audio MP3 files can be made ready on a Web site for downloading. You can produce video podcasts for realtors, marketing research firms, distributors, and any company wishing to create video or slide-show advertisements as video podcasts. Anything you produce as a podcast also can be recorded on DVDs to mail out to customers and saved in your hard disk drive for updating.

ADDITIONAL INFORMATION:

Associations of Interest

> **American Medical Writers Association**
> **40 West Gude Drive, Suite 101**
> **Rockville, MD 20850-1192**
> **http://www.amwa.org/default.asp?ID=1**

> **National Association of**
> **Science Writers, Inc.**
> **P.O. Box 890, Hedgesville, WV 25427**
> **http://www.nasw.org/**

American Society of Journalists and Authors
1501 Broadway, Suite 302
New York, NY 10036
http://www.asja.org

Society for Technical Communication
http://www.stc.org/

Association of Professional Writing Consultants
http://www.consultingsuccess.org/index.htm

Council of the Advancement of Science Writing
P.O. Box 910
Hedgesville, WV 25427
http://www.casw.org/

Careers in Science Writing:
http://www.casw.org/careers.htm

World Association of Medical Editors
http://www.wame.org/
http://www.wame.org/index.htm

Text and Academic Authors Association
TAA
P.O. Box 76477
St. Petersburg, FL
http://www.taaonline.net/

Education Writers Association
2122 P Street, NW Suite 201
Washington, DC 20037
http://www.ewa.org/

Council of Biology Editors
http://www.monroecc.edu/depts/library/cbe.htm

American Society of Indexers (for indexing careers)
10200 West 44th Avenue, Suite 304,
Wheat Ridge, CO 80033
http://www.asindexing.org/site/index.html

Society of Professional Journalists
Eugene S. Pulliam National Journalism Center,
3909 N. Meridian St., Indianapolis, IN 46208
http://www.spj.org/

Diversified Media Associations

American Business Press
http://www.americanbusinesspress.com/

American Society of Business Press Editors
http://www.asbpe.org/

Associated Business Writers of America
http://www.poewar.com/articles/associations.htm

Associazioni ed Enti Professionali-America
http://www.alice.it/writers/grp.wri/wgrpame.htm
Contains a list of South American, Canadian, and US writers' organizations, including language translation firms.

American Marketing Association
http://www.marketingpower.com/content1539.php

Association of Professional Communications Consultants
http://www.consultingsuccess.org/index.htm

Writer's Encyclopedia A-Z List
WritersMarket.com
http://www.writersmarket.com/encyc/azlist.asp

Editorial Freelancers Association
http://www.the-efa.org/

Editor's Guild
http://www.edsguild.org/become.htm
The current online Yellow Pages, published annually since 1997 includes listings by skills as well as a specialties index. This association published the hardcopy, Yellow Pages, a listing of Association members who wished to advertise their skills and specialties, between 1989 and 1999.
http://www.tiac.net/users/freelanc/YP.html

International Women's Writing Guild
http://www.iwwg.com/index.php, Or: http://www.iwwg.com
The International Women's Writing Guild, headquartered in New York and founded in 1976, is a network for the personal and professional empowerment of women through writing.

Video Software Dealers Association
http://www.vsda.org/Resource.phx/vsda/index.htx

Public Relations Society of America
http://www.prsa.org/

Deep Dish TV
http://www.deepdishtv.org/pages/catalogue13.htm

Video History Project
http://www.experimentaltvcenter.org/history/groups/gtext.php3?id=37

Advertising Research Foundation
http://www.arfsite.org/

The Mail Preference Service
http://www.dmaconsumers.org/offmailinglist.html

Advertising Associations Directory
http://paintedcows.com/associations.html

Mailing Fulfillment Service Association
http://www.mfsanet.org/pages/index.cfm?pageid=1

Television Bureau of Advertising
http://www.tvb.org/nav/build_frameset.asp?url=/docs/homepage.asp

Home Improvement Research Institute
http://www.hiri.org/abouthiri.htm

Writers-Editors Network
http://www.writers-editors.com/

Professional and Technical Consultants Association
http://www.patca.org/html/articles/ratesurvey/ratesurvey1.htm

Association of Independent Commercial Producers
http://www.aicp.com/splash-noswf.html

National Cable & Telecommunications Association
http://www.ncta.com/

International Association of Women in Radio and Television
http://www.iawrt.org/

National Communication Association
http://www.natcom.org/nca/Template2.asp

The Association for Women in Communications
http://www.womcom.org/

Society of Telecommunications Consultants
http://www.stcconsultants.org/

European Training Media Association
http://www.etma.org/

Advertising Research Foundation
641 Lexington Avenue • New York, NY 10022
http://www.arfsite.org/

International Women's Media Foundation
http://www.iwmf.org/training/womensmedia.php

Videotex Industry Association
http://www.iit.edu/departments/csep/codes/coe/
Videotex_Industry_Association.html

Independent Publishers Group
http://www.ipgbook.com/index.cfm?userid=36155756

American Society of Media Photographers
150 North Second Street, Philadelphia, PA 19106
(Electronic imaging and digital technology)
http://www.asmp.org/

International Interactive Communications Society
http://users.rcn.com/sfiics/

International Multimedia Association
http://www.emmac.org/

National Cable Television Association
http://www.museum.tv/archives/etv/N/htmlN/nationalcabl/national-cabl.htm

Information Technology Association of America
http://www.itaa.org/eweb/StartPage.aspx

Electronic Retailing Association (Formerly, the National Infomercial Marketing Association)
http://www.retailing.org/new_site/default.asp

Association of Independent Commercial Producers
http://www.aicp.com/

Directory of PR Consultancies and Press Release Writers
http://www.pro-talk.com/pr-directory/
public_relations_consultancies_list.html

2

Who Are the Audiences for Video Podcasts, and How Do You Produce Video Podcasts?

What consumers of video podcasts want are "killer applications" so anyone easily can produce a video podcast from a traveling van, spare room, factory, tradeshow, school, or office now that the devices such as video iPods and its competition are available. Video podcasts can be viewed in transit, at school, work, or at home.

Extreme telecommuting for many jobs also is open to video podcasting producers. Do you want to be the premier resource for video podcasting content? Apple currently is the premier Podcast content and hardware resource, but the competition is growing. Each week about a thousand podcasts are added to Apple's iTunes music store. In 2005, the music store featured more than 15,000 podcasts. As an entrepreneur, you can use the popularity of the growing number of video podcasts to direct your own production emphasis.

The biggest corporations are getting into the video podcasting act. When iPod recorded a second filing seeking a trademark on the term iPodcsat, it included not only the usual "hardware devices and apparatus for recording, transmission, and reproduction of sounds, images, data, and magnetic data carriers," but also "telecommunications services such as telephone services and leasing of communications apparatus." It's first filing seeking a trademark for the term iPodcast included images, sounds, and other data such as electronic bulletin board services," according to the September 4, 2005 *Apple files for Podcasting Trademark* article. There's a vast RSS community online that has opinions on what Apple should be offering or trademarking.

Branding is a big issue in the video podcast revolution. When video iPod and iPod-like devices are widespread in the student and young adult community, there will have to be content with variety to meet the needs of the types of viewers most likely to use video podcasting content. The gerontology community also has a wide intergeneration community emphasizing expression of creativity for memory enhancement in the golden years. Life stories and lifelong learning content has vast potential with both the older community of retirees seeking information, leisure, hobbies, life story recording for family, and learning, travel, and fun material for mental stimulation.

There's a video podcasting audience among home schoolers, children, and teenagers, and a potential for tutoring and learning new skills or for armchair travel and family auto travel. Research the trends in job-training, corporate seminars, trade shows, and professional associations. Human resource personnel can use the video conferencing and branding aspect of video podcasting. Besides music TV or entertainment, there are virtual museum tours, and libraries offering a video version of narrated audio books, live plays, and entertainment for fun or learning.

Distance learning is another aspect of teaching online through the video podcast. If you want to open a business, find a job, or have a career in the video podcasting revolution, you need to partner with those who can help you optimize video podcasts and/or produce them for a targeted audience.

Branding and infomercials at trade shows are only one aspect of networking, learning, or relaxing with video content in a podcast format. Software support is where the jobs will be. Who's creating software to optimize and produce video podcasts? Microsoft? Apple? iLife?

How many other companies are making the software that makes it possible for anyone without technical background to make a video with a Web camera or camcorder, save it in a computer, publish it online, and save it to a DVD for mailing? In the direction of the corporations that are making video podcasting simple to produce for most anyone online is where you follow the money. What affordable software is there that is supported by Windows?

Video podcasting support has been around for a decade, but on May 13, 2005, the Wall Street Journal had only spotlighted audio podcasting, but not the potential of video podcasting at that time. See the May 13, 2005 article titled, *Papers Turn to 'Podcasting.'* It's cached on the Web.

The article reported that the Denver Post, Seattle Post-Intelligencer, Philadelphia Daily News, Washington Post and Forbes have started podcasts. Most people would rather look at video podcasts than listen to audio, unless they're operating machinery or driving while listening. Listening to audio podcasts while driving is as distracting as listening to music with lyrics, or lectures and news. However, listening to music without lyrics is less distracting unless the music is hypnotic or promotes sleep.

The low-tech, low-budget 'podcasted' audio files are on each newspaper's Web site. The Wall Street Journal article noted that podcasts can be automated and that numerous university journalism students recorded audio podcasts as volunteers but were negotiating for pay. But major newspapers have been producing their own *video* podcasts since the Internet went public. The video podcasts of news reach younger audiences raised in front of TVs and Web sites.

All you need to start an audio podcast are one or more professional microphones, a beginner's level audio mixer, and recording software. However, video is the media of the present and near future, if it can be sufficiently compressed. The Daily News podcast features advertising. It has a sponsor. To open an advertising agency offering video podcast production, you need a sponsor.

You could open up a business that only offers creative advertising to clients in the form of video and audio podcasts, much like you'd sell TV and radio advertising time. Depending upon what type of advertising you'd specialize in, you'd need to find yourself a sponsor who specializes in that the type of business that supplies the news industry, such as a computer retailer. The problem you'd need to solve for your clients is how to drive traffic to your video podcasting site and once there, how to persuade the traffic to buy what's advertised. You'd make your money by selling ads.

Have you listened to the sound on most amateur podcasts? Does the podcast take too long to download? If you do interviews, keep them about 15 minutes in length. Attention span for podcasts is short. Interviews are the way to go if you're a beginner with video podcasting. There is always someone interested in being interviewed.

Start with print-on-demand book authors who have to publicize and promote their own books because it's difficult to get reporters to review books that may or may not be copyedited by experienced copyeditors. The greatest fear of those who buy print-on-demand books is that the books aren't organized by people experienced in organizing books. That's why interviews are easy to find among authors promoting books. You could also interview retailers with a product to sell who want customers, teachers, clergy, psychologists, or tutors and teachers who have a lecture or how-to instruction in a niche area.

C/Net's "News.com" (News of Change) posted an article online on October 14, 2005, titled, *"Podcasters Prepare to Launch Video Era."* One of the biggest fears stated in the article emphasized the video revolution in podcasting attracting a flood of pornographers. Not only the sex trade, but religious sermons are expected along with comments from the almost anyone.

It seems as if Apple's portable media player and the competition from Microsoft and other manufacturers of similar devices will let anyone download free video segments. Sure, students already know anyone can download audio MP3 files to an iPod or similar device. Ever since MP3 players of all sizes have been on the market for several years, students, parents, and senior citizens have been downloading a medley of favorite radio programs from business to alternative health.

The video revolution is termed that way in most major newspapers. Although it's the 'amateurs' most often referred to in newspaper articles around the world, most of these 'amateurs' are interested in how to make money from their creative expressions in the way of video podcast productions.

In mid-October of 2005, Apple announced its first video-enabled iPod models. Local talent and local broadcasters, people of all ages that dream of having their own radio talk show, entertainment, or teaching with video podcasting on the Web are the probable consumers of the video-enabled iPods and other similar devices made by any company that can and will make video devices.

What entrepreneurs ripe for producing video content for these iPod and related devices want is to be able to combine technologies and software to produce content that draw in larger numbers of viewers. What's most popular currently is opinionated programs and sex. Anyone with a Web camera or camcorder who longs to be an opinionated, perhaps controversial or volatile radio or TV talk show personality now can have his or her own Internet-based 'video' or 'radio' reality program with podcasting.

Video podcasting technology can be used to train employees, home school, teach courses, or lead seminars in subjects that draw niche audiences. The how-to audience is in demand. People want to see free video on how to make money from a hobby, travel, stay healthy, build, craft, or sew an item, find a job, or how to make a business presentation using a certain type of software.

One of the most useful ways to sell a book is by presenting school librarians with the title before the book is written and asking whether the librarian might buy such a title. Video podcasting can be fine-tuned to cater to the needs of certain groups such as high-school and college librarians, if the entrepreneurs knew where they could get a list of the email addresses of librarians from their professional associations.

Major publishers that sell books to these types of customers have such lists. The question is, can video podcast producers find out how to reach their intended market without spamming and annoying anyone in a position of buying the video podcasting content or advertising?

The way to get around this is to set up interviews with authors whose books are targeted to audiences that include school and public librarians, teachers, students, and parents. Then, without spamming, let the customers view freely the authors discussing their book titles and content that appeal to a specialized audience that might be interested in the information.

Clergy—preachers and other religious speakers were among the first to show an interest in video podcasting. Fundraisers also find a niche audience when they ask for donations to charities by podcasting video segments of their charity work around the world. When it comes to religious audio podcasts, check out iTunes' listings. According to the article, *Podcasters Prepare to Launch Video Era,* there are about "1,400 religious offerings available on iTunes."

The type of entrepreneurial person most likely to start a video podcast from home is a journalist interested in economics. This can be consumer economics communications or finance. Journalists who also are media analysts would be interested. If an average retailer opens a video podcast, the individual may not have the necessary funding or may not know where to start or what to post on the Web in the way of quality video that already has a built-in audience.

If you're already a video content producer and can do fundraising to get the money, such as a professor of documentary production, you can become a Web-based documentarian offering specialized video, such as personal history, life-story reality podcasts, business advice, or consulting/counseling. Since a huge number of first-time businesses fail before going online, you have a lot to overcome to stay afloat. It's not for someone who hasn't researched the intended audience's preferences and needs. Video is so much more involved than audio MP3 broadcasts. You need to start by learning from documentary video producers before you learn about putting the content online.

You can start by looking at the materials published by the International Documentary Association (IDA). See the IDA Web site at: http://www.documentary.org/. Or you can start your own national association for video podcasting. Who is going to fund your video production projects? Do you have an industrial-quality camcorder? Are your documentaries short enough? Can you use software to compress your documentaries?

What software is best? Who will judge the quality of your video objectively? Can you ask a video professor in a university to help you judge the quality or someone in the video profession? Get at least three opinions as they may differ as to the quality of your editing. Who will edit your work, or will you use software and edit on your own computer? Are you experienced in editing videos for podcasting on the Web? Who is around who is that you can hire—or learn from?

Find out who your audience will be. Young people look at video iPods when they are waiting in restaurants, malls, sports centers, food courts, or traveling in public transportation. Young people view videos during lunch breaks at school or while shopping and waiting for others to try on clothing. They also view while hanging around the malls. Can people view your content in public?

For those who want to put pornography on video podcasts, they have a magazine all their own for this industry. There's the Adult Video News, a trade magazine of the industry. Those entrepreneurs will probably gear content to be watched by couples at home, parked in cars which would bring back the 'private' drive in, or otherwise view the content where the public isn't watching what they're seeing—certainly not in libraries or schools. On the other hand, educational content can be viewed in libraries or schools.

Entrepreneurs might want to create online virtual worlds that residents of a community can offer ideas on 3-D models of prototypes of parks. These virtual worlds are in some ways similar in theory to the interactive learning materials, simulators, avatars, role-playing games, hypertext interactive fiction, and video worlds that existed in the early 1990s.

For example, Democracy Island is a three-dimensional testing ground inside an online virtual world called Second Life. The virtual world is funded by the $50,000 grant from the International Center for Automated Information Research that went to the New York Law School's Institute for Information Law and Policy. See the November 8, 2004 Internet Week article titled, *Online Virtual World is Part Fantasy, Part Civics Experiment* by Christopher T. Heun at: http://internetweek.cmp.com/173600540. The idea of a Web site is now not merely a Web site but a place and state of mind known as "your island" or "your virtual world." The idea isn't really new. Before the Internet became public, people played virtual world role-playing games with interactive computer software, most often in virtual reality video arcades at shopping malls.

Business Presentations with Video Podcasting

If you're making a presentation for yourself or any of your clients, make a video podcast using Powerpoint or Keynote. Your intended audience can save your video in their video iPods and similar devices and play your presentation when they get back to the office or home on their own computers.

The video also can be saved to a DVD and mailed. For videoconferencing globally, your business can be built and based on synchronizing MP3 audio files with video or changes your MP3 files into MP4 files. You'd need video compression software. If you have Powerpoint slides, you can import each slide individually as an image. Check out Keynote software.

Another software to try out is iMovie, which lets you import each image as a separate clip. After all your clips are imported into the software called iMovie, you'd have to record your audio track. The only problem left to solve then would be to adjust the amount of time for each still image. The time adjustment is done in order to synchronize your video with your audio. But if it's a slide show you want to turn into a video podcast, your job would be to make sure the video slides "lined up" in time with the correct audio tracks. Also, iTunes lets you import audio files for each of your slides.

The video podcast revolution happened because people were not comfortable sitting in front of a computer staring at a bright screen while trying to listen to audio. There's enough unread blogs out there to fatigue the eyes. What consumers want is mobility—the listening or viewing while in a setting such as the beach, hiking, out in nature, or viewing anywhere outside or in bed, but not sitting with aching shoulders in front of an eye-fatiguing computer screen.

Children riding in the back seat of a car on a long vacation automobile trip enjoy watching DVDs on a DVD player. Teenagers and college students can afford iPods and simlar devices to take on the run or from room to room. The mobility is what video podcasts are about, not the tiny viewing screen. At home, your large-screen TV can play that same file saved on a DVD using a DVD R/RW instead of the old fashioned DVD or CD player.

Games are a big market for video podcasts that don't necessarily have to be played on a video iPod or its competition. Video podcast games also can be played on game video players. Try Sony PSPs, GameBoy Micros, PlayYans, Series 60 smart phones, and ZVue movie players. No doubt hand-held size computers will soon feature video podcasts. Some MP3 players could be enhanced for video in the future.

Consumers buying video iPods already loaded with videos usually don't have time to download videos from computer sites. You also could walk in a used game store and buy UMDs (interactive videos).

Another alternative is to look at the DVD-to-PSP Web site at: http://www.gamerbots.com/DVD2PSP/index.htm. With this software, you can convert your DVDs, and play them on your PsP. The Web site reads, "We are also throwing in with this auction—Directions on how to activate the hidden browser in PSP. Use it to Surf the internet over a wireless network! We'll show you how step by step with pictures." Your system requirements would be Microsoft Windows, Internet Explorer, a USB cable, and a DVD drive on your PC.

If you want to provide video podcasts for customers, you need cost-effective ways to obtain movies already formatted for any video podcast device you might buy. Companies that create video content include iFilm http://www.ifilm.com/?htv=12, AtomFilms http://www.atomfilms.com/ (watch short films and animation) and JibJab http://www.jibjab.com/Home.aspx (animated cartoons and riddles featuring Nasty Santa, Hoola Boy and the Riddle King).

Videoblogs

To create video content for iPods and other small, portable viewing and listening devices, you need to get an RSS feed. Check out RocketBoom, a three minute daily videoblog based in New York City at: http://www.rocketboom.com/vlog/about.html. According to the RocketBoom Web site, it covers and creates "a wide range of information and commentary from top news stories to quirky internet culture. Agenda includes releasing each new clip at 9am EST, Monday through Friday. With a heavy emphasis on international arts, technology and weblog drama, Rocketboom is presented via online video and widely distributed through RSS."

An RSS feed stands for "Real Simple Syndication". Read an in-depth definition and explanation by Mark Pilgrim at the O'Reilly XML.com Web site at: http://www.xml.com/pub/a/2002/12/18/dive-into-xml.html. Also, an excellent book on RSS feeds is titled, Developing Feeds with RSS and Atom *By Ben Hammersley. April 2005. ISBN: 0-596-00881-3.*

RSS is actually a format for syndicating content. It's used primarily for news and similar Web sites. Examples of news content online using RSS feeds include Wired and Slashdot. Actually RSS feeds are used for articles, book excerpts, reviews and other personal Web log materials.

To organize your writing for RSS format, you need to divide your material into small enough articles that are able to be syndicated with RSS feeds. Don't put your unpublished novel into an RSS feed. People spend only a few minutes reading each syndicated news story online.

If you edit books online through RSS feeds or do tutoring, break items down into news-size chunks of text. The average attention span looking at video is only seven minutes, and people need breaks from reading on screen material. After you put your writing in an RSS format, a program that syndicates RSS news can keep returning to the feed and pick up your frequent news updates or include your other changes.

RSS technology lets people subscribe to your site. What you put up there in the way of newly published content can be downloaded to any portable player or computer. This means not only text, but also video and audio are considered content for RSS feeds.

Each subscriber (at no cost to them) can view the *free* video you've put up on the RSS feed. Subscribers don't have to download your video and waste time for buffer delays. If you're interested in video blogs, check out MobuzzTV, a video log (vlog) at: http://www.mobuzz.com/. Watch the latest shows.

The old fashioned way is to upload your mpeg videos to your Web site, use up a lot of bandwidth, and keep people waiting until your hour-long video is saved in their hard disks where they can save each video to a DVD.

It takes a long time to download that way, without an RSS feed, and some people are not on faster-loading DSL, cable, or other ways to download material from the Internet. Those who still have slower modems may run out of patience. That's why video blogs using RSS feeds cut the downtime waiting for any video to load.

Mobile phones are getting into the video podcasting arena with video player phones just as they got into the game with video recording and camera phones. Check out Verizon's VCast. See the article from the PC.com Web site titled "*Verizon's VCAST: Video Over EVDO Phones* at: http://www.pcmag.com/article2/0,1759,1749429,00.asp. According to the article by Sascha Segan, on February 1, 2005 the carrier, Verizon began "selling three phones for its high-speed EVDO (Evolution Data Only) network: one from LG, one from UTStarcom (formerly Audiovox) and one from Samsung."

You can open a business charging people a monthly fee to download your videos. With Verizon, the company charges a monthly fee plus what the corporation also charges for existing voice plans. As of February 2005, Verizon's customers in 32 cities could download, if they chose to, video clips: news from CNN and NBC, weather from AccuWeather, and entertainment content from channels like VH1 and Comedy Central.

It looks like the entertainment industry is getting into the production act as well. According to the PC.com's article, *Verizon's VCAST: Video Over EVDO Phones,* "Fox will produce exclusive serials for Verizon's new VCAST video service, too, including one based on the TV show '24'."

Let's suppose you want to produce video content that video podcasting phones would receive. Do you approach the phone companies or the phone manufacturers? You start with the phone companies and at the same time, you approach large production corporations and small, independent producers with your sample video clips. Keep your video podcasts short. Verizon's clips run two to five minutes. Your business might start out with a dozen or a hundred video podcast clips. Verizon makes available about 300 video clips every day.

What if you're out of cash, but still want to produce video podcasts for the Web that can be downloaded to iPods or video phones and similar gadgets? You could post your videos on iTunes Podcast Directory where people can download your video clips to their iPods if you have the software called Quick Time 7 Pro. You can buy the software at a very affordable price online at: http://www.apple.com/quicktime/download/win.html.

The Quick Time 7 Pro Web site reads, "The perfect companion for your Windows PC, QuickTime 7 Pro will convert you from a video watcher to a video maker. Harness the power of QuickTime 7 Pro for everything from creating podcasts to transcoding media in more than a dozen formats. Create video using the Web's premier codec: H.264 Record audio for producing podcasts Create movies for iPod New full-screen controls Convert media to more than a dozen formats."

What helps you to become familiar with QuickTime is to first to try out before you upgrade to the Pro version is the free QuickTime 7.03 or later version download. It's at: http://www.apple.com/quicktime/download/win.html. Click on Download the Free Player. Connect your camcorder or digital video Web camera with a Fire Wire 1394 cable to your computer. Shut off any versions of AOL Instant Messenger or iChat AV. If you don't have a camcorder, most digital video cameras are fine. One example would be the iSight. You don't have to use this equipment if you don't have a Mac. Most any digital video Web camera or camcorder will be fine.

If you use the Mac, according to Apple Hardware's Web site at: http://www.apple.com/isight/, iSight is a "state-of-the-art video camera that's the easiest way to video conference with your colleagues, friends and family over broadband. Featuring an autofocusing autoexposure F/2.8 lens which captures high-quality pictures even in low lighting, iSight also includes a dual-element microphone in its stylish compact aluminum body."

You can either open Quick Time 7 Pro and use it according to directions or use QuickTime 7 Pro for Mac OS Video Podcast: iPod Edition. The software lets you "Create video for iPod" and easily "convert your existing movie collection for playback on iPod." If you have a PC, purchase the Windows version for Windows XP.

3

DESCRIPTION OF BUSINESS

Travel and Free Walking Tours Video Podcasts

Two types of free tours exist if you're looking for free travel. The first kind is where you visit a city and take advantage of the free tours offered of the city. These usually are walking tours of streets, galleries, government buildings, theaters, or museums on free admission day. Make a list of cities and check the Web at sites such as Chicago Traveler at: http://www.chicagotraveler.com/attractions/chicago-greeter-free-tours.html, or New York City for Visitors at: http://gonyc.about.com/cs/toursbr/a/bigapplegreeter.htm, or The Paramount (free theater tour) at: http://www.theparamount.com/artists/public-tour.asp. When you use your search engine with the key words "free tours," you'll see a list of cities or places that offer free guided walking tours of an area or buildings.

When you visit a city and don't know anyone, don't have a car, don't know the bus, trolley, or train schedule, and don't know where to go, a free tour can help you to meet new people, walk in safety with a group, and learn some historic or contemporary information about a particular area. In New York City, for example, check out the free walking tours by viewing the Web site at: http://www.newyorkmetro.com/urban/guides/nyonthecheap/pleasures/walkingtours.htm.

The advantage of a free walking tour is that you learn details that people who lived there may never have heard. The New York metro.com site contains a headline from an article that explains: "Free walking tours dish the dirt on neighborhoods, landmarks, parks, and celebrities. Rediscover City classics or set out for the road less traveled."

Check out the San Francisco City Guides site at: http://www.sfcityguides.org/ where free walking tours of San Francisco have been offered for the past 25 or more years. If you really love any city, its history, lore and legends, you can volunteer to offer free walking tours. Build experience by volunteering in your area.

When you've learned the lore of any city you want to travel too, consider gathering a group of tourists or travelers who will pay to travel with you to a particular city. You go to that part of the world free in exchange for conducting a walking tour of that city.

There are in many cities, people who give walking tours for pay. They usually negotiate with a tour bus or travel service to give a number of tours in an agreed upon time frame for commission or pay.

You can offer walking tours free as a volunteer, or organize a walking tour business of your own. To get paid and still go free on the tour, you'd have to get a certain number of people to pay for the tour and work out a deal with the airlines, cruise ship, hotel, hostel, school, tour bus or travel service whereby you work by giving a certain number of tours in exchange for free travel.

Another way to go free is to run your business from scratch. Tourists pay you a fee. You make all the arrangements, and take them on a walking tour of a certain country or city. Your fee per person would be enough to pay for your lodging and travel expenses.

After you've taken several free walking tours of any city, consider whether you'd like to start a home-based business offering walking tours of any city, anywhere in the world that you'd like to see and where walking tours are relatively safe.

Find out what kind of insurance you need and which travel agencies you want to contact. Promote your walking tours in travel and entertainment publications and Web sites that reach tourists and travelers, including business travelers and those attending conventions.

You could conduct walking tours of any city, anywhere. Often travel agencies have arrangements. Some stipulate that if you find a certain number of paying tourists to go take a tour of a particular area that you can come along free as the tour guide.

Or start your own independent walking tour that specializes in taking people to another part of the world. If you sign up enough paying tourists, you can go free, if those type of arrangements are made with your travel agent, a particular cruise company, hotel, hostel, or as part of your own independent business.

Walking as a Business

You can produce podcasts on the subject of guides to neighborhoods for walkers. The walkers can download your podcasts on their devices, such as iPods and listen to the historic description of a neighborhood as they walk. These audio guides can be developed for any city in the world that walkers can stride or tour.

If you love to walk, contact various offices of any type where the people usually sit all day. Offer to take groups on lunch hour walks in a particular area of the city in which you live. Take the office employees—whether you work there or not—on long walks during the flexible lunch hour.

Start a home-based weekend-only neighborhood walking tour business on a shoestring budget. Give your walking tour business a name such as "Inside Details" or "Images and History." Pick an original name for your business that explains in two words what you offer on your walking tour. Start with sedentary office workers and offer lunchtime walks with a stop so they can sit somewhere and eat or buy lunch, sit down, and eat for 15 minutes before walking back to the office as a group.

During vacation periods from your usual weekday job, take tourists on walking tours all over the most fascinating cities of different countries. Pick a country that's relatively safe for walking. Eventually, your walking tour business can offer international walking tours of foreign cities as well as local, neighborhood, and wilderness sites.

You start local at first, obtain knowledge of where to walk in which countries or cities, and finally, turn your small business, into an international walking business with a new name that explains where you walk. Finally, turn your international walking business into a nonprofit group dedicated to promoting neighborhood walking in urban, suburban, and rural environments throughout the world. As you expand, you'll have to hire people to run the walking tours seven days a week. You also can work with volunteers as well as paid employees. You decide how far you want to go as a nonprofit group with a commitment to promoting safe walking around the world.

You can charge a small fee, such as $3 or walking, or let everyone walk free and operate as a nonprofit business to promote safe walking for health and stress reduction. You can cater to older adults or office workers or all age groups, or specialize in walking for people with special needs.

If you operate as a nonprofit agency, you can offer free walking tours and run on donations to your nonprofit agency. You'll be able to maintain a rented office with a volunteer staff if enough donations come in for your nonprofit safe walking tour group.

Most people would not like to spend a fee for walking. You'll probably find your people dropping because the walks cover the same area repeatedly. So it's best to operate as a nonprofit agency and run on donations with a volunteer staff rather than a paid staff.

To bring in more money, publish a newsletter listing walking times for an annual $10 or $12 subscription. When running your non-profit walking tour service, make a list of categories to which people can contribute money.

Out-of-town trips will generate more income. In addition, the volunteer walking leaders can arrange their own trips and go through your nonprofit safe walking tour service to take walkers on tours of foreign cities or national locations if they can find enough walkers willing to walk through the cities selected at an agreed-upon price. They have to work up a budget.

For the working crowds, keep offering midweek lunch break walks. Some of these office workers will be happy to take your walking tours to other countries when they get vacation time. Your clients would be sedentary office workers.

Other features offered by your free and safe walking tours in addition to offering walking the various neighborhoods of your area could include a once-a week lunch group that visits different ethnic restaurants. You can offer a Saturday walk for older adults or singles so they can walk and chat.

Offer free walks through local parks focusing on older adults or singles groups to meet, walk, and talk. One day of the week offer a walk through various wilderness sites in your area. Schedule different types of walks throughout the week depending upon demand and needs of various age groups and special interest groups.

Besides walking within one city, take a group for a weekend trip to another nearby city to see a show and spend two days overnight for a reasonable price—perhaps for under $200. Contact a reputable bus line and take your group to mountain resorts or other areas where they can walk safely. Make sure you and everyone else has insurance in case something happens to someone on a walk. Keep insured for surprises.

Take walkers to see a play or other event combined with a day of walking. Let them see a show and rest after a walk, and make sure there are places for them to eat, perhaps at different ethnic restaurants or have a take out lunch. Take the walkers to a resort where they can have a wine and cheese party and in the summer, use of a swimming pool (provided the resort, you, and the walkers are insured against accidents or other surprises). Make sure you have liability insurance.

Your walkers would enjoy a Sunday spent with breakfast at a hotel followed by a tram ride and a sightseeing walk. Let them look at lakes. Keep rules, such as never allowing a tourist to pass the leader. If they walk ahead of the leader, don't let them participate again in the walk. You need to follow these rules for safety. No one can walk ahead of the leader or move out of site. You don't want people getting lost in a mountain or wilderness setting or moving out of site and being late or missing for the ride home.

To start your walking regimen, lead a downtown walking group. Specialize in older adults or the group you want. Morning walks starting at about 10 or 11 AM are excellent for older adults. Take your walkers on a golf course walk around dinner time—between 5 and 6 PM.

Another walking group can start with a train ride to the old town of your city followed by an hour and a half walk with a stop for a refreshing snack and water, including breaks for restroom use. Older adults and non-drivers who use public transportation usually prefer morning, afternoon, or early evening walks.

For all ages, Saturday night walks are excellent as free entertainment. In addition, Saturday night walks traditionally draw younger singles and those who still drive. Families with young children in strollers enjoy morning or afternoon walks on weekends.

You also can offer an early Saturday morning hike if you live near a mountain. Volunteers can take this tour with walkers in good condition who like steep and strenuous walks. For persons who need to take it easy, Saturdays could unfold at 8:30 AM, beginning with eating together at the Y or elsewhere, meeting people, and chatting, followed by a volunteer-led mild walking tour of downtown or another area that offers historic and cultural points of interest.

As a nonprofit service, your walks can continue all day with a variety of volunteers focusing on different areas such as a river walk, a beachcomber walk. At 6:00 PM, you could have a volunteer conduct an evening walk. Offer a Sunday breakfast walk at 7:00 or 9:00 AM, followed by a merry-go-round walk at 8:00 AM. By 3:30 PM, you could offer a coffee or high tea walk led by volunteers. Different volunteers would offer the walking tours each day of the week.

Your high tea walk could offer herbal tea followed by walks along your harbor or other point of interest to enjoy sights and sounds. In winter, volunteers could show the walkers the colorful sunset on a 5:00 pm. Spend Sunday evenings at a coffee or tea house for an optional visit after the walk. Offer flat walks for those who can't climb steep sidewalks or hills. Classify your walks into mild and moderate. Offer a large variety of walks and give your walking group a name.

Find fit volunteers to offer family fitness walks at 9:00 AM one day a week when families can walk together. At 10:45, a good time for older adults who don't like getting up early in the morning for 7:00 or 9:00 am walks, offer a mild walk. Award a price for the oldest walker.

Take senior citizens from various senior community centers on a mild one-hour stroll that emphasizes spectacular views, including views from high-rise buildings from the inside as well as outdoors. For example, many seniors like to look at views from the 40th floor or higher of a building to see the panorama of their city. Others like to stroll outdoors. Include wheelchair walks for those who use power chairs and scooters as well. Walk at the pace of the slowest walker and have volunteers trained to work with older adults. Patience is a virtue when people need to walk slowly. The goal is enjoyment of the walk, stress reduction, and relaxation.

Take walkers on tours of high-priced homes or home tours when available. Looking at the outside of expensive homes is free, whereas looking inside a home, usually around the holidays, usually costs money that often is donated to charities to raise funds for various causes. Morning tours are best for viewing expensive homes from the street. Make sure the homes don't have loose dogs running in the street before you take a group on a walk of neighborhood sidewalks.

Your nonprofit walking service needs several vice presidents, a treasurer, secretary, and numerous corresponding secretaries. Have an emphasis for your nonprofit group dedicated to walking—such as family fitness. Make sure special groups are taken on walks, such as those with disabilities. To contribute to causes, do fundraising as a nonprofit group.

Make sure any leaders are trained and certified where fitness is concerned. Conduct several walks as fundraisers. Shoes are important in the walking business. Contact shoe manufacturers. Negotiate with companies that sell walking shoes to help you arrange a shoe fund and annual picnic. Ask the manufacturers and sellers of walking shoes to provide shoes to needy children in your area. Support your shoe fund.

You'll find that there will be some people who like to walk for miles. Others want to stroll around posh areas. Volunteers who are trained, certified, and fit can conduct walks for those who are fit enough to take eight-mile hikes. Schedule the walks around the lovely areas of your town. Include the expensive and beautiful country clubs, the places famous for attracting vacationing movie stars, and resorts or hotels with golf courses that attract the wealthy and world-class golf professionals.

What you need for your nonprofit walking group are high teas and coffee klatches. The best day for these events is on each Fridays morning after the walk or at noon lunches after the walk. It's one of the "Thank God It's Friday" type of events. After a Friday morning walk or at lunch time after the noontime walk, a lot of office workers still have spare time to get back to the office. So make time for lunch. Or offer your high tea at 9:45 instead of the usual 4:00 PM.

Walkers will look forward to stops for scrumptious breakfasts are made after the early morning walks that might typically run from 7:45 to 9:45. Friday morning walks followed by breakfast or lunch are for those with flexible working hours and retirees. Early morning, lunch, and after-work hours draw a crowd of office workers, work-at-home parents, people who work afternoon shifts, and those into family fitness.

Total family fitness walks can be your most popular offering. Schedule at 9:00 AM a toddlers and grandparents walk together around flat areas such as lakes or beach areas that run about a mile in length. Allow families to decide how many laps around a lake, beach, park, or other area they want to walk. They can choose a nature trail or the sidewalk to finish the workout.

Include training and walking, a jaunt with lunch, or a midweek wilderness walk on trails plus lunch. Train and certify your volunteers on how to lead people on walks. Give them awards.

Talk to newspaper reporters about your need to recruit volunteers to lead the walks with free training provided. The training is not only about safe walking. It's also about the sights and events discussed on the walks. Leaders can earn money by taking walkers on their own customized walking tours anywhere.

On one of your walks, include seeing a musical play. For example, an hour's walk can complement taking in a dramatic theater play at a discounted fee. The walkers could meet in front of the theater at matinee or evening time, walk for an hour, and return at 1:45 PM or 6:45 PM to wait for the play performance in the theater.

Focus on walking throughout the world as a fitness recreation. Classify your walkers and volunteer leaders as casual, moderate, moderate/plus, brisk, and very brisk, depending upon the speed at which the group walks. Casual is clocked at 2–3 miles per hour, moderate, 3 miles per hour, moderate/plus, 3 ½ miles per hour, brisk, 4 miles per hour, and very brisk, more than 4 miles per hour.

Start a nonprofit walking group that attracts a certain group of people—for example, families with children, fitness enthusiasts, older adults and retirees, singles, sedentary office workers, persons with special needs, mall walkers, artists, photographers looking for a clearer focus, birdwatchers, dog-walkers, or a job/client-hunting community seeking to net-walk. Your photographers, artists, or birdwatchers may want to stroll with cameras, camcorders, or sketch pads ready for the unexpected in nature.

Don't forget the large number of people, including older adults who enjoy morning or noontime mall walking as exercise. If you want to learn how an actual nonprofit walking group operates, contact the National Organization of Mall Walkers, at PO Box

191, Hermann, MO 65041. Check out Web sites at: http://www.peternielsen.com/walking.htm and at: http://www.chiropractic-software.com/mall_walking.htm. If you want to bring more walkers to malls for walking combined with culture rather than shopping, offer poetry or drama readings in shopping malls, perhaps near food courts and book stores. Reading excerpts from books near a bookstore might also bring in the walkers, and the food courts may look inviting even to rest, after a long mall walk.

Design your own walking program. See the Web site at: http://www.peternielsen.com/walking.htm. For more information, *The Rockport Guide to Lifelong Fitness* tells you more about an easy-to-use test that helps you design your own walking program. Send a self-addressed, 45-cent stamped envelope to Walking Test, The Rockport Walking Institute, 220 Donald Lynch Blvd. PO Box 480, Marlboro, MA 01752.

4

DESCRIPTION OF BUSINESS:

Inventory Comparative Shopping Checker and Events/Contests Video Podcast

Show people the records on how to cut expenses by comparatively recording the items and prices of stock of various competitors, including model and serial numbers of stores, schools, hospitals, homes, insurance firms, law enforcement agencies, attorneys offices, and warehouses with a video camera as the employees take periodic inventory.

You combine the inventory taking/recording with event video. For example, a large food or product manufacturer or distributor runs national contests where there are many winners. Each winner gets a video DVD of the event.

Videos are ordered for a low price from the manufacturer or distributor. The video DVD or podcasting MP3 audio producer asks for a 15 percent share of the gross profit.

INCOME POTENTIAL:

The current rate for independent contractors who take inventory varies from $6 an hour to $10 an hour. Videographers who record data on tape charge from $15 an hour up to $75 an hour for taping only, depending on the job complexity required.

Taking simple inventory and recording the results on tape for security is competitive with freelance inventory takers hired by temporary employment services. For contests and events video taping, the current rate is about 15 percent of the employer's gross profit going to the independent video producer.

Current rates for syndication of any video is divided like this: The distributor gets 30 percent. The Producer pockets 70 percent. In business videos, the current rate or fee is 25 percent royalty going to the video producer.

BEST LOCALE TO OPERATE THE BUSINESS:

Taking inventory with a video camera may be operated in any medium sized to large city, or anywhere in the world. In foreign countries, concentrate on export firms and insurance companies.

TRAINING REQUIRED:

Learning to use your video camera to record information is necessary. Learning to take inventory can be learned by watching any retailer or wholesaler take inventory or by volunteering to take inventory at a warehouse and watching the employees as you learn or apprentice.

GENERAL APTITUDE OR EXPERIENCE:

An eye for detail is necessary. It's important to have patience to record minute detail such as serial numbers on the backs of products and many items. It's routine, repetitive work.

EQUIPMENT NEEDED:

You'll need a video camera and editing system or access to editing. A lot of inventorying is straight taping without much editing.

OPERATING YOUR BUSINESS:

Send insurance firms, department and toy stores, hospitals, offices, warehouses, manufacturer's representatives or locators, and even detective agencies your flyer or brochure stating that you will take inventory by video tape and record serial numbers for security and insurance purposes.

Hire a door-to-door flyer delivery service to slip on each doorknob your notice that you videotape for security or inventory. For events, try advertising in the trade journals and business publications and contact manufacturer's representatives or locators.

The business and industry video market made more than $500 million in gross revenues during the eighties, mainly from videocassette sales to other businesses. There's a 70 percent annual compounded growth rate in the business video market, according to CBS/Fox. Keep in mind that whatever you tape with your video camera, it's wise to include workbooks or training materials with your tape.

TARGET MARKET:

To take video inventories, target warehouses, stores, shopping malls, department stores and supermarkets, schools, and hospitals as well as manufacturer's representatives and locators. For taping events and contents target manufacturers of products and foods that sponsor contests where there are many winners who would all enjoy having a videocassette of the contest or event.

RELATED VIDEO OPPORTUNITIES:

Security for home or office—taping of serial numbers. Take inventory of furniture and possessions in people's homes as well as office equipment and summarized inventory items. Tape events and contest winners at ceremonies and provide videocassettes to thousands of contest winners for a percentage of the manufacturer's gross profit. Firms that hire temporary security guards or temporary retail employees may also work with inventory takers.

ADDITIONAL INFORMATION:

North American Association of Inventory Services
http://www.naais.com/

Inventory Services Network
http://www.isninv.com/main.asp

The Association for Operations Management
http://www.apics.org/default.htm

American Production and Inventory Control Society (APICS)
http://www.bsu.edu/cob/article/0,1370,11012-2631-3987,00.html

International Recording Media Association
http://www.recordingmedia.org/news/press-vhsanniversary.html

Audio Publishers Association (APA)
http://www.audiopub.org/i4a/pages/index.cfm?pageid=1

5

DESCRIPTION OF BUSINESS

Cleaning Products—Make Your Own Basics Video Podcast

Show people how black tea puts a shine on hardwood floors. To start a business showing others how to make their own cleaning products from natural products found at home, start by buying four basic products and make your own cleaning mixes: Instead of detergent, stock washing soda, baking soda, vinegar, and black tea to use for cleaning of different surfaces. Be sure not to use caustic washing soda on aluminum, waxed floors, or fiberglass. Washing soda strips wax.

Make a basic washing mix from a gallon of water and ½ cup of washing soda. For ceramic tile floors, use a gallon of water and a ¼ cup of vinegar. Black tea and water put a shine on your hardwood floors.

Make your own cleaning compounds. You can control the amount of any ingredients you include. Also, you know what you put into the cleaning solutions or mixes that you make from scratch. According to Stony Mountain Botanicals, adding black tea to your floor washing water helps to make floors shiny.

See the Stony Mountain Botanicals Web site: http://www.wildroots.com/natural_cleansers.html.

Black tea mixed with water—about three teabags to a gallon of hot water works well on my hardwood floor. Three tea bags to a gallon of warm water shine a hardwood floor. It's what I experimented with after trying different strengths of tea on my hardwood floor. Don't put tea stains on a light-colored hardwood floor. Wash your tea-colored hardwood floors with black tea.

My hardwood floor is close to the color of a regular cup of black tea. Don't use a lot of water on hardwood. Water turns hardwood floors black. The water is absorbed and bows the wood or rots it. Water makes the wood swell.

Instead, clean off the dirt with a little water and black tea. Then use an oil-based hardwood floor cleaner to protect the wood.

Black tea in water works best on hardwood floors when very little water is used on the wood. For ceramic tile in the kitchen or bathroom, use a micro-mop first to remove all dust and scratchy debris before you wash with vinegar and water. Wash ceramic tile floors with a half cup of vinegar mixed with each gallon of water.

Click on the Do It Yourself Network at http://www.diynet.com/diy/lv_household_tips/article/0,2041,DIY_14119_2275102,00.html. Check out the cleaning tips from Linda Cobb. For example, you can clean ceramic tile floors with water, but don't use a sponge because it drags the grime into the grout. Use a micro mop or vacuum the dirt first before you wash the floor. Check out the Do It Yourself Network Fact Sheet PDF files at: http://www.ncta.com/guidebook_pdfs/DIY.pdf.

Make your own ceramic tile floor washing mixes by mixing a quarter cup of ammonia with a quarter cup of Borax mixed in a gallon of water. Or wash the floor with plain water. Check out Linda Cobb's Queen of Clean Web site for tips on how to clean and make your own cleaning mixes at: http://www.queenofclean.com/tips/index.html and http://www.queenofclean.com/. You can make so many of your own cleaning mixes easily from simple ideas such as a little white vinegar in water in your washing machine or use plain water for simple ceramic tile floor washes.

She has excellent cleaning tips such as using unseasoned meat tenderizer as a stain remover or tips on conquering clutter. I highly recommend these tips. They have saved me so much money by creating my own cleaning products from simpler and less costly, less processed materials.

If Linda Cobb, the *Queen of Clean*, can create a TV show and books on how to clean and organize, you too can find ways to share and experience living the more unprocessed and balanced life.

Why Washing Soda?

The generic term, "washing soda" with a pH of 11, is a salt. Washing soda is sodium carbonate and a lot more caustic than baking soda, although it is a soda processed to be a lot more alkaline and caustic enough for you to wear protective gloves to protect your hands. There are no harmful fumes. To buy washing soda, check the laundry shelves in supermarkets. Use a generic brand from your supermarket or a brand such as Arm & Hammer.

Baking soda is less caustic. It's called sodium bicarbonate. You also can make generic or basic cleaning mixes and compounds using baking soda. Besides putting an open box of baking soda in your refrigerator to get rid of odors, you can use it as a cleaner. Wear your gloves when you handle anything with baking soda and washing soda. Alkaline products are caustic to the skin. Never use washing soda the way you use baking soda.

You'll use washing soda to get rid of soot after a fire or to cut grease and oil. Washing soda will strip wax or lipstick and other oily coatings. It's good for getting rid of petroleum oil. It's not for fiberglass. To make a generic cleaner, mix a bucket of warm water with ½ of washing soda. For a less caustic cleaner, mix a bucket of warm water with ½ cup baking soda. Baking soda is a bit less caustic on the hands, but gloves are recommended because of the sodium and the alkaline effect on your skin.

Whenever you wash with baking soda or washing soda, always rinse whatever you washed, and keep wearing your gloves. If you want a generic drain cleaner, put white vinegar down the drain followed by baking soda. Let the fizz come up and then rinse well after the fizzing stops.

You can make a paste of baking soda or washing soda and water. Spread paste on soot or other dirt and put a mixture of either baking or washing soda in a spray bottle with water, mix, and spray. Leave on for a few hours and rinse thoroughly. Only use this mixture on glass or stone. Remember that washing soda usually peels off paint as well as wax.

INCOME POTENTIAL

You'll be able to price your product according to affordability, price of ingredients, time budgeting, and what the market will bear. Look at comparable natural products and research the market to see how well those competitive products are selling. Look at the natural and organic products market research for your specific product.

BEST LOCALE TO OPERATE YOUR BUSINESS

At home, online, any geographic location where you can buy your basic products for the price you can afford.

TRAINING REQUIRED

It's a good idea to learn from people who teach classes in making products from scratch such as home-made soaps, cleaning materials and deodorants. Look at the organic and holistic health magazines as well for do-it-yourself instruction as well as the variety of frugal living publications and books.

GENERAL APTITUDE OR EXPERIENCE

Learn to make a safe product yourself and test your markets. Is the product you made appealing to others?

EQUIPMENT NEEDED

Home-Made Deodorant

If you want to make your own deodorant without artificial additives such as aluminum, just take a teaspoon of baking soda, a pinch of cornstarch, and a dab of petroleum jelly. Mix the petroleum jelly with the baking soda and a pinch of cornstarch.

When it looks like a facial cream or smoothes on like a cream, use it under your arms. It works better if you swab the area with rubbing alcohol first and then apply the petroleum jelly and baking soda mix with a little cornstarch to make it go on smoother. Wash this off after a few hours. Don't use petroleum jelly near your nostrils.

Make your own hard soap from recipes on the Internet's World Wide Web starting at Miller's Homemade Soap Pages at: http://www.millersoap.com/ and also at: http://www.millersoap.com/soapproc.html.

Also check out the home made soap recipe at this other Web site at: http://nvnv.essortment.com/homemadesoaps_rbzq.htm. When you make soap, you might make an olive oil and grape seed oil soap.

OPERATING YOUR BUSINESS

How Do You Make A Basic Face And Bath Soap?

It's amazing what you can make with glycerin. Use it to get out stains from clothing by soaking glycerin and water on the spot. Or add a teaspoon of glycerin to soaps and home-made shampoos to add a moisturizing, lotion-like effect. Can you make soap for yourself at less cost than buying it commercially at the market?

Yes, if you have the time to make soap, including melting the bits of soap you already have and remolding it or making soap from scratch. You have control over the scent and ingredients. If you want a soap to smell like your favorite scent, make your own soap and add your favorite scent and oils, such as roses and olive oil.

Why make home-made soap with lard when you can make soap with herbs, vegetable oils, or beeswax? Make soap containing almond meal, oat meal, or other ingredients. You can even sell your soap or put in gift baskets.

Soap can be made cheaply in the old fashioned way or creatively with olive and grape seed oils. It's all about what you want to do with your soap, use it frugally yourself. Sell special hand-made soaps as gifts to earn money at home. When you make soap from scratch, using a cold process, you're performing *saponification*. This is a chemical process which converts most types of fat into soap by reaction with an alkali called lye.

Use distilled water when making soap. Soap-making kits are for sale online. All of these kits and special soaps with expensive ingredients are fine. Check out the soap making supplies at: http://www.soapmakersupplies.com/soapmaking/Index.html. You can spend more money buying soap making supplies, kits, and making expensive soaps to sell or use for yourself. Or you can live on less by making soap cheaper than you'd pay for commercial soap. What you have is control over the ingredients.

Compare what it cost you to make soap to what you spend to buy commercial soap. Depending upon the ingredients you put into the soap, home-made soap can be made for less, if you have the time and want to work with the ingredients such as lye and certain fats, beeswax, or olive oil. See the Web site at: http://www.soapmakersupplies.com/soapmaking/HowTo_ColdProcess.html for making basic cold-process soap using either fats or oils.

The SoapMakersSupplies.com Web site at: http://www.soapmakersupplies.com/soapmaking/HowToColdProcess.html lists the following Soap Making Supplies Needed:

Oils (fats)
Caustic Soda (lye)
Distilled Water
Newspaper
Safety Glasses or Goggles
Rubber or Plastic Gloves
Scale
Glass Jar
1 Lye Pitcher (plastic). Mark pitcher and use it only for lye water
Long-handled Wooden Spoon
2 Thermometers (one for oils and one for lye water)
Stainless Steel Soap Pot (do not use aluminum pot)
Mold. Use a Plastic or Wood Box or other Container

Insulating Materials (blankets work well)
Freezer or Butcher Paper
Fragrance or Essential Oils
Colorant

When at Soap Maker Supplies Web site, click on one of the site's soap-making recipes. You can choose the cold process or the melting process. Read their thorough processes on how to make soap. If you want to make soap from scratch the way it was done historically, choose the cold process method.

The melting process involves simply melting soap you already have and re-shaping it or adding scents, textures such as oatmeal or almond meal, and oils—for example olive or grape seed oil. You can melt soap by putting it in a sealed plastic bag and heating it in 120 degree F. water. The cold process of making soap from scratch requires that you work with lye and fats or oils.

Lay out all the ingredients and equipment first before starting. Don't forget essentials such as safety glasses, vinyl or latex gloves, and a water and vinegar solution for washing and neutralizing any caustic lye that touches you or other equipment.

Other Web sites list similar supplies needed. Check out the soap-making recipes at the Pioneer Thinking Web site at: http://www.pioneerthinking.com/soaps.html

You can start from scratch and make your own soap using lye and fats as people did in historic times. Or you can grate a bar of ivory soap with a cheese or potato grater and then melt it in a pan over a very low heat adding food flavorings such as vanilla or almond. Add any scent that appeals to you and pour the melted soap into a bowl.

Add oat meal and chopped nuts or a scent of jasmine, lavender, melon, or musk oil perfume. The scent would be expensive, though. Artificial vanilla would be more frugal. The price of real vanilla has risen dramatically, but you can look for vanilla seeds and see what you can do with them in a warm greenhouse. You might put the scent of lemon, lime or orange in your soap, or add the essence of lemon or citrus fragrance meant for perfumed oils. Or you might want the scent of chocolate in soaps.

Don't put sugar or honey in your soaps. It's okay to add oatmeal for a scrub-type soap. These hand-made soaps can be put in gift baskets. You also can add olive oil or grape seed oil to your soaps. Adding olive oil to the soap helps the soap keep the skin smoother. No one wants to use soap heavy in lye for a facial, but olive oil is well-known in the homemade or 'natural' soap-making industry.

If you're starting from scratch, you'll need to use lye. You can't make soap without lye unless you make soap out of your old bits of soap such as pan-melted ivory soap with added ingredients such as meal (oat meal) or scents. You also can use an old bottle of rose cologne or rose-petal water, orange-blossom water, or any type of safe and healthy scent that doesn't cost more than the original soap.

Here's how to make lye soap from scratch. Since lye is caustic and has extremely bad fumes, keep the lye away from children and use a child-proof cover on its container. Lye burns skin. Don't touch it with your hands. If you want to make your own soap from scratch, here is the recipe. The Pioneer Thinking Web site at: **http://www.pioneerthinking.com/soaps.html** lists the following soap making supplies needed:

Ingredients:

1 can (12 oz or 340 grams) Lewis Red Devil 100% lye

21 1/2 oz (605 grams) ice cold or part frozen *distilled* water

5 lbs, 7 1/3 oz (2.48 kg) lard or all vegetable shortening. You can add olive oil or grape seed oil. Any type of vegetable shortening works well. Use the type of hard fat that you feel comfortable with knowing the finished soap comes in contact with your skin.

Equipment:

1 each of 1–2 quart Pyrex or oven ware bowl

1 each of a 4–6 quart plastic bowl or stainless or cast iron pot

1 each of plastic, wooden or stainless big spoon

1 each of shallow cardboard box lined with plastic trash bag

Latex or vinyl gloves

Canning pot (for water bath if you use plastic reaction bowl)

Instructions:

Prepare a wooden or plastic box to be used as a mold that won't allow hot liquid fat to leak out. Line it with plastic such as a transparent painter's drop sheet cut to size or a plastic garbage bag or cat litter box liner. I like to use a square of plastic painter's drop cloth that comes on a roll, which I can cut to fit the box. You can cut it to fit the inside of the box and the outside, so there are no seams with openings for liquids to spill out. Check the box by putting water in it first to make sure there are no leaks. Then spill out the water. Put the box aside.

Keep handy a container of water mixed 10% with vinegar and a sponge to neutralize what splashes on you or on any surface. Remember that lye is alkaline and caustic. To neutralize the burning effects of lye, you need vinegar, which is an acid that won't burn you if it splashes on you when mixed with water. (Use 10 percent vinegar and 90 percent water in your solution.)

Keep that vinegar mixture in a container handy whenever you work with lye nearby. When you mix acid with alkaline, the effect is to neutralize the burning, caustic alkaline lye that splashes on you or on your furniture or clothing.

Put on your vinyl or latex gloves and any goggles to protect your eyes from caustic chemical splashes. Freeze half of your water into ice cubes. Put the ice cubes and the rest of the water into the 1 to 2 quart bowl. Use the stirring spoon (known to soap makers as the 'crutch'). Add the lye very slowly to the ice and water, stirring until the lye is all dissolved. Go slowly.

If the lye splatters on you, it will burn you. Immediately wash with a mixture of 10 percent vinegar and 90 percent water to neutralize the caustic alkaline lye. Place next to you that bottle of water mixed with vinegar to neutralize and washing any lye that touches you or any other surface on which you're working.

Lye gives off caustic fumes. Make sure the window is open and the room ventilated. Keep pets and children out of the room. Use a fume-proof cover over the solution. You don't want to expose the solution to air. Let it rest until it reaches 85 degrees F. You can cover the pot with a glass cover. Keep glass, plastic, or wooden covers for the working pot or the box in which the soap hardens. Don't let anything stay exposed to the open air.

Use a glass bowl or pot, never aluminum or galvanized metal. You're working with hard fats such as vegetable shortening. Melt the fat in the 4–6 quart bowl or pot. When the fat is melted, cool it down to 95 degrees F. Don't pour anything into your lined box yet. You're still working with your large glass pot.

Put aside your wooden box to use as a square mold. Line the box with plastic transparent or plastic trash bag lining. Make sure the liquid soap when poured into your wooden box that will be used as a mold, will not spill or leak in any way. You're dealing with hot liquid, melted fat.

You're box is put aside, and now you're still working with the ingredients in your large glass pot. Into the pot, stir the liquid fat in a clockwise direction while pouring the lye water into it in a stream so thin that it looks like a skinny pencil.

After all the lye water is added to the liquid fat, stir the mix using an "s" pattern. Soap makers use the verb "to crutch" instead of "to mix." Use a circular pattern. You also can use a hand blender as long as the circular pattern is repeated until the mix cools and slightly thickens. Keep stirring. If you stop, the mix separates.

The mix will begin to take on the consistency of cream and then thicken to look more like a pudding. Keep stirring from 10 to 45 minutes. If you use a hand blender, you'll be able to stop stirring much sooner. To tell when it's time to stop, dribble a stream from your stir stick. The batch should show traces. How long it takes for your soap to thicken depends upon the ingredients and the temperature in your work room or kitchen.

Many home-made soap crafters say that pure ingredients take less time, perhaps 10 minutes. Your trace is what appears when you dribble a stream from your stirring stick onto the liquid in the middle of your pot. What you want to see in your trace is the dribble from the stream that drips from your stirring stick. Make sure the dribble doesn't drown into the surface.

If the dribbled stream doesn't sink, then the soap is ready to pour into the lined box. Careful—wear rubber gloves and treat the raw soap like you treated the lye water. Wash off all splatters immediately. Now you're carefully pouring your soap into your lined box.

Cover your box to keep out the air. Use a wooden or plastic cover. Let stand for three to five hours. Then cut into bars with a dull table knife. Never use a sharp knife. Allow the soap to cure in the box for about a week before breaking it up and handling it, and another month before using it.

Centuries ago, the early New England settlers on farm wives who made soap actually put their tongues on the new bars of hardened soap to see whether the un-reacted lye burned. Don't try this because it's unknown how it will affect your ability to taste or your taste buds. The soap that this recipe makes can be used for your face or for bath soap. You can add olive or grape seed oil in small amounts while the fat is liquid.

There's another kind of soap that was used in the past for washing floors called Lye Soap. It uses less fat. One recipe asks for 5 pounds, five ounces of fat, and the soap had to rest for six months before using it. Don't use lye soap on your face. The more fat and oils such as olive oil, grape seed oil, or face creams you put into your soap, the more suitable it becomes for face and bath use.

For colorful soap, you can add food coloring or non toxic children's tempura paint powder—about 20 grams, according to one recipe on the Web at: the Home Made Soap Recipe site at: http://nvnv.essortment.com/homemadesoaps_rbzq.htm. You add the coloring when the soap mix reaches the heavy cream stage, according to the Web site mentioned above. My feeling is that soap touches your skin and is absorbed somewhat. So I wouldn't want to put nontoxic tempura paint powder into soap that constantly touches my skin.

Instead, my personal feeling is that safe food coloring or coloring from vegetables such as spinach juice, beet juice, or similar natural food colorings used in foods would be preferable. You can try various colorings made from natural vegetables that are labeled safe to eat. This is not because you're eating the soap, but because it contacts your skin and pores.

Not everyone likes scented soap. If you want a scent, such as vanilla or almond, orange or rose, you can add about two ounces (60 grams) of rose petal or orange blossom water, jasmine, vanilla, almond, or other scented essential oil or perfume before the soap is thick enough to pour.

Another way of added scent is to finish curing the soap. According to the Home Made Soap Recipe site, you can dip a muslin cloth in scented oil and wrap it around the soap. Then seal in the scent with aluminum foil.

I like to use rose petal water and rose petal extract scented oil. I dip a cloth in the rose petal scented oil. Then I wrap the cloth tightly in plastic and keep it airtight for two months. The Web site recommends wrapping the soap in muslin dipped in scented oil and then wrapping that in aluminum foil for six weeks. Your objective is to have the perfume sink into the soap all the way to its core and not just on the outer layer.

When I want to change the form of the bar of soap, I put the bar of soap into a plastic bag that seals tightly. Then I lower the soap into hot water (120 degrees) for a half hour. That makes the soap soft enough to cut and roll into balls or press into a mold. My favorite molds are animal figures or oval shapes. When the soap cools, it hardens. After reshaping, let the soap rest for a few hours.

You can melt down most types of soaps, even glycerin soaps that are translucent. Any type of hard soap can be melted and remolded to a new shape. An interesting shape is to make a mold of your portrait in three dimensions, like a sculpture and give soap bars as gifts molded into the shape of someone's face.

RELATED OPPORTUNITIES

Pesticides-Home-Made from Spices and Vegetables

Cinnamon oil kills mosquitoes according to the Web site Dirt Doctor at http://www.dirtdoctor.com/view_org_research.php?id=26. I first noticed how fast the mosquitoes disappeared when I bought air freshener spray made with cinnamon oil. See the article researching cinnamon oil as an insecticide in the July14, 2004 issue of the *Journal of Agricultural and Food Chemistry.* The study looked at essential oils such as cinnamon and catnip. Cinnamon oil is easier to find in household products.

It's amazing how popular Borax, boric acid, garlic, basil, and vinegar and cinnamon oil are as insect repellents. Citronella also wards off mosquitoes. Also see the Web site at: http://www.mercola.com/2004/aug/7/cinnamon_oil_deet.htm which compares cinnamon to Deet for mosquito control in your home.

An old recipe for getting rid of insects is to leave fresh basil leaves in the corners and behind furniture. Back on the farm, another recipe for getting rid of fleas in furniture and pet bedding recipe is to sprinkle Borax around a dog's blankets and bedding to get rid of fleas. Then vacuum it up so the dog doesn't lick the Borax.

Make your own non-toxic pesticides from natural ingredients. The Web site at eHow, http://www.ehow.com/how_4034_make-own-nontoxic.html gives recipes for using condiments and foods around the house to make non-toxic pesticide sprays. The pesticides last for a short time because they come from food products. So you can't store them. Spray them on, let dry, and reapply after the surface gets wet from rain or in the case of plants, from watering.

One of the recipes is to combine food ingredients such as chopped garlic and hot peppers or pepper sauce with a little liquid detergent and spray on a household surface to keep insects away. Another recipe for the garden is to blind three white onions and one garlic bulb with three cups of water. Then strain out the vegetables and use the water which should be left standing overnight. You can add enough water to make a gallon of liquid spray for your garden.

Other recipes for natural non-toxic (to humans) pesticides include mixing mineral oil with garlic cloves to make a spray on garden plants that are infested with bugs. It's the garlic that gets them to run, and the oil serves as a means of keeping the garlic essence working. Before you put anything on your garden plants test one to see how it reacts. Most plants are sensitive to soap and acid. So be cautious and wait before you put the solutions on all your plants.

The Web site at http://www.ehow.com/how_4033_rid-home-fleas.html shows you how to rid your house of fleas. Some of the recipes include boric acid. A simpler recipe is to mixing eight parts Borax cleaning powder with one part table salt. Sprinkle around and leave for a week before vacuuming several times. The salt and Borax mixture dries out the flea eggs and the area where the fleas live. Keep your pets and small children away from the areas that you sprinkle with the mixture.

You don't want people with respiratory problems breathing the Borax and salt in the air. And you don't want pets or children eating the Borax and salt mixture. Sprinkle the mixture on areas of the house you can vacuum, not on your pets' bodies.

See the Web site for the actual recipes. There are several there for making various types of pesticides that use ingredients made from vegetables and condiments or products you normally find around your home. Some handy tips at the Web site include preventing termites from invading your home by building sand barriers in crawl spaces and under fence posts, patios, and steps. According to the Web site, "Termites cannot tunnel through sand."

An abstract of a recent study published in Environmental Health Perspectives that's posted at the Care2 Web site at: http://www.care2.com/channels/solutions/guides/226, notes that 99 percent of children tested for that study show pesticide exposure. It's time to make natural pesticides from vegetables and spices.

Cinnamon and the skin of cucumbers are products also used to get rid of insects. Wood scraps draw termites, and cardboard and paper draw in mice. See the Coleoptera Web site at: http://www.coleoptera.org/p1020.htm. According to the Web site, "If ants are coming in through doors or windows, put a cinnamon stick across the path. They will not cross it." The site also has a tip noting that ceramic tile floors are too cold for mice and roaches to cross.

Other repellents mentioned on the Web site include garlic salt, a mix of borax and sugar on ant hills, and other combinations of food and detergents to get rid of bugs. Other tips include mixing bay leaves and Listerine mouthwash to get rid of cupboard ants. Wiping olive oil on plant leaves also helps repel bugs. Borax repels roaches and boric acid chases away ants. At the Antbuster.com Web site at: http://www.antbuster.com/ants-articles/ants-in-plants.asp, you'll find recipes for making ant-repelling with cinnamon. According to the site, "Cinnamon is both repugnant and fatal to ants."

Pens

Instructions for making your own writing pen are on the Rockler.com Woodworking Superstore at: http://www.rockler.com/articles/display_article.cfm?&cookietest=1&&story_id=41.

You don't need a lathe to make your own custom pen. The instructions at the Web site come, with permission, from Alice's Workshop (Woodworking and Crafts) at: http://members.fortunecity.com/alices_workshop/. Basically, you cut in half a pen blank using your box and mitre saw. If you don't own a mitre saw, use what you have that will cut through a piece of material about a half inch in diameter. Pen blanks come in strips 5" X 1/2" X 1/2" wood or corian.

If you don't want to buy pre-cut pen blanks, then cut your own pen blank from 1/2" stock. Use scrap wood or corian. According to the Web site, you'll be "drilling a hole all the way through the center of both pieces lengthwise using a drill press and a 7 mm drill bit."

The site also mentions using a pen kit and also has a link to a *Jet Pen Lathe* that you can use to make your own pens and pencils. Pen turning can be a hobby or a business that makes customized pens. Make your own pens and pencils for your family, or make them to sell online or at swap meets. Also, you can make your own bleach pen by putting bleach in a fountain pen or dipping a dry, clean fine-pointed marking pen in bleach.

Permanent Plastic Seal

At the Web site ThriftyFun.com, there are thousands of tips, articles, and requests such as sealing plastic bags with foil and an iron. You just put the foil over the plastic bag parts that you want sealed and iron the spot with a warm iron. See the Web site for these handy tips at http://www.thriftyfun.com/tf644813.tip.html.

Seal your keepsakes to keep mice from eating cardboard or paper by placing any type of metal or aluminum foil over the plastic and sealing the plastic like a big laminating machine. It works well with garments sealed in plastic wrap as well. The kind of plastic bags that can be sealed don't come in all sizes in most supermarkets.

So you can make your own sealed plastic bags by ironing them. If you don't use aluminum foil or other metal over the plastic the warm iron will melt the plastic all over your fabric and probably rip the fabric when you try to peel off the plastic. Always use something that will not melt when you put a warm iron on anything like plastic that can't take the heat without melting.

Once you seal the plastic by laminating, it's sealed until you rip it open. To make your own customized vinyl or plastic garment bags with zippers or Velcro, use an inexpensive roll of transparent plastic painter's drop cloth. Cut to the size you want and with fabric glue, glue in a zipper or Velcro.

Or sew in a zipper or Velcro using thread and sewing machine needles suitable for sewing on plastic or vinyl. If what you want to put in a garment-sized or customized bag is sensitive to ultra violet light from the sun or other lighting, use black or dark colored vinyl or plastic of the type used for table cloths. Buy from a fabric store to customize the size you want by buying the vinyl or plastic by the yard. Then blue or sew the zipper or Velcro at the top to seal in the garment, film, or whatever else you want to keep from light damage.

Draining Duties

Baking soda and vinegar drain cleaner

Make more environmentally-safe cleaning mixes. Add a quarter cup of white, distilled vinegar to your laundry in the rinse water. It won't leave an odor. And it will help to soften the laundry water, dissolve the minerals, and give your clothes that soft, fresh feel so you won't need a commercial fabric softener.

Use multi-purpose cleaners that you can make from *simple, less hazardous* household products such as white distilled vinegar and baking soda. Not only can you live on less expense when you work with basic ingredients such as baking soda and vinegar (drain freshener) or *olive oil and vinegar* (furniture polish), but you'll be using less hazardous substances. See the cleaning recipes at the Web site of the NC State University, College of Agriculture& Life Sciences, and Family & Consumer Sciences Department at: http://www.ces.ncsu.edu/depts/fcs/housing/pubs/fcs3682r.html.

Make your own drain cleaner with baking soda and vinegar. Assemble 1/2 cup baking soda and 1/2 cup white vinegar or any equal parts of baking soda and vinegar if you're working on several drains.

Put a quart of water in a pot or tea kettle and heat it so that you have a pot of boiling water available. First slowly pour the half cup of baking soda down the drain. Add the half cup of white vinegar and cover the drain.

Let the baking soda and vinegar fizz and set for 5 minutes. Then pour a pot of boiling water down the drain.

According to the publication, *as a section of publication he-368-2 (January 1991) by Dr. Wilma Hammett, Extension Housing Specialist, North Carolina Cooperative Extension Service, North Carolina State University, Raleigh, NC,* at the NC State University's Web site mentioned above, when you mix vinegar and baking soda, the fizz that occurs is the process of the vinegar and baking soda breaking down fatty acids into soap and glycerin.

This process allows the clog to wash down the drain. Do not use this method if you have used a commercial drain opener and it may still be present in the drain. Remember that you can't use these methods if you have been using chlorine bleach or commercial drain openers that are still in the drain.

Mixing certain products create poisonous and hazardous gasses such as chlorine gas which can be fatal. Do not mix any products if you have a commercial drain cleaner, chlorine, or anything other than water still present in the drain.

See the section on reducing hazardous substances in your home at: http://www.ces.ncsu.edu/depts/fcs/housing/pubs/fcs3682.html.

Simple All Purpose Cleaners

To make an all-purpose cleaner, simply mix 4 tablespoons baking soda with
1 quart warm water. Dissolve the baking soda in warm water. Apply with a soft cloth, terry cloth, micro cloth or micro mop or other soft, absorbent cloth or plastic scourer. Don't use a sponge as it drags grime into the grout of ceramic tile.

Rinse with clear water. Sponges hold bacteria in their pits and craters. Use a soft cloth that can be cleaned thoroughly. For metal surfaces, such as frying pans, use a plastic scouring pad. For sinks use a soft dish cloth or disposable wiping cloth, or plastic. You don't want to scratch the surfaces.

Furniture Cleaner and Polish

First wipe furniture with a damp washcloth and dry immediately. Then mix two cups of cups olive oil with ½ cup of vinegar. If you have a lot of furniture, mix 3 cups of olive oil with a cup of vinegar. Blend the olive oil and vinegar mixture well.

With a soft, dry cloth, apply a small amount of the mixture to wipe your furniture. If you don't like the acidic vinegar eating your furniture, use a small amount of olive oil and wipe dry. Don't use it on your hardwood floor. Instead use black tea and water to shine your hardwood floor. That way, you won't slip on an oily surface.

Lime and Mineral Deposit Remover

Soak disposable wipes or paper towels in distilled white vinegar. Apply the wipes or paper towels to the calcium or lime deposits around the faucet. Leave them on for an hour. The softened deposits can be removed with a few wipes of vinegar and water. To dissolve black or manganese mineral stains, make a paste of cream of tartar and hydrogen peroxide. Let the paste stand on the stain. Then wash the object with water and wipe dry.

Aluminum

Don't use aluminum cookware. It's unhealthy. Aluminum leeches out and ends up in your brain and other organs. It's a toxic metal when it collects inside your organs. Instead use stainless steel cookware.

If you have anything that's made of aluminum in your house and want to clean it, mix a quart of water with two tablespoons of cream of tartar. Boil the water and cream of tartar for 10 minutes with the aluminum object in the mixture. If the aluminum object is large, soak paper towels in the boiled water and cream of tartar mixture and apply for an hour, then wipe dry.

Brass Cleaner

There are two ways to clean brass. The first is to mix a little lemon juice, a half-cup for example, with an equal amount of baking soda. Make a paste that looks like toothpaste or wall paper paste. Rub the paste onto brass with a soft cloth. Rinse with water and dry.

The second method is to use lemon juice and cream of tartar. Mix in equal amounts the lemon juice and cream of tartar. Or mix in small amounts until you have the consistency of a paste, such as toothpaste or wallpaper paste. Apply to the brass and let stay for five minutes. Wipe or wash with warm water and dry with a soft cloth that doesn't leave lint.

Stainless Steel Cookware Cleaner

Dip a soft cloth or disposable wipe in undiluted white vinegar. Wipe the surface. You also can use this method to clean chrome such as sink faucets.

Oven Cleaner

Baking soda and water cleans your oven. Buy a large, empty spray bottle in a hardware store and some paper towels or disposable or re-usable wiping cloths. You can use this combination for many purposes.

Fill the spray bottle with water and spray your oven. Then take some baking soda and a plastic scouring pad. Scour gently in circles. Wipe off the grime with the paper towels or re-usable or disposable wipes. Give another spray with the water bottle and then wipe dry.

For really stubborn stains, sprinkle table salt inside a warm oven. When it cools, scrape off the salt that now has absorbed the grime. Then wash the area with water and baking soda or plain water and wipe dry.

Less Toxic Toilet Bowl Cleaners

Pour a cup of baking soda into the toilet bowl. Add a cup of vinegar. After the fizzing stops, scour the bowl with a toilet brush or toilet wand. Another method that uses borax, which is a toxic ingredient, works on tougher toilet stains.

Be careful where you store the borax so no animal or child can reach it, and handle it carefully. Baking soda is less toxic because small amounts (such as a . quarter teaspoon) are used in cooking. Baking soda is the less hazardous ingredient.

Here's the toilet bowl or sink cleaning method using borax. Mix a cup of borax with a half cup of lemon juice or equal parts of borax and lemon juice until you get a paste the consistency of wall paper paste or toothpaste.

Flush the toilet so that the bowl gets coated with a thin film of water. Rub the paste inside the toilet bowl and under the rim. Leave the paste in the toilet for two hours. Then scrub and flush.

Chlorine bleach dulls porcelain enamel surfaces when left standing a long time. So don't let it stand in your toilet. It's also a toxic substance. Make more use of common household products such as lemon juice, vinegar, and baking soda.

Removing Mineral Deposits and Rust with Cream of Tartar

Use white vinegar and baking soda mixed to form a paste for dissolving soap scum and hard water marks. It certainly beats sniffing the odor of many commercial products for cleaning showers, tubs, and bathroom sinks. Check out the article, *Removing Mineral Deposits from Household Surfaces* at: http://www.ces.ncsu.edu/depts/fcs/housing/pubs/fcs397.html.

According to the publication prepared by Dr. Sandra A. Zaslow, Extension District Director, North Carolina Cooperative Extension Service, North Carolina State University, Raleigh, NC, issued in print by the North Carolina Cooperative Extension Service as publication FCS-397 and WQWM-12 (February 1993), published by North Carolina Cooperative Extension Service North Carolina State University, Raleigh, NC, you can use these techniques for removing a variety of household mineral deposits. View the Web site's "Stains at a Glance" summary.

What I like most about the publications at the university's Web sites are the recipes for making household cleaning products and mineral deposit removers with common household products. Such products normally are used in cooking such as lemon juice, cream of tartar, vinegar, and baking soda. Another surprise is making furniture polish from olive oil.

There also are products mentioned that are definitely not used in cooking such as ammonia or borax. The make it yourself recipes mostly call for less toxic, less hazardous, less expensive, and more environment friendly ingredients. What I liked most about this Web site was the recipes for multi-uses of cream of tartar as a cleaning agent and rust remover.

If your gadget or fixture is covered with mineral deposits or rust and *is not acid resistant*, use *cream of tartar*. It's a mild acid. Cream of tartar may be mixed with water to form a paste **rust** remover. Acids help remove hard water deposits. Some acid cleaners help remove discoloration from aluminum, brass, bronze, and copper. Other acids remove iron rust stains. Commercial toilet bowl cleaners, rust removers, metal cleaners, and kitchen and bath cleaners that remove mineral products usually are acids.

Commercial products may have stronger and more toxic acids. Make your own *milder* acid by using white vinegar. It's about 5 percent acetic acid. White vinegar may remove hard water deposits from glass, rust stains from sinks, and tarnish from brass and copper. Another mild acid is lemon juice.

Lemon juice contains citric acid, which can be used in much the same way as vinegar. However, it's easier to open a plastic jug of white vinegar and pour compared to squeezing a dozen fresh lemons to collect the juice and fill a cup. Unless you have a lemon tree in your backyard, the cost of lemons is a price to consider. What if you have pitted surfaces from abrasive cleaners, and you need to remove the rust?

Make a paste of borax and lemon juice. After the paste dries, rinse with water. For really stubborn rust, make a paste of mild scouring powder, cream of tartar, and peroxide. Let it set for 1/2 hour, and then rinse.

To get rid of copper stains (blue-green stains from acidic water) use a mixture of equal parts of water and ammonia. Ventilate the room. Mix a cup of water with a cup of ammonia. Be careful of those caustic fumes. Wear goggles and gloves.

Let the mixture stand on the stained area or wipe after the stains soften. Then rinse and flush pipes with water. Always flush pipes after using anything containing ammonia.

For black stains from manganese and a variety of other minerals, make a paste of cream of tartar and hydrogen peroxide. Let the mixture stand on the object, and then rinse thoroughly. For construction, maintenance, and repair solutions, the North Carolina State University's Web site at http://www.ces.ncsu.edu/

depts/fcs/housing/repair.html offers excellent techniques. Check out their index to publications on the Web at: http://www.ces.ncsu.edu/depts/fcs/housing/index.html on these how-to subjects and links.

Wood Moisture, Decay, and Mold

Is wood moisture causing allergies, toxic mold, or other damage problems in your house or apartment? Take wood moisture readings. See the North Carolina State University's site at http://www.ces.ncsu.edu/depts/fcs/housing/pubs/fcs486.html for tips on how to take wood moisture readings. At that Web site you'll see their publication called *Moisture Control and Prevention Guide.*

Buy a moisture meter at your local hardware or home improvement center. Insert the probes into the wood and read the indicator. It will tell you the percent of moisture in the surface. Take readings from every corner of a crawl space and the damp areas around plumbing fixtures in kitchens, laundry rooms, garages, and bathrooms. Take readings around the sills under sliding glass doors. Also get readings from places where chimneys, porches, garages, and patios attach to the house.

If you use a pest control firm, ask them to take moisture readings and stay round so you can get a copy of the recordings and watch how they do it so you can do it yourself periodically.

In addition to the toxic mold that grows on wood, fungi will only decay wood with moisture content above the fiber saturation point, which is 30 percent by weight for most species used in construction, according to the NC State University's publication at the Web site mentioned above.

They publication also states that wood with a moisture content of 20 percent and above is susceptible to decay. Make sure the moisture readings of wood in your home or apartment are below the fungi, decay, or mold levels.

Learn how to check for moisture levels before your wood decays or becomes moldy, infested, decayed, and toxic. Think about other products made from wood such as paper and cardboard. Cardboard and paper stored in closets and garages draw insects and mice that feed on paper. Store in plastic containers or jars, not in cardboard and paper. Make sure your books and paper documents are not subject to moisture or light or in open areas where bugs and worms can eat the paper or glue. Book or display cases need doors to protect the objects from dust, sunlight, moisture, acid, and mites.

6

DESCRIPTION OF BUSINESS

Clothing Selection Bargains and Image Coaching Video Podcasts

Buy shelf-pulls. Look for surplus clothing from overstocked wholesalers, warehouses, and liquidators. Look for clothing and other items returned to department stores that sell at a deep discount at warehouses. Shop for surplus goods, close outs, and liquidation items. One example of a one-stop shop surplus warehouse is Via Trading Corporation. The company's Web site is at: http://www.viatrading.com/.

If you want to live on less and make a living that way, consider selling on eBay or your own Web site products that are drop-shipped to you. Also check out the flea markets, swap meets, and garage sales.

You can buy clothing or books very inexpensively at garage sales. Buy by the pallet and not by the piece.

INCOME POTENTIAL

Buy at wholesale rate. Sell at low retail rate. For custom-designed shoes, charge what the current rate for custom shoes cost around the world, considering you are casting a separate mold of each individual's feet to design and sew the shoe. Consider learning to make prescription shoes, customized shoes, and shoes based on the sculpture mold casting of the feet of adults and children.

Call shoe repair shops that used to repair shoes but now only make a living from creating shoes from prescriptions. Also contact specialized shoe stores and manufacturers catering to special type of shoes made for unique feet by taking castings and creating molds.

BEST LOCALE TO OPERATE THE BUSINESS

Work at home online. Any geographic area is good where you can work online and send out catalogues, either electronic or print (more costly) are fine. Target areas where there are many Internet users or busy working people or others who are online and need to order lower priced surplus clothing, shelf-pulls, and over-stocked items or discontinued lines. Don't buy clothes that are 'mistakes', stained, or sewed wrong.

EQUIPMENT NEEDED

You'll need software that creates retail parts catalogues or fashion catalogues and brochures. Put up a Web site with links to all your items. Use Web-creating soft-ware or hire a Web designer to put up an electronic catalogue online. Also have the same on discs if you need to mail them to a customer. Consider print cata-logues, but those on discs are cheaper to duplicate or store.

OPERATING YOUR BUSINESS

Keep what you need and sell the rest online at eBay or other Web sites or at swap meets, garage sales, or throw clothing parties with your friends, neighbors, or rel-atives to sell clothing, especially children's clothing or other items. Buy items in bulk, including clothing, if you will need it. It's cheaper to buy in bulk.

New merchandise that's surplus or overstocked sells in warehouses at a huge discount. The surplus is sold both to the public and to those who resell the prod-ucts or clothing online or at swap meets.

Also check out the clothing or electronics brokers. When you buy an item, ask whether you can pay the reseller's price.

That way you can buy several of the same items at that price, keep an item for yourself and sell the rest online such as on eBay. It pays to get a business license from your local Board of Equalization as a reseller of the items you want to pur-chase to keep one, and resell the rest.

Is making your own clothing too time consuming? You'd have to spend money for a sewing machine, patterns or pattern supplies, thread, needles, scis-sors and other sewing equipment.

Where else can you get *quality* clothing that lasts as long as you need it—for less? Second-hand stores that handle "upscale neighborhood" clothing are fine if you don't mind cleaning the clothes all over again when you get them home.

No one is suggesting you look for clothing in dumpsters. However, some astute dressers actually look over designer clothing and fabrics from dumpsters in upper class neighborhoods or from the discarded samples of fashion design salons, manufacturers and designing schools. Clothing from upper-East Side NY trash bins may be searched for throwaway wearable clothing and usable items.

There's usually someone hunting for discarded fabrics from wholesalers and remnants from fabric stores. Many second hand or thrift shops depend upon people that bring in clothes.

Not all people bring in cleaned clothing, although stores usually ask you to have a garment cleaned before you donate it. Where else can you look to buy new clothes that don't fall apart quickly?

RELATED OPPORTUNITIES

Track down the less costly imports along with those made locally from the discount clubs, wholesalers, and surplus stores that buy clothing as well as food and other items in bulk. Also try eBay at http://www.eBay.com. New as well as used clothing and fabrics are bargains if you watch the shipping and handling costs.

Try some of the military surplus stores for clothing and equipment such as Army-Surplus.com at: http://www.army-surplus.com/. Surplus military clothing such as walking boots, camping gear, jackets, and pants generally take more wear and tear than similar department store bought clothing. Try the Army Surplus Online Super Store at the Web site: http://www.army-surplus.com/ss_store/index.html. Check out the duffle bags, boots, and bags.

Shoes

How do you craft and sew custom-made-to-fit shoes from scratch? To get an idea of how to make your own shoes for comfort and tailored fit, first explore online instructions for making your own shoes. Keep in mind that if you have growing children or grand children, making custom-made shoes is a wonderful gift, and it does cut expenses and at the same offer comfort and benefits.

Making your family's shoes is another way to live on less while having more. It enhances your creativity and thinking skills. The shoes can be of better quality. And it fits under the label of household necessities to enjoy within the basic food, shelter, and clothing category.

Put your own designer label on your home-made shoes and offer to design custom-fit shoes for others. That's one more way to make money at home or online with your creativity. You can make shoes for yourself and your family or for others. Crafting, sewing, and practical creativity give you more choices when you're aiming to cut expenses and enjoy more comfort.

Start with the Web sites and books on how to make your own shoes. Excellent Web sites include Make Your Own Shoes, a step-by-step guide for high fashion, low-cost, and perfect fit. The Web site features illustrated instructions for making shoes from scratch. Every step is illustrated. The site is at: http://www.marywalesloomis.com/page3.html.

What I like about these instructions is that the author, Mary Wales Loomis, also has written a book on how to make your own shoes. The details are at: http://www.marywalesloomis.com/page10.html. In addition to her book, which you can order, her Web site gives instructions on how to make shoes.

The instructions show how you use your existing shoes to make a last by reshaping plaster of Paris to change width or toe shape on the last. Included are detailed instructions for casting your feet to make a custom-made last from which you can make different types of shoes to match your clothing or accessories. At the site: http://www.marywalesloomis.com/page4.html illustrations include a list of the materials you will need and instructions on how to make a muslin pattern and sew the shoe. The illustrations show the materials you'll need in forming the uppers to join the lasts.

You learn with illustrations and explanations how to sew the back seam and put the uppers onto the lasts. For example, you wet the upper and form it onto the last so it can dry in the shape of the last. This is illustrated at the site. The instructions are excellent, especially in recommending strong thread so the upper can be sewn tightly to the last and left to dry.

The site shows you how to apply a certain type of cement to the heels and attach the sole. For those who aren't able to access the Web or use computers, the book is full of excellent illustrated instructions on how to make your own shoes.

You can make them at far less cost than you'd ever buy custom-made shoes that fit perfectly. You have the power to control what materials you want to use for your shoes. The benefit is you get to make shoes for yourself or anyone else that match other clothing or accessories. There are several other sites on the Web on making your own shoes.

What you need to do before you make anything such as shoes is to take a shoe apart or anything else apart to make a pattern and to see how they are made. It's a type of back-engineering with basic clothing that mystifies a lot of us.

You start by putting in front of you two comfortable pairs of shoes that will be 'sacrificed.' Begin by assembling a hammer, screwdriver, and pliers. Then take apart an old shoe that was very comfortable and broken-in to the shape of your foot.

Now take another complete pair of shoes that have not been taken apart. Use your most comfortable shoes that have seen their day, but are stretched and molded to fit your foot. The key word is comfortable. Use the most comfortable pair of shoes you have.

You're going to make a mold by filling your most comfortable pair of shoes with plaster of Paris. When the plaster dries, you carefully cut the shoe away from the plaster, saving the tops of the shoes for your pattern. Now you have your mold. This mold is called a set of 'lasts.' Save those tops to make a pattern out of muslin fabric.

You'll use fabric that matches your other clothing or accessories for the outside of the shoe. Buckram is used to shape the inside of the shoe and give it some support for your foot.

When you sew it all together, you will be putting water on the upper part of the shoe to form it onto the plaster lasts. Then you let it dry on the last so that it makes a custom fit in the shape of your old comfortable shoe.

You'll need finer details of what type of shoe to make. Some books show you how to make a ladies' pump. So for making shoes for men or boys, you'll need to use men's shoes. The best way to start is to buy a book on how to make shoes and learn the finer details of materials to use.

You'll need to learn how to change the plaster of Paris mold of your foot into the shape of a shoe. The crude type of shape from your shoe is different from the exact plaster of Paris cast of your foot that you'll need to customize the shoe to fit comfortably on your foot. That's why it's best to start by reading a book on how to use the plaster of Paris cast of your foot and how to change it into the shape of a shoe.

Mary's book illustrates how to make the soles of your shoes by hand-cutting them from tooling leather. She also lists resources to buy the leather. There's a chapter on making flat shoes. Some people don't wear leather shoes. So you choose what materials you want. To order Mary's book, see her Web site at: http://www.marywalesloomis.com/page10.html.

There are other Web sites on how to make your own shoes. For example, learn to make your own shoes at the Web site at: http://www.inquiry.net/outdoor/winter/gear/snowshoes/.

The site gives instructions for making "Indian" snowshoes made from wood, pioneer snowshoes from ash or hickory sticks, Alaskan shoes (includes patterns and plans), Chippewa snowshoes with pointers on variations including bear paw, co-Yukon, Sioux, Oregon, Utah, Montreal, and Iroquois snowshoes.

There also are instructions on making snowshoe bindings for use with snow-shoe moccasins, and bindings made for boots. Look at Web sites emphasizing prescription shoes such as shoes for diabetics. One such Web site is Lucha's Comfort Footware at: http://www.comfortfootwear.com/.

Some food conditions include:

• **Achilles Tendonitis**	• **Hammer Toes**	• **Neuropathy**
• **Arch Pain/Strain**	• **Heel Fissures**	• **Overlapping Toes**
• **Arthritis**	• **Heel Pain**	• **Over Pronation**
• **Athletes Foot**	• **Heel Spurs**	• **Plantar Fasciitis**
• **Bunions**	• **HIV & Your Feet**	• **Post-Tib Tendonitis**
• **Calluses**	• **Ingrown Toenails**	• **Pregnancy**
• **Claw Toes**	• **Mallet Toes**	• **Sesamoiditis**
• **Corns**	• **Metatarsalgia**	• **Shin Splints**
• **Diabetic Foot**	• **Mortons Neuroma**	• **Toenail Fungus**

What you can do is specialize in creating shoes for various foot conditions by talking with podiatrists and owners of special shoe stores and schools that train people to make prescription shoes customized to order by taking casts of feet and making molds for designing the shoes. Some shoe stores accept Medi-Care payments.

Check out how these craftspeople learned to make and/or sell prescription shoes. You'll be helping people cut expenses by buying shoes that fit right and last longer.

Import specialized shoes from around the world to sell if you don't want to craft the shoes yourself. Check out the frequently-asked questions at the Dr. Zen's Shoes Web site at: http://www.drzen.net/faq.htm. For example, according to the Web site, Ulcers or sores on the feet (…of diabetics) can be caused by improper shoe gear that can result in infection and possible amputations. Diabetic shoes with moldable insoles reduce the development of these ulcers and sores."

Your business would be about helping people find the right shoes or crafting specialized or prescription shoes yourself. Look for instruction online or in your area on how to design and make shoes taken from making a mold or cast of individual feet. By making your own shoes for different uses, you can match the material and color of the shoe as well, and cut expenses along with getting higher quality by customizing the shoe to the individual.

ADDITIONAL INFORMATION

Contacts

The Simple Living Network
http://www.simpleliving.net/
http://www.simpleliving.net/ecoliving/default.asp

Your Money or Your Life Online Study Networks—A Nine-Step Program
http://www.simpleliving.net/ymoyl/default.asp

Study Groups Database
http://www.simpleliving.net/studygroups/default.asp

Building Sustainable Communities
http://www.simpleliving.net/ecoliving/community-default.asp?title=Building+Sustainable+Communities

Manual for Group Facilitators
http://www.simpleliving.net/ecoliving/community-default.asp?title=Manuals

Simple Living Resources Database
http://www.simpleliving.net/resources/default.asp

EscapeArtist.com (Moving to Thailand)
http://www.escapeartist.com/Thailand/Thailand.html

Mother Earth News. Com
http://www.motherearthnews.com/index.php?page=main&ref=mothermisc

Choosing a Log Home (article)
http://www.motherearthnews.com/article/2151/

Log Homes and Log Cabins from Scratch
http://www.loghomebuilders.org/
Also: http://www.loghomebuilders.org/articles_about_log_homes.htm

Contracts

USA Contract Categories
http://www.lawdepot.com/contracts/usa/?pid=google-contracts_usa-contracts_b

Legal Database
http://www.legal-database.com/contractlaw.htm

Find Legal Forms.com-Easy to Use Legal Forms for the Right Job
http://www.findlegalforms.com/xcart/customer/
home.php?partner=google&alphabetical=yes

Consumer Report
http://consumerreport.ca/

ConsumerReports.org
http://www.consumerreports.org/main/home.jsp

ConsumersUnion.org
http://www.consumersunion.org/

7

DESCRIPTION OF BUSINESS

Branding, Logos, & Business Creativity Video Podcasts

Branding is your mark of creativity. Use video podcasts to create and promote brands for a variety of products and people—from public speakers to manufacturers. Create a title for yourself and your experience of living on less to make a living. Read the advice of professionals.

For example, Linda Cobb is known professionally as The Queen of Clean. She writes excellent, helpful books on how to organize, clean, and remove clutter. And she has her own TV show featuring tips on how to clean and make your own cleaning products from less costly materials such as vinegar, borax, ammonia, water, and unseasoned meat tenderizer for removing stains.

Her books and shows feature an enormous number of helpful tips that save money and work right on the materials they clean or organize. For example, there are tips such as when sitting at the dinner table, as soon as something spills on your clothing or carpet, putting salt on stains from gravy or food takes out the stains in an emergency.

Club soda removes red wine, coffee, tea, and even red pop soda if you put it on the stain right away. What all these tips show is practical creativity. You can live on less and make a living at it by sharing creativity about your helpful, practical applications that show people how to improve and simplify their lives through step-by-step useful how-to information.

Become aware of a community need. Work with inspiration and motivation. Research niche areas not yet covered to create your own original video podcast.

Find out through research what people want most in the way of a video podcast. Help people solve problems such as getting rid of clutter, organizing a home-based office, cleaning, repairing, or planning creative home schooling experiences. What else do people need answers or solutions to in your area?

INCOME POTENTIAL

Charge a flat fee or by the hour to create branding logos and themes for other businesses. Use the current rate for other people who design logos and branding themes as well as publicity. About $100 an hour for creating a logo works in areas where other designers make that sum. Charging $25–$35 an hour works in other areas. It all depends on your reputation and how well you are known in the business community. Competition exists with graphic designers who design logos, book covers, brochures, and press kits.

BEST LOCALE TO OPERATE THE BUSINESS

Work in an area where there is a lot of industry. You need contacts with new businesses and stores.

TRAINING REQUIRED

Anywhere you can find creativity enhancement courses or practice in creating logos and branding themes. This would include courses in advertising, branding, graphic design, and logo design, desktop publishing, and typesetting.

EQUIPMENT NEEDED

You'll need graphic design software and a computer with a color printer/photo printer as well as a text printer. You might want to add a machine that binds books if you are hired to create booklets or small books for corporations.

OPERATING YOUR BUSINESS

To express creativity about living on less and sharing the experiences, first create your own logo, title, and plan of how you will share useful information. Will you be the next ogre of organization, curmudgeon of clutter, duke of drains, prince of plumbing, or cloisonné of clean?

Will you be the next earl of examples, marques of mothering, sovereign of simplicity, viscount of ventilation, lady of less, sultan of sources, sheik of shopping, or baron of bargains? You get the picture.

Put creativity into the elbow work. Use a term that's familiar to many or a proverb that you expand into ***branding.***

If you're going to show people how to use branding as a business that teaches people how to cut expenses, instead of showing them how do you live on less, show people how to get higher quality for less money. Show them how they can have more, and get what they pay for. Start with the hidden markets like the wholesalers, shelf-pulls, and overstocked items or the imports and exports.

Teaching branding is about emphasizing simplicity and commitment. That's what you market in your buzz appeal campaign to the media and to the public as your customers and clients.

Your first step would be to use branding to make a 'brand' or trade name or logo and slogan for yourself that represents your basic concept and message. That's a proverb or quotation that in one sentence or less tells the public what you represent, to what you are committed. Keep it simple and short. After you have your branding complete with slogans and proverbs, launch your *get what you pay for* theme in the media.

To select a reporter from the media, find out by reading publications and newspapers who is writing a story similar to your concept or who has recently written a similar article. That reporter may not do another similar story, but can refer you to someone who might. Call the features editor and ask who has written similar articles or will be assigned a similar topic on bargain hunting for quality, getting what you pay for, simplifying your life, or living on less, saving, and enjoying the lifestyle more.

If you emphasize extreme telecommuting, travel, working outdoors, mobile lifestyle, working at home, or any other lifestyle, work style or attitude, focus on publications that emphasize publishing information or advertising those types of products.

If your writing is honest and dramatic, it will appeal to the newspaper reporter who is writing on a subject similar to yours. If that reporter from a national newspaper or other national publication with a very wide circulation writes about your story or interviews you and incorporates passages into the reporter's piece, quoting your story—fiction or biography—you have a great chance of publishers and agents contacting you. Usually, it will be an agent who is willing to bid your story to publishers.

Here's a famous example. Jessie Lee Foveaux, at the age of 98, sold her memoir for a million dollars, and she had never published before. She sold her book and movie rights. Was it luck or buzz appeal? The Life of Jessie Lee Brown from Birth up to 80 years had been written in longhand for an adult education class in writing for senior citizens writing their life stories.

In fact, she wrote the book manuscript 18 years before it found a market. How did she get it auctioned to competing book publishers and movie producers? How did she find her agent? Her life story is all about how she, as a battered wife married to an alcoholic husband, managed to raise eight children alone after leaving her husband and how hard she struggled to put food on the table. It is because she is from Kansas and spent her time knitting cross-shaped bookmarks for her church members that the story had universal appeal to agents?

The message of the book emphasized commitment and simplicity. It's hard to find an agent who would take on a 98-year old great, great grandma and sell her life story for a million dollars. Foveaux wrote her memoir back in 1979 when friends encouraged her to enroll in an adult education writing class. Her writing teacher, who also is a farmer, gave out assignments to the senior citizens in the class to write the story of their lives.

Foveaux even protested to her writing teacher at adult school that she didn't have the time to write. He insisted that she make the time and encouraged her to write. She took his advice and brought in her assignments each week with up to four thousand words of her life story.

When you try to sell simplicity and commitment in any item, whether it's your diary or a gift basket of hand-made products, write down what's different about what you have to offer? Foveaux wrote the details of how she spent her childhood, the characters who inhabited towns in which she lived, and details of her relatives.

Then she started on a narrative and got to the deeper story of her life. That's what you have to do—get to the deeper story of how to get what you pay for. Details and information are what sells—the facts and how to apply them in a practical, yet simple way to improve. Foveaux wrote about commitment using a simple plot with lots of details of her life story. She worked as a grocery clerk and other jobs to support all her children.

What in this story differed from the thousands of memoirs that are written by seniors in adult education classes? It's this story that brought in a million dollars from publishers, plus movie rights. How did this story differ from the others? The visibility or "buzz" appeal began with Foveaux's writing teacher who put her writing in his newsletter that contained the writing of all the students in the senior citizen writing class.

When we analyze how the first step led to the next, we have to look at her writing teacher's credibility adding to her credibility by publishing the writing of all the students in a newsletter. Normally, that would have been the end of the . line. Except, by mailing the newsletter to a reporter from The Wall Street Journal, this reporter wrote about the author. That article published in the Wall Street Journal helped to give visibility and credibility to significant highlights of the book. The book soon sold to major publishers for a lot of money.

So you have to have a similar leap from adult education class newsletter of writing to actually being published in a national publication that has national credibility. The most important step of buzz appeal occurred when the Wall Street Journal reporter actually took a step forward to make Foveaux's writings known to the wider world of Wall Street Journal readers.

Your approach and product or attitude needs to be the perfect forum for a particular newspaper or magazine or other media venture. There had to be a reason why the newsletter went to this particular reporter at The Wall Street Journal. After all, most people think of The Wall Street Journal as a financial newspaper full of articles on stocks, investments and mergers. The newspaper's focus is far removed from a senior citizen's memoirs of raising a large family in an unhappy marriage, yet it made the perfect forum because it has universal appeal.

The writing teacher had read a previous article in The Wall Street Journal by that reporter who wrote an in-depth article on senior citizens that attracted the interest of the writing teacher in the Midwest. He sent the article to the reporter because it emphasized the **commitment to family and faith**. To create buzz, your writing, product, or application of your idea **must have some redemptive value to a universal audience.** That's the most important point.

What you need for your idea is **momentum.** You need to have a practical application—details, facts, and step-by-step instruction people can follow in what you present to the public. The Wall Street Journal reporter drew close to the writings of the 98-year old woman. Those writings had such redemptive value to create buzz (universal appeal). The Wall Street Journal reporter developed more buzz (appeal) around the manuscript by writing an article about the author and the manuscript.

Momentum resulted. The momentum moved it along the pipeline so that all the right connections had access by reading the Wall Street Journal. The point is if you want to reach all the right connections for your applications of ideas, you need a pipeline, a publication or other media that is credible enough for the people in power to view.

Make sure the people you want to reach read or view the publication or media to which you send your promotional writings. Do these people you want to reach even read or watch the media that is publishing your work? Before you launch anything in the media, think about who you want to reach.

Do these powerful people actually see that publication daily? Would they be interested in your information on how to get what you pay for or how to live on less and enjoy it more? Would you be better off sharing information not on how to live on less, but on strategies that the wealthy and famous use to get richer and happier at the same time? Think about it. Two very simple values sell to the rich and poor alike. They emphasize commitment. Those two values are *doing the best you can* under the circumstances, and *trusting in your faith*. It's like the old proverb, "You know that I care more than you care what I know."

A front-page story ran in the Wall Street Journal on March 7, 1997. Offers from publishers immediately flooded the writer. A lawyer hired by the writer's relative helped to find a literary agent to look at all the publisher's offers and select the best one. When 20 publishers called and 20 movie producers, offering six-figure movie contracts, the power of buzz—of **credibility** created through **visibility** in the major national press—spun into action.

The point is that without "buzz" (as they say in the publishing world), would that book have gotten the attention it deserved before the author had an agent? If you sent a book manuscript directly to a publisher, it most likely would come back with a note that unsolicited manuscripts are not read.

You'd most likely be told to find a literary agent willing to send your book to publishers. That manuscript might stay on the agent's desk for a year before you finally received it back with a rejection form letter. Who wants to spend that many years trying to find an agent who thinks your book will earn a commission or sell widely?

No matter how great your idea or product is, unless you find someone to buzz you into the national press, you aren't going to be noticed that easily. That's where creativity plays a role. Forget the cliché of thinking outside the box. Instead view the familiar box from a different angle.

To be more creative, find out what's in vogue. What's the current interest? Simplicity and commitment always is in vogue, but you need the next step—time. Look at trends. Research the trends to find out whether what you have to offer is coming at a time when people are trying to hold a family together and put bread on the table at the same time. Now get even more creative. You have buzz appeal.

In any video podcast offer *simple* solutions using step-by-step instructions people can follow. Solve problems. Emphasize results, benefits, and advantages. Use facts that can be checked for credibility. Make sure claims are scientifically substantiated, and show viewers where and how to check your facts. Focus more narrowly. Are you appealing to American women? Do the trends say that this is the time when American women are working to support families? What practical steps can you offer them to make life and work easier, less costly, and of better quality?

Foveaux's book was auctioned at more than a million dollars, and Warner cast the top bid. Think about how the author's manuscript went through certain steps to get to the person at Warner with the power to make things happen for the author. Think of what happened in between, the lawyer who helped the auction to happen and the publishers who took an interest. What made all these people take an interest?

Look at the value of your writing or information. Is what you have **simple** enough to sell for a million dollars? It has to be really simple to make so much money. Simple means *understandable* by the average viewer, and that's buzz (universal) appeal.

If you want to make a living by living on less, share what's simple and earthy about what you have and what you do. Be yourself. Publishers can spot phoniness in a minute. Can your customers or clients do the same?

If you write, be a real person in your writing. Be true to yourself. What's worth a million? The book emphasized morals, faith, and values. If you analyze what powerful publishers buy for universal appeal, it's a steady focus on values. Publishers look for faith in something greater than our lives. They seek stories of commitment and simplicity of values.

Publishers who buy a book or any other item on its buzz value are buying simplicity. It is simplicity that sells and nothing else but simplicity. This is true for computers, MP3 players, books, or items that have to be assembled by the buyer. Simplicity sells in instructional manuals and in how-to kits. It's good storytelling to say it simply. People want user-friendly gadgets, stories, and information.

Simplicity means what you have to offer gives your customer all the answers everyone looks for in exotic places, but finds close by. What's the great proverb that sells anything to anyone? It's to stand on your own two feet and put bread on your own table for your family.

Living on less and enjoying it more or you get what you pay for are moral points telling you to pull your own weight. And pulling your own weight is a buzz word that sells any product or application of an idea that teaches and reaches through simplicity.

The backbone of the media emphasizes the values of simplicity, morals and faith (or trust). These are universal values. Doing the best to take care of your family sells. That's the buzz appeal you need to emphasize.

Consumers and publishers go through fads every two years—angel books, managing techniques books, computer home-based business books, novels about ancient historical characters or tribes, science fiction, children's programming.

The genres shift emphasis, but values are consistent in the bestselling books, toys, and any other product.

You need to offer simplicity, values, morals, and commitment in whatever you want to share to make a living. Look at trends. To live on less and have more, find the highways to simplicity. Target those values. Emphasize commitment.

Buzz is universal, but you need national press to get publishers bidding. National press gives you credibility in the eyes of major publishers. The world is impressed by front page coverage in The Wall Street Journal because of what it symbolizes—stability, dependability, security, centeredness.

Find a newspaper article that relates to what information you want to share. Write to the reporter covering the feature. Query to see whether there is an interest in your story or feature. Make sure you have a new angle on your project. Does your item emphasize universal values, morals, simplicity, and commitment?

Does it span real history in a way that reads and works well? Quality is the most important trait. Visibility and credibility give your product momentum. Buzz appeal gives momentum to the practical application of your idea. Universal values and simple lifestyles sell each time they solve problems, give results, and offer benefits with balance.

Take drop-ship products from a company at no cost to you. Sell the products online, on eBay, for example. The products are stored in the company's warehouse, not in your home. You could have the company mail the product directly to the customer after you collect the payment, take your share or commission, and notify the company of the sale and customer's shipping address.

ADDITIONAL INFORMATION

Resources: Simplicity, Balance, & Commitment

Living the Simple Life
http://www.cottagesoft.com/~cynthia/nfbkrevw/simplife.htm

Books and Magazines about Balance
http://www.marciaconner.com/fav/balancereading.html

Right on the Money
http://www.rightonthemoney.org/shows/116_simplify/

8

DESCRIPTION OF BUSINESS

Video Podcasts on Comparison or Mystery Shopping with Decorating and Design & Marketing/Opinion Surveys

Pay Less for High-Quality Items and Services Using Focused Practical Comparison Shopping Strategies

Your video podcasts can emphasize high-quality bargains and simplicity, including commitment to a brand or style. The more creative you become, the more you need to simplify your life style. Simplicity sells because it offers commitment to basic values. To be more creative in purchasing and saving, simplify your lifestyle. Make the complex clearer to understand. Apply simplicity and commitment to shopping.

To sell your concept of getting what you pay for, simplifying your life, or bargain-hunting in hidden markets, you need to develop buzz appeal. You have to package your strategies, tips, and techniques to the media in a way that has universal appeal. What you're marketing is a concept.

The concept emphasizes simplicity, commitment, and time-tested values. This concept is all about making what is difficult to understand clear and easier to understand. You're looking for a concept that unites everyone, a type of simplicity that is universal, with which nearly everyone can identify.

You're looking for a concept that gives people the power to choose what helps them reach their maximum potential, make their own decisions, and think about what's right. You want a concept that makes people feel good about themselves and important. What's that concept? It's getting what you pay for.

Everyone wants a bargain as long as the bargain is of high quality and long-lasting. You want to live the concept of living on less and having more. More what? You're emphasizing quality of life. Your bargains represent products or ideas that stand up to the test of time. In your concept of you get what you pay for, emphasize better quality when it comes to wear and tear. Include decorating, design, and mystery shopping services.

EQUIPMENT NEEDED

Make a budget of money and of time. Set aside another 20 percent to cover expenses if you go over the budget. Live on less by making your own decorations and designs from scratch. To make a table, use a polished thick tree trunk with a flat bottom and top for a middle base and an oval piece of wood for the top. For drapes use easy-to-clean vertical blinds. Make curtains out of colorful sheets. Or sew scraps together like a patch quilt to make tapestry hangings for the walls.

You can use stencils to paint murals on your walls to give the feeling of a larger room. For example, a seascape or trees with perspective give an in-depth feeling of distance. An open road painted on a wall or mirrors from floor to ceiling give the impression that the room is larger.

Paint your walls white and stencil murals if you want to give the impression of depth perspective. Look at the walls of restaurants painted in murals of balconies and palm trees with a seascape in the distance.

Work on the kitchen and bath. The living room can be redecorating simply by changing the color of the walls, sofa pillows, drapes or blinds, and slip covers. Wooden tables or other furniture can be stained the same color.

On the floor hardwood stands up longer than carpets. Use hardwood or ceramic tile and two inexpensive throw rugs that imitate in design the more expensive oriental rugs.

Match any throw rugs on the floor to the tapestries on the walls if you use wall tapestries. They harbor dust and insects. So you might want to paint murals on the walls using stencils.

What you probably need most are new faucets in the kitchen and bath or new sinks if your basins are cracked. Accessorize. If you don't like your old color scheme, put new colors over your old furniture. It's easier to sew slip covers than to buy a new sofa as long as the basic framework is holding up and there are no tears to the fabric.

The inexpensive quilts you find in discount stores for a queen or king size bed make excellent slip cover throws on sofas. Use a queen size for a love seat and king size for larger sofas. Pick the color scheme you want.

Use the pillow slips that come with the quilts to put on your arm rests or sofa pillow throws in matching colors. Video podcasts may emphasize interior design or house remodeling techniques that offer a different emphasis from the popular do-it-yourself shows currently on satellite television. One example would be how to make a home more child or pet-friendly using technology or techniques that have stood the test of time.

INCOME POTENTIAL

What can you do to earn money in a hurry and be proud of it—if you don't have a job? Your first step, assuming you have no capital to start with is to provide a service. You can provide a wide variety of services from recording the highlights of people's lives on video and making copies on DVDs as gifts and greetings. Or you could become a secret shopper. Check out the mystery shopper information Web sites, such as the one at Volition.com ® at: http://www.volition.com/mystery.html.

Secret shoppers visit businesses posing as customers. They evaluate the services received and complete an evaluation form. Entrepreneurs use comparative shopping reports to insure that their employees are practicing appropriate selling techniques and providing quality service to customers.

If you want to be a comparison or secret shopper, check out the many Web sites that offer to pay you to shop for them or their clients. Never send any money to anyone for information.

Use the key word "mystery shoppers" to find a listing of these firms on the Web. Visit sites for information only from reputable companies. Make sure you don't sign any agreement where there is an obligation or cost. You can research both USA and international firms. After you check out national or international companies based on their reputation, ask secret shoppers who already work for them to evaluate the company before you sign up.

When you have a credible list of national and international firms, you can sign up as long as there's no clause in the contract that keeps you from leaving without any cost to you. They companies with which you sign on will eventually contact you when they have a store in your area.

OPERATING YOUR BUSINESS

Check out the Mystery Shopping Bulletin Board and USA Mystery Shopping Companies List at http://www.volition.com/mysteryUSA1.html. Look at the International Companies Shopping Companies List at: http://www.volition.com/mysteryint.html. ON these and other bulletin boards companies post immediate needs. There's also information regarding what companies other shoppers have used. View the information on who pays on time and who does not. Checking the Web sites for up-to-date information is an excellent way to learn from those who are already secret shoppers.

Comparison shopping can be done for the media or when you write a column on retailing advice. Look at the lists for Canada, Australia, New Zealand and other areas such as Taiwan, Puerto Rico, Guam, Hong Kong, and Japan by clicking on the International Companies List. If you don't like comparison shopping by driving to various stores, try online comparative shopping where you can sit at home and order online using your computer and Internet connection.

You could make money starting bartering clubs or joining one. The idea is to swap goods that you can keep or sell with online sites. Most barter clubs let you swap products rather than pay for them in cash. You can check out the barter clubs to join.

National barter clubs have not done well. Locally, barter clubs do work when people can look over the merchandise in their neighborhood rather than send anything unseen through the mail far away.

Membership fees to barter clubs can run in the hundreds of dollars. Then there are the commissions per trade of up to 15 percent. Some commissions are still only five percent. Other clubs charge a monthly fee, perhaps $20. So the idea of working with someone else's barter club is not exactly living with fewer expenses.

You can start your own local club. Instead of trading products, trade your time. Help someone on a per hour basis, such as tutoring, mentoring, cleaning, sorting, organizing, indexing, editing, speaking, writing, watching, or coaching. You could offer services house sitting or watching and waiting for delivery or construction crews.

Exchange your time for someone else's time. Anything from beauty treatments to cooking lessons can be exchanged. Research the type of credit given or what is given in return for your time and services. Watch out. Barter credit runs out of time. You don't want to lose any opportunity to earn cash for your time rather than spend time and get in return something you don't really need like more knick-knacks to clutter or small living area.

RELATED OPPORTUNITIES: Video Podcasts of Opinion Survey Interviews

Your opinions are worth pay. Check out the Web site at http://www.fieldwork.com. How the process works in getting paid for your opinion is that marketing research firms are the companies to apply to for work. The marketing firms form focus groups that research what consumers think and feel about individual products. A typical payment is $100 for a few hours of your time spent filling out forms or answering questions about using the product in a group meeting.

Make money from your opinions. Apply to firms that pay cash. Some pay only in coupons. Coupons are fine when you want to buy a product at a discount, but cash pays bills. Careful, your name and address may end up on endless lists to receive unsolicited junk mail. Then again, you may receive coupons.

You make the decision. If you supply a post office box number, the junk mail or sales material may come to that address instead of flooding your home. Not all companies sell your address to lists, but some may.

That's why it's best not to put personal information such as a social security number into any application. What you fill out may end up on hundreds of lists of addresses to send junk mail to—that is unsolicited mail asking you to buy something or donate money.

Post office boxes can direct mail to the box and not to your home. Never give out your home phone if there's a chance the marketing company might sell your name to another list. Instead use an answering service or a special email address to see to how many lists your name is sold.

Several years ago I was paid $50 for my opinion for using two competing products for a week and then answering questions and filling out forms regarding what I thought about different aspects of each product. Your local phone directly has a category titled "Market Research." Contact all the market research firms in your area and tell them you want paid work for offering your opinion or evaluation of products by using them comparatively.

Another way of generating income in a hurry is to be paid for your opinions by answering *online surveys*. Check out the site at: http://www.volition.com/opinions.html. Some companies pay you only by entering you in sweepstakes for answering their opinion surveys.

When you need cash in a hurry, only look for companies that actually pay you in cash right after you answer their surveys. Try companies such as American Consumer Opinion ®. Their Web site is at: http://www.acop.com/. Most survey companies pay a small amount for your opinion. Some companies require you to be selected before you are paid. So check out the companies online before you spend time filling out opinion surveys. Look at the trends influencing the various age groups, such as the Baby Boomers and grandchildren of the Boomers

Empty Nesters

Check out the statistics on Baby Boomers and Empty Nesters at the EscapeHomes.com Web site at: http://www.escapehomes.com/articles/Baby_Boomers_Statistics_on_Empty_Nests_and_Retirement.htm. According to the 2004 Del Webb Baby Boomer Survey, getting out of debt are the Baby

Boomers' first priority as empty nesters. When empty nesters that also are Baby Boomers (or beyond) want to live on less and earn more, what the Boomers actually are feeling, according to the 2004 Del Webb Baby Boomer Survey, is an increase in freedom to be themselves.

The survey notes that 75 percent of Boomers don't miss the parenting roles, such as being soccer moms or tutoring school work. However, 64 percent of Boomers do miss the family vacations.

Forty percent of Boomers believe their children will be better off financially than they are. Only 2 percent say they wished they would not have had children. 46 percent would advise future parents to spend less time at work and more time with their children. And 74 percent say they have been good role models.

Twenty-seven percent would not let their grown children move back in with them assuming that their children were in good health and financially secure. Forty percent of Boomers anticipate that their adult children will move back in with them.

Thirty percent anticipate that their parents will move in with them. Do Boomers charge their children rent and their parents rent? Actually, the study noted that 28 percent of Boomers would charge their kids rent, but only eight percent of Boomers would bill their parents who move in with them for rent and/ or food.

What if you are a Baby Boomer, an empty nester with adult children? You've paid for their education with your retirement money. Now you decide to travel around the world or across the country to relax and enjoy.

You've spent your life helping your children grow up, graduate from college or trade school, marry, and have their own children. Your goal focused on helping your children to become employable, friendly, and financially responsible.

Your parents live in another city. Suddenly, your parents retire from paid income. Because of health problems, they can't take care of themselves. They can't afford long term care insurance. They sell their home to make ends meet. Declines in investments take away your parents' savings.

At the same time, your children move back in with you with their children. Your daughter becomes pregnant and loses her job.

Your son has health or emotional problems that keep him from working, or he can't find a new job. Now your parents move back in with you taking your son's room. Your children move back in with you taking your daughter's room.

Your grandchildren occupy a spare room. You're about to take your first trip around the world as an empty nester. Do you tell your children, grandchildren, and parents to move in and house sit while you board the cruise ship with your spouse?

Of course you do. It's your turn now. If you wait to become dependent and penniless, will you really have the chance to travel? The message is to list your priorities, plan, and live each day at a time while looking ahead to the future.

Empty nesters who want to live on less should consider putting their parents and adult children to work for them either house sitting while they travel or in a family business that allows each family member to work together in a cottage industry at home doing what they do best—where their natural talents take them. What do you want to do for the long term that you can live on and at the same time promotes your general health?

For example, parents can watch the property. Adult children can work at telecommuting, and grandchildren can do promotional such as voice over work in commercials or help illustrate children's story books. There's a creative endeavor for those who insist they don't have a creative bone in their bodies.

The whole idea is to encourage people to reach their maximum potential by working together as a family unit on living the positive attitude by being of service to others or working on creative expression projects that fill a need in the community.

How can you make working together as an empty nester a step-by-step how to useful skill to share with others? From publishing print-on-demand genealogy research booklets to making time capsules, there's a place for everyone with every type of skill. For the number counters, there are budgeting, planning, and logistics. For the artists, creative projects to expand, and for the people-oriented members, bringing more people together through event planning and budgeting.

Another way to earn money quickly is to sell what you have around the house on eBay auctions. Sell used DVDs (documentaries only of interest to teachers and students), old textbooks, used books, audio books, software, and remnants of new fabric with unusual historic designs, (for quilters or costumers) and classical music or multi-ethnic dance music CDs from the world music dance genre. To place an item for auction, look at the instructions on eBay at http://www.eBay.com.

Put love letters on CDs or DVDs and send them as greeting cards for clients who want the perfect poem or letter send with a slide show, video clips, or public domain music clips in the background.

You can buy reasonably-priced software with public domain music, clip art, and add your own photos, text, or video and audio clips to create love letters or gifts for any reason from graduations and grand openings of stores to rites of passage, eulogies, and wedding greetings or anniversaries. Create multimedia tributes and greetings on DVDs or CDs and mail them for your clients. Charge what the market will bear for these multimedia services. This is one way to market poetry in motion through sound, music, imagery, and text. You can also save Web sites to DVDs for clients.

You can earn money in a hurry by recording family reunion videos. Contact genealogists and groups online for various family surnames. Ask whether they would like an event set up with a DVD time capsule recorded. Use your camcorder to record these meetings. As a family history event planner and videographer, it would be fun to bring people together and produce time capsules such as DVDs of family reunions. This enterprise would combine skills in event planning with an interest in genealogy or history.

Everyone has an interest that could be developed into a skill in which you package and sell information, facts, recorded life stories, history, or events. Some people's interests focus on the how-to step-by-step variety that others can follow. Other people like to deal with intangible ideas. Facts and ideas as well as step-by-step instruction can be researched and recorded on video and audio.

You can make time capsules or reunions and present events to celebrate a historic event and a person. Or disseminate information to those who want to know more local history, genealogy, or learn specific skills. An event also can be about any subject. You can plan an event for people to meet more people with similar interests and goals.

Decide what categories of people or ages you want to emphasize, what type of special interest groups, and list your plan of events, speakers, or other contacts.

An example would be to plan a special interest group that meets in community centers, schools, churches, or convention centers.

You can offer a service to convention attendees by providing a service such as child care or pet sitting, or finding rooms to rent in private homes for people who attend business conventions in various cities.

List the services needed in your local area. Would you like to help match seniors to share homes, provide child or pet care services to shoppers or travelers, or shop and locate items for individuals or corporations, provide company gift baskets, or write instructional how-to booklets to provide a needed skill in your community? Match your special interests with the need in your area.

The quickest way to make money is to find something to sell that someone else wants and advertise it online. Look into drop-ship services, where without any investment on your part, you can have products delivered directly to someone who buys a product you offer to sell online, for example, on eBay or other online sites set up for people to sell items.

Would you like to become a print-on-demand publisher one book at a time? You need to write a contract first that you'd send to prospective clients. What can you do with that novel that you can't sell to a publisher after four decades of trying?

You can use your computer to offer a service for a small fee. Advertise that you'll write a novel using the name of the person you sell to as the hero character. As long as the person sends a written letter of permission and pays a small fee, all you have to do is insert the person's name on the cover and substitute that person's name for your hero character. Make sure the novel shows the person as likeable and reputable, something the owner will be proud to show to friends.

Your computer's software would substitute any name with the find and replace word menu. You can send the same novel to many people as long as you keep changing the name of the hero and have their permission. Print up the book as a print on demand publication using print on demand software.

You can type set the book as a PDF file. Offer the book either as an e-book or printed as a paperback with nicely designed cover using your graphic design or photo imaging software, (for example, Adobe PhotoShop).

Your client would have a nice paperback book with his or her photo on the cover or any other design emailed to you for the cover or one you select for yourself. Always obtain written permission to use anyone's name.

Charge a fee covering your expenses so you make a small profit on each book. Create any type of book using an individual's name with written permission and send copies of the book as a print-on-demand paperback.

Each book would be typeset as a PDF file, printed and mailed to your client. You can study how a large print-on-demand publisher does it for hundreds of books per month by looking at the Web sites of several publishers. One example would be iUniverse, Inc. at http://www.iUniverse.com. Click on their bookstore and browse. Look at the company's contracts as a guide to writing a contract for your own business, should you desire to print anyone's manuscript as a print-on-demand publication.

Compare the contracts of several different print-on-demand publishers online. Then write a business plan of how many books you might like to handle at one time. You might try this with your own book and see whether anything sells.

You'd have to work out a deal with distributors such as Ingram or other large, national book distributors to make sure your published book appeared in books-in-print. People should be able to order the book by walking into a local book-store.

Many people ask to see a book listed in various books in print online or listed in the actual books in print publications. Not everyone is online.

Bookstore clerks usually look online to find the book listed in the distributor's books in print publication. Ask in bookstores which distributors the bookstores use in your area.

Not everyone is interested in disseminating information. Some people like to build projects such as making palaces for cats out of doll houses. Others like to sew items such as quilts or cushiony igloos for cats or build dog houses or other pet-centric items to sell at pet fairs or offer to stores.

If you like to make gift items rather than distribute information in unique ways, then focus on researching your special interest, skills, or learning goals. You can also cater to the needs of various age groups such as new parents or empty nesters, or parents of home-schooled children and teens regarding their learning resources.

What do people need that you can supply at little cost to you? As an example, I review audio books for a national magazine. Make a list of what you would like to do to earn money in unique ways that bring not only income but contacts who also can be your sources of feedback. Use this feedback to develop better skills and services.

RELATED OPPORTUNITIES:

Barter

Barter consists of trading products and services for other products and services of equal value. Provide centralized accounting systems, national computer and video networks, comprehensive sales and marketing programs, and comprehensive training for all barter dealers on your videos, in essence creating an exchange of barter dealers.

You would pay members interest on positive balances, sign up new clients for cash income, receive cash income on each trade transaction and on every account you sign, and charge your members a one-time dealer's fee on a per-client basis.

INCOME POTENTIAL

Charge each owner of a barter-exchange business an annual membership fee of $300 to $2,000, with an additional fee paid in trade credits. You can market your barter and trade videos to your club members at a discount, offer events, seminars, conferences, or other networking opportunities to market your videos live, and continue to market videos through mail orders to members and also to the public at large.

Advertise your videos in bartering newspapers, entrepreneurial publications, and in shopping-type newsletters and newspapers which use lots of classified ads. Your income depends on people who want to trade services, products, and property. Make use of direct mail videos with advertising on the videos of products to barter or trade.

Use your video camera to create video ads. You can add electronic mail with your computer or interactive multimedia shopping services to members and/or subscribers for a fee plus a 15 to 20 percent profit margin for yourself.

BEST LOCALE TO OPERATE THE BUSINESS

You can market your barter videos anywhere, but there is special appeal to people in rural areas and small towns or overseas, especially if you want to tap the import/export market. People can barter products from any location, anywhere in the world.

Many people would love to see a barter/trade video to exchange houses for the summer or winter with someone in a far-away country. With the interior of the house and surrounding town on video, easy vacation home bartering can be arranged.

People buy what they can see on video first. Barter may not work for you online if done on a large scale. People want to see the goods. Try it on a small scale.

Barter works better locally where people can see, turn, and touch the merchandise to view all sides of a product. Selling for cash online works well globally, but bartering for services or exchanging items works better offline, with the exception of trading homes in different countries to tourists for a short amount of time such as renting a timeshare for a few days or weeks.

TRAINING REQUIRED

Interview the key people who run reputable barter associations. Prepare a list of questions. From the answers that explain step-by-step procedures, learn how to bring the people together with products that are in demand for barter. Study the barter magazines to see what products would have barter appeal. You also can re-sell online what you receive by bartering locally.

Study how the business brokers handle their business sales and propositions. Contact your local Small Business Association, SCORE. The retired executives in

SCORE are available to advise you how to startup your new business and give you the benefits of their lifelong experience running businesses. Choose someone from SCORE who has had video experience or bartering trade experience.

GENERAL APTITUDE OR EXPERIENCE

You need patience, an artistic flair, good camera skills, and an interest in business and bartering of products and services of fair and equal value. Experience in bartering or trading goods helps, but all can be learned on the job. Begin small at first with one barter/trade video tape. Form your barter video club first and see how many people join and how fast membership grows. Get feedback from your customers on what they expect.

EQUIPMENT NEEDED

You need a camcorder for recording interviews or making instructional videos, lighting and editing equipment, and people to record who have products or services to barter or trade. You also can hook your video camera and VCR player into your personal computer with a FireWire or other video cable that connects your camcorder to your DVD recorder/player and computer.

You need a computer printer and broadband or modem to network with other businesses. The estimated cost is $2,500 to $3,500.

Besides tapes and your camera, you need a good word-processing program, a spread-sheet accounting program, blank disks for writing your barter newsletter or enough tape for creating a monthly video newsletter, or less expensive, an electronic mail newsletter about your barter videos, sales reports, fliers, and paper supplies.

Discuss trade and bartering on video or even begin to barter special niche videos with other video collectors. The estimated cost for computer software, tapes, and paperwork office supplies is $800 to $1,000.

OPERATING YOUR BUSINESS:

Your computer can maintain files of your new video-advertising barter and trade club members who represent the largest single source of professional expertise in the financial, legal, and economic aspects of bartering in the world. Members of your trade exchange would be entrepreneurs who cooperate in bartering—either bartering videos on any high-demand topic, or bartering and trading any product or service from real estate to independent contracting. You can also put video ads on tape to barter, trade, or sell anything from garage sale items to recycling appliances, homes, apartment rentals, cars, or anything else.

You could also conduct studies and surveys on barter around the world, using your computer to generate reports and publications that monitor the barter industry. Currently over 130 trade exchanges are members of the International Association of Trade Exchanges.

Many barterers are starting franchises of their barter services. Such franchises must be registered with their state authorities in accordance with the state's franchising laws. Bartering franchises must also demonstrate that they're in compliance with the Federal Trade Commission trade franchising regulations.

Ask members of your barter exchange to submit franchise disclosure statements and organizational documents to your exchange for review. Use your video camera to generate evaluations, to give advice to the public, and to answer questions on how to enter the bartering business.

TARGET MARKET:

Form a video bartering club. Your members can be owners of bartering businesses and franchises or people who are interested in bartering and trading any product, service, or property—from apartment houses to occupational services in exchange for a car or boat.

There are more than two hundred trade exchanges in the United States owned by independent business persons. To reach owners of bartering businesses, write to the International Association of Trade Exchanges, 2948 University Terrace NW, Washington, DC 20016. Or start your own association of bartering business entrepreneurs to whom you can market bartering videos.

RELATED VIDEO OPPORTUNITIES:

Related to creating bartering/trade videos, is the art of putting business case histories on video. You can combine the two in one service. Corporate video biographies can be made by dealing with businesses and entrepreneurs. Also, you can create shopping videos for garage sales and later go electronic into multimedia, offering interactive shopping videos on computer software.

ADDITIONAL INFORMATION:

International Association of Trade Exchanges,
2948 University Terrace NW,
Washington, DC 20016

American Video Association
557 East Juanita
Mesa, AZ 85204

Mail Advertising Service Association International
7315 Wisconsin Ave, Suite 440-W
Bethesda, MD 20814

Direct Marketing Computer Association
60 East 42nd St.
New York, NY 10165

Do-It-Yourself Research Institute
770 North High School Road
Indianapolis, IN 46224

Institute of Certified Professional Business Consultants
221 N. La Salle St.
Suite 2026
Chicago, Il 60601

Bureau of Wholesale Sales Representatives
1819 Peachtree Road NE
Atlanta, GA 30309

Professional and Technical Consultants Association
1190 Lincoln Ave
San Jose, CA 95125

National Business League
4324 Georgia Ave NW
Washington, DC 20011

Institute of Business Appraisers
PO Box 1447
Boynton Beach, FL 33435

International Association of Merger and Acquisitions Consultants
11258 Goodnight Lane
Dallas, TX 75229

9

DESCRIPTION OF BUSINESS

DNA-Driven Genealogy Video Podcast Reporting Service

How to Open Your Own DNA Test Results or Molecular Genealogy Video Podcast Reporting Company

Did you ever wonder what the next money-making step for entrepreneurs in genealogy is-searching records for family history and ancestry? It's about opening a genealogy-driven DNA testing service reported by video podcast and DVD to be saved for inclusion in time capsules and keepsake albums.

Take your pick: tracking ancestry by DNA for pets or people. You don't need any science courses or degrees to start or operate this small business. It can be done online, at home, or in an office. A video podcast saved on a playable DVD and put into a mobile player also is a great gift for family history buffs.

INCOME POTENTIAL

What should you charge per test? About $200 is affordable. You'll have to pay a laboratory to do the testing. Work out your budget with the laboratory.

Laboratories that do the testing can take up to fifty percent of what you make on each test unless they have research grants to test a particular ethnic group and need donors to give DNA for testing. Each lab is different. Shop around for an affordable, reputable laboratory.

BEST LOCALE TO OPERATE THE BUSINESS

Find a university or private laboratory with easy access to your location. Your first step would be to ask the genetics and/or molecular anthropology departments of universities who's applying for a grant to do DNA testing.

Also check out the oral history libraries which usually are based at universities and ethnic museums. You're bringing together two different groups-genealogists and geneticists. You'd work with the laboratories that do the testing. Customers want to see online message boards to discuss their DNA test results and find people whose DNA sequences match their own.

TRAINING REQUIRED

Familiarize yourself with how DNA-driven genealogy reports are interpreted and generated by reading books on how to interpret DNA tests for family history. If you deal with generating reports for genetic risks or predispositions, interview physicians trained in genetics and genetics counselors and get a bibliography to read on how to interpret the DNA tests.

Practice interpreting them in plain language for consumers. You could audit some lifelong learning courses in human evolutionary genetics or read several books to get started. Your job is not to test or analyze DNA, but only to provide reports to customers on what the findings of the laboratories are and what they mean in plain language.

Most people taking DNA tests for ancestry information want to know where their sequences originated geographically. They are curious about in what geographic locations the DNA sequences are found today.

People who take DNA tests for discovering genetic risks and predispositions are more interested in what food, medicine, or lifestyle changes to make so they can tailor their foods, medicines, and lifestyles to their genetic signatures.

They turn to a physician trained in genetics and genetics counselors to interpret reports in plain language for them. As a middleperson or liaison, your business would be to generate reports explaining the results of DNA tests for those with little or no science background. Most DNA-for-ancestry testing reports are put in time capsules or other keepsake albums.

The information is passed to the next generation as a medical history and ancestry history. Sometimes genealogists include DNA sequence reports where written records stop, mostly to show clients where the most people with those DNA sequences tested for ancestry live today. Studies on evolutionary and migratory genetics or archaeogenetics are published in scientific journals. To get started, you'd first have to partner with a laboratory, preferably a well-known university DNA-testing laboratory doing current research on population genetics. You'd offer to generate reports for clients.

EQUIPMENT NEEDED

You'd need a Web site with databases of the customers, message boards, and any type of interactive communication system that allows privacy and communication. DNA database material would not show real names or identify the people. So you'd use numbers.

Those who want to contact others could use regular email addresses. People want ethnic privacy, but at the same time love to find DNA matches. At this point you might want to work only with dogs, horses, or other pets or farm animals providing a DNA testing service for ancestry or nutrition.

OPERATING YOUR BUSINESS

Take your choice as an entrepreneur: sending the DNA of people to laboratories to be tested for ancestry or having the DNA of dogs, horses or other pets and animals sent out to be tested for ancestry and supplying reports to owners regarding ancestry or for information on how to tailor food to the genetic signatures of people or animals. For animals, you'd contact breeders.

For people, your next step is to contact genealogists and genealogy online and print publications. You'd focus on specific ethnic groups as a niche market. The major groups interested in ancestry using DNA testing include Northern European, Ashkenazi, Italian, Greek, Armenian, Eastern European, African, Asian, Latin American, and Middle Eastern.

Many successful entrepreneurs in the DNA testing for ancestry businesses started with a hobby of looking up family history records-genealogy. So if you're a history buff, or if your hobby is family history research, oral history, archaeology, or genealogy, you now can turn to DNA testing.

What you actually sell to customers are DNA test kits and DNA test reports. To promote your business, offer free access to your Web site database with all your clients listed by important DNA sequences. Keep names private and use only assigned numbers or letters to protect the privacy of your clients. Never give private and confidential genetic test information to insurance companies or employers. Clients who want to have their DNA tested for ancestry do not want their names and DNA stored to fall into the "wrong hands." So honor privacy requests. Some people will actually ask you to store DNA for future generations.

If you want to include this service, offer a time capsule. For your clients, you would create a time capsule, which is like a secure scrap book on acid-free paper and on technology that can be transferred in the future when technology changes.

Don't store anything on materials that can't be transferred from one technology to another. For example, have reports on acid-free paper.

You can include a CD or DVD also, but make sure that in the future when the CD players aren't around any longer, the well-preserved report, perhaps laminated or on vellum or other acid-free materials that don't crumble with age can be put into the time capsule. You can include a scrap book with family photos and video on a CD if you wish, or simply offer the DNA test report and comments explaining to the customer what the DNA shows.

Use plain language and no technical terms unless you define them on the same page. Your goal is to help people find other people who match DNA sequences and to use this knowledge to send your customers reports. If no matches can be found, then supply your clients with a thorough report. Keep out any confusing jargon. Show with illustrations how your customer's DNA was tested. In plain language tell them what was done.

Your report will show the results, and tell simply what the results mean. You can offer clients a list of how many people in what countries have their same DNA sequences. Include the present day city or town and the geographic location using longitude and latitude.

For example, when I had my mtDNA (maternal lineages) tested, the report included my DNA matches by geographic coordinates. The geographic center is 48.30N 4.65E, Bar sur Aube, France with a deviation of 669.62 miles as done by "Roots for Real," a London company that tests DNA for ancestry. The exact sequences are in the Roots for Real Database (and other mtDNA databases) for my markers.

Later, with Family Tree DNA, my mtDNA H1b haplogroup came with a report of possible areas of origin. Maps of the possible geographic origin at different periods of time in prehistory expanded the report. Charts and articles explained the prehistory of how the mtDNA migrated and expanded at the end of the Ice Age. Paragraphs explained where the mtDNA (female lineage) might have originated and where it is found today.

There were charts, maps, and tables tracing the migrations of the mtDNA as it expanded from prehistoric refuges in the Pyrenees to where it is found today on the East coast of the Baltic Sea. The colorful report came in a press kit type folder.

Another company that I highly recommend and have done business with is AncestryByDNA. The company sent me a CD with my report, a colorful folder, and boxed appropriately with images of maps on the box. There were certificates with the DNA haplogroup printed along with my name. AncestryByDNA at:

https://www.ancestrybydna.com/default.asp also did a racial percentages test and gave me a certificate with the results printed in graphs and text.

You're going to ask, with no science background yourself, how will you know what to put in the report? That's the second step. You contact a university laboratory that does DNA testing for outside companies. They will generate all the reports for you. What you do with the report is to promote it by making it look visually appealing. Define any words you think the customer won't understand with simpler words that fully explain what the DNA sequences mean and what the various letters and numbers mean. Any dictionary of genetic terms will give you the meaning in one sentence using plain language. Use short sentences in your reports and plain language.

Your new service targets genealogists who help their own customers find lost relatives. Your secondary market is the general public. Most people taking a DNA test for ancestry want information on where their DNA roamed 20,000 years ago and in the last 10,000 years. DNA testing shows people only where their ancient ancestors camped. However, when sequences with other people match exactly, it could point the way to an ancient common ancestor whose descendants went in a straight line from someone with those sequences who lived 10,000 years ago to a common ancestor who lived only a few generations ago.

Those people may or may not actually be related, but they share the same sequences. The relationship could be back in a straight line 20,000 years or more or only a few centuries. Ancient DNA sequences are spread over a huge area, like mine-from Iceland to Bashkortostan in the Urals. DNA sequences that sprung up only a few generations ago generally are limited to a more narrow geographic area, except for those who lived in isolation in one area for thousands of years, such as the Basques.

You would purchase wholesale DNA kits from laboratory suppliers and send the kits to your customer. The customer takes a painless cheek scraping with a felt or cotton type swab or uses mouthwash put into a small container to obtain DNA that can help accurately determine a relationship with either a 99.9% probability of YES or a 100% certainly that no near term relationship existed.

The DNA sample is sealed and mailed to a laboratory address where it is tested. The laboratory then disposes of the DNA after a report is generated. Then you package the report like a gift card portfolio, a time capsule, or other fancy packaging to look like a gift. You add your promotional material and a thorough explanation of what to expect from the DNA test-the results.

The best way to learn this business is to check out on the Web all the businesses that are doing this successfully. Have your own DNA tested and look at the printout or report of the results. Is it thorough? Does it eliminate jargon?

Include in the report materials the client would like to see. Make it look like a press kit. For example, you take a folder such as a report folder. On the outside cover print the name of your company printed and a logo or photograph of something related to DNA that won't frighten away the consumer. Simple graphic art such as a map or globe of the world, a prehistoric statue, for example the Willendorf Venus, or some other symbol is appropriate.

Inside, you'd have maps, charts, and locations for the client to look at. Keep the material visual. Include a CD with the DNA sequences if you can. The explanation would show the customer the steps taken to test the DNA.

Keep that visual with charts and graphs. Don't use small print fonts or scientific terminology to any extent so your customer won't feel your report is over his or her head. Instead use illustrations, geographic maps. Put colorful circles on the cities or geographic locations where that person's DNA is found.

Put a bright color or arrow on the possible geographic area of origin for those DNA sequences. Nobody can pinpoint an exact town for certain, but scientists know where certain DNA sequences are found and where they might have sat out the last Ice Age 20,000 years ago, and survived to pass those same DNA sequences on to their direct descendants, that customer of yours who has those sequences.

In the last decade, businesses have opened offering personality profilers. This decade, since the human genome code was cracked and scientists know a lot more about DNA testing for the courtroom, DNA testing businesses have opened to test DNA for information other than who committed a crime or to prove who's innocent.

Applications of DNA testing now are used for finding ancient and not-so-ancient ancestry. DNA testing is not only used for paternity and maternity testing, but for tailoring what you eat to your genetic signature. The new field of pharmacogenetics also tests DNA for markers that allow a client to customize medicine to his or her genetic expression.

Perhaps you're an entrepreneur with no science background. That's your skill as long as your laboratory contacts are reputable scientists. Contact DNA testing laboratories. Show them how you can package their reports. Results could go into folders, press kits, and on CDs. You can make colorful packages of information with explanations, maps, or charts and graphs.

A liaison service for connecting the DNA testing companies to the media is another service, offering electronic press kits. Another service would be to write and package the reports so that genealogists would understand what the DNA reports revealed as pertaining to ancestry where written records are not found.

Your goal would be to explain the report is explained in plain language and visually to their customers. Find out who the various DNA testing companies contract with as far as testing laboratories.

For example, Family Tree DNA at the Web site: http://www.familytreedna.com/faq.html#q1 sends its DNA samples to be tested by the DNA testing laboratories at the University of Arizona. I've done business with them several times for family members and with surname groups and also highly recommend them.

Here's an example of one of the DNA testing companies for ancestry that provides extensive reports on their Web site and sends customers their DNA results with explanations in plain language of what the results mean. Bennett Greenspan, President and CEO of Family Tree DNA founded Family Tree in 1999. Greenspan is an entrepreneur and life-long genealogy enthusiast. He successfully turned his family history and ancestry hobby into a full-time vocation running a DNA testing-for-ancestry company.

Together with Max Blankfeld, they founded in 1997 GoCollege.com a website for college-bound students which survived the.COM implosion. Max Blankfeld is Greenspan's Vice President of Operations/Marketing. Before entering the business world, Blankfeld was a journalist.

After that, he started and managed several successful ventures in the area of public relations as well as consumer goods both in Brazil and the US. Today, the highly successful Family Tree DNA is America's first genealogy-driven DNA testing service.

At the University of Arizona, top DNA research scientists such as geneticist, Mike Hammer, PhD, population geneticist Bruce Walsh, PhD, geneticist Max F. Rothschild, molecular anthropologist, Theodore G. Schurr, and lab manager, Matthew Kaplan along with the rest of the DNA testing team do the testing and analysis.

So it's important if you want to open your own DNA for ancestry testing company to contract with a reputable laboratory to do the testing. Find out whether the lab you're going to be dealing with will answer a client's questions in case of problems with a test that might require re-testing.

Clients will come to you to answer questions rather than go to the busy laboratory. Most laboratories are either part of a university, a medical school, or are independent DNA testing laboratories run by scientists and their technicians and technologists.

Your business will have a very different focus if you're only dealing with genealogy buffs testing their DNA for ancestry than would a business testing DNA for genetic risk markers in order to tailor a special diet or foods to someone's genetic risk markers. For that more specialized business, you'd have to partner with a nutritionist, scientist, or physician trained in customizing diets to genetic signatures.

If you're dealing with DNA testing for risk and predispositions rather than ancestry and family history, partner with a laboratory doing testing and research for risk and predisposition rather than for ancestry and population genetics/evolutionary biology. Align yourself with a physician trained in interpreting the tests and read articles and books on how the physician is trained to interpret the tests in plain language for clients.

The physician will be working with the client, not you. What your business would be about is simply writing and editing the report in the style of a press kit with folder, booklets, brochures, and interpretation of sequences typeset and written in an easy to read and visual or colorful format.

RELATED OPPORTUNITIES

Many independent laboratories do test genes for the purpose of tailoring diets to genes. The new field is called nutrigenomics. Check out the various Web sites devoted to nutrigenomics if you're interested in this type of DNA testing business. For example, there is Alpha-Genetics at http:// www.Alpha-Genics.com.

According to Dr. Fredric D. Abramson, PhD, S.M., President and CEO of AlphaGenics, Inc., "The key to using diet to manage genes and health lies in managing gene expression (which we call the Expressitype). Knowing your genotype merely tells you a starting point.

Genotype is like knowing where the entrance ramps to an interstate can be found. They are important to know, but tell you absolutely nothing about what direction to travel or how the journey will go. That is why Expressitype must be the focus." You can contact AlphaGenics, Inc. at: http:// www.Alpha-Genics.com or write to: Maryland Technology Incubator, 9700 Great Seneca Highway, Rockville, MD 20850.

Why open any kind of a DNA testing business? It's because the entrepreneur is at the forefront of a revolution in our concept of ancestry, diet, and medicines. Genes are tested to reveal how your body metabolizes medicine as well as food, and genes are tested for ancient ancestry or recent relationships such as paternity. Genes are tested for courtroom evidence.

So you have the choice of opening a DNA testing service focusing on diet, ancestry, skin care product matches, or medicine. You can have scientists contract with you to test genes for risk or relationships. Some companies claim to test DNA in order to determine whether the skin care products are right for your genetic signature. It goes beyond the old allergy tests of the eighties.

"Each of us is a unique organism, and for the first time in human history, genetic research is confirming that one diet is not optimum for everyone," says Abramson. Because your genes differ from someone else's, you process food and supplements in a unique way. Your ancestry is unique also.

Do you want to open a business that tunes nutrition to meet the optimum health needs of each person? If so, you need to contract with scientists to do the testing. If you have no science background, it would be an easier first step to open a business that tests DNA only for ancestry and contract with university laboratories who know about genes and ancestry.

Your client would receive a report on only the ancestry. This means the maternal and/or paternal sequences. For a woman it's the mtDNA that's tested. You're testing the maternal lineages. It's ancient and goes back thousands of years. For the man, you can have a lab test the Y-chromosome, the paternal lineages and the mtDNA, the maternal lineages.

What you supply your clients with is a printout report and explanation of the individual's sequences and mtDNA group called the haplogroup and/or the Y-chromosome ancestral genetic markers. For a male, you can test the Y-chromosome and provide those markers, usually 25 markers and the mtDNA. For a woman, you can only test the mtDNA, the maternal line for haplogroup letter and what is called the HVS-1 and HVS-2 sequences. These sequences show the maternal lineages back thousands of years. To get started, look at the Web sites and databases of all the companies that test for ancestry using DNA.

What most of the DNA testing entrepreneurs have in common is that they can do business online. People order the DNA testing kit online. The companies send out a DNA testing kit. The client sends back DNA to a lab to be tested.

The process does not involve any blood drawing to test for ancestry. Then the company sends a report directly to the customer about what the DNA test revealed solely in regard to ancient ancestry-maternal or paternal lines.

Reports include the possible geographic location where the DNA sequences originated. Customers usually want to see the name of an actual town, even though towns didn't exist 10,000 years ago when the sequences might have arisen.

The whole genome is not tested, only the few ancestral markers, usually 500 base pairs of genes. Testing DNA for ancestry does not have anything to do with testing genes for health risks because only certain genes are tested-genes related to ancestry. And all the testing is done at a laboratory, not at your online business.

If you're interested in a career in genetics counseling and wish to pursue a graduate degree in genetics counseling, that's another career route. For information, contact The American Board of Genetic Counseling. Sometimes social workers with some coursework in biology take a graduate degree in genetic counseling since it combines counseling skills with training in genetics and in interpreting genetics tests for your clients.

Most people in a hurry to make a living by offering a home-based online service need not think about going to school and spending money with the hope of being hired. Instead, think in terms of providing a unique, inexpensive service to people interested in exploring their ancestry, DNA, nutrition, or genealogy. Think in terms of offering reports and time capsules.

Think of creating heirlooms. Offer genealogy dolls or puppets and personal history videos on DVDs. What new ways can you develop to bring people together joining family history to technology? Think in terms of virtual reunions, event planning, running a speaker's bureau, or giving information and history on media that stands up to the test of time and technology.

Help people trace their female ancestors' through lists of maiden names from hidden sources. You too, can provide services and skills regardless of your training emphasis. The way to tap into creativity is to take a proverb or quotation and expand on it, personalize it, and find your niche in its goal.

Here's one example: *"Destiny is not a matter of chance, it is a matter of choice. It is not a thing to be waited for; it is a thing to be achieved."* (William Jennings). How can you make that proverb your goal and use it to serve others in order to make a living by living with fewer expenses?

Find a way to package and sell new ways to help people make choices and decisions. Develop a list of pros and cons, a plan, and a course or seminar on how to make better choices and decisions. Package it, and offer it to speakers, teachers, and students, as extended studies seminars, courses, and training materials.

It can be offered in the form of CDs, DVDs, tapes, books, course syllabi, or live presentations. If you don't like to speak in public, offer your self-published package to speakers' bureaus, convention-panel speakers, and public speakers on the topic of your interest.

ADDITIONAL INFORMATION

Resources for DNA Testing

The American Board of Genetic Counseling.
9650 Rockville Pike
Bethesda, MD 20814-3998
Phone: (301) 571-1825
FAX: (301) 571-1895
http://www.abgc.net/

Below is a list of several DNA-testing companies. Some of these companies test DNA only for ancestry. Other companies listed below test genes for personalized medicine and nutrigenomics, and some companies test for nutrigenomics, pharmacogenetics, and ancestry.

You'll also find several companies listed that only test the DNA of animals. So you have a choice of testing DNA for a variety of purposes, for testing human DNA only, or for testing animal DNA. And the applications for testing genetic signatures are growing, since this science is still in its infancy in regard to applications of genetic and genomic testing.

Roots for Real
http://www.rootsforreal.com
Address: PO Box 43708
London W14 8WG UK

Family Tree DNA—Genealogy by Genetics, Ltd.
World Headquarters
1919 North Loop West, Suite 110 Houston, Texas 77008, USA
Phone: (713) 868-1438 | Fax: (713) 868-4584
info@FamilyTreeDNA.com
http://www.familytreedna.com/

Oxford Ancestors
Oxford Ancestors, London,
http://www.oxfordancestors.com/

AncestrybyDNA, DNAPrint genomics, Inc.
900 Cocoanut Ave, Sarasota, FL 34236. USA
Tel: 941-366-3400 Fax: 941-952-9770 Web site: http://www.ancestrybydna.com/

GeneTree DNA Testing Center
2495 South West Temple
Salt Lake City, UT 84115
Toll Free: (888) 404-GENE
Phone: (801) 461-9757
Fax: (801) 461-9761, http://www.genetree.com/

Trace Genetics LLC
P.O. Box 2010
Davis, California 95617
info@tracegenetics.com
http://www.tracegenetics.com/aboutus.html

Predictive Genomics for Personalized Medicine including Nutrigenomics
AlphaGenics Inc.
9700 Great Seneca Highway
Rockville, Maryland 20850
Email: info@alpha-genics.com
http://www.alpha-genics.com/index.php

Genovations TM
Great Smokies Diagnostic Laboratory/Genovations(tm)
63 Zillicoa Street
Asheville, NC 28801 USA
http://www.genovations.com/

Centre for Human Nutrigenomics
http://www.nutrigenomics.nl/
According to its Web site, "The Centre for Human NutriGenomics aims at establishing an international centre of expertise combining excellent pre-competitive research and high quality (post)graduate training on the interface of genomics, nutrition and human health."
Nutrigenomics Links: http://nutrigene.4t.com/nutrigen.htm

Veterinary DNA Testing

Veterinary Genetics Laboratory
University of California, Davis
One Shields Avenue
Davis, CA 95616-8744
http://www.vgl.ucdavis.edu/

According to their Web site, "The Veterinary Genetics Laboratory is internationally recognized for its expertise in parentage verification and genetic diagnostics for animals. VGL has provided services to breed registries, practitioners, individual owners and breeders since 1955." The Veterinary Genetics Laboratory performs contracted DNA testing.
Alpaca/Llama
Beefalo
Cat
Cattle
Dog
Elk
Goat
Horse
Sheep

DNA Testing of Dogs and Horses:
VetGen, 3728 Plaza Drive, Suite 1, Ann Arbor, Michigan, 48108 USA
http://www.vetgen.com/

♦   ♦   ♦

Ethnic Genealogy Web Sites

(Usually, there are several genealogy sites on the Web for each ethnic group.)

Acadian/Cajun: & French Canadian: http://www.acadian.org/tidbits.html

Afghanistan Genealogy: http://www.kindredtrails.com/afghanistan.html

African-American: http://www.cyndislist.com/african.htm

African Royalty Genealogy: http://www.uq.net.au/~zzhsoszy/

Albanian Research List: http://feefhs.org/al/alrl.html

Armenian Genealogical Society: http://feefhs.org/am/frg-amgs.html

Asia and the Pacific: http://www.cyndislist.com/asia.htm

Austria-Hungary Empire: http://feefhs.org/ah/indexah.html

Baltic-Russian Information Center: http://feefhs.org/blitz/frgblitz.html

Belarusian—Association of the Belarusian Nobility: http://feefhs.org/by/frg-zbs.html

Bukovina Genealogy: http://feefhs.org/bukovina/bukovina.html

Carpatho-Rusyn Knowledge Base: http://feefhs.org/rusyn/frg-crkb.html

Chinese Genealogy: http://www.chineseroots.com.

Croatia Genealogy Cross Index: http://feefhs.org/cro/indexcro.html

Czechoslovak Genealogical Society Int'l, Inc.: http://feefhs.org/czs/cgsi/frg-cgsi.html

Eastern Europe: http://www.cyndislist.com/easteuro.htm

Eastern European Genealogical Society, Inc.: http://feefhs.org/ca/frg-eegs.html

Eastern Europe Ethnic, Religious, and National Index with Home Pages includes the FEEFHS Resource Guide that lists organizations associated with FEEFHS from 14 Countries. It also includes Finnish and Armenian genealogy resources: http://feefhs.org/ethnic.html

Ethnic, Religious, and National Index 14 countries: http://feefhs.org/ethnic.html

(Finland) Genealogical Society of Finland: http://www.genealogia.fi/indexe.htm

Finnish Genealogy Group: http://feefhs.org/misc/frgfinmn.html

Galicia Jewish SIG: http://feefhs.org/jsig/frg-gsig.html

German Genealogical Digest: http://feefhs.org/pub/frg-ggdp.html

Greek Genealogy Sources on the Internet:
http://www-personal.umich.edu/~cgaunt/greece.html

Genealogy Societies Online List:
http://www.daddezio.com/catalog/grkndx04.html

German Research Association: http://feefhs.org/gra/frg-gra.html

Greek Genealogy (Hellenes-Diaspora Greek Genealogy):
http://www.geocities.com/SouthBeach/Cove/4537/

Greek Genealogy Home Page: http://www.daddezio.com/grekgen.html

Greek Genealogy Articles: http://www.daddezio.com/catalog/grkndx01.html

India Genealogy: http://genforum.genealogy.com/india/

India Family Histories:
http://www.mycinnamontoast.com/perl/results.cgi?region=79&sort=n

India-Anglo-Indian/Europeans in India genealogy:
http://members.ozemail.com.au/~clday/

Irish Travellers: http://www.pitt.edu/~alkst3/Traveller.html

Japanese Genealogy: http://www.rootsweb.com/~jpnwgw/

Jewish Genealogy: http://www.jewishgen.org/infofiles/

Latvian Jewish Genealogy Page: http://feefhs.org/jsig/frg-lsig.html

Lebanese Genealogy: http://www.rootsweb.com/~lbnwgw/

Lithuanian American Genealogy Society: http://feefhs.org/frg-lags.html

Melungeon: http://www.geocities.com/Paris/5121/melungeon.htm

Mennonite Heritage Center: http://feefhs.org/men/frg-mhc.html

Middle East Genealogy: http://www.rootsweb.com/~mdeastgw/index.html

Middle East Genealogy by country: http://www.rootsweb.com/~mdeastgw/index.html#country

Native American: http://www.cyndislist.com/native.htm

Polish Genealogical Society of America: http://feefhs.org/pol/frg-pgsa.html

Quebec and Francophone: http://www.francogene.com/quebec/amerin.html

Romanian American Heritage Center: http://feefhs.org/ro/frg-rahc.html

Slovak World: http://feefhs.org/slovak/frg-sw.html

Slavs, South: Cultural Society: http://feefhs.org/frg-csss.html

Syrian and Lebanese Genealogy:
http://www.genealogytoday.com/family/syrian/

Syria Genealogy: http://www.rootsweb.com/~syrwgw/

Tibetan Genealogy:
http://www.distantcousin.com/Links/Ethnic/China/Tibetan.html

Turkish Genealogy Discussion Group:
http://www.turkey.com/forums/forumdisplay.php3?forumid=18

Ukrainian Genealogical and Historical Society of Canada:
http://feefhs.org/ca/frgughsc.html

Unique Peoples: http://www.cyndislist.com/peoples.htm **Note: The Unique People's list includes: Black Dutch, Doukhobors, Gypsy, Romani, Romany & Travellers, Melungeons, Metis, Miscellaneous, and Wends/Sorbs**

◆   ◆   ◆

Genealogy, (General):

Ancestry.com: http://www.ancestry.com/main.htm?lfl=m

BMD Certificates, London, England, UK:
http://www.bmd-certificates.co.uk

Cyndi's List of Genealogy on the Internet: http://www.cyndislist.com/

Cyndi's List is a categorized & cross-referenced index to genealogical resources on the Internet with thousands of links.

DistantCousin.com (Uniting Cousins Worldwide)
http://distantcousin.com/Links/surname.html

Ellis Island Online: http://www.ellisisland.org/

Family History Library: http://www.familysearch.org/Eng/default.asp

http://www.familysearch.org/Eng/Search/frameset_search.asp

(The Church of Jesus Christ of Latter Day Saints) International Genealogical Index

Female Ancestors: http://www.cyndislist.com/female.htm

Genealogist's Index to the Web: http://www.genealogytoday.com/GIWWW/?

Genealogy Web: http://www.genealogyweb.com/

Genealogy Authors and Speakers: http://feefhs.org/frg/frg-a&l.html

Genealogy Today: http://www.genealogytoday.com/

My Genealogy.com: http://www.genealogy.com/cgi-bin/my_main.cgi

Scriver, Dr. Charles: The Canadian Medical Hall of Fame
http://www.virtualmuseum.ca/Exhibitions/Medicentre/en/scri_print.htm

Surname Sites: http://www.cyndislist.com/surn-gen.htm

National Genealogical Society: http://www.ngsgenealogy.org/index.htm

United States List of Local by State Genealogical Societies:
http://www.daddezio.com/society/hill/index.html

United States Vital Records List:
http://www.daddezio.com/records/room/index.html or
http://www.cyndislist.com/usvital.htm

10

DESCRIPTION OF BUSINESS

Free Entertainment Directories on Video Podcasts

Help others cut expenses by publishing electronically or in print directories showing people how to find free or low-cost entertainment in any city of the world or locally. Most university campuses offer free concerts where graduate or advanced music students present rehearsals or master's thesis concerts and similar free performances, plays, or lectures open to the public.

With a library card, you can view free educational, business, scientific and literary videos, attend the free days for museums and galleries, and enjoy free concerts given in places such as shopping malls, museums, or library galleries. On the Web, you'll find The FreeBay.com site at: http://www.thefreebay.com/.

There is a Freebie site also at: http://www.eversave.com/eversave/consumers/CampaignReg.jsp?sourceid=7632&cid=163. You can find free coupons and other free offers. Discover ideas about what people buy from sites such as Shop.com at: http://www.shop.com/.

INCOME POTENTIAL

Sell advertising for the directories and leave them at various stores and hotels, convention centers, and chambers of commerce meeting rooms. The directories of free entertainment also can be free which dramatically increases circulation, a positive selling point when trying to sell display or classified advertising in the directories from companies that provide free entertainment.

Use current rates for free newspapers and other publications to sell advertising. For example, you can charge $25 or $50 for a small display advertisement or as high as $100 depending on what type of businesses advertise.

Good targets are restaurants, theme parks, museums, zoos, and any other establishment that has a free day or offers free entertainment or walking tours on any particular day of the year, perhaps as a sideline to some other product being sold. Free lectures and seminars offered at convention centers or meeting rooms are an excellent source of advertising. Also try mall walking clubs, food courts, and shopping malls as well as park and recreation district offerings, free classes, adult education or continuing education, writers' clubs, craft and hobby clubs, library lectures, concerts, and folk dancing classes.

BEST LOCALE TO OPERATE THE BUSINESS

Look for free entertainment by various music bands that come to malls on certain days of the week at certain times, such as a noon lunch hour. Some churches offer free concerts at noon or evenings for downtown works to spend their lunch hour.

Check out FreebieDot.com at the Web site: http://www.freebiedot.com/3p1.htm. Look at FreeMovieMayhem.com at http://www.freemoviemayhem.com/index.cgi?src=WC-31275aaa:33320:

Look at sites such as Memolink.com or FreeDVDs.com at: http://www.freedvds.com/Default.aspx?N=1&P=168. In short, there are freebie sites on the Web. Check them out as to what the conditions are. Free entertainment is available without having to go online. Find out what free entertainment such as music exists at your local college campuses, high schools, churches, public libraries, art galleries, concert halls, museums, and community centers or shopping malls. Public places often have days of the year offering free entertainment or admission.

OPERATING YOUR BUSINESS

Publish a directory online and/or in print of free entertainment at parks, museums, church picnics, church concerts, brown-bag luncheon concerts downtown for workers, poetry readings, recreational presentations, street entertainment, art walks and art shows, student concerts, campus lectures open to the public, free film presentations at campuses and other public places, club meetings open to guests, community centers, galleries and libraries, targeting days with free admissions.

Explore the possibilities for video podcasting on various media players. Demonstrate your podcasts at exhibits, conventions and city information offices, local visitors' bureaus, chambers of commerce, hotels and convention centers, tourist industries, museums. Podcast videos of historic homes open to the public, galleries, and professional association meetings.

Video podcasts may be shown on various media players at expos, public lectures, and national association meetings. Trade shows and events related to a wide variety of industries and educational programs are shown. Look at listings of free offerings from professional associations and their meetings announced in newsletters and trade journals.

Sell advertising to make income from your directory. It's logical and easier to sell the advertising and give the publication away free than by trying to persuade any consumer to pay for a directory of free entertainment.

If the zoo or museum cost too much to bring your family to frequently, buy a year membership at a discount or volunteer to work there as a docent a few days a year in exchange for a free pass for you and a guest.

Zoos also have one day a year with free admission. To cut expenses, show up early. If there's a particular museum, gallery, or exhibit you want to attend, offer to volunteer there a few days a year in exchange for a free admittance to the exhibit.

Conventions, conferences, meetings, and theatrical presentations also offer free attendance in exchange for volunteer work as an usher or registrar, people-greeter, ticket-taker or other helpful work.

When various theaters present plays and music concerts, they usually need volunteer ushers who get to attend the play or concert free. Call a few weeks in advance and offer to be a volunteer usher, people greeter, helper, or ticket-taker in exchange for getting to attend the particular function.

If you like to attend a lot of plays or, offer to volunteer for university or even high school plays. If you're an older adult, contact various senior centers and theaters and volunteer to give information or help people when the plays or concerts open. You'll get a free admittance in exchange. The same works for art galleries and museums.

If you enjoy hanging around radio or TV stations, call in advance and ask to be put on their volunteer list. Most duties involve answering questions for people who call. Galleries and museums use volunteers as docents. You can do fund-raising work for public TV and radio stations in exchange for free tickets to various functions, such as theatrical or musical productions or live shows.

If you want to work in public relations roles, volunteer to help out at conferences, conventions, or concerts. If you want to become more involved as an event planner, join professional associations for event planners and offer to help find speakers for a panel.

By volunteering, you can learn more about how event planners put together an event or how artists or musicians are promoted.

Another field in the entertainment business is selling the music of professional musicians to the movie industry. You'd be the middle person or go-between finding the right musicians and placing their work with various movie producers and directors.

For those who only want free entertainment without much complexity or involvement in the industry, by volunteering a few days a year in any media, you can ask for free tickets to an event in exchange for being a helper when help is needed. Helpers in the entertainment industry answer phone calls at a radio station or greet and register people at a convention. It's a form of bartering a few hours a year of volunteering in exchange for tickets for you and a guest to attend specific entertainment events.

Not everyone wants an actual career in the entertainment industry You may only want free tickets to see a show or look around in a museum, zoo, or at a convention. Another form of free entertainment is to become an independent tour guide.

You find a required number of persons to pay for a cruise or tour, and you go free on the tour or cruise. Check out the cruise lines and various tours and travel businesses that allow you to go free if you find a required number of paid guests.

Take advantage of free walking tours of various cities. For example at the Web site: http://www.newyorkmetro.com/urban/guides/nyonthecheap/pleasures/walkingtours. htm, you'll find New York metro.com. The site explains that the free walking tours give specific details and history of a neighborhood.

Almost every city offers free walking tours. That's another type of free entertainment. To find free walking tours for other cities, just use your Internet's Web search engine and put in the key word "free walking tours." What pops up, for example, at http://www.google.com is a list of Web sites from various cities offering free walking tours.

Look for docent organizations, and consider giving a free walking tour yourself of your city to meet a lot of new people. Become a docent, a volunteer who offers a tour of a place, city, neighborhood, museum or gallery. Join docent groups and receive free training to be a docent. Or just take advantage of the free walking tours of any city. You'll see online free walking tours of various European cities. It's your choice of where you want to take your free walking tour or offer one in your neighborhood.

If you're looking for free entertainment, the walking tour will give you some exercise and outdoors experience. You can choose where you'd like to walk.

RELATED OPPORTUNITIES:

Live Docents and Video Podcast Docents

Talk to docents from various museums and outdoor events programs or groups to list free entertainment. An example of docent training and free walking tours would include Las Angelitas in California. If you attend their docent training when it's offered, you can learn about early California and Los Angeles history and how to give small group tours.

After completion, requirements are to give tours 2 weekday mornings per month or 1 Saturday morning. Las Angelitas is a diverse group of people from all over Southern California who also go on historical tours and have social gatherings.

With free entertainment such as walking tours, they are useful if you're interested in history. Most docent groups include social gatherings. It's a good way to make new friends with similar interests and experience the free entertainment.

Historical walking tours can be started in almost any place where people are willing to take walks and discuss the historical events of that community.

Every spot in the world has its own history. And history is as much entertainment as walking. For persons with disabilities, for example, wheelchair historical tours or tours for the deaf community also are resources to help others learn the history of a neighborhood, institution or city. Also try campus walking tours. For example, the University of California, Berkeley has walking tours of the campus where there also are nearby museums. Cultural tours are forms of entertainment where you learn where your values direct you.

Join professional or trade associations and offer to find people to give presentations or speakers for their panels. Whenever an expo, trade show, conference, convention or meeting is scheduled, the professional association or society needs volunteers to help run the show. You get to attend the expo or show free, listen to speakers or enjoy the entertainment.

To find speakers for panels, you contact speakers' bureaus and members of the association with expertise in an area and experience in public speaking. Bring the speaker to the convention and get rewarded with free entertainment. You work through either event planners or the trade association/professional group, or volunteer to work on the group's newsletter.

Another way to work the conventions is to greet people and register newcomers. You can be a ticket-taker or help the event planner. If you're looking for a career as a party-planner, working with event planners is one way to learn the ropes.

Entertainment is a broad area to define. Looking for free entertainment can be found at libraries or theme parks, hotels, casinos, and at performances of musicians or artists at college campuses. A quick way to find out what's free is to call talent agents and promotional companies in advance and ask what you can do to help in exchange for free tickets. Of course, the easiest way is to check with convention and visitor's bureaus and information bureaus for any city and ask what the free admission days are for the local events such as zoos, museums, galleries, theaters, concert halls, and theme parks.

Free university lectures are given almost daily. Check the particular college's newspaper for dates of free lectures. Also check each department's list of events. My field of interest is listening to anthropology lectures. I'd call the department of anthropology at several universities nearby as well as the museums and ask what days free lectures are given that are open to the public.

You'd be surprised at how many people are speaking at university ballrooms and auditoriums, for which most of these lectures are free and open to the public interested in that particular subject. Some people giving an oral presentation for a graduate thesis welcome strangers to quietly sit in the room or auditorium and listen to their presentation to their faculty advisers.

Entertainment that's free can come in the form of seminars. For example, the Federal Technology Center presented a free seminar on negotiation. Business information is a form of entertainment. Contact your local small business and economic development center. Free seminars are frequently offered.

Newspapers that emphasize niche markets such as job listings and information often present career fairs. Attend a free career fair. It usually offers free lectures, seminars, and sometimes entertainment. Attend the free franchise expo circuit. These franchise expos at hotels offer seminars, exhibits, or entertainment, and sometimes free giveaway items such as pens, note pads, samples of products, mugs, book marks, or paperweights.

Make the rounds of exhibits and trade shows. The vendors' rooms are often free to attend. You can also ask a local weekly paper for an assignment to write up the highlights of the convention in exchange for a letter asking for a free press badge.

With a press pass or free press badge, you can attend the lectures and entertainment of the convention or trade show. When you're done, turn in a one-page media release of any important facts you've learned from attending the conference.

Interview the vendors and emphasize what's the upcoming trend and what's most popular on the agenda. Then turn in to the publication your typed two-page story. Or email it.

Ask the editor of any professional association's newsletter if you could review the convention in exchange for a free press pass to the convention. You wouldn't get paid for the article, but you'd get a press pass to attend the convention free. Trade publications, professional associations' newsletters, niche market magazines, such as local computer publications, popular Web sites, and weekly business publications are most likely to be interested.

Attend the job fairs at your local convention center. Usually, there's some form of free entertainment. If you have young children, volunteer at various children's theater projects. Most cities have a children's theater or drama group. If you want to attend expensive business awards banquets, ask whether you can be a volunteer.

Besides the general chamber of commerce groups, there's also the various ethnic chamber of commerce associations that present annual business awards at banquets. Although tickets to these affairs cost upwards of $100, there may be a spot for someone who volunteers to be of help where needed for the event, if you call well in advance.

Most ethnic chambers of commerce include the name of a city followed by the ethnic group such as "Hispanic chamber of commerce" or "African-American Women's chamber of commerce" or "Asian chamber of commerce." How many different ethnic chambers of commerce can you locate?

The smaller the niche, the more opportunity you have to get to work with people in exchange for a free ticket to entertainment offered or a chance to help promote projects, causes, or raise money for the group. You can work with church groups also that offer entertainment in connection with a project.

Look in your area. Call your local college's ethnic studies department. Find out how many different ethnic or other category chambers of commerce in your area are giving business awards and recognition banquets.

ADDITIONAL INFORMATION

Other forms of video podcast entertainment can occur in your home. Free CDs or DVDs can be obtained if you volunteer or perform paid work part time as an audio book reviewer. Check out the various audio publishers' associations. Then contact magazines that publish short reviews, usually about 100 to 110 words per review. Offer your reviewing services, and you'll be placed on the publisher's or the publication's list to receive several audio books each month.

In exchange for reviewing the audio book for a publication, you'll receive the books free which you can keep or sell on eBay or other online sales sites or sell at garage sales. Or you can just enjoy the free entertainment and eventually donate your audio CDs or cassettes to libraries, libraries for the blind, or schools where they are needed.

Some publications pay writers to review audio books. You can contact the publishers of the audio books directly or go through magazines that publish reviews. When you've made yourself known as an audio book reviewer, video or DVD reviewer, or print book reviewer, publishers and publications will contact you.

Also, your Web site can be used to practice writing reviews. Keep them one paragraph in length and about 110 words. Emphasize the audio presentation, not the literary review, unless you're reviewing a print book.

Contact authors for "author interviews" in addition to reviews, and offer the interviews to magazines with the approval of the author for a taped interview. Ask the magazine in advance for a go-ahead before you contact the author.

Give the author the chance to change anything he or she said before you send out a transcribed and edited tape interview. Keep the number of words to what the publication wants as space is very limited.

11

DESCRIPTION OF BUSINESS

Inspirational Markets and Experiences: Video Podcasting Combined with Publishing

Video podcasts are distracting. Don't watch videos while driving. When riding for hours in trains, planes, and busses, you may want to be motivated, distracted, and inspired by sermons, alternative healing, and all types of inspirational talks or dramatizations. One example would be video podcasts on nutrition and special diets.

Inspirational and motivational video segments emphasize human experience with solutions to problems. Some fall under the mind-body-spirit or self-help classifications. Your inspirational podcast shows others how to solve problems, learn from and transcend prior mistakes, end bad habits by replacing them with healthier habits, or cut expenses and obtain higher quality products and services. Your video podcast can explore your previous writing for the inspirational markets by producing inspirational materials.

Videos of significant events, turning points, or highlights of life stories can show that by sharing people can learn alternatives and possibilities for healthier and happier choices. Help people make more informed decisions. You can focus either on religious video podcasts or self-help and inspirational solutions and turning points that reveal positive results.

It makes no difference what religion or spirituality essence you select, but writing a life story for the religious or inspirational markets is in demand and expanding its need for sharing life story experience in the form of books, stories, or featured articles and columns.

What many religious, self-help, or inspirational markets are looking for are steps that others can follow showing the viewer how to arrive at a decision or choice by growth and transformation.

Your message of self-help could be about how you or someone gained wisdom that everyone can share. Inspirational video podcasts are about how you searched for answers in exotic or complex places but found close to home, usually right in front of you. And the answer (growth) wasn't complex at all, but simple as commitment to family, faith, and universal values.

By sharing your experiences and life story, readers will learn how you made decisions and why, what wisdom you gained from your growth or transformation, and what made it possible for you to grow and change and become a stronger and better person. The stories you'd write about would be those universal messages we all go through, such as rites of passage, dealing with the stages of life in new ways, finding alternatives, and how you handled the challenges.

The podcast's theme could be on how you found the answer close to home that helped you make a choice, what caused your transformation, how and why you changed or grew, and what you learned from your prior mistakes. Include step-by-step guidelines that achieved results.

INCOME POTENTIAL

After you produce your video podcast, write a short article of about 1,500–1,800 words and submit a query letter and then the article to magazines interested in inspirational, religious, self-help, health, mind-body-spirit, or new age markets. Each magazine may offer a different payment based on the number of words published after editing. Some publications pay a nickel a word or ten cents a word and others pay a dollar a word or more. Income depends on whether you write articles for magazines, newspaper columns, books, or go on public speaking tours on a specific inspirational subject.

Try the religious, new age, holistic health, and inspirational markets, and the book publishers under the title Mind-Body-Spirit or "inspirational books." You can earn from making your own CDs or DVDs with inspirational messages, lectures, or humor. Or create audio books with inspirational and life story themes.

Join various small publishers' groups such as Publishers' Marketing Association (PMA) at: http://www.pma-online.org/ or Small Publishers Association of North America at: http://www.spannet.org/ for instruction and information in operating an inspirational publishing business if you want to publish your own material.

BEST LOCALE TO OPERATE THE BUSINESS

Working at home online is the cheapest way to get started in publishing or writing inspirational material. You can work from small offices in the libraries of churches or church offices, any office in a house of worship or inspirational organization.

The Bible belt location also is helpful if you're writing or publishing religious books. Being close to a center of inspirational, new age, trendy, or alternative healing conventions works best if you need foot traffic.

If your business comes from selling at trade show or convention booths, locate to where most of the alternative health and healing conventions take place, where the foot traffic is high if you want to take a booth at conventions. Otherwise, work online or by catalogue. Otherwise, working at home and online can be done from most locations.

TRAINING REQUIRED

Read inspirational books and articles and study what the publications want most, especially in new trends in publishing. Every two years there's a new fashion in publishing such as angel books or published diaries. Familiarize yourself with what the inspirational market needs by talking to booksellers, publishers, and those who buy inspirational books. Ask them what sells more each year.

The religious and spiritual or inspirational markets want stories that offer pictures and choices and show how you solved your problems. The reason people read your story is to find out how to solve their own problems and make decisions. Give them information they can use to make decisions, even if you write fiction. Have some authority and truth in the fiction, particularly about facts and historical information.

People buy your story to make choices, including choices in the later stages of life or choices in growing up and making transitions. As people move from one career to another or from one stage of life to the next, they want to read about how you made that passage in time and space, and what choices you made.

Life story writing should be more preventive than reactive. Biography writing is reactive because it responds only when people are in need, in transition, or in turmoil. What sells is preventive story writing.

Give transformation, growth, and problem solving information so people will be able to prevent making your past mistakes. Show readers, viewers, or listeners how you've learned from your mistakes and pass on your wisdom, growth, and change. Readers want to share your understanding.

OPERATING YOUR BUSINESS

Put rewards and possibilities for personal growth into your life story. Don't merely dump your pain and prior abuse on readers or your history of how you were tortured. That's not going to solve their problems.

What will is writing about how you've worked at understanding challenges. Look at your readers as your future selves.

Approach life story writing as you would approach writing song lyrics. Pick an industry and focus on the industry as you develop a life story built around an industry or event. If you write about your own life story, do interviews. Gather many different views.

You'll discover blind spots you would never have noticed about yourself. Treat your life story not only as a diary with a one-sided view, but as a biography. Interview many people who have had contact with you as you grew up or during the experience you're targeting.

Writing the Forward

If you write a biography of another person as a book, story or article, or as fiction in a novel, you'll need a foreword. This is what you're doing as you first meet the person you're interviewing. Have two tape recorders going at the same time in case one isn't working properly. Get permission to record. Write what you're doing as you first meet the person you're interviewing. It should be about 16 double-spaced pages or 8 printed pages, or less.

Writing the Preface

What is the person most conscious of? What is the individual whose biography you're writing doing right now as you first interview that person? What's the biography going to zoom in on? Describe the body language.

In Andrew Morton's Monica's Story, Monica stifles a yawn and pulls on black leggings as the preface opens with the title "Betrayal at Pentagon City." The preface summarizes the most important event in the entire biography.

It should be about 10 double-spaced pages or 5 printed pages. Is your character going to be the right person at the right time in the wrong place? Or the wrong person at the wrong time in the right place?

Writing your First Chapter

Begin with the person immediately becoming involved in the action if he is not well-known. If your person is in the news and a known celebrity or royalty, start with the date and season.

It's all right to begin with the birth of your biographical character if the childhood has some relationship to the biography. You can describe the parents of the character if their relationship has a bearing on the life of the main character you're portraying.

The less famous or news-worthy your character, the more you need to start with the character involved in the middle of the action or crisis, the most important event. Avoid any scenes where the book or story opens and the character is in transit flying to some destination. Start after the arrival, when the action pace is fast and eventful.

Characters

You can make a great career writing true story books about people in the news, celebrities, and the famous. If these are the type of books you want to write, focus on the character's difficult childhood if it's important to the story and the character is famous or in the news frequently. To create the tension, get into any betrayals by the third chapter. Show how your character's trusting nature snared the individual in a treacherous web, if that's in your story. If not, highlight your main crisis here in the third chapter.

By the fourth chapter, show the gauntlet or inquiry your character is going through. How did it affect your character and the person's family? How will it haunt your character? Where will your character go from here? What are the person's plans?

Focus on an industry or career, whether it be the world of modern art or computers to get the inside story of the people and the industry and how they react and interact. What is your character's dream? How does your character realize his or her dream?

How does the person achieve goals in the wake of the event, scandal, or other true story happening? Take your reader beyond the headlines and sound bits. Discover your character in your story and show how readers also can understand the person whose life story you're writing.

It makes no difference if it's your own or another's. You may want to bring out your story's texture more by adding a pet character and focusing also on the pet's reactions to your characters. For further information, below is a list of several book publishers and magazines in the field of religious and inspirational markets. Contact the various inspirational or religious booksellers associations, publishers associations, and religious or ethnic publishers associations.

Some Religious and Spiritual Book Publishers

Abingdon Press
Augsburg Fortress Publishing
Baker Book House
Behrman House
Bethany House Publishers
ChariotVictor Publishing
Dharma Publishing
Discipleship Resources
Feldheim Books
Gefen Publishing House Ltd.
Gospel Advocate Company
Hachai Publishing
Hazelden Publishing Group
Herald Press
Hope Publishing House
InterVarsity Press
Jason Aronson Inc. Publishers
Jewish Lights Publishing
Jewish Publication Society
Jonathan David Co., Inc. Publishers Joy Publishing
Judson Press
Kar-Ben Copies
Ktav Publishing House
Liguori Publications
The Littman Library of Jewish Civilization
Llewellyn Publications
Moody Press
Numata Center
Paraclete Press
Paulist Press
Pilgrim Press
Pitspopany Press
Red Heifer Press
St. Anthony Messenger Press

Targum Press
Thomas Nelson
Tyndale House Publishers
United Methodist Publishing House
Urim Publications
Vendanta Press
Westminster John Knox
Zondervan Publishing House

Magazines

Alive Now
Angels on Earth
Bible Advocate
Campus Life Magazine
Catholic Digest
Celebrations
Christian Families Online·
Christian Home & School
Christian Science Monitor
ChristianWeek
Catholic Peace Voice
Catholic Rural Life
Children's Ministry
Church Herald and Holiness Banner,
Companion Magazine
Expression Christian NewspaperGreen
Cross Magazine
Guideposts for Kids
Indian Life
Moody Magazine
New Writing Magazine
Our Little Friend (Weekly take-home paper for 1–6 yr olds)
Presbyterian Record
Spiritual Life
Teens Mission Launch Pad
The Upper Room
The Quiet Hour Echoes

Alphabetical Listing of Periodical Publishers
http://www.colc.com/pubbook/periodical.htm

Association of Jewish Book Publishers
http://www.avotaynu.com/ajbp.html

Christian Book Publishers
http://www.colc.com/Publish.htm

Secular Newspapers with Religion Editors
http://www.colc.com/pubbook/reli-ed.htm

Podcasting News: Religion and Spirituality Directory
http://www.podcastingnews.com/forum/links.php?id=73

12

DESCRIPTION OF BUSINESS

Health Video Podcasts

Your video podcats can cover seminars, lectures, and conventions. Show people at seminars and in other situations finding higher quality and/or alternative nutrition and health care. If you don't have insurance or need to save money on your health, make sure you take advantage of free health screenings offered at health fairs. Senior centers, shopping malls, health departments, and other health agencies or businesses have frequent health fairs. Some items you can get for free include blood pressure and bone density screenings, cholesterol and blood glucose readings, weight, and other measures.

Flu shots usually are given free or at very low cost to certain age groups such as older adults. Call each health fair and ask the requirements.

Many screenings don't have age requirements. Ask that copies of the reports be sent to you as well as your doctor. Keep a record of your numbers and measurements. Different health fairs emphasize screening for different health issues such as bone density, blood sugar, blood pressure, or other research. Your health department and the sponsors of the health fair will have the schedules.

Study the health Web sites for factual material that you can research in magazines and journals. Health food stores have free booklets and pamphlets on various supplements and health food products.

INCOME POTENTIAL

There's income in referring people to various health establishments ranging from clinical trials that pay people or give them free examinations to spas, rehabilitation centers, home health care services, senior services, assisted living apartments, anti-aging conventions, alternative medicine and health treatments, nutrition retreats, free plastic surgery from physicians who donate their time free and travel around the world on hospital ships, to reducing farms.

Usually, you would earn a commission much like a travel agent from the health care establishment you refer people to by educating them with facts about the establishment or the research as in clinical trials of various new treatments. Ask the establishment what percentage of a commission for referrals you'd be paid.

You can also publish material or reports about the health service or offer marketing communications services and information dissemination. You're acting as "an observer" reporting information about the health care establishment, procedure, clinical trial, or other service. Or you're making referrals by finding new clients for the establishment for a commission or flat fee.

Use your public library to read about what foods and nutrients work best. Make use of any offers for paid-for DNA testing for ancestry. Some genealogy surname groups on the Web offer to pay for DNA tests for ancestry.

Find out whether your surname fits the projects being researched. These tests usually are for males, and the Y chromosome is tested for ancestry research connected to some surname groups. Ask the various DNA testing companies that emphasize testing for ancestry whether there is a surname group offering to pay for DNA Y chromosome ancestry tests for males with the same surname, if there's a project researching the ancestry of that particular surname.

Besides attending conventions or expos and trade shows, referring people for clinical trials, or traveling to give lectures as a medical journalist or health referral agent, you could write and/or publish alternative health booklets. Here's how to publish these types of pamphlets.

OPERATING YOUR BUSINESS

Produce video podcasts of the highlights and significant points of your own or with permission, other authors' 72-page or 98-page pamphlets and booklets on alternative health, clinical trials, nutrition, spas, procedures, or contemporary issues, pet training, animal behavior, parenting, or school-related subjects such as biographies of historical characters, ethnic studies, or any other subject of interest to a wide or niche audience. You can publish the pamphlets, write them yourself or use with permission other writers' pamphlets, and then produce video segments dramatizing, reviewing, or discussing the materials. Also, you could narrate the video podcasts.

Before you produce podcasts based on booklets or pamphlets on controversial issues in the news or controversies in health, nutrition, or other issues, you'd have to write and publish those pamphlets. Your video podcast can publicize what you write and publish yourself.

Pamphlets can be of the general consumer type found at supermarket check-out counters or specialty pamphlets on how-to subjects. Or they can be genre fiction such as children's stories, romances, or biography. Another form of pamphlet is the one-act 45 minute play suitable for high-school drama classes.

Here's how to write and sell a fast-selling paperback 98-page (when published) pamphlet or booklet, the kind you see on supermarket impulse racks at the check stand. They can sell quite a number of copies, or you can sell them by mail order or online from your Web site.

Start by writing about twice the number of pages that will be published. For a 98-page booklet, about 196 double spaced typed pages produces, usually a single-spaced booklet with double spaces and headlines between the sections. You may come out with having to write less than 196 pages, it depends upon the font and size of the booklet. However, here are the dimensions you'll need.

The size of the booklet may either be six inches wide by nine inches in length or five and a half inches wide by 8 inches or 8 1/2 inches in length. Take your choice. The difference is that trade paperbacks of 6 by 9 inches fit on supermarket impulse racks at checkout counters, whereas the mass market paperbacks you see in supermarkets and book stores in the back areas on special 5 by 8 book-size racks are standard for novels in the mass paperback market.

Let's say you choose the 6 by 9 size, which is the best fit for the impulse check out stand supermarket size. It will also fit into gift shops and specialty store racks. You'll have a soft, glossy cover with your price, usually $2.99 printed on the upper right hand corner of the book cover. The title will be placed in the middle of the book cover toward the upper half. It will be centered and have a two-word to five-word title that speaks volumes about what's in your little paper book.

In the middle of the cover, explain in one short sentence in smaller font, about 24 point what your book shows people how to do. It must be a how-to book such as how to find and keep a soul-mate, or some other how-to theme.

Below the explanation is the author's name: By: Joe John, or whatever name you want on the cover. Inside the cover on the left hand side you print the name of your publishing company. Assuming you're publishing the booklet yourself, put an intelligent-sounding two-word name for your publishing company such as Behavioral Digests and trade mark your publishing firm, even if it's only you at home.

Then under than you can put a longer publishing company name, just in case you want to publish other items besides these little paperback booklets. Put something light Published by International Palm-sized Books, Inc., and your address. You can incorporate your publishing company. Use an office address or a PO Box number, not your home address. You don't want people showing up on the front steps.

Under your mailing address, write: "Copyright, the year, by, your publishing company, address and e-mail address." Leave out your home phone.

You can add a disclaimer in small font at the bottom that "Reproduction in whole or part of any (your publishing company's name) without written authorization is prohibited. Then add at the bottom, "printed in the USA" or wherever you send the booklet to be printed. I understand printing prices in Singapore are great, so I hear from greeting card publishers nowadays.

On your first page's right hand side, print the name of the book centered up close to the top of the page, leaving a 2 inch margin from the top. Put in a small clip art illustration or your own art, and then a line and a by (author's name) at the bottom, leaving another 2 inch margin from the bottom.

The left hand side of the first page can have an illustration centered. On the right hand side put your table of contents. Label it Contents. Divide your booklet into six small chapters and list them. Let's say your book is on how to find a rich mate. Label it with a title, such as why am I single? Then have a second chapter on your cure-all for loneliness.

A third chapter on raising your feeling of importance, a fourth chapter on how to appreciate being by yourself in various settings, a fifth chapter on how to find your soul mate and where to look, and a last or sixth chapter on how to keep your mate once you found him or her. Mostly women will buy this book on impulse, but if the book is labeled, how to pick up girls, of course it will attract guys or anyone who wants to meet girls.

The left hand side of your table of contents page should have artwork on it centered. Then on page 7, a right-hand side page, your first chapter begins with the title, self-explanatory and short, usually asking a question which you will answer in your first chapter. Define your question and answer it. Keep each chapter four printed pages, which is eight double spaced type written pages. When made single-spaced, each chapter runs to about four printed pages each.

Then start your second chapter on page eleven. Break your booklet up into segments or chunks. The printing will be singled spaced with double spaces between each section heading. Show the reader how to solve a problem or fill a need. The problem could be technical or personal, business-oriented or relationship-oriented, health-directed, or about healing and nutrition, parenting, or any subject likely to land on a supermarket check out counter's impulse rack.

After every 14 or 14 chapters, usually 13 to 15 chapters, you'll need a segment or section break with a new title, perhaps outline your case histories, success stories, anecdotes, interviews, or using someone as an example. Don't use real names unless you have signed permission letters and can footnote that at the end of each chapter in a list of references that's numbered. For brevity, use a first name only and an initial, usually a fake false name approved by whomever you interview with an asterisk saying the name was changed to preserve privacy.

Use more than one example, usually two or three case histories. You can also use celebrity examples if you can get permission for success stories that run about 13 paragraphs each.

Have sections divided if you can around page 19, 21, 23, and start another chapter heading around page 28. Every two pages should have section breaks with new headings. You might write and publish a booklet on journaling and describe how it's related to a feeling of self-importance or of accepting oneself as "good," or write a technical or business how-to if you're not an expert on relationships.

More women will buy these booklets if they're about relationships. You can focus on instructional booklets on any topic from needlepoint and crafts to how to paint furniture and offer it to do-it-yourself stores, such as the big chain stores that customers frequent to buy do-it yourself materials for home repair and building. Another fast-selling area is travel writing.

This would focus on where to go and how to find specifics from antiques to restaurants and entertainment for various ages, education, visual anthropology, or special needs, such as traveling with multiple disabilities or traveling with one's dog or cat. One person trains his cat to use any toilet so he can take it into motel rooms without a litter box.

Your main focus is on how to do something, build something, solve a problem, make choices, or fill various needs, from quilting to relationships. Most people buy booklets with general titles such as how to keep a mate from leaving or how to save a troubled marriage.

Your six-chapter booklet should take up about 98 pages when printed, so don't make it longer or it won't fit into the small books rack in supermarkets and gift shops. It's easier to mail that way. Break your six chapters into three sections that run about two pages each per section with each chapter about four to six pages in length, but vary the length throughout the booklet.

Distribute it yourself or find a distributor who handles the supermarket impulse checkout counter rack. Or you can use gift shops or mail order. Another way to go is to offer your booklet to the tabloids as they have publishing divisions for these types of little books. They'll take a lot of your profit, so my advice is do everything yourself from writing to selling.

A print run of 1,500 copies would test your markets, but do your market research first to make sure someone would buy your book in large numbers. You might try a test run in a supermarket to see if the booklet moves and whether it competes with the tabloid-published booklets of similar size and length.

Will the tabloids let you compete with them in their supermarket client's racks? If not, you have the small gift shops and the malls. If you want to move the booklet, also offer it on tape or online for the e-publishing download market or on a CD ROM or DVD disk. Look at all the marketing alternatives and give your booklet visibility in place where people gather. Career booklets belong in community college and high school career counseling libraries.

Non-Fiction Booklets and Pamphlet on Controversial or Contemporary Issues

Write and publish sixty-six-page pamphlets or booklets that are about 4 inches wide and about 6 inches in length. These booklets fill up quickly with your articles. Don't forget to reduce the number of pages you write that first start out as double-spaced typed pages.

You can also provide marketing research for corporations or information for advertising and public relations agencies, employment agencies, or college career centers in this format or mystery shopper news if updates aren't required more frequently than annually.

If you're printing up an 8 1/2 by 11 inch page, usually it takes up to twice as much writing to reduce the size in half when you print up single spaced content with a double space between paragraphs and allow for a 16 point type size font for each heading or larger fonts for chapter headings.

Make Small Booklets with Fresh Information

When you print up small booklets, you'll need much less writing to fill up a whole little booklet. These small booklets are bought by school libraries to fill research folders on a variety of topics that are current issues in the news. If you are marketing to the general public through supermarket racks on impulse shelves near the checkout counter, usually near the checkout person, you'll want to supply each supermarket with your own racks the size of your tiny booklets.

The subjects that sell best are topics that tell the reader how something affects or changes something else. For example, how different foods affect your moods, and subtitle the booklet how people can change their behavior or their lives by adjusting the foods to their moods or any other topic telling readers how to improve themselves with the specific information.

Price your booklets anywhere from $1 to $2. Usually $1.19 in the US and $1.49 in Canada is fine, keeping the price plus tax adding up to an even amount. Find out what the tax would be on your booklets to one person at a checkout counter for the booklet. Then adjust the price so the reader can pay the tax and your price and have it add up to an easy to come up with amount, like $1.20 or $1.50. Calculate your expenses so you can arrive at a price that looks inviting.

Keep your pages around 66. Use an even number of pages. Your cover would have a title and a subtitle explaining what the title can do for the reader, how changing the behavior can change the person's life. Print your company or publishing name and address on the inside cover in the center.

On the first page, label it "Contents" and list you six or seven chapters and the page numbers. At the bottom of the contents page, about two inches up from the bottom of the page have the authors name in small, but easily readable font, such as 10 point Times New Roman or italics.

The left hand side of the contents page should have a disclaimer saying that your book is intended as a reference volume, not a medical manual so you won't be sued for giving medical advice without a license or credentials. Put in there that your booklet doesn't presume to give medical advice.

You really need this in there. Add a "consult your physician before beginning any therapeutic program," to protect yourself from being sued or accused of giving medical advice. You need this disclaimer on any booklet that gives information based on material provided by actual researchers and experts, even if you are using medical articles with simplified English or anything where people are told what to eat to change their health or behavior.

Always put this disclaimer or a similar one into a booklet you write and publish. This is especially true when you interview doctors or read their articles and report what they wrote, even with their written permission, which you always need to have. You don't need this disclaimer of your booklet is about how to knit costumes for animals or how to fix a leaky faucet or repair and antique furniture, but you need it for special diet, food, and nutrition booklets.

Each chapter can run four to 12 pages in this tiny booklet with the chapter divided every few paragraphs into new headings so you break up your booklet in chunks. Try to balance the size of your chapters. Usually four-page chapters work best in this size booklet totaling about 6 or 7 chapters, and total amount of pages being about 66.

Keep your pages an even number. Don't leave blank pages in this size booklet. Place a one or two-sentence description of the booklet centered about one inch down from the top of your glossy back cover.

Put it in a box if you like, and place or print your bar code below with the price on the back. You'll also have the price on the front cover, your logo in the upper left hand corner of the front cover, the title, subtitle, and any illustration, usually a photo in color of a person working with the items in the book or doing some action that sums up what the book says.

Have the book cover put on with two staples in the spine that are not readily noticeable to the reader. Only the backs of the staples should be seen on the spine, and flat into the crease of the spine of the book so as not to catch on any object. You don't need an ISBN number for this kind of booklet, only a bar code so the scanning machine in the supermarket can scan it. Provide your own racks if ones there belong to other merchants and distributors. Have the price on the front and back cover in addition to the bar code so readers can see the price immediately.

If you write on health topics, keep the English simple, writing at 5th grade level. Keep sentences short and paragraphs short, about two sentences per paragraph. Use Times New Roman 12 point type, nothing smaller, or older people won't want to look unless they have their reading glasses. So keep the font large enough for most people to see at most ages.

You can find distributors who specialize in small pamphlets and booklets. Print your own catalogue listing all your pamphlet/booklet titles. Place a catalogue copy on the Internet's Web to reach people around the world. Specialize in supplying college and high school career counseling offices with booklets on each type of career in a group of related careers. Or focus on foods and health or psychology and behavior for self-help.

Inspirational, religious, New Age, nutritional, and holistic health booklets each have individual, customized, expanding markets associated with conferences, conventions, suppliers, vendors, publications, and members of the various groups with similar interests.

If you want people to pay for your booklets, give readers information that's not easy to find and is not usually found among the free literature available in health food stores, community centers, self-help magazines, or religious organizations. Also try specialty gift stores, home building centers, discount stores, libraries, business, professional, and trade associations, corporations, schools, and employee organizations.

Supermarkets have special display racks with informational booklets and short romances. Some of these publishers are parts of larger publishing companies, such as the tabloids. Try gift shops, museums, libraries, bookstores, schools, churches, hotel lobby shops, sports stores such as golf and tennis shops at hotels and resorts, golf courses, and sports clubs.

Keep trying the supermarkets and smaller convenience stores until you find a store that lets you put in your own display rack for your catalogue of booklets or pamphlets. Sometimes used bookstores will allow you to put in a display case or rack of your short romances or historical fiction. School supply stores may be interested in your pamphlets with biographies of historical characters or vocational biographies.

Writing on contemporary and controversial issues in the news supplies school libraries with information for student research. Pamphlets need a bar code and a price more than they need an ISBN, but you can get one in case you want your booklet to go to libraries and schools or be sold by online booksellers and distributed by national distributors.

ADDITIONAL INFORMATION: Podcast Feed Urls

Podcasting News: Health and Fitness Podcast Directory
http://www.podcastingnews.com/forum/link_13.htm

Sanoviv Alternative Health Care Medical Institute
Podcast Feed URL:
http://feeds.feedburner.com/SanovivMedicalInstituteAchievePerfectHealth

A Better Day (Helping to make everyday a better day)
http://feeds.feedburner.com/ABetterDaysMedia

2Down (Weight Loss) Podcast News Feed:
http://feeds.feedburner.com/TwoDown

Fitness
Podcast Feed Url:
http://feeds.feedburner.com/ABetterDaysMedia

13

Romance Fiction Video Podcasts

DESCRIPTION OF BUSINESS

Romance Stories as Video Podcasts: Write and Publish Short & Sweet Romance Stories as Booklets. Then Produce Video Segments of Romantic Stories or Excerpts

First create a following with romantic fiction dramatized and/or promoted on your video podcasts. Interview a panel of authors of published romance fiction and videos. Then publish your own romantic fiction collection as 72-page booklets consisting of romance stories or novelettes.

Set up a display rack near check-out counters of gift, book, and grocery stores. These are called the impulse racks in supermarkets. Turn your sweet or historical romance stories into a 4 inch by 6 inch small, 72-page booklets of either collected stories or one novelette, and sell your work in supermarkets and gift shops, candy gift stores, or packaged with other products.

Don't forget those wonderful romance novelettes and stories you have that are shorter than book length. Keep producing video podcasts of your short romance novelettes, especially those published in nontraditional formats, such as print-on-demand books or written as dramatized story scripts. These can be dramatizations of the entire story or a collection of excerpts from your publications, or author interviews and reviews.

Promote them on holidays such as St. Valentine's Day. Take your booklets to romance writers' conventions and club meetings. Write and publish pamphlets of holiday stories for Christmas, Easter, or any other religious holiday with appropriate stories or historical research articles. Promote them a month before the holidays. Animal stories are good such as cat or dog stories for Christmas or other holiday themes.

If they are sweet romances, short stories in three parts or "acts," of about 23 pages for each act, totaling around 72 pages or so, you can turn them into 72-page, 4 inch by 6 inch booklets, promote, and sell the little pamphlets at super-markets. They go in the impulse racks at the checkout counters. Most of these small size mini-racks hold booklets about four inches wide by six inches long. This is the ideal size for romance stories or novelettes.

You'll get about a maximum of 300 words on a page: that's a maximum of 10 or 11 words across a line and about a maximum of 30 lines on a page. For first pages of new sections, and you'll have three sections or "acts," you start about two inches down from the top of the page with the first letter of your beginning sentence capitalized and highlighted in a larger font than the rest of the letters.

Print or place a bar code on the back of each booklet. It's a good idea to get an ISBN. It's a number placed on the back cover of books used as a code to find the book or to locate it in The Library of Congress and in the catalogue of the original publisher.

Publishers, libraries, and book sellers locate books through that number. You don't necessarily need an ISBN unless you want to send your booklets to gift shops, libraries, schools, booksellers, or other publishers.

You'll need or put your own racks up to match your customized size in super-markets if they have room, but the small size that holds the four by six inch book-let is fine.

How to Get an IBSN for Your Book, Pamphlet, or Booklet

If you plan to sell your booklet by mail order to gift shops in hospitals or to libraries, get the ISBN as well as the bar code. The ISBN is a unique machine-readable identification number, which marks any book.

If you need instructions on how to send away for an ISBN number to print on the back cover of your booklet, contact the national or regional ISBN agency in your own country. Presently, more than 160 countries or territories are official ISBN members. Check out the Web site of ISBN information titled, How to Get an IBSN number at: http://www.isbn-international.org/en/howtoget.html. The site for the USA regional office is at: http://www.isbn-international.org/en/agencies/usa.html. It's called The ISBN Agency for the United States. And it's in operation since 1968. It is located at the R. R. Bowker Co., LLC. Write to them at the following address:

R.R. Bowker Co., LLC
Att. Ms. Doreen Gravesande
Senior Director ISBN/SAN/PAD
630 Central Ave.
New Providence, NJ 07974

Tel: Toll Free/United States: 877-310-7333
     All others: (+1 908) 286-1090
Fax: (+1 908) 219-0188
E-mail: isbn-san@bowker.com
URL: http://www.isbn.org

Decide whether you'd like to put an ISBN on the back cover of your book or only a bar code and the price. A typical booklet that is four inches wide by six inches in length has no ISBN number on the back cover. Instead, it has the price and a bar code at the bottom. In the middle of the back cover would be a title and subtitle and three sentences or two paragraphs explaining the main message of your booklet or pamphlet. The typical number of pages would be about 66 for this type of booklet.

The size is suitable for supermarket racks. One excellent example is a booklet titled *What Do Dogs Dream About?* It is published by Mini Mags in Boca Raton, Florida, copyrighted in 2000. The back cover tells you what the booklet is about. And it has a bar code and price on the back cover. The last page contains a box with the sentence: "We Want Your Cute Dog Stories."

When you publish your booklet, use the bottom of the last page, if space allows, to ask readers for feedback and to collect ideas and stories for your next pamphlet. And always obtain written permission from anyone who sends you anything before you use it in any way. A good way to collect ideas or stories is to run writing contests and publish the winning story. Decide what the prize will be and whether one-time publishing rights would be what the author and you agree on. Or work only with your own stories.

Writing and Publishing Your Own Sweet or Historical Romances or Biographies

Here's how to organize your little book of sweet romances or biographies of historical characters. The cover should be a glossy heavier weight paper that can fold easily enough to fit into a small pocket or purse so people can carry the book easily onto transportation. Your book also can contain an envelope inside the back cover with a DVD or CD of your dramatized romance novelette.

Market your video romances and books at racks in airports, train, and bus stations or at transit centers in vending machines if you buy the empty ones and place them where you can get permission. Hotel lobbies have racks that could fit your book, but usually you supply your own racks to hotels and convention centers.

Resorts and antique malls also are great places for your little book. Tourist attraction shops in the "old town" sections of cities are great. Any establishment that sells tourist souvenirs makes a great place to sell your little romances. People staying in hotels and motels can read the little books, and you can offer the same size booklets with adventure stories or romances related to the particular town or resort history.

On the cover have an illustration in color of the couple featured in the romance story, usually a cameo of the couple featured against a pristine background of countryside, or local resort attractions. On the top you can put a ribbon-like title "Your (logo or name) Romance Library" or "Historical Romances of the resort city___" or whatever you want to feature as your own publishing and writing library.

This represents your collection of booklets. You can publish your own writing or those from other romance or historical fiction writers. Travel booklets, auto travel games for kids, or travel romances also can be published in this format.

Usually sweet romances sell better than other genres in this type and size of booklet. People want a sweet romance to escape to and to read at night, especially people traveling on business at hotels. The books will be bought by women and female students of all ages, with the highest demographic being in the 18 to 44 age range and the next highest, 44 to 54 age range.

INCOME POTENTIAL

Sell your pamphlets or booklets for one or two dollars. Keep the price low and similar to the commercial romances and how-to booklets on sale at the impulse counters or racks of supermarket shelves, right next to the check-out counters.

To help sell your romance against the competition, put in a pet character, usually a cat or kitten or a pair of cats in the story that bring the couple together. Your story can feature a female who works at an animal shelter. In this way you can bring in a real animal shelter and dedicate your booklet to animal rescue volunteers, which helps move the story. You can also donate a percentage of your income from the booklet to help animal rescue shelters of your choice.

Make sure your story is universal and familiar enough to sell anywhere in the country or even overseas. Your booklet also can be translated into languages if you sell to various countries. Keep your pamphlet-sized library focused on sweet romance. These supermarket rack pamphlets appeal to a wider and older audience than the actual full-length romance novels found in bookstores.

TRAINING REQUIRED

Read short romance novels found at supermarket check-out stands. Study the pages, how they are stapled and the quality of paper on the cover. Look at the printing. Take a pamphlet or small novel to a printer and get a price quote for these short novels. Ask the supermarket how to get your novel on their rack. Try small bookstores and gift shops first, including hotel gift shops and airport, bus, and train station impulse racks at the food counters. Ask people who buy these booklets what they are looking for in a story.

EQUIPMENT NEEDED

You'll need a computer and a printer. Also, the kind of printer you go to in order to have a booklet published. Decide what kind of art work or photo you want on the cover and what type and size of lettering. Check rates out of the country to see whether printing is cheaper abroad or locally. Make sure the printer staples the covers to the booklets. Proofread everything several times before giving to the printer as they don't usually read the material or check for typos.

To follow a template, buy several of these little romantic stories at your local supermarket counters and study every detail—not only the story, but the way the book is put together. Look at the cover and the art work. Then make your own original template for the cover and layout. Never use the same template of an existing book because everything always is copyrighted. Just use the work to study for inspiration. Then design your own details.

People want to believe that love, commitment, and faith in your ability to hold a family together while standing on your own two feet and pulling your weight conquers all. People buy these little stories to relax, to be nourished, to feel good and important and to escape the real world. Yet the story must be real enough so that it could believably happen to the reader.

Your little booklet will be a tiny version of a magazine. In the romance story, keep it around 72 pages as the best-size and weight for handling, mailing, and reading in one sitting. Most people will buy these as they leave the supermarket to take with them during that long hour or two wait in doctors and dentists offices or while taking a two-hour train ride or while on vacation on the beach or in a hotel or during anytime when waiting is necessary.

The non-fiction informational booklet can be around 66 pages in length. It's not going to make a difference whether your pages run to 66 or 72 as long as the last page isn't a blank waste of space and the two staples on the spine that binds the glossy front and back covers will easily hold together the booklet.

OPERATING YOUR BUSINESS

How to Format Your Book or Booklet Manuscript

Start your story halfway down page 3 with the title of your little book. You'll find about six paragraphs can fit on one page. In a sweet romance story, don't have chapter headings or a table of contents. Instead of chapter headings, you only have the title page with author's name and dedication "to the____." Fill in to whomever you dedicate the story.

Use three asterisks (***) at the end of each part or chapter of the story instead of chapter headings. The asterisks represent the breaks in the story when the action changes instead of having chapter headings. Your story can run about an average of 23 to 26 pages before the chapter ends with the three asterisks and new action begins, for example, on page 27. Then run the action on to about page 36 and have three asterisks there.

On page 38 the first sentence starts about two inches down with the first letter of the first sentence in larger and highlighted capital letters than the rest of the text. Your middle chapter ends about on page 62 with page 63 started with new action about two inches in margin from the top of the page and the first letter of the first sentence in highlighted, larger capital letters.

You'll notice that the book or story has three acts or three parts. Each chapter can be of unequal or equal length. It doesn't matter as long as it adds up to a total of about 72 pages. So you see, the sweet romance story has, like a full-length stage play or short cinema film, 72 pages made up of three acts. Each act takes up a third of the booklet or story. You have a beginning, middle, and end. It follows the rules for a romance novel with romantic push-and-pull tension between the characters.

In the story you bring together an unlikely couple that conquer the push and pull tension of first impressions that don't prove true as you flesh out the second and third act where sweet romance proves love conquers all.

Build up your own romance library of titles from your own writing or those of other authors. Some authors might want to start a cooperative where they share the cost of publication and distribution, but this is up to you.

You'd do well with only your own stories and publishing your own work. Distribute to supermarkets and gift stores. Then add other sources such as racks in hotels, waiting rooms, airports, hospitals, senior centers, community centers, bus or train stations, cruise ships' libraries, schools, or doctors' and dentists' offices, lawyers' offices, and any place people travel or wait, including tourist gift stores in resort areas and theme parks.

Book stores and libraries or vending machines in rest rooms or on the street near supermarkets are good bets for little books. Romance novelettes should run around 72 pages. Keep them even numbers. On the back cover place a two paragraph review of each character the starring male and female of the couple and tell something about the person in one sentence for each character. Use only two characters on the back cover.

Your third paragraph, a one-sentence statement tells what the story is about in a 15-word sentence that is centered in the middle of the page. Below this three sentence/three paragraph description, put a short statement about your romance library or book, such as "welcome to a cornucopia of sweet romance, where love brings different people together" or love conquers all (this one has been used on Mini-Mags).

So use your own original statement, "romance unites all." Pick your own logo. The bar code goes at the bottom of your back cover, usually in the lower left hand corner. Your own logo image goes at the lower right hand corner. Put your banner and initials centered beneath your "Welcome to the world of sweet romance" or other statement. Use your own statement, not the one Mini-Mags uses. Use them for inspiration only or marketing research.

On your front cover have your banner and logo, an illustration in the center, and your price at the lower left hand corner. Pick your own prices, but don't go over $2.00 or you won't compete with the $1.59 of the current ones. Have your 72-page romance novelettes or stories bound.

Don't use staples in a fiction booklet. That's only for how to booklets or tiny pamphlets on how to change something or improve one's behavior or booklets on food and nutrition or health. So be sure to have a bound booklet for romance that has no staples. Research the booklets in existence and show your printer.

This is one way to find winning strategies or guerilla tactics to salvage your wonderful stories if they are rejected and you know they are really as good or better than similar stories in print and selling wonderfully.

If you have revised your stories and have logical reasons and concrete research and marketing tests showing the content appeals to all audiences and could sell well if published, then a 72-page romance story printed and promoted would cost you far less than publishing a romance novel with no way to distribute it.

Do your research first. Talk to distributors, and find out how to get your small racks into supermarkets or other sources where you can sell them. Try news stands and vending machines or packaging your romance stories. Other products can be packaged with your booklet and offered as promotions. These might include honeymoon packages, lingerie, and mail order products such as gift baskets for bridal showers or booklets sold at writer's conventions.

You can review audio books and send the 110-word reviews to magazines publishing audio book reviews. Concentrate on the audio presentation and narrator rather than on the literary print format for an audio book review. Pamphlets and booklets can be converted to audio format.

You can narrate your own stories or informational pamphlets on audio CDs and market them alone or as package deals with other products or books. Audio material should run an hour on each CD, MP3 CD, DVD, or other format. Most people need a break after listening for an hour. Some tapes and CDs run about an hour and a half. Keep yours in that parameter, an hour to an hour and a half of listening, similar to a feature film.

Formatting Book Manuscripts for an Editor

Here's how to format a book manuscript. The acquisitions editor will hand your book to a group of readers after spending about 20 seconds getting a first impression. Your book manuscript is read as if it were a resume. They expect white 20 pound 8.5" X 11x" paper without textures. The acquisitions editor will photocopy your outline, proposal, synopsis, cover letter, and sample chapters or if fiction, completed book when requested.

If the paper weighs more than 20 pounds, it will be hard to photocopy, and thin, onion-skin paper will tear in the automatic photocopying machine. If you're in another country, send a clear photocopy of your work on this type of paper, if possible. Your book, again, is your resume and application for a business partnership or employment and needs to reflect that business mood.

The cover page will contain your book title, the division of the publishing house for which your book is intended, and the number of words and pages. You put your name and address on the cover sheet and the date. After your cover page, insert a blank sheet and put another blank sheet after the last page to protect the last page of your book from creasing and tearing.

My favorite romance of this size is author, Kathleen Dreesen's sweet romance story, *Loving Touch*. It runs the standard 72 pages, and the novelette booklet is published by American Media Mini Mags Inc., MicroMags logo. Her booklet is dedicated to the staff and volunteers at We Care Animal Rescue, St. Helena, California. The characters are fiction. Only their love is real, says the statement on the first page. I highly recommend reading this booklet to get an idea of the size and type of story that sells well.

On the inside of your cover, put your name, business address, and email. Put the date of the copyright and where it was printed, in the USA or elsewhere. Your title page would have the title centered, the author's name beneath it, and any dedication. On the back of your title page, print any information regarding your decision to accept or not accept unsolicited manuscripts from other writers.

Otherwise, you may get everyone sending you their romance stories in hopes you'll publish them. You don't want your mail or email blocked, so print a statement that you'll only take one-page queries if you're interested, or whether you don't want anyone sending you their own stories to publish.

Editors want a standard of one inch margins all around each page, on everything. Leave room for the reader's and editor's notes on top of the page. Your header is standardized at one inch from the top page and a half inch higher than where your text starts. Make sure your header is the same width as the text line.

On this page, you put the title of your book, your name, and the page number on the upper right corner. Use your full or last name (last name is preferred by most editors). Use the same font throughout, preferably Times New Roman 12 point.

Don't send books in any other font as editors are required to convert for type-setting departments to Times New Roman 12. So convert it if it's in Courier, Ariel or another font. Make sure the font is as black as you can get it and the paper is really white, not tan. It has to be photocopied without a shadow.

Most books accepted had more white space and paragraphs under ten lines. Rejected books almost always didn't have these appearances. When mailing your book, put it in a clear plastic bag, the kind you get from the supermarket or meat counter, with no printing on the bag.

The green or red printing comes off with moisture and ruins the book with stains. So no print is placed on the bag. After your book is in the clear plastic (transparent) bag, fold it over so it fits well around the book and put a small bit of transparent tape in the middle. Then put two rubber bands around your manuscript. One rubber band will be at the top and the other at the bottom to hold the plastic bag in place better and to keep pages together.

Don't send a manuscript in a loose leaf binder and don't put clips on it. Leave off any file folders. Put the manuscript along with a sturdy self-addressed stamped envelope inside a large envelope with book padding. Make sure the return envelope won't tear in shipping and handling when it's returned. Have the correct number of stamps on the envelope.

Also add to this before sealing, a self-addressed stamped post card the editor can return to let you know your book is received. You'd be surprised at the long way this courtesy goes and the effect it has on readers or editors about your attitude to save them the postage of a receipt reply. Print up some business cards and put this into a small envelope with your return card, so you'll look more like a professional writer with a business card.

Have a query letter or cover letter on top of everything so the editor will know what you want done with the book and what it's about, and perhaps a guide to the synopsis. In one paragraph or preferably one sentence, state or pitch what your book is about: For example, it has been said that "Star Trek is Wagon Train in Space."

Never embarrass an editor by sending a gift or artsy crafty item with a manuscript because everything will be returned after going in the slush pile. Manuscripts must never be faxed. They use up the editor's paper supply and make an awful impression on your attitude and boldness. You want to make an impact of courtesy and business-like manners, an aura of professionalism.

Every time someone faxes a manuscript or synopsis, usually it's rejected and taken as an insult for tying up the fax machine and using up the paper at the other end. So treat your manuscript as if it were your best resume. Show your enthusiasm by a professional, business-like attitude and common courtesy. When finished, produce a video podcast dramatizing what's in your book—either the whole story, excerpts, or reviews. You can include the CD or DVD of your video podcast in a sleeve inside the book's back cover. Keep the romance short so you don't have to publish at an expense. Or use print-on-demand software technology to turn out books and videos that dramatize the romantic or historical story.

ADDITIONAL INFORMATION

Place of Pines (The First Australian Novel to be Podcast)
Romance and Historical Fiction
http://www.podcastdirectory.com/podcasts/index.php?iid=831

Life Matters
http://www.podcastdirectory.com/podcasts/index.php?iid=2289

National Public Radio Romance Novel Cover Stories
http://www.npr.org/templates/story/story.php?storyId=1138053

Podcast.Net
http://www.podcast.net/tag/romance

Harlequin to Offer Mobile Romances (Cell Phone-Based Entertainment)
http://www.engadget.com/entry/1234000977043124/

Blogcritics.Org
http://blogcritics.org/archives/2003/04/16/131311.php

Romance Writers of America
http://www.rwanational.org/

14

DESCRIPTION OF BUSINESS:

Playology (Play Behavior/Laughter and Playography (Commentary on Stage Plays)

Show duplications your video podcasts on hundreds of cruise ships. Or be there in person for one cruise. How would you like to work on cruise ships showing passengers and crew how to play for stress reduction and health benefits or work at home selling your play-for-health videos? Your videos can improve the quality of life for others. Wouldn't it be wonderful to make a video on the healing power of play (playography) linking research with dolphins and autistic children to show beneficial mutual effects? Your videos help therapists take clients to the next level of recovery.

The video therapist technician assists a psychologist, interpreter for the deaf, psychiatrist, social worker, counselor, teacher, or psychotherapist by operating a video camera, editing the tape, and monitoring a television set to help children and adults with emotional or behavioral problems. In some videos people and animals interact to show the beneficial or healing results from play between the two.

Scriptwriting is another option. The best market today is producing and distributing exercise, fitness, or healing-through-play videos for target populations and special groups of clients or patients such as preschool, seniors, persons with certain illnesses or disabilities.

Video therapy is done also with schizophrenics to show them how to have emotion, and with the elderly for therapeutic communication. It is a new biofeedback technique that teaches speech volume and coping mechanisms. It condenses behavior into "well" role models on video tape and shows a person how others see him or her.

Video therapy teaches pro-social behavior in prisons, schools, geriatric homes, on-the-job, in psychologists' offices, and in numerous institutional settings. Experience is telescoped. The video therapist's duties are to film the counseling session and carefully to edit the tape to include only appropriate behavior.

The patient then sees the edited tape and becomes his or her own teaching resource. It's also important to videotape interpreters for the deaf as they do their hand and finger signing in American Sign Language.

These interpreters need to be videotaped so that the speaker in the background of the tape can be hand signed for deaf video viewers. Or you can close-caption video tapes and put in written words on the tape.

INCOME POTENTIAL:

A video therapist technician can create applications and uses for niche markets in video therapy, virtual reality, and fitness. As a video therapist technician you can write and/or produce training materials and multimedia for home-based persons or for people who work with a wide variety of clients in the self-help field. Create your own videos and sell them each in the range of $20 to $40 to helping professionals, allied health workers, and the public.

Place and watch advertisements at online auctions for other people or companies if you had nothing to sell. Your business would be a type of sales assistant who takes care of business for others who have lots of items to sell online and little time to watch when an item is sold or whether questions are asked. Mail packages for people who have sold an item online.

BEST LOCALE TO OPERATE THE BUSINESS:

Institutional centers, childhood development centers, schools, geriatric centers, psychiatrist's offices, marketing and advertising research firms, cable television stations, exercise spas, and educational psychology research programs.

Exercise, acupressure, Yoga, and playography videos appeal to stressed-out salespersons, therapists, teachers, attorneys, public speakers, holistic health workers, nurses, physicians, and other allied health workers, sedentary people, and anyone interested in personal growth, fitness, or nutrition.

Operate your video business or distribute your tapes in areas where holistic health and alternative fitness instruction is popular—such as large cities, the whole state of California, the entire West coast, New York, large cities, ski resorts, health spas, vacation areas, Colorado, and especially, Arizona.

TRAINING REQUIRED:

Video school courses in camera operation and videotape editing are helpful. By learning how to edit videotape, you can save yourself the cost of hiring a video editor.

Many video production supplies stores offer short courses in how to edit tape and in video production techniques. They can also refer you to low-cost adult education courses in the community.

Community college courses in recreational therapy assisting, gerontology, or nursery school teaching also are helpful

You can even earn a certificate as a "certified" recreational therapy aide or recreational therapist from a community or two-year college and produce videos on recreation for the institutionalized person or for senior centers and nursing homes. In addition, you can earn a certificate as a health and fitness trainer or health promoter from the extended studies division of many major universities. Extension courses (extended studies departments) are open to adults and usually have no-prerequisites.

GENERAL APTITUDE OR EXPERIENCE:

The ability to relate to all kinds of people under extremes of behavior is essential. An aptitude for editing video in an artistic way following specific directions is necessary.

EQUIPMENT NEEDED:

Purchase a broadcast quality video camera or super digital high 8 camcorder or DVD camcorder, video tape, editing machine, VCR player, computer for desktop video, and equipment to produce titles on your videotape. This can be either standalone title makers or computer software that produces titles on videotape and can be hooked up to your video camera. Call your local video supplies store to outfit you with camera, editing machines, title makers, and tape.

It's important that your video doesn't lose quality the more times it's played. Don't use a VHS home camcorder because the tapes lose quality when reproduced and when played over and over. You'll be making many copies of your tapes for distribution to a wide variety of helping professionals.

OPERATING YOUR BUSINESS:

How would you like to work on cruise ships showing passengers and crew how to play for stress reduction and health benefits? Contact psychotherapists, hypnotherapists, prison wardens, psychiatrists, hospitals, schools for special education, speech pathology centers, rehabilitation centers, psycho-dramatists and schools teaching psychodrama, art therapy, or the expressive and recreational therapies, home healthcare nursing departments of hospitals and home care agencies, nursing homes, senior citizens centers, recreational facilities, hospices, fitness centers, weight loss centers, nutrition companies, holistic health clinics, acupuncture schools, allied health care schools, and crises centers to find a therapist you can apprentice to as a video therapy technician.

You can teach Yoga exercises, acupressure, infant massage, exercises for pregnant women or senior citizens, holistic health, personal growth, preschooler's fitness training, alternative fitness techniques, playography (geographic diversity of types of play and their applications) or playology (the healing power of play) for beginners, seniors, the disabled, children, or any targeted audience.

Put the Yoga or acupressure instruction or other mild, stretching exercises on tape for relaxation or rehabilitation. Asian exercises such as Yoga or Tai Chi Chuan (Chinese slow exercises favored by seniors) are available on tape. Read studies of how Tai Chi for mature adults helps strengthen their ability to balance.

There are health benefits to certain other exercises that you could interview people about to make an instructional video. The type of exercise varies from belly dancing to Yoga and Tai Chi to wheelchair aerobics.

You can become an independent practitioner of exercise technology. Call the local spas, nursing homes, assisted living centers, and gerontology-oriented social and community centers. Ask whether they can hire you to work as a video therapist exercise technician. Or make a video on a DVD and offer the video to these types of establishments. Work with the elderly in homes, spas, and gerontology centers.

A decade later, we find acupressure, playography, Yoga, Tai Chi Chuan (Chinese exercise), infant massage, preschool children's exercise, exercises for pregnant women, and slow Oriental exercises for senior citizens tapes popular and in demand by people seeking alternative ways to physical fitness, personal growth, and relaxation techniques.

For example, infant massage tapes and exercise videos for pregnant women can be sold in maternity clothes stores. Alternative exercise tapes for senior citizens can be sold in stores and community centers older people frequent, and playography videos can be marketed at hospital workshops where patients learn stress release techniques or in classes, that nurses, psychologists, and social workers attend to fulfill continuing education licensing renewal requirements.

Playology videos focus on discovering the healing power of laughter and play, especially for people suffering from the fear of play. Playography videos emphasize the diverse and similar types of play around the world, at different periods of history, or within various ethnic groups. You could make videos using scientific data validating the healing power of play, including problem solving by using the creative process.

Compare play among tribal peoples or in contrasting areas of the world such as India, Scandinavia, Africa, Latin America, the USA, Australia, Oceania, the Middle East, Central Asia and Europe. Your videos could help viewers lighten up and learn to play more, laugh to promote health, and have fun wherever they happen to be at the moment in order to relieve stress.

Ellie Katz, R.N., PhD coined the word "*playology.*" Highly recommended is her wonderful 10-minute video, "*Change Your Mind,*" on the healing power of laughter and play. Ellie Katz traveled all over the world giving *playology* workshops and seminars on cruise ships.

Her 10-minute video is on the subject of how to play in your office, home, with groups, and how to stay healthy, do what you are and get better. The field of *playology*, (the healing power of play and laughter) or *playography* (defined as the geographic and demographic study of play) are field open for you to make videos, audios or other learning materials, including board games.

Show others how to get over the fear of playing and how to use scientific data validating the healing power of play. Or show others in a video DVD how play is enjoyed in different areas of the world—a visual geography or anthropology of play.

In addition to play therapy, you can view the healing power of oriental exercise on video. If you don't know anything about Yoga or Tai Chi, then join a class at your community center or extended studies for life-long learning group. Rent a video on any of these relaxation and healing-oriented exercises. Study scientific and behavioral studies of play as a combination of relaxation, laughter, and mild exercise.

Work with an instructor to make a video of any new approaches to healing or stress reduction through play or slow exercises. Make a video with the instructor giving beginning instructions on a 30 to 60 minute DVD, or produce a series of instructional video discs for beginners, intermediate, and advanced students.

Find out from the instructor, based on market surveys and the instructor's class numbers which tapes are most likely to sell—usually the beginner's tapes or intermediate. Variety for beginners is more important in the workouts than advanced studies that would appeal to fewer students.

Offer your services to work with the patients or clients in offering fitness or health-related videos for instructional or recreational purposes in the field of health and fitness, recreation, activities training, or creative and expressive arts.

When you find the centers you want to work for or the therapists you want to apprentice with, ask them what their specific needs are in video or videotaping to teach their clients pro-social behavior, such as self-esteem realities. Then produce the tapes to meet their exact requirements to help individual clients or patients. Video therapy is about transformation.

TARGET MARKET:

Find manufacturers of exercise equipment and ask them to include your videos prepackaged with their equipment. You can work out a barter deal with them so you can include your advertising on the back of your video package along with their advertising copy. Also ask specialty shops such as maternity or children's stores for permission to put your video display rack in their window or at their checkout counter for impulse buys as people pay for their merchandise.

Cooking videos frequently are sold along with new convection ovens. Exercise videos and booklets, or videos go well with prepackaged products.
Examples include the following:
Tai Chi Chuan
Infant massage
Pet massage,
Play for various age groups
Special interest organizations,
Exercise for pregnant women
Walking tours for older adults.

You can prepackage your video or instructional material with products related to exercise or relaxation equipment and healing music, memory-enhancing devices, furniture, sandals, clothing, appliances, and related types of devices and musical instruments. Some producers put relaxing sounds and sights, like nature and clouds with music on videotape for stress reduction.

Approach the maternity hospitals, birthing centers, or nurseries. Offer your video to new mothers leaving the hospital with their babies. Capture a niche market by focusing your tape on a subject like infant exercise and massage, exercises for postpartum women, acupressure, playography, tummy flattening tapes, or other health and fitness information on video appealing to a specifically targeted market interested in new possibilities for fitness.

Your videos can also come with booklets on the same subject or any type of exercise equipment, holistic health products, food supplements, etc. You could do demonstrations at holistic health fairs and conventions or rent booths to other videocassette producers at theme conventions.

Therapists, hospitals, prisons, and fitness centers use therapeutic video or interactive video to observe people interacting and to record their behavior for study, research, and therapy. You want to reach all helping professionals, such as the following:

1. interpreters for the deaf who want you to put their sign-language expert on videotape to explain their instructional tapes.

2. prison psychologists, who may want you to make a videotape about pro-social behavior and self worth training for the prison population.

3. speech pathologists who may want you to make videos to train stroke victims to look into mirrors to see their opposite hand and try to move it.

4. acupuncturists, acupressurists, and holistic health practitioners or alternative fitness experts who may ask you to make instructional videos for specific audiences.

5. cruise ships, airlines, hospitals, and nursing homes—who may wish to show your uplifting videos on how to improve the quality of life.

You can specialize in creating videos for children. Target preschools, children's centers, hospitals, and schools of education where preschool teachers are trained. Another specialty is creating exercise, fitness, and eating-the-right foods videos for preschoolers and children in daycare, nursery schools, after-school care, and at children's hospitals. Create a children's or preschooler's gym on video by targeting corporate daycare centers and gyms.

RELATED OPPORTUNITIES:

Recreational video exercise therapist, instructional media technologist, cable television programmer, playographer, cruise seminar and event planner, and holistic health practitioner videographer.

Your exercises could focus on preschoolers or infants. Appeal to family gym classes where parents take their infants for workouts and to learn more about play between parents and children. Provide videos so that the whole family, including grandparents can exercise together and get fit.

ADDITIONAL INFORMATION:

American Kinesiotherapy Association (exercise therapists)
259-08 148th Rd.
Rosedale, NY 11422

American Association for Rehabilitative Therapy, Inc.
PO Box 6412
Gulf Port, Mississippi 39506

National Association of the Deaf
814 Thayer Ave.
Silver Spring, MD 20910

National Therapeutic Recreation Society
3101 Park Center Dr., Suite 1200
Alexandria, VA 22302

National Council for Therapeutic Recreation Certification
49 S. Main St., Suite 005
Spring Valley, NY 10977-5635

American Association of Advertising Agencies (AAAA)
666 Third Avenue, 13th floor
New York, NY 10017

American Yoga Association
3130 Mayfield Rd., W-103
Cleveland Heights, OH 44118

15

DESCRIPTION OF BUSINESS

Publicity & Promotion: Making Media Kits as Video Podcasts

Video podcasts are age-targeted hubs to launch your creative works in the media before you have pre-sold your creative ideas to publishers. Pre-sell your creative work with video podcasts. Launch it in the media before you publish. To persuade the press, create an age-elated hub. This can be a mature adult, parenting, or teen hub. Look at any teen hub from the 1990s, such as Goosehead. There's still room for other shows like Goosehead, and one could feature your unpublished writing, learning, parenting, or merchandising ideas.

Create a similar venture yourself online by first developing the content. You could create content for shows similar to Goosehead or create your own concept. After call, a concept is actually made up of facts built around a foundation or basic message. Think of a concept as a sculpture built step-by-step over a wire frame skeleton.

The idea of a teen hub came about when a 14-year old girl named Ashley Power with her personal Web site caught the attention of Richard Dreyfuss. He made a deal to create content for Goosehead. How did such publicity come to a 14-year olds personal Web site?

Thousands of girls from 11 to 15 daily have personal Web sites and need content. One day actor Richard Dreyfuss's niece appeared in a Goosehead video series. It's quite a leap and rare that the niece of an actor appears in a video series that springs out of a 14-year old girl's Web site. Such rarity is what makes for fame. What part did destiny play? According to media reports, Dreyfuss got in touch with Power and made a deal to create at least two interactive episodes to Goosehead.

What can you do that's interactive? If you're a parent, start with what's familiar to you in parenting. Look at similar sites yourself, and decide what about it made the teen hub or senior citizen life-long learning hubs ripe. How did the concept of a teenage hub move from a 14-year old girl's personal Web site into a video series that caught the eye of a star who writes content for interactive Web?

The episodes, by the way, were called Webisodes. Actually, the technical term is multicasting content as opposed to multimedia that's not always online. Before you test the waters, look at the following sites that use stars to plug products they like. Then think of ways how you can *launch* your unpublished writing in the credible media by *plugging a product* you like and that a star also likes. Look at www.gooshead.com, www.babystyle.com, www.voxxy.com, www.sightsound.com, www.shockwave.com, and www.generationa.com. What did you notice about teen hub sites?

Is there anything similar (based on what you love to do most) that you can do with your sites to produce content or plug a product you like for the age group you want to emphasize? Use your unpublished writing to move your content, be your content, plug your content, or launch someone else's product you use for a fee, and enjoy. That's one other way to launch your unpublished books, booklets, scripts, plays, stories, poems, lyrics, content, or learning material.

INCOME POTENTIAL

Charge a flat free and/or a retainer for publicity and promotion, such as getting authors on radio and TV programs. You might acquire space on a radio program and ask authors or other people with trendy occupations and interests to be interviewed by you on your own radio show.

Try pod-casting on the Internet as a way to interview people with audio file-based 'radio' shows that people can download to their iPods or other audio devices. What's the current fee? Charge anything from $25 up to have a four to ten-minute radio interview or whatever the market will bear. For half-hour radio interviews, charge double. Don't overcharge authors.

It's better to have a higher volume of clients paying less than be talked about on chat groups as overcharging. You can upload an MP3 audio file and 'pod-cast' the audio on the Internet for less than it costs to buy time on a radio station and charge people to interview them on the air to publicize their books or other items.

In promotion of someone's product, never make the language seem as if the author or inventor is talking down to the consumer. You want to make people feel important and positive about their choices. The selling point is to put value on people's decisions and to emphasize commitment to what works well and is healthy in the long run. Help make people feel good about their choices.

Scripts, books, and stories that are unpublished can still find a market on the Web if they are customized to the tastes of those who produce such works. If you have ambition and drive, you could aim to producing your own unpublished direct-to-Web material, called entertainment content.

Your creativity doesn't have to be fiction. It could be learning materials or documentaries. If you don't want to compete with the entertainment industry, there are audiences who want how-to films or videos that were never videos in the first place, but produced direct-to-Web with good multimedia authoring software such as Macromedia's *Director* and other software.

Let your unpublished writing plug, launch, or promote any product you like or a star likes and do it online and on TV. Or package your material with someone else's product. If you're into performing arts, start a Web site for teenagers or any other age group.

GENERAL APTITUDE OR EXPERIENCE

You can make yourself or anyone else, even a star, spokesperson. The trick is to produce and star in 12–26 half-hour shows aimed at a specific audience, such as teenagers, where you can use your unpublished book to plug the products advertised on the teen magazine Web and/or cable TV show.

You get visibility, publicity, and market your work all at once. If you go for the teen market, produce shows for a Web site, where you'll get to talk honestly with teens about issues they're interested in. Shows can focus in on niche audiences that need Web sites or cable TV teen magazine shows only for them, such as girls from 11–17.

There's one site www.voxxy.com that did that in new ways. If you have a lot of unpublished writing, you want to sell your work in by these two methods: 1. Use a Web site to draw in the stars of TV looking for shows to produce or be spokesperson for. 2. Ask those starts to endorse your writing as they endorse products they enjoy.

Find out what they want. Then provide that niche of content, branding, or redemptive value. Keep your idea simple to understand and explain everything clearly in a short paragraph or in one sentence.

TRAINING REQUIRED

Join public relations trade associations and attend seminars to learn the techniques of promotion. Read books on public relations strategies and buzz appeal.

The idea of plugging products you like by using your unpublished books and scripts is a form of packaging your books or booklets with products going to be bought. Before the Internet, you'd approach a warehouse or manufacturer and ask that your book be packaged with the products being shipped as a way to give customers a free instructional manual on a product or a sideline, like a cookbook on how to cook with wines or sauces being shipped with packaged wines or sauces.

Now, you do similarly on a Web site, called a Web venture. If you write about baby care, target a Web site for this subject and for your video podcast. Observe sites such as www.babystyle.com if you're writing books or booklets about baby wear and care, focus your Web site or content on everything about style and babies. Compare text and image-based Web sites to video segments on the Web.

Start your own site focusing on baby style, elder style, teen style, or any other age or other group of interest to parents, women, men, teenage girls, or wherever there is a high demand for information, content, and products. Video podcasts appeal to young people and to life-long learning groups of all ages. Parents and adolescents alike use video podcasts. Primarily, though, high-school and university students download podcasts for lectures, language-learning, and entertainment. Expand the use of video podcasting for travel planning.

Women and senior citizens are increasingly on the Web. So you might want to study new *trends* to get a handle on the latest women's interests. Before you get too narrow, pick the audience for the widest possible number of visits to your site. You need to research your markets. Where do people in different targeted groups really want to spend their valuable time visiting?

EQUIPMENT NEEDED

A spinoff of the 1990s-style 'Docu-tech' machine helps, but you really need access to a printing company. Your computer and laser printer can generate brochures and press kits. A four-color printer helps as well as a scanner that can produce photos scanned at 300 DPI in CMYK color. Check out the CMYK Color Space: The Colors of Printing Web site at: http://www.techcolor.com/help/cmyk.html. You need Adobe Photoshop software or the equivalent to put photos or graphics in your publicity brochures or press kits.

Find a way to endorse a product or keep asking powerful and popular people to endorse a product that will include your unpublished book along with a product being endorsed as a gift or giveaway. Your content and a manufacturer's product must offer specific benefits and advantages to the buyer.

OPERATING YOUR BUSINESS

Use your writing or research to plug someone else's products. If you have an unpublished romance novel, personalize it with the name of the happy couple and package it along with the wedding gifts ordered. Or leave a personalized novel you wrote in guest rooms of hotels with the name of the guests, *if they order it*. Honeymooners might, or it might be of interest to those planning bridal or baby showers, anniversary cruises, or office parties. Always ask the buyer first and show in advance what the product will contain before having anything printed with someone's name.

The quickest way to launch your book is to stage an around the world online launch and media party. Pick a time when most media people are available. Invite the specialty and general press, publishers, agents, entertainment attorneys, producers, directors, book talent managers, book packagers, famous writers, newspaper reporters and columnists. Also invite the members of various public relations and press clubs from your local area chapters.

Include the print media, small press publishers, book sellers, event planners for booksellers events overseas and nationally, and those who come to book sales parties in people's homes. Invite software, book and video distributors to meet you for a conference online where you'll have a chat and put up a presentation with sound, text, and video clips or visuals all about your unpublished book or script.

Did you see the pre release publicity the Harry Potter books received, even coverage on the cover of Newsweek several years ago? What can you do for your unpublished book to create spin that will add to your credibility as well as visibility in the media all over the world?

It all starts with a story board and a press kit that reveals your main character's measured change, transformation, or growth, or if your book's nonfiction, how much everyone needs to know the information you're about to tell. It's not whom you know, but whom you tell—and how you tell it that brings people together. If you want to earn income and cut expenses, you need to be a catalyst.

How Do You Make A Storyboard?

Storyboards can help launch your unpublished book if you use them as a kind of mind map that uses the right hemisphere of the brain to express visually with thumbnail sketches and dialogue bubbles what goes into a novel or script. If you write your story as a play first and flesh out the dialogue into a novel, it will flow easier when based on a storyboard.

You can move to a springboard, where you can bounce the story off of the springboard's role as a summary or synopses of significant events and turning points in your book or script. A springboard runs up to 15 pages long.

A story board can go the length of the book summarizing the highlights in half that number of pages. A synopsis runs about one or two pages, and a high concept pitch is one sentence that tells your whole story such as Star Trek is Wagon Train in space.

What's a storyboard? Storyboards are pages of panel cartoon-like visual images of how a chapter or scene looks visually before the dialogue is spoken. Draw in thumbnail sketches your storyboard for each scene of your novel, autobiography, or script as you write it or adapt it from a novel, news clipping, or story.

To pre sell your unpublished book to the media or publishers, write the significant events, turning points, or highlights of your confrontation where the hero and the opponent come into conflict for the last time. The battle scene is the major test that results in a major change both inside the hero morally and externally so he/she can reach the goal and end the story. This is what you hand to the press and to publishers, agents, or producers. You're highlighting and summarizing the significant events of your book.

1. Hold a mid-night launch party for your life story or other book.

2. Hold a noon launch party for readers who can't drive or go out at night, and have the location near a bus line.

3. Hold a weekend launch party at a department or discount store such as Wal-Mart or any similar store. Or combine with any store's grand opening party.

4. Hold a launch party in a school cafeteria, library, gym, yard, or auditorium for the appropriate age group. Combine launch party with a lecture to elementary or high school classes. Or if more appropriate, to special interest groups and clubs, professional associations, or women's clubs and organizations or related societies.

5. Hold a launch party at a college campus or rent a room or auditorium or space on the lawn.

6. Hold a launch party in a senior citizens apartment complex, recreational center, adult education center, hospital gift shop, or nursing home.

7. Hold a launch party in a place where you can set up an international or national day so that everyone, especially children, if your book is appropriate, can read your book on the same day, in case they do order it. Have all the children across the nation experience *Your Life Story* or *Your Book* on the same day.

8. Hold a launch party in a church recreation hall, park, museum, library, art gallery, zoo, space theater, or social center.

9. Hold a launch party in a mall or on the lawn of a public park or skating rink on a Sunday or at a sports center or field.

10. Hold a launch party on a cruise ship before it sails or in a bus or train station or airport.

Put up a temporary kiosk for your launch party. Or get permission and a permit to launch your book near or in front of a supermarket or convention center or a hotel lobby. Use cruises and travel situations to launch your party. Or charter a flight and launch it in transit to help passengers pass the time. Cruise ships are you best bet.

Ask newspaper reporters from national press associations and public relations associations to cover your book or life story in their articles on lifestyle or business subjects or whatever the subject of your book covers. Societies of professional journalists have monthly meetings. Ask to have your launch party at one of their meetings or invite the whole organization to your meeting.

Gather other writers of similar books and life stories into a pool of vendors and sell booths or tables in a large hall, Masonic center, or other meeting place, like an association of Realtor's Hall, or building you can rent. Have all the writers self-publish their books or photocopy with cardstock cover and illustration or photo and comb binding. Print on demand.

Have numerous copies of books on tables. A group of 10 or 20 writers can have a group launch party and invite the press or sponsor a press club meeting, perhaps on board a docked yacht that's rented for the day or in a hotel or university rented room or meeting hall. Books can be printed on demand and given as press copies to reporters.

Invite entertainment and copyright attorneys, agents, publishers, editors, the media, and writers, also the potential readers of your book such as children and parents or business people. Have your launch party at a convention or conference on a related theme, such as a conference of small press publishers or a book buyer's convention or annual meeting in the US or abroad. Or take a group of writers on a cruise and present books to the press.

You can go free if you gather enough paying people to take the tour with you. Have stationery printed with a logo or slogan. Print the letterhead with enlarged slogan or logo onto a supply of two-pocket folders. Print a scriptwriting logo onto adhesive labels. Stick the labels onto the cover of the folders. The multi-colored two-pocket folders are available in any office supply outlet.

Create a brochure, preferably in color. Include the brochure in the press kit. Make an electronic media kit as well as a print press kit. The brochure could list a writer's services and credentials or credits. If there are no past credits, print all the services provided such as the following:

1. Quality circles for writers
2. Individual instruction
3. Seminars, event planning for communications professionals
4. Freelance technical writing, manual writing, corporate scriptwriting, desktop publishing, word processing, editing, tutoring, instructional courseware design, children's writing instruction, corporate scriptwriting
5. English as a second language writing instruction
6. Fiction written for adults with 2nd grade reading ability
7. Science journalism
8. Writer's speakers bureau
9. Art
10. Publicity writing, or any other type of writing services offered.

Nourishment is a Fountain

What's your most powerful resource you can call on when you need it? It is not only the source within, but the source without also. How do you write about this source? How can you use this source to both cut expenses and bring in income while expanding your creative abilities? Nourishment is all about offering the public and the media positive magnets. Decades ago these magnets or catalysts were called positive hooks because they hooked the readers or viewers. You had a captured audience.

The idea behind nourishment or positive incentives is that people don't want a steady diet of pain, fear, and horror—all the time. If they did, then books such as the *Chicken Soup* series would come in second place to gladiatorial blood sport movies. Nourishment sells. There is a market for joy. Don't dump pain on readers all the way through your writing—not if you are writing for a large audience.

People buy audio books, videos, learning materials, and information books to learn more about health, mind, spirit, investments, or contemporary culture issues. Which sells more books or videos—works about poverty or the habits of billionaires?

The habits of billionaires and efficient people are of more interest than documentaries and books on poverty. Why don't enough people buy books surveying the plight of those in poverty or pain? The media will help you launch your work if you provide solutions to problems and results. Offer easy and quick solutions backed up by detailed step-by-step information people can follow.

Large audiences want to hear about the secrets of healing, love, wealth, and happiness. Nourishment sells along with commitment and inspiration. People also want to improve their memory, enhance creativity, and be happy. Instruction is in high demand. People want instructions that they can easily understand. They want to know how to build, make, or repair an object. Most people have little time or money to spend on luxuries.

Look at the success of home improvement centers. Those with time to "build it at home" want to create a device better in quality, safer, and at lower cost than can be bought commercially. An example would be instructions on how to make your own shampoo from scratch. With home-made shampoo, you could customize a non-toxic formula for your own hair's needs using natural flower essences, oils, moisturizes, scents, or spices. People are looking for safer hair tints, depilatories, and other products that are absorbed by the pores. That's why you need a professional-looking electronic and portfolio-type print media kit.

Whatever your creative project entails, include a press kit when giving presentations, seminars, interviews, radio or T.V. appearances or querying editors, producers, publishers, agents, and entertainment attorneys. Send the press kit to newspaper and magazine editors, television producers, and radio talk show hosts seeking guests from the writing community. Even mystery and suspense novels or true crime accounts have to offer more than violence and justice.

The purpose of a press kit is to inform people that scriptwriting is being done on a full-time basis and assignments are wanted either re-writing other writer's scripts or created fiction or non-fiction video and film scripts for production. Industrial video and the trade magazines are constant users of video scripts for training.

Media kits, also called press kits are included in presentations, pitching, written proposals, sales packets, query letters, and in general correspondence. Marketing and sales for home-based scriptwriters are fields worth writing about in print and in training video script format.

How Do You Create A Powerful Media Magnet?

Every scriptwriter needs an online press kit to pre-sell a script to the video or film market. Most print press kits are discarded by the media without being opened, unless you're well-known. The only way the media will pay attention to a press kit is if it contains a powerful hook. Have one sentence or question that will repeat at the beginning, middle, and end of the press kit. Bring the media to your

Web site before you mail out expensive printed material to someone who doesn't contact you and ask for a review copy or press kit of your work.

Use a question hook that makes a busy editor stop and think. Make the question personal and universal. Put on the press kit's cover a hook question that makes the media do some introverted thinking. In large type letters have the question make an impact. You can ask the reader to name his or her strongest source. In the past, media kits used words like "powerful resource" or "strongest magnet."

Notice that that question that holds the reader's attention is the same as the one you ask of your hero when creating a screenplay, novel, or short story. Another powerful hook question that has been used in media press kits and in presentations to the press in the past is, "How many times have you sold out on your plans and settled for something less?" However, today, this type of question might get a response like, "None of your business." So use something that makes your content more *approachable* such as "You don't have to settle for reality anymore. Your dreams just woke up your imagination."

You want the reader in the media to feel important and good about himself while reading your press kit. You want to nourish the press. You don't want to frighten, shock, or remind the reader of human mortality or frailty. Media kits are there to make you likeable.

Use a statement instead of a question to draw the reader in. Questions often bring knee-jerk hostility responses. Soothe the reader. Put the statement on the cover of your press kit folder and also inside the press release.

If you want to launch anything in the media, you need to show commitment and credibility. You're a media strategist, an architect and designer of 'models' on paper that create visibility in the media for your unsold, pre-sold, or in-development content or product.

In the middle of the press release, exert power. Write about how the reader can do something to increase his or her power. You could show the reader what one act he or she could perform to become more powerful. Don't ask a question in the middle of your press release.

A question wastes the limited time available, usually 20 seconds spent to read a one-page media release. Instead, illustrate in words how to solve a problem, obtain a result, or get more powerful by performing one act. That one act would directly relate to your product, premise, or content. In one sentence, tell the reader exactly what he or she has to do to become more powerful. That's the selling point of your item.

Professional-looking press kits publicize any item inexpensively. Paid advertising would cost hundreds of dollars for a two-inch display ad in daily newspaper or high-circulation trade journal.

A press kit is an open invitation for the writer to be hired by colleges of extended studies at $50 an hour or 50% of the gross of student's fees to give a one-day seminar on writing. Experience is more important than a degree at such adult education seminars in private schools. Exposure, such as giving seminars for producers and directors on script analysis and consulting, leads to better chances to have personal screenplays seen by producers.

Stop using fear as an advertisement to draw in people. There are enough ads on TV that start with a screeching ambulance or loud, fast heartbeats, screams, or a man shouting how he's dying or crying. These ads often are broadcast after midnight or late at night, when most frail seniors are up watching TV and just dozing off. It shocks people out of sleep, particularly the frail elderly or people with disabilities who are not able to sleep easily.

So if you fell asleep in front of your TV set, these types of ads may shock you out of your sweet dream with fearful possible reality scenarios that remind you of your mortality, pain, or diseases. The shock ads are there to get you to buy safety products. Older people feel anxiety when such ads come on. It reminds them of what's ahead. Instead of making them think about preparing for possible events or their final expenses, people sometimes are shocked awake into a panic attack or worse by the sudden noise of screaming sirens and shouting or loud rapidly beating sounds. Shock ads are unwelcome by those with panic disorder or sensitized nervous systems.

What ads do seniors like? Serenity is one. You can sell serenity to the media. Instead of wondering how many people get sick watching other people getting sick, use the opposite to attract attention. Offer gently bubbling fountains, quiet rivers and sunsets, beaches, mountains, pine trees, gardens, and anything that brings joy and contentment in TV ads that appear in the wee hours of the night.

To promote a product, use "two word" titles. Or use the word "Why" in your title if you're giving information. For nonfiction, use an insightful, popular, and commercial short two-word title such as "Robot Cowboys" Or a trendy title that tells the whole story of the nonfiction book: "Why Writers Want More Monies and Publishers Want More Funnies." Or "Why Women Want More_(drama)____and Men Want More_(sports)____"

What Do Media Professionals Expect To See in a Media Kit?

Newspaper and magazine editors, radio and T.V. producers, agents, publicists, entertainment attorneys, directors, actors, film, and video creative directors are used to receiving professionally printed press kits. They only read material sent in an "acceptable format."

An acceptable press kit consists of a double-pocketed file folder, the question hook printed on the cover (not typed on a regular typewriter, but typeset with desktop publishing fonts). Inside the flap pocket is another question hook on the inside cover. In the flap-pocket is a black and white glossy photo of the writer (matte for television producers).

On top of the photo is a four-page press release about what the writer has to offer that needs visibility—and how the information will help the community or readers. A short, one-page press release goes on top of the four-page release. The short press release gives the writer's biography, credits, credentials, and anything else important the writer has done in relation to what the longer press release covers.

News clippings about the writer or the script are put over the short press release. The clippings are cut out, dated, titled, and pasted on a sheet of paper and then photocopied onto a slick, camera-ready white sheet. Include in the second flap pocket a copy of any article, booklet, book, sample, or tape for media review. This press kit goes to agents as well as media editors and producers. Make sure you have an electric press kit on a Web site and also sent to the media as well as print folders. Too many paper print media kit folders are thrown away or recycled without being read. No one is paying anyone to read media kits sent unsolicited, and there's very little time to read them. The exception would be those on a newspaper staff paid to write book reviews or producers that book radio and TV authors as guests on programs.

*Start a reporting service. Create **press kits** containing DNA-driven ancestry reports. Create folder-type press kits as well as electronic media kits. Mail the paper press kits with reports to clients who have had their DNA tested for ancestry. Or make time capsules on genealogy, ancestry, family history, and DNA testing reports for ancestry.*

With very little capital, you can write a business plan to start *a reporting* service that brings business and client together. One of the easiest enterprises to start with only your computer, printer, and Internet connection is a DNA-driven genealogy reporting service.

You wouldn't have to spend money on equipment such as gifts for gift baskets or fabric, cameras, or other investments. With only your computer, printer, paper, press kit folders, DVD/CD recorder, DVDs and CDs, and email, you can offer information packaged in unique ways. Instead only offering administrative assistant services, typing, or editing and proofreading, you can offer DNA reporting presented in a media kit or package-type folder.

What does a press kit pitch? Place a two-page pitch release on top of all the other information in the kit tells the media why the script is so extraordinary, so unique and different and who can benefit by seeing it. Include a marketability study of who would be buying the script, book, or tape. The new age video market is on the rise.

On top of every release, place the final cover letter as a courtesy, telling why you want the media to print selected press releases and the photo inside. The cover letter is one page or less in length. The first paragraph of the cover letter contains a premise—of the release. What's important is summarized in one sentence.

Use concrete credentials that can be checked. If the press kit is going to a publisher to sell a book/script package deal, include a chapter breakdown. The titles of the chapters sell the book just as the title of a video script determines its commercial appeal.

Book chapter summaries vary from three paragraphs to under a page for highlights. Tell the media exactly what viewers will be told when they view the script. For script/booklet combinations such as book and audio tape combinations, or video and instructional manual packages, write down the components of the book in a press kit, and send a sample. This technique holds true for self-published and self-produced video/book packages used for instruction or motivation.

The first chapter of a book is like the first scene of a video script. It's the selling chapter. In a media kit designed to sell and outline a book and video package, tell the reader why she needs to read the book and view the video. Include photos or a mock-up copy of the video or book combination.

The fastest way to impress a reader about a video is to have an advertisement or poster with a black background and white print. The print is superimposed over a photo in the background. Viewers will remember that video above one on a white background with black lettering and design.

It's possible to create an infomercial to mail out to potential buyers who might be interested in purchasing a produced video or a published book, but it's expensive. A press kit creating visibility for a video, a script, or a book is more direct. Use one sentence to summarize your book, pamphlet, article, or script's premise.

Marketing researchers often report that readers will respond faster to an article written by a reporter about a person, business, or product than to a paid advertisement placed by the entrepreneur. An article I wrote for a high-circulation paper brought in 600 requests for information when I included my post office box number.

The tiny, classified ad I placed in the back of the paper (which was expensive for me) brought no responses. Visibility influences marketing.

Contacts with video software distributors lead to contacts with producers. A commercial title can pre-sell a script. Free publicity and press coverage pulls more weight than small, paid display ads announcing "script for sale." Press coverage is free, and can be obtained by a phone call and a news angle or a press kit.

ADDITIONAL INFORMATION

Press Kit (The Author's Guide to Self Promotion)
http://www.writing-world.com/columns/promotion/press12.shtml

American Library Association (Professional Tools)
http://www.ala.org/ala/proftools/professional.htm

Press Kits (American Library Association)
http://www.ala.org/ala/pio/piopresskits/alanationalconference2004/acma2004.htm

16

DESCRIPTION OF BUSINESS:

Reunions by Video Podcast

How to Startup A Family Reunions Business on the Internet, or Satellite for Videoconferencing

You can bring long-separated family members together even though each member may live in a different corner of the globe by creating video reunions. Similar videos can be created for retired military, school and college alumni, and other long-separated friends and co-workers.

INCOME POTENTIAL:

For a small fee—the cost of taping plus a margin of profit, a few dollars per minute, plus a little more than the cost of each copy of the videotape, you can unite families on the Internet, by video or videoconferencing, and give each family member a copy of the family reunion tape.

Back in 1994, the cost came out to about $4 a minute to reunite people on television through a hookup to a satellite. One company, *Canal Uno*, helped to unite families or hold business videoconferences.

Today, you can charge sliding scale fees for family members, refugees, retired military, co-workers, school alumni, missing persons, or the physically ill, depending on the budget, your cost, and the ability to pay of the client. Your goal is to bring together people long separated for a reunion on tape because none of the members could come in person due to financial inability, distance, work obligations, age, or illness.

BEST LOCALE TO OPERATE THE BUSINESS:

Locate anywhere there are large populations of immigrants and refugees, or anywhere your target populations congregate. You will be linking together people at a distance by video and phone.

On the video will be relatives, friends, co-workers, immigrants, refugees, or former soldiers who now live anywhere in the world. These people may not have seen their relatives and friends for decades. What they all have in common is that they want a reunion on non-broadcast television.

TRAINING REQUIRED:

You'll need to know how to operate your camcorder and television videoconferencing equipment. Or work with Internet connections. If you can't afford to buy satellite time, then you can limit your service to putting family reunions on DVDs or on the Web or other Internet arrangement, or plan videoconferencing with the client footing the bill for any satellite hookup.

Recommended are books or a course on how to produce with your video camera and how to produce videoconferences using satellite hookups. Contact the satellite companies for training offers or inquire in the telecommunications department of your local community college.

GENERAL APTITUDE OR EXPERIENCE:

You'll need to stand on your feet a lot and operate a camera. You should learn how to hook up television cables and devices. The best experience is hands-on volunteering with other small producers. Experience can be gained by joining professional associations related to video or satellites and volunteer to be on their teams or get available short and low-cost training offered by the business associations. Attend or volunteer to help out at conventions and conferences.

EQUIPMENT NEEDED:

You'll need a telephone line open to whatever countries you're hooking up to as well as a satellite connection. Your office can be in your home or in a small building. You'll need a room or studio to operate in or space to put your television screen and camera. A home office or garage can be used for your equipment. Perhaps a spare bedroom can be outfitted with camcorders and computers.

OPERATING YOUR BUSINESS:

Expect the reunions to be emotional. You could create a high-tech video network in a small building that brings families together from a part of the world you choose.

You are allowing families to be close for a short time on television. Seat relatives in a small room with a big television camera mounted in the back wall.

Here's one example from the mid-nineties. Canal Uno (Channel One) debuted on January 15, 1994. It provided the technology for families to talk to each member instantaneously on television, usually for 20 minutes. By satellite connection, each family member talked and viewed one another on a television screen.

If you start your own reunion business at home to make spare cash or to cut your own expenses, your reunions can last for what ever time slot you make—20 minutes—for example, depending upon the time you're allowed to use. You can work with the Internet or where there is no Internet connection, a satellite connection.

To look back at the Canal Uno example of 1994, El Salvadorans in Texas, California, Maryland, New Jersey, Washington, D.C., Virginia, and Florida could use this high-tech link to Central America. Canal Uno, in June 1994, handled about 100 links a week between the United States and El Salvador.

The courier firm, Gigante Express' opened back in 1983 when a young El Salvadoran entrepreneur, Jose Carlos Perez Saleh, had a plan to bring Canal Uno to Nicaragua, Honduras and Guatemala.

Before Canal Uno began operating, Gigante Express carried 30,000 letters a week as a major courier service from the firm's 52 offices in the United States and Canada to El Salvador, Nicaragua, Honduras and Guatemala.

This is one example of how successful high technology can be when applied to bringing people together or acting as a courier service. Look at how successful giants became successful. For example, it has been reported in the media during the nineties that Gigante as the first Central American courier company soon became the largest of more than 100 courier companies in El Salvador. How does this success case history apply to you at home?

You, too, as a family reunion video producer, also can make use of any type of technology that's affordable—from broadband Internet connections to satellite hookups feeding into your camcorder, monitor, or TV set. Your goal would be to bring long-separated people together and give them discs of their family members or long-lost friends anywhere in the world.

As a sideline, you can also do videoconferencing for corporation executives who need to attend interviews, seminars, and meetings around the globe without the bother and expense of jet lag.

What do consumers want? Connectivity is at the top of the list. Particularly in demand are satellite hookups to the Pacific Rim nations such as Japan, China, Taiwan, the Philippines, and Australia with the rest of the Far East linked to the West Coast of the United States for executive merger and business talk.

TARGET MARKET:

If you find out how many thousands of people from specific countries live in your area, you'll be able to estimate your target market. How many people from a given country live in the city you're in today?

Work with population demographics. Your goal is to reach interested people to make the distance between their old country and their new homeland seem smaller through the use of the home camcorder, wireless Internet, phone lines, or a satellite hookup.

Also contact realtors, vacation housing exchange firms, travel agents, and tour guides as well as executives at Fortune 500 companies to see whether they would like your videoconferencing services.

Reunions are not only for long-separated family members. They can be for business executives from around the world who need to connect via satellite and video.

RELATED VIDEO OPPORTUNITIES:

You can use your satellite time slot to broadcast election returns from foreign countries and tape them for distribution to community members or researchers. Team up with persons who speak foreign languages, Track how many people from the various countries live in your area and research what their needs are and what type of reunions would interest them. Cater to their videoconferencing needs by Internet, satellite hookup, camcorder, and DVDs or other compact discs.

ADDITIONAL INFORMATION:

International Teleconferencing Association
1150 Connecticut Ave NW, Ste. 1050
Washington, DC 20036

Satellite Video Exchange Society
1102 Homer St.
Vancouver, BC Canada V6B 2X6

Satellite Broadcasting & Communications Association
225 Reinekers Lane
Station 600
Alexandria, VA 22314

International Association of Satellite Users
PO Box DD
6845 Elm St.
McLean, VA 22101

Society for Private and Commercial Earth Stations
c/o Richard L. Brown
1920 N St. NW
Washington, DC 20036

Society of Telecommunications Consultants
One Rockefeller Plaza, Suite 1912
New York, NY 10020

Envirovideos
PO Box 629000
El Dorado Hills, CA 95762

El Salvador Media Project
335 W. 38th St., 5th fl.
New York, NY 10018

17

DESCRIPTION OF BUSINESS

Video Podcast Time Capsules

Scrap Booking & Life Story Skits: Personal History Keepsakes, and Genealogy Slide Shows

Plan, write, produce, and syndicate digital scrapbooking video podcasting news releases. Scrapbooking is so big that news releases emphasize the customer's needs and new products available for the craft of keepsake albums and memorabilia—from photos to time capsules. Additionally, turn oral or personal history significant events and life story highlights into video podcasts of 45-minute one-act plays for student audiences. Skits and plays are *time capsules* that can be included with family history and genealogy keepsakes. Record and transcribe the skits, monologues, life stories, oral histories, or plays.

Here are the steps you need to take in order to gather life story highlights to turn into skits, plays, monologues, vignettes, or other time capsules for high-school, college, or junior-high student audiences.

Anything recorded needs to have a text transcription in case the technology advances and the recording medium disappears before the material can be transferred to a newer medium. Digital scrap booking of oral history and photos or videos can be put in a variety of multimedia formats.

Examples would be records made for 'Victrolas' or old-time phonographs would not be able to play on current DVD players. If one generation forgets to transfer the time capsule from video tape or DVD to the next technology, at least photos and transcribed text would be viewable.

INCOME POTENTIAL

Charge a flat fee such as $100 for putting an edited one-hour life story oral history on a CD or DVD. Or charge less for an unedited oral history on disc or tape. You can charge $75 or more to put the life story on the Web at a Web site where space is bought, or make time capsules—containers of keepsake memorabilia and albums. Another alternative is to charge $100 to transcribe a one-hour oral history tape into a printed out transcription.

The purpose of a transcription of what's on a video or audio recording is to have the words on paper in case the technology evolves so that a disc or tape cannot be played in another generation or in a century or more in the future. Just in case someone forgets to transfer the recording to the newest technology, you have a library file of the printed out text that can be translated and emailed or put in a database.

BEST LOCALE TO OPERATE THE BUSINESS

Scrap booking stores operate in any locality where there is family life. Houses of worship, libraries, online at home, and in suburban, family-type neighborhoods and community centers or schools are good places as are supplies in educational settings. Craft, art, and hobby supply stores also carry scrap booking supplies.

TRAINING REQUIRED

Classes in scrap booking are given in continuing and adult education centers as well as in shops selling supplies for scrap booking, crafts, artists' tools, and hobbies.

EQUIPMENT NEEDED

You'll need scrap booking supplies you can get from suppliers of craft, hobby, art, and scrap booking stores. Some suppliers and vendors also sell kits where you can be trained to teach others how to scrap book.

Digital scrap booking uses software with clip art and photograph album-creating as well as genealogy and pedigree chart software. Contact the suppliers listed under scrap booking supplies. One excellent Web site for scrap booking supplies you also can sell to your students is at: Y

Set up classes of your own and train others. Contact your local church or house of worship and community center to see whether they already have scrap booking classes. You can teach at any adult education, park, or informal craft class and charge fees for a class ranging from $25 to $35 per person (or what your market will bear) for instruction in scrap booking, either paper hard copy with photos or digital with scanned and digital photos.

OPERATING YOUR BUSINESS

Use the following sequence when gathering oral/aural histories:

1. Develop one central issue and divide that issue into a few important questions that highlight or focus on that one central issue.

2. Write out a plan just like a business plan for your oral history project. You may have to use that plan later to ask for a grant for funding, if required. Make a list of all your products that will result from the oral history when it's done.

3. Write out a plan for publicity or public relations and media relations. How are you going to get the message to the public or special audiences?

4. Develop a budget. This is important if you want a grant or to see how much you'll have to spend on creating an oral history project.

5. List the cost of video taping and editing, packaging, publicity, and help with audio or special effects and stock shot photos of required.

6. What kind of equipment will you need? List that and the time slots you give to each part of the project. How much time is available? What are your deadlines?

7. What's your plan for a research? How are you going to approach the people to get the interviews? What questions will you ask?

8. Do the interviews. Arrive prepared with a list of questions. It's okay to ask the people the kind of questions they would like to be asked. Know what dates the interviews will cover in terms of time. Are you covering the economic depression of the thirties? World Wars? Fifties? Sixties? Pick the time parameters.

9. Edit the interviews so you get the highlights of experiences and events, the important parts. Make sure what's important to you also is important to the person you interviewed.

10. Find out what the interviewee wants to emphasize perhaps to highlight events in a life story. Create a video-biography of the highlights of one person's life or an oral history of an event or series of events.

11. Process audio as well as video, and make sure you have written transcripts of anything on audio and/or video in case the technology changes or the tapes go bad.

12. Save the tapes to compact disks, DVDs, a computer hard disk and several other ways to preserve your oral history time capsule. Donate any tapes or CDs to appropriate archives, museums, relatives of the interviewee, and one or more oral history libraries. They are usually found at universities that have an oral history department and library such as UC Berkeley and others.

13. Check the Web for oral history libraries at universities in various states and abroad.

14. Evaluate what you have edited. Make sure the central issue and central questions have been covered in the interview. Find out whether newspapers or magazines want summarized transcripts of the audio and/or video with photos.

15. Contact libraries, archives, university oral history departments and relevant associations and various ethnic genealogy societies that focus on the subject matter of your central topic.

16. Keep organizing what you have until you have long and short versions of your oral history for various archives and publications. Contact magazines and newspapers to see whether editors would assign reporters to do a story on the oral history project.

17. Create a scrapbook with photos and summarized oral histories. Write a synopsis of each oral history on a central topic or issue. Have speakers give public presentations of what you have for each person interviewed and/or for the entire project using highlights of several interviews with the media for publicity. Be sure your project is archived properly and stored in a place devoted to oral history archives and available to researchers and authors.

Video Podcasting Using Oral History Interviewing/Recording Techniques

1. Begin with easy to answer questions that don't require you explore and probe deeply in your first question. Focus on one central issue when asking questions. Don't use abstract questions. A plain question would be

"What's your purpose?" An abstract question with connotations would be "What's your crusade?" Use questions with denotations instead of connotations. Keep questions short and plain—easy to understand. Examples would be, "What did you want to accomplish? How did you solve those problems? How did you find closure?" Ask the familiar "what, when, who, where, how, and why."

2. First research written or visual resources before you begin to seek an oral history of a central issue, experience, or event.

3. Who is your intended audience?

4. What kind of population niche or sample will you target?

5. What means will you select to choose who you will interview? What group of people will be central to your interview?

6. Write down how you'll explain your project. Have a script ready so you don't digress or forget what to say on your feet.

7. Consult oral history professionals if you need more information. Make sure what you write in your script will be clear to understand by your intended audience.

8. Have all the equipment you need ready and keep a list of what you'll use and the cost. Work up your budget.

9. Choose what kind of recording device is best—video, audio, multimedia, photos, and text transcript. Make sure your video is broadcast quality. I use a Sony Digital eight (high eight) camera.

10. Make sure from cable TV stations or news stations that what type of video and audio you choose ahead of time is broadcast quality.

11. Make sure you have an external microphone and also a second microphone as a second person also tapes the interview in case the quality of your camera breaks down. You can also keep a tape recorder going to capture the audio in case your battery dies.

12. Make sure your battery is fully charged right before the interview. Many batteries die down after a day or two of nonuse.

13. Test all equipment before the interview and before you leave your office or home. I've had batteries go down unexpectedly and happy there was

another person ready with another video camera waiting and also an audio tape version going.

14. Make sure the equipment works if it's raining, hot, cold, or other weather variations. Test it before the interview. Practice interviewing someone on your equipment several times to get the hang of it before you show up at the interview.

15. Make up your mind how long the interview will go before a break and use tape of that length, so you have one tape for each segment of the interview. Make several copies of your interview questions.

16. Be sure the interviewee has a copy of the questions long before the interview so the person can practice answering the questions and think of what to say or even take notes. Keep checking your list of what you need to do.

17. Let the interviewee make up his own questions if he wants. Perhaps your questions miss the point. Present your questions first. Then let him embellish the questions or change them as he wants to fit the central issue with his own experiences.

18. Call the person two days and then one day before the interview to make sure the individual will be there on time and understands how to travel to the location. Or if you are going to the person's home, make sure you understand how to get there.

19. Allow yourself one extra hour in case of traffic jams.

20. Choose a quiet place. Turn off cell phones and any ringing noises. Make sure you are away from barking dogs, street noise, and other distractions.

21. Before you interview make sure the person knows he or she is going to be video and audio-taped.

22. If you don't want anyone swearing, make that clear it's for public archives and perhaps broadcast to families.

23. Your interview questions should follow the journalist's information-seeking format of asking, who, what, where, where, how, and why. Oral history is a branch of journalistic research.

24. Let the person talk and don't interrupt. You be the listener and think of oral history as aural history from your perspective.

25. Make sure only one person speaks without being interrupted before someone else takes his turn to speak.

26. Understand silent pauses are for thinking of what to say.

27. Ask one question and let the person gather his thoughts.

28. Finish all your research on one question before jumping to the next question. Keep it organized by not jumping back to the first question after the second is done. Stay in a linear format.

29. Follow up what you can about any one question, finish with it, and move on to the next question without circling back. Focus on listening instead of asking rapid fire questions as they would confuse the speaker.

30. Ask questions that allow the speaker to begin to give a story, anecdote, life experience, or opinion along with facts. Don't ask questions that can be answered only be yes or no. This is not a courtroom. Let the speaker elaborate with facts and feelings or thoughts.

31. Late in the interview, start to ask questions that explore and probe for deeper answers.

32. Wrap up with how the person solved the problem, achieved results, reached a conclusion, or developed an attitude, or found the answer. Keep the wrap-up on a light, uplifting note.

33. Don't leave the individual hanging in emotion after any intensity of. Respect the feelings and opinions of the person. He or she may see the situation from a different point of view than someone else. So respect the person's right to feel as he does. Respect his need to recollect his own experiences.

34. Interview for only one hour at a time. If you have only one chance, interview for an hour. Take a few minutes break. Then interview for the second hour. Don't interview more than two hours at any one meeting.

35. Use prompts such as paintings, photos, music, video, diaries, vintage clothing, crafts, antiques, or memorabilia when appropriate. Carry the photos in labeled files or envelopes to show at appropriate times in order to prime the memory of the interviewee. For example, you may show a

childhood photo and ask "What was it like in that orphanage where these pictures were taken?" Or travel photos might suggest a trip to America as a child, or whatever the photo suggests. For example, "Do you remember when this ice cream parlor inside the ABC movie house stood at the corner of X and Y Street? Did you go there as a teenager? What was your funniest memory of this movie theater or the ice cream store inside back in the fifties?"

36. As soon as the interview is over, label all the tapes and put the numbers in order.

37. A signed release form is required before you can broadcast anything. So have the interviewee sign a release form before the interview.

38. Make sure the interviewee gets a copy of the tape and a transcript of what he or she said on tape. If the person insists on making corrections, send the paper transcript of the tape for correction to the interviewee. Edit the tape as best you can or have it edited professionally.

39. Make sure you comply with all the corrections the interviewee wants changed. He or she may have given inaccurate facts that need to be corrected on the paper transcript.

40. Have the tape edited with the corrections, even if you have to make a tape at the end of the interviewee putting in the corrections that couldn't be edited out or changed.

41. As a last resort, have the interviewee redo the part of the tape that needs correction and have it edited in the tape at the correct place marked on the tape. Keep the paper transcript accurate and up to date, signed with a release form by the interviewee.

42. Oral historians write a journal of field notes about each interview. Make sure these get saved and archived so they can be read with the transcript.

43. Have the field notes go into a computer where someone can read them along with the transcript of the oral history tape or CD.

44. Thank the interviewee in writing for taking the time to do an interview for broadcast and transcript.

45. Put a label on everything you do from the interview to the field notes. Make a file and sub file folders and have everything stored in a computer, in archived storage, and in paper transcript.

46. Make copies and digital copies of all photos and put into the records in a computer. Return originals to owners.

47. Make sure you keep your fingerprints off the photos by wearing white cotton gloves. Use cardboard when sending the photos back and pack securely. Also photocopy the photos and scan the photos into your computer. Treat photos as antique art history in preservation.

48. Make copies for yourself of all photos, tapes, and transcripts. Use your duplicates, and store the original as the master tape in a place that won't be used often, such as a time capsule or safe, or return to a library or museum where the original belongs.

49. Return all original photos to the owners. An oral history archive library or museum also is suitable for original tapes. Use copies only to work from, copy, or distribute.

50. Index your tapes and transcripts. To use oral history library and museum terminology, recordings and transcripts are given "accession numbers."

51. Phone a librarian in an oral history library of a university for directions on how to assign accession numbers to your tapes and transcripts if the materials are going to be stored at that particular library. Store copies in separate places in case of loss or damage.

52. If you don't know where the materials will be stored, use generic accession numbers to label your tapes and transcripts. Always keep copies available for yourself in case you have to duplicate the tapes to send to an institution, museum, or library, or to a broadcast company.

53. Make synopses available to public broadcasting radio and TV stations.

54. Check your facts.

55. Are you missing anything you want to include?

56. Is there some place you want to send these tapes and transcripts such as an ethnic museum, radio show, or TV satellite station specializing in the topics on the tapes, such as public TV stations? Would it be suitable for a world music station? A documentary station?

57. If you need more interviews, arrange them if possible.

58. Give the interviewee a copy of the finished product with the corrections. Make sure the interviewee signs a release form that he or she is satisfied with the corrections and is releasing the tape to you and your project.

59. Store the tapes and transcripts in a library or museum or at a university or other public place where it will be maintained and preserved for many generations and restored when necessary.

60. You can also send copies to a film repository or film library that takes video tapes, an archive for radio or audio tapes for radio broadcast or cable TV.

61. Copies may be sent to various archives for storage that lasts for many generations. Always ask whether there are facilities for restoring the tape. A museum would most likely have these provisions as would a large library that has an oral history library project or section.

62. Make sure the master copy is well protected and set up for long-term storage in a place where it will be protected and preserved.

63. If the oral history is about events in history, various network news TV stations might be interested. Film stock companies may be interested in copies of old photos.

64. Find out from the subject matter what type of archives, repository, or storage museums and libraries would be interested in receiving copies of the oral history tapes and transcripts.

Print media libraries would be interested in the hard paper copy transcripts and photos as would various ethnic associations and historical preservation societies. Find out whether the materials will go to microfiche, film, or be digitized and put on CDs and DVDs, or on the World Wide Web. If you want to create a time capsule for the Web, you can ask the interviewee whether he or she wants the materials or selected materials to be put online or on CD as multimedia or other. Then you would get a signed release from the interviewee authorizing you to put the materials or excerpts online. Also find out in whose name the materials are copyrighted and whether you have print and electronic rights to the material or do the owners-authors-interviewees—or you, the videographer-producer? Get it all in writing, signed by those who have given you any interviews, even if you have to call your local intellectual property rights attorney

How Accurate Are Autobiographies, Biographies, Personal Histories, Plays and Monologues Based on Life Stories?

Autobiographies, biographies, personal histories, plays, and monologues present a point of view. Are all sides given equal emphasis? Will the audience choose favorite characters? Cameras give fragments, points of view, and bits and pieces. Viewers will see what the videographer or photographer intends to be seen. The interviewee will also be trying to put his point of view across and tell the story from his perspective.

Will the photographer or videographer be in agreement with the interviewee? Or if you are recording for print transcript, will your point of view agree with the interviewee's perspective and experience if your basic 'premise,' where you two are coming from, are not in agreement? Think this over as you write your list of questions. Do both of you agree on your central issue on which you'll focus for the interview?

How are you going to turn spoken words into text for your paper hard copy transcript? Will you transcribe verbatim, correct the grammar, or quote as you hear the spoken words? Oral historians really need to transcribe the exact spoken word. You can leave out the 'ahs' and 'oms' or loud pauses, as the interviewee thinks what to say next. You don't want to sound like a court reporter, but you do want to have an accurate record transcribed of what was spoken.

You're also not editing for a movie, unless you have permission to turn the oral history into a TV broadcast, where a lot gets cut out of the interview for time constraints. For that, you'd need written permission so words won't be taken out of context and strung together in the editing room to say something different from what the interviewee intended to say.

Someone talking could put in wrong names, forget what they wanted to say, or repeat themselves. They could mumble, ramble, or do almost anything. So you would have to sit down and weed out redundancy when you can or decide on presenting exactly what you've heard as transcript.

When someone reads the transcript in text, they won't have what you had in front of you, and they didn't see and hear the live presentation or the videotape. It's possible to misinterpret gestures or how something is spoken, the mood or tone, when reading a text transcript. Examine all your sources. Use an ice-breaker to get someone talking.

If a woman is talking about female-interest issues, she may feel more comfortable talking to another woman. Find out whether the interviewee is more comfortable speaking to someone of his or her own age. Some older persons feel they can relate better to someone close to their own age than someone in high school, but it varies. Sometimes older people can speak more freely to a teenager.

The interviewee must be able to feel comfortable with the interviewer and know he or she will not be judged. Sometimes it helps if the interviewer is the same ethnic group or there is someone present of the same group or if new to the language, a translator is present.

Read some books on oral history field techniques. Read the National Genealogical Society Quarterly (NGSQ). Also look at The American Genealogist (TAG), The Genealogist, and The New England Historical and Genealogical Register (The Register). If you don't know the maiden name of say, your grandmother's mother, and no relative knows either because it wasn't on her death certificate, try to reconstruct the lives of the males who had ever met the woman whose maiden name is unknown.

Maybe she did business with someone before marriage or went to school or court. Someone may have recorded the person's maiden name before her marriage. Try medical records if any were kept. There was no way to find my mother's grandmother's maiden name until I started searching to see whether she had any brothers in this country. She had to have come as a passenger on a ship around 1880 as she bought a farm. Did her husband come with her?

Was the farm in his name? How many brothers did she have in this country with her maiden surname? If the brothers were not in this country, what countries did they come from and what cities did they live in before they bought the farm in Albany? If I could find out what my great grandmother's maiden name was through any brothers living at the time, I could contact their descendants perhaps and see whether any male or female lines are still in this country or where else on the globe.

Perhaps a list of midwives in the village at the time is recorded in a church or training school for midwives. Fix the person in time and place. Find out whom she might have done business with and whether any records of that business exist. What businesses did she patronize? Look for divorce or court records, change of name records, and other legal documents.

Look at local sources. Did anyone save records from bills of sale for weddings, purchases of homes, furniture, debutante parties, infant supplies, or even medical records? Look at nurses' licenses, midwives' registers, employment contracts, and teachers' contracts, alumni associations for various schools, passports, passenger lists, alien registration cards, naturalization records, immigrant aid societies, city directories, and cross-references.

Try religious and women's clubs, lineage and village societies, girl scouts and similar groups, orphanages, sanatoriums, hospitals, police records. Years ago there was even a Eugenics Record Office. What about the women's prisons? The first one opened in 1839—Mount Pleasant Female Prison, NY.

Try voters' lists. If your relative is from another country, try records in those villages or cities abroad. Who kept the person's diaries? Have you checked the Orphan Train records? Try ethnic and religious societies and genealogy associations for that country. Most ethnic genealogy societies have a special interest group for even the smallest villages in various countries.

You can start one and put up a Web site for people who also come from there in past centuries. Check alimony, divorce, and court records, widow's pensions of veterans, adoptions, orphanages, foster homes, medical records, birth, marriage, and death certificates, social security, immigration, pet license owners' files, prisons, alumni groups from schools, passenger lists, military, and other legal records.

When all historical records are being tied together, you can add the DNA testing to link all those cousins. Check military pensions on microfilms in the National Archives. See the bibliography section of this book for further resources on highly recommended books and articles on oral history field techniques and similar historical subjects.

ADDITIONAL INFORMATION

The Digital Scrapbook Place
http://www.digitalscrapbookplace.com/

Accents 2 (Scrapbooking Shopping Director)
http://www.accents2scrapbooking.com/scrapbooking_links.htm

Scrapbooking Press Releases
http://www.topix.net/hobbies/scrapbooking/pr

18

DESCRIPTION OF BUSINESS

Make Your Own Toys Instruction by Video Podcast

Video podcasts about building or using toys may help families interact and communicate in new ways. Help buyers of toys cut expenses by offering kits on how parents and children as a family may interact together to create original toys. Help parents and children invent toys together or even assemble toys for the fun of making one's own toys. It brings parents and children together to spend quality time and enhances creativity.

Teach children how to think creatively, assemble toys, and perhaps show others how to make their own toys to cut expenses and at the same time find higher quality toys. With toys you make yourself, the goal is to get more for less and also to learn more about design.

Grand River Toys at: http://www.grandrivertoys.com/pages/MakeYourOwn.html offers kits on making your own toys. One example is the kit for making your own ice cream. There's another kit for making your own chocolate. Kits include making your own comic book, talking clock, bubble gum, jigsaw puzzle, a volcano-making kit, a milk carton radio, a tooth fairy treasure chest, a sensory dome, and lots of other kits for making toys, digital recording labs, crystal wonders, pinhole cameras, and food items.

The easiest way to make a toy is to take one apart and back-engineer it to see how it fits together, piece by piece. Old-fashioned toys made of wood or fabric or toys focused on making CDs have different methods of construction. Toys, fabric, and pillows can easily be turned turn into soft pet beds.

The Web site, Physics Toys at: http://fog.ccsf.cc.ca.us/~tbardin/ has a section on how to make your own toys that explain physics. It's at: http://fog.ccsf.cc.ca.us/~tbardin/html/toys.html. Check out this site to learn how to make toys illustrating the principles of electrostatics, magnetism electromagnetism, buoyancy, fluid pressures, fluid dynamics, heat energy, evaporation, phase changes, forces, motion, momentum, energy, light waves, image formations, sound waves, standing waves and wave motions. How about making a toy the whole family can enjoy and continuously contribute to?

What kind of toys or board games can you make from item you have around the house? Games from cardboard boxes, craft items, and knitted toys such as teddy bears all can be made from existing objects such as pillows and sweaters. It enhances your creativity to think of new items to make out of what you already have or could easily and inexpensively obtain. The whole idea is to have fun, and increase benefits, comfort, health, quality, and custom-fit while decreases expenses. You also want to be good to the environment and exercise your brain and body. It's the redemptive value that's your motivation for making it yourself from scratch.

Open an Online 'Toybrary'

Look at the success of a popular videotape game called Clue, from Parker Brothers. As soon as the tape was released, it immediately sold more than 100,000 units. By the mid-eighties, Park Brothers sold more than 300,000, about 90 percent marketed to toy stores.

Today, the trend moves from camcorder to DVD to computer. Visual anthropology and sociology, current issues, and life stories move from camcorder to DVD in one take. Life stories feed into computer hard disks to be downloaded by anyone anywhere with fast broadband and saved on a disk. Education and toys mix so that learning can be fun again.

Earn money with your video camcorder by producing, editing, distributing, or selling your videos to toy stores. You can create a video toy library: a toybrary, where children can rent video games as if they were toys donated to a library.

Sell or rent children's videos by mail order, out of your home, or in your own video thrift store—operating like an old time radio tape rental library. If your video focuses on activities children enjoy, or can be viewed by families, try the toy store market for your video game or video storytelling. Create videos to be used as toys.

INCOME POTENTIAL:

If you sell your video game at low prices, or have a low-priced (under $30) videocassette, it might interest toy stores. The toy market recently represented more than $10 billion in sales.

If you can price your video really low, it might interest the more than 375 super toy stores in the United States and the more than 1,200 toy specialty outlets. Children's video sales are big business. A growing market exists in interactive children's videos also.

Price your videos for children under $30, and contact the children's video libraries. The video genre of children's programming is the fastest and largest growing market of non-movie videos carried by both toy stores and video stores.

You can also sell to the publishing market. Well known children's book publishers have entered the video business. Like them, you, too can produce, acquire, or distribute children's videos.

Children's bookstores usually prefer videos priced under $15. Many bookstores carry children's videos priced as cheaply as $9 or less. The cheaper you can price your videos, the more stores will be interested in taking them in to sell.

BEST LOCALE TO OPERATE THE BUSINESS:

Try the toy stores first. Bookstores that carry videos really want outstanding video hits. However, there is an expanding market for children's educational videos, teen magazine videos, calendars, information, health, children's animation, and music videos. Books on video are popular, particularly favorite children's books that can be brought to life on tape and marketed to toy chains.

Here's a list of the most interesting businesses to buy books to put on video: mystery, suspense, romance, mainstream, historical romance, adventure, science fiction, western, humor/comedy, supernatural, scientific toy research, and war/military. Pick a genre after you've done your market research to find out the exact products where there exists a high demand.

If your video is nonfiction storytelling for kids, the favorite genres are instruction, reference, biography, religious, health, exercise, and for adults, home repair, gardening, how-to, craft, leisure/travel, investments, and last—doing your tax paperwork.

If you try to get your videos in bookstores, be aware that bookstores expect a 45 percent margin or higher. Orders take quite a while to fill. As a video-maker, the bookstore long margins may bother you.

New video titles are announced two months before release. So orders are demanded long before the video is available. This does not agree with bookstores who order only quarterly. If you're dealing with mass market merchandisers, they also order only quarterly.

Since video has carved a permanent niche in bookstores, the two fields—publishing and video-making have a lot to learn from one another to make production go smoother. The outlook is that whatever is a hit in book form could soon become a videocassette meant for home viewing by the family.

In the industry, children's video represents more than a $50 million wholesale business for toy stores, including educational tapes sold by toy stores. Video tapes are even sold in the children's department of many stores. Some new video makers are putting greeting card videos for children on tape.

If the average parent spends more than $170 a year on toys for each child, about 50 percent are impulse items. Toy stores like to push videocassettes displayed as customers walk in or as they wait to pay the cashier—as one of their favorite impulse items.

If you want to begin as a video vendor before you make your own videos, try the toy stores first—before the book stores. Video retailers put their orders in for new cassettes every 30 days. When the toy stores finally orders, they want big profit margins and high return agreements.

People who make videos don't like giving these lee ways to the toy store owners. To make money, focus on giving a unique presentation or game on your video.

TRAINING REQUIRED:

To make a video for toy store sales, focus on children's or family programming. You don't need formal training, but learn what sells to children by reading the toy trade journals and joining the business trade associations.

GENERAL APTITUDE OR EXPERIENCE:

You should like to entertain children and know what's popular. Animation, games, storytelling, or putting your writings on video, if they are popular with children helps. You can also try storytelling for an adult audience or a video game the whole family can play.

If you invent a new kind of video bingo-type game, or use your original cartoon character, training in animation design helps. You can get such training or hire an animation artist by consulting "animators" in your local Yellow Pages directory.

EQUIPMENT NEEDED:

You'll need a video camera, editing equipment, and good story material, animation, and special effects. The quickest way to obtain animation on tape is to ask a student in animation or a hungry new animator to design from your story script and go 50-50 on any profits made from sales. Copyright your work.

For animation, a computer is necessary with animation software. You'll need equipment that interfaces your video camera, VCR, and personal computer, and any other special effects and animation software.

The cheapest route is to approach any community college that has a major in animation and ask for students to help you or to intern with you in exchange for college credits, or to hire a new animator who needs experience and a tape to use as a portfolio piece.

OPERATING YOUR BUSINESS:

Begin to design your game or tell your story on video with either live actors using your material in script or play form, or if a game, computer animation and voice-over simulations. If you're going interactive, you'll need a freelance crew of programmers, technicians, artists, writers, and yourself as producer-packager to deal with distributors and toy stores.

To get specific instruction, step-by-step in creating original video games, network with members of video and computer game designers' professional associations and inquire of animation students how they get their ideas. That will inspire and motivate you to invent your own video game. Everyone's is original and unique, yet appeals to popular tastes in video games. So study the video game market thoroughly.

One great annual conference of video, computer, and interactive game designers is the TED Conferences, Inc., The Orchard, 180 Narragansett Ave., Newport Rhode Island 02840.

To make money putting your storytelling on video, you can round up actors, readers, writers, and professional storytellers and create a unique character such as a foster grandparent who reads children's stories on video for special occasions—birthday party entertainment, bedtime stories for preschoolers, or any unique audience you want to target with your stories on video.

Add the spice of special effects and animation combined with live actors and readers, and you have a great storytelling experience on video. You can begin by showing your video at professional storyteller's associations, and then market to retailers, bookstores, record stores, video chains, toy stores, and the rental market.

Find out whether your storytelling videos or your video game cassettes would be better suited to the sell-through market or the rental market. These two separate markets for video product have different prices and different material.

Videos that are rented by consumers are geared for quick turnover. The videos go to stores at higher prices than the cheaper videos meant for sale.

Most movies are high-priced videos going to rental markets. Most toy-store videos are cheap videos or video games meant to sell to parents and children.

Don't price your video, toy, or board game higher than the average cost of books, records, audio tapes, and music compact disks. Your video can sell in convenience stores, through mass merchants, at sports stores if it has to do with athletics, exercise, or health, through direct mail, or through direct response television infomercials.

You'll have to package your video or toy to attract attention. Advertising and pricing will determine whether your video will become popular. Nobody can look at a DVD in a toy store, unlike books that can be read in the store. *Packaging* sells your video, board game, or toy, not 'browsability'.

If you go in for storytelling and video games, you'll be competing in the children's market and in toystores, competing against Disney, Family Home Entertainment, Kids Klassics, Scholastic, and all the big names in book publishing and home video production, like Vestron, Sony, and Western Publishing. You'll also be competing against the interactive multimedia computer game market that uses video interactively with computer animation and story telling—music, lights, text, and art.

Keep your tape for children under one hour in length. Price it under $20. Storytelling works best around a theme, especially a holiday theme. If you aren't doing animation themes, focus on a holiday celebration or animal themes.

You can also do an exercise for children's tape, focusing on preschoolers, or present on video your own children's books, featuring live actors. One excellent example is the Beatrice Potter stories on video. Classic characters from children's story books, if you can get the rights or write great stories, make classic children's video.

TARGET MARKET:

You want your video games or storytelling on tape to reach toy stores and bookstores. You can also market through direct mail order to clients whose names already appear on lists which you can buy—people who have bought videos my mail order before.

Storytelling video markets include schools and parents, bookstores, and writer's circles.

RELATED TOY OPPORTUNITIES:

Besides video games or storytelling videos, you can work with animators to create unique characters to fit special occasions, such as children's birthday parties. Or you can use videos to present themes to schools, such as tapes on self-esteem for children, cultural diversity, or psychological themes, such as why some children need to be the center of attention, others need approval, and others need to be the class clown. Another theme is dealing with difficult people such as the school bully or finding ways to deal with learning disabilities and discovering aptitudes or enhancing creativity.

Social studies and controversial themes also make good videos. A related opportunity is to acquire pamphlets on hot issues in the news or controversy and create videos for the junior high school social studies classes. Entertainment and learning are often combined on popular-selling videos.

ADDITIONAL INFORMATION:

Toy Industry Association
http://www.toy-tia.org/template.cfm

Toy Manufacturer's Association
http://www.tmhk.net/English_Version/index_e.htm

Toy Source
http://www.toysource.com/resources/trade/

Toy Surplus
http://www.toysource.com/surplus/

Toy Auctions/Global
http://www.toysource.com/global/

American Specialty Toy Retailing Association
http://www.astratoy.org/i4a/pages/index.cfm?pageid=1

Commission on Instructional Technology
C/O Superintendent of Documents
US Government Printing Office
Washington, DC 20402

19

DESCRIPTION OF BUSINESS

Writing and Producing Video Podcast Animation Destined to Become Children's Video Books or Segments

Writing Video Podcasts for Puppet Theatre

Adapting Scriptwriting for Animation to Puppet Theater for Children

Re-write this animation script as a video podcast for children using the concept
of animal puppets in costume. It's 24 pages in length and runs about 6,367
words. You can write this video podcast script for puppets, your own animated
cartoons, avatars, or for children in costume or puppets that children can make.

Puppet movements on a puppet stage substitute for camera angles or camera
frames. Write in the direction choosing either puppet actions or live children
dressed in animal costumes. With puppets you can simulate the flight of birds
across a puppet stage.

This makes it easier to adapt as a puppet theater script. This exercise gives you
practice and experience in writing for puppet theater, children's theater, and animation scriptwriting. Camera direction such as "fade in" can be substituted for
lighting variations and sounds on a puppet stage.

◆   ◆   ◆

THE AMAZON HATCHLINGS

In
"PICKLES, THE PARROT"
A 12-Minute Pilot Script for a New Animation Series
(12 minutes)

THE AMAZON HATCHLINGS
In PICKLES, THE PARROT
Copyright 2005
words
pages
THE AMAZON HATCHLINGS
in
PICKLES, THE PARROT
By:
Anne Hart
FADE IN:
ON A CLOSE SHOT OF A LARGE RAINBOW TOUCAN
rapidly chewing down an Amazon Parrotberry tree. CAMERA WIDENS to reveal a whole flock of toucans stripping the tree of all berries and leaves. The tree is soon chewed down to a nub.

CLOSER ON PICKLES, THE AMAZON YELLOW NAPE PARROT, as he sticks his head out of a window putting a steaming Parrotberry pie on his window sill to cool.

PICKLES
Those toucans are eating all
our Parrotberry trees.

CAMERA WIDENS to reveal the parrot family: Old Macaw, Parette, Hatchling, a tiny ball of fluff with a beak, Nestling, and Fledgling inside the highrise bamboo birdcage house building scarecrows to chase the toucans away from the parrotberry tree. OLD MACAW is building a bird cage in the middle of the floor instead of a scarecrow.

CLOSER ON OLD MACAW
MACAW
Your scarecrow won't scare 'em
for long. But I'm building them a
home of their own.

PICKLES
When there aren't any more
Parrotberries left, the toucans
will move to another spot.

CLOSER ON PICKLES
PICKLES takes a magical salt shaker out of his pocket and seasons a bowl of fruit from the table.

PICKLES

This will attract the toucans
away from the Parrotberry tree.
When they smell these salts,
they'll stop eating Parrotberries.
Pickles stuffs fruit into his pockets and into the pockets
of all the Amazon Babies, including Hatchling, also putting
seasoned plums under Hatchling's bonnet.

FLEDGLING

You mean our last Parrotberry
tree.

PICKLES

I'll sprinkle my toucan bait
powder on all this fruit.
PICKLES grabs a cord he's attached to the bird cage and gives
it a pull. SFX: OUTBOARD MOTOR SPUTTER

WIDER ANGLE

as the birdcage starts to glide across the floor. PICKLES
points ahead. All the AMAZON HATCHLINGS hop aboard through the
open door of the cage and hold onto one another as they sit
on the bird cage swing and perches.

PICKLES

That tree over there looks swell.
As they move out of shot we cut to:

THE TREETOPS OF A LARGE GROVE OF PARROTBERRY TREES

The HATCHLINGS gain into shot in an animated bird cage
helicopter/motorboat combo. They take fruit and nuts
out of their pockets and bait the birdcage to attract
the toucans. Fledgling leans over the edge, looks
down at the toucans on the Parrotberry tree branches.

FLEDGLING

Amazonadoodle! I hope the toucans
find the fruit in their new home
tastes better than our Parrotberry
branches.

CLOSER ON FLEDGLING AND PICKLES

FLEDGLING screeches as the chewed branch gives way.

PICKLES

Oh, no! There's nothing to
hang the cage on up here. Help.
WIDE ON CAGE
as cage begins to crash through the hollow, eaten out
tree. The tree falls over, entirely stripped of branches
and berries. In mid-air PICKLES pulls a balloon out of
his pocket and, huffing and puffing, inflates it. He
attaches the balloon to the top of the birdcage and it
floats above the next treetop.
CLOSE ON GRANDPA MACAW IN CAGE
GRANDPA MACAW
Look! That tree still has some
Parrotberries left on it.
WIDE ON CAGE
as it floats to the next treetop and settles on a branch.
HATCHLING holds out a plum and a toucan flies over and takes it
out of the HATCHLING's hand.
THREE-SHOT PICKLES, GRANDPA MACAW, AND HATCHLING
GRANDPA MACAW
They are taking the fruit.
PICKLES
Now, if only they'll all fly
into the nice birdcage.
CLOSE ON HATCHLING
HATCHLING burbles, flaps his tiny wings and climbs out on the tree
branch to pet the nice toucan as the bird gobbles up the plum.
NESTLING
No, Hatchling, don't follow
that toucan.
The toucan looks up at Hatchliing with a mischievous twinkle in
its blue eye as it flies under Hatchling. Hatchling wraps his baby wings
around the toucan's outstretched neck as it takes off into a rainbow with
Hatchling holding on, riding the toucan.
GRANDPA MACAW
Come back, Hatchling!
ANGLE ON PICKLES, GRANDPA MACAW AND NESTLING
PICKLES
We must find out where the

toucans are coming from.
GRANDPA MACAW
They're probably taking
Hatchling to toucan's cove.
NESTLING
With all that fruit I
stuffed in Hatchling's knapsack,
it will attract every
bird in the Amazon.
ANGLE ON SILLY AND JESTER
SILLY takes a little yellow wormlike noodle out of a
container, and grimaces.
JESTER
Yeuk! What kind of birds
would want to eat those?
JESTER holds a similar container. He takes a noodle
wormlike thing out of his container.
SILLY
These vegetarian worms
are great for toucans.
They only eat veggies,
just like parrots.
SILLY pops it into his mouth, swallows it, and licks
his lips. JESTER frowns.
WIDER ANGLE
JESTER
Yeuck! Vanity swallowed
a worm or a baby snake.
SILLY
Toucans don't eat real
worms! These are fried fruit noodles.
He takes another handful, stuffs them into his mouth.
SILLY looks at his container.
JESTER
No, they're my fish-bait worms.
These are fried fruit noodles!
CLOSE ON SILLY
as he does an abrupt take, his cheeks stuffed. SILLY looks

down into his container. A little yellow baby snake pokes
its head up, looks and him and gurgles, making an evil,
angry face. SILLY looks into camera, swallows hard, then
breaks out into loud laughter.

SILLY
Well, if it's good enough
for the toucans, it's okay
with me.

ANGLE ON FLEDGLING AND DROOPY
as they walk into shot. FLEDGLING wears a bird-house hat with all types of
bird lures on it. DROOPY wears a vest with pockets from which hang transparent bags of seeds. They both wear artificial wings. DROOPY holds a long
pole with a radar screen on the handle and artificial wings and a guided missile lure on the end of the pole that detects birds before they reach a Parrotberry tree. DROOPY puts on a toucan's beak mask.

DROOPY
This is my toucan-detecting missile.
It's a radar detector that shows me
when strange birds are
approaching our Parrotberry trees.
All you have to do is turn it on
and it automatically finds those toucans.

FLEDGLING
Why don't you try it out?

FLEDGLING hands the pole to DROOPY who presses a button on
the radar controller and the guided missile fires up,
shooting away with a LOUD ROCKET ENGINE SOUND, dragging
out the line. DROOPY jumps back as the bird detecting
missile spirals around DROOPY'S wings. The missile springs a net and ties
DROOPY into a bird's nest of twigs and twine.

FLEDGLING
Amazoneroops! My device thought
you were a toucan. Better take
off that toucan bannana beak.

Now we can see DROOPY'S eyes blink in a perplexed way and his feathers
stand on end like a ruffled bird.

DISSOLVE TO:

INT. PAPA YELLOW NAPE'S HOUSE—SHORT TIME LATER

Carrying a large bird net, PAPA YELLOW NAPE ENTERS SHOT from the
stairway.
PAPA YELLOW NAPE
Everybody knows eagles taste awful.
WIDER ON EAGLE IN SKYEAGLE soars again until the bird becomes a
black dot on top of the mountain's peak.
CLOSER ON EAGLE, FLEDGLING,
EAGLE
He thinks that you'd send
eagles and hawks to chase
the toucans away from your
parrotberries.
FLEDGLING
So if we get your eaglets
back for you, then will you promise
never to take our parrotlings?
ANGLE ON EAGLE
EAGLE
Sure. I don't like cream of
hookbill soup anyway. My
eaglets would much rather
have leftover chicken.
WIDER ON PICKLES, GRANDPA MACAW, EAGLE
PICKLES
Let's sneak into Hawk's castle.
EAGLE
If I snatch his pet iguana in my claws,
as I fly, Hawk will follow me.
GRANDPA MACAW
Then we can return the eaglets
to you.
DISSOLVE
EXT.—NEAR THE EDGE OF THE AMAZON—THE NEXT MORNING
HATCHLING sits in the shade of a hollowed tree, playing with his
magical bracelet. Parette looks overhead to see hundreds of
new toucans swarming through the groves of parrrotberry trees.
WIDER ON PICKLES AND EAGLE
PICKLES is putting together a type of harness on the EAGLE'S back.

The harness has three seats on it. PICKLES, PAPA YELLOW NAPE, and FLEDGLING hop on board the EAGLE'S back and put on goggles. The eagle soars skyward as PARETTE and HATCHLING wave to the three. The EAGLE grows smaller and finally disappears into the sky toward Bald Eagle Mountain and the EAGLE'S nest.

CUT TO:

EXT. EAGLE'S NEST ON TOP OF BALD EAGLE MOUNTAIN—DAY
There is sunshine, blue sky with clouds, and lots of grass
and greenery. It is pleasant and warm. We see the EAGLE'S nest
with hatched, empty cracked eggshells strewn around the
outside of the nest. The EAGLE paces to and fro awkwardly
with her wings spread.

PICKLES, PAPA YELLOW NAPE, AND FLEDGLING strut around following in back of the EAGLE, pacing, copying the same movements as the EAGLE.

CUT TO:

HAWK'S PET IGUANA PICKS UP THE EAGLETS, ONE BY ONE, AND DROPS THEM INTO A BASKET TO HAWK, WAITING BELOW.

CUT TO:

ANGLE ON PICKLES as he
peers over the ledge of the enormously steep cliff,
a yawning ravine.

PICKLES
There's a ledge down there to land on.

FLEDGLING peers over.

FLEDGLING
Look! There's a yawning ravine.

FLEDGLING points. Below is a grey stone rock that looks like a huge open yawning mouth. It's an entrance to a cave.

CLOSE ON PICKLES, FLEDGLING, AND EAGLE

PICKLES takes a rope out of his back pack and ties it to a rock near the EAGLE'S nest. The EAGLE takes its big nest in its beak and moves it to PICKLES. FLEDGLING helps PICKLES tie the rope onto a loop in the nest.

FLEDGLING
I'll stay up here with Eagle
and build a trap in case Hawk
comes back to the scene of the crime.

PICKLES

If we're not back by sundown, Eagle,

come and parrot us to safety.

EAGLE nods his head up and down agreeably.

FLEDGLING gently lowers the basket holding PAPA YELLOW NAPE and PICKLES as EAGLE helps by holding the rope in its beak. EAGLE and FLEDGLING peer over the ledge of the vertical cliff as FLEDGLING ties the rope to the rock even more securely.

DISSOLVE TO:

INT. INSIDE DARKISH CAVE.

WIDER ON ENORMOUS CAVE.

STALAGTITES AND STALAGMITES, hang like limestone needles from the cave. (It looks like the interior of Carlsbad Caverns). It is dark, but with an eerie red light coming from an opening in the

distance ahead. This is Hawk's summer palace.

WIDE ON PAPA YELLOW NAPE, AND PICKLES

as they enter a brightly lighted room. There is a huge swimming pool surrounded by classical Roman and Greek statues. The pool is rimmed by turquoise, blue and white mosaic tile. There are tall, gothic windows. The white marble statues circle the large, kidney-shaped pool. The walls are tiled in the blue, white and turquoise fleur-de-lis mosaic tile. The pool has an open skylight roof—an atrium where the sun's rays shine down into the pool to show hazy beams of light.

PAPA YELLOW NAPE and PICKLES tiptoe around the pool.

CLOSER ON PICKLES AND PAPA YELLOW NAPE

PICKLES

Look how real those marble statues look.

ANGLE ON ONE "GREEK" STATUE

One tear drop begins to trickle down the cheek on one male marble statue standing beside the pool. SFX: The tears plink into the pool.

PAPA YELLOWNAPE

Slithering sparrows!

That statue's crying real tears.

PICKLES sidles up to the statue and looks deeply into its eyes.

CLOSE ON EYES OF STATUE

The eyes give PICKLES a pleading look for help.

PICKLES

You're right. These aren't statues.

Hawk's turned these people to
marble to line his swimming pool.
ANGLE ON STATUE'S ARM
as it points to a bend in the cavern ahead.
WIDER ON PICKLES AND PAPA YELLOW NAPE
PAPA YELLOW NAPE
That statue's pointing to the light
ahead.
The two scramble in the direction the statue is pointing.
They stumble upon a huge aviary filled with the eaglets
and other very rare birds, including blue macaws, green parrots, red cardinals, etc. The aviary is perched on a ledge high on the stalagmites and under the stalactites. Brainy climbs up on the ledge and unlocks the birdcage door.
PICKLES
Okay eaglets and other birds.
You're free now, and big enough to fly away home.
All the BIRDS make an exit from the huge cage, except for the
eaglets. They look up sadly and vulnerable at PICKLES.
PAPA YELLOWNAPE
Those eaglets are babies. They're too
young to fly. Let's stuff them in
our pockets.
PICKLES puts out his wing and the eaglets crawl onto the wing and into his pockets. The two eaglets, Vali and Vanda, sit on top of Pickles' wings. He gives one to PAPA.
EAGLET VALI
I'm Vali.
EAGLET VANDA
And I'm Vanda.
VALI AND VANDA
(speaking together)
We wander.
The eaglet nestlings are cute and irresistable little cottony puffballs.
VALI
Would you happen to have a
chili dog on you?
ANGLE ON PAPA YELLOW NAPE
PAPA

Don't worry. We'll return you
to your mother.
WIDER ON HAWK'S IGUANA, SCREECHER
hiding on the ledge, posed to leap.
SCREECHER is perched on a ledge above the empty aviary. He snarls
angrily, baring his teeth, and leaps for the eaglets on PAPA YELLOW
NAPE'S wings. PAPA YELLOW NAPES flaps his wings and a strong wind
blows them into his claws in time to save the eaglet from SCREECHER'S
grasp.
VANDA
Help! That iguana's going to have
us all for dinner.
IGUANA SCREECHER snarls viciously, snaps and screeches.
Stars appear and a beam swirls bright light as HAWK appears in his royal
evil magician's robes.
ANGLE ON HAWK, PAPA YELLOW NAPE, PICKLES.
HAWK shoves PAPA YELLOW NAPE and PICKLES back into the aviary.
He slams the door of the bird cage as the two eaglets peer out of each of
PAPA YELLOW NAPE'S pockets.
HAWK
(laughing menacingly and rubbing his wings)
Guard them well, Screecher.
SCREECHER circles and paces around the cage like a dragon.
CLOSER on the SHADOW of SCREECHER, which looms much larger as a
black silhouette of dragon doom on the walls of the cave. HAWK pulls a
torch off the wall and lights it with a candle on a table. He places the lighted
torch back in its slot on the cave wall. An eerie light flickers as SCREECHER
paces back and forth around
the bird cage, guarding the captured parrots and eaglets.
DISSOLVE TO:
HAWK'S KITCHEN
HAWK is rapidly slicing carrots and throwing them into a pot of boiling
water.
HAWK
Oh, there's nothing more delicious
than a parrot casserole over a crusty
eaglet pie. For dessert I'll have
stuffed mushrooms and cloves

on sizzling parrot steak.
ANGLE ON SCREECHER
As the iguana watches HAWK dice his veggies.
WIDER ON HAWK AND SCREECHER
HAWK looks up at SCREECHER.
HAWK
I thought you're supposed to be watching
that bird cage.
SCREECHER
(looks down sheepishly)
HAWK
Naughty iguana. We'll you can stay here
for now and help me prepare the pie
crust.
SCREECHER
(delighted growl)
CLOSER ON SCREECHER
HAWK
Soon we'll have a real parrotberry pie
with the eaglets buried in the crust.
(CACKLES)
DISSOLVE TO:
INT. CAVE—DARKISH
WIDE ON PAPA YELLOW NAPE AND PICKLES
in bird cage.
In the distance, an opening to the cave shows the setting sun slipping below
the horizon.
PAPA YELLOWNAPE
Hawks like to eat their parrots in the dark.
BRAINY
We've got to get outta here before
dinnertime.
The eaglets stick their heads out of PAPA' YELLOW NAPE'S and PICK-
LES'S pockets and begin to peep loudly for their mother.
CUT TO:
WIDE ON TOP OF BALD EAGLE MOUNTAIN
as the eagle perks up its head, hearing the loud peeps of its eaglets inside the
yawning ravine.

FLEDGLING
What's that?
EAGLE
They said if they weren't back by sundown,
we must go and get them.
FLEDGLING
Hey, take it easy!
CLOSER ON EAGLE
FLEDGLING ties a knapsack and saddle on the EAGLE'S back.
The EAGLE lifts FLEDGLING up in its beak and takes off like a plane down the vertical cliffs and into the dark bowels of the cave. FLEDGLING hollers, but the EAGLE tosses him on his back
EAGLE
Hold on tight. A mother eagle will go
to any extreme to save its eaglets.
FLEDGLING
Just like a parrot!
WIDER ANGLE
SFX: Buzzing of a jet fighter plane, a loud drone as the eagle finally lands next to the bird cage, pushing up a cloud of
dust in its tracks. SFX: a screeching halt of a plane landing.
CLOSE ON PAPA YELLOW NAPE
PAPA YELLOW NAPE
Hurry and get this lock open.
We must get out before Hawk
returns for us.
PICKLES
When Hawk's bird's nest soup boils,
so do we.
WIDER ON EAGLE, PICKLES, PAPA YELLOW NAPE, and FLEDGLING
as the eagle pecks away at the lock, breaking it open.
The cage door springs open and PICKLES, PAPA YELLOW NAPE, and FLEDGLING speed away. SFX: We hear a peeping sound of chirps coming from the cage.
The EAGLE does a double take, perks up her head, tilts head
and runs back toward the cage, squawking.
EAGLE
My eaglets!

CLOSER ON PAPA YELLOW NAPE
PAPA YELLOW NAPE
Parrotoops! They must have fallen
from our pockets.
The EAGLE swoops up her eaglets and tucks them in a knapsack
on her back. They peer out of the sack and blink innocently,
peeping softly. The eagle stuffs the eaglets back inside the
pockets on the knapsack.
PAPA YELLOW NAPE and PICKLES mount the EAGLE's saddle and ride
away, up into the dark, reddish air of the caverns, dodging the many stalagmites and stalactites as water drips from these limestone needles growing
down from the cave ceiling and up from the cave floor.
WIDE ON SWIMMING POOL ROOM—THE ATRIUM
as we get a view of the classical marble statues lined around the pool pointing to the way to freedom out of the cave, toward the light at the end of the
cave.
CLOSER ON EAGLE
EAGLE
That awful Hawk made all these
people into statues. Maybe your
magical bracelet will also bring them
back to life.
ANGLE ON ONE STATUE'S FACE
as a tear drop runs down its marble cheeks.
CLOSER ON PAPA YELLOW NAPE AND PICKLES
PICKLES
Let's give it a try. Give me that
bracelet.
PICKLES takes the bracelet from Fledgling's outstretched wing and punches
a white button on the bracelet. It lights up and pulsates for a moment. Then
in an explosion of light, all the
statues are restored to life. The statues run free in all directions, cheering
and shouting.
WIDER ON STATUES
as all statues with the exception of TWO scatter to the light at the end of the
cave.
STATUES
(scattering wildly)

We're free at last,
after all these years.
Let's head home for our village.
CLOSE ON THE ONE REMAINING PAIR OF MALE AND FEMALE
STATUES
One marble statue runs over to greet PICKLES and PAPA YELLOW NAPE
MALE STATUE
Oh, thank you.
The last thing I remember
is that Hawk asked me to model
for his sculpture lesson.
WIDE ON FEMALE STATUE
as she runs towards EAGLE, PICKLES, PAPA YELLOW NAPE, and
FLEDGLING.
Then WIDER on FEMALE STATUE, PICKLES, FLEDGING, and EAGLE
together.
CLOSER ON FEMALE STATUE as she embraces and kisses PICKLES in
gratitude.
PICKLES makes a shy, cringing face and shows tense embarrassment.
TWO SHOT—STATUE AND PICKLES
FEMALE STATUE
I didn't realize that when Hawk
advertised for an interior decorator
that I'd be the decoration.
CLOSE ON FLEDGLING
FLEDGLING
It looks like this bracelet does
more than attract birds. It also
reverses all of Hawk's tricks.
I wonder what would happen if we
pointed it at Hawk and Screecher
and pressed this little blue button?
PAPA YELLOW NAPE
Not now, beaky bird.
WIDER on flying EAGLE
As she flaps her wings, creating high winds and a dust storm of many rain-
bow colors and flashing stars, whirling colors.

EAGLE soars. They fly out the mouth of the yawning ravine and into the bright blue air. HAWK sees them fly through the sky over his summer palace as he looks out of his kitchen window while stirring his pot of stew.
CUT TO:
WIDE SHOT
EXT. FLYING OVER THE ROOFTOPS AND TREE TOPS IN THE CLOUDS
CUT TO:
CLOSE on HAWK and SCREECHER who are sitting on the window sill looking at the flying EAGLE with PAPA YELLOW NAPE, FLEDGLING, and PICKLES on its back growing smaller as they head toward the Amazon village.
HAWK
Great hounds of hallucinations!
Get me Archy the archaeopteryx.
SFX: CLASH OF THUNDER and lightning.
As HAWK flings his curled fingers to cast a magical spell, in a cloud of pink smoke an archaeopteryx (ancient bird, half bird-half dinosaur or lizard bird) appears. It's all saddled
up and ready to fly.
WIDER ON HAWK, SCREECHER, AND ARCHY
HAWK
Come, Screecher, fly with me
on this dinosaur of birds.
Leap on this lizard, the
first bird that ever was.
CLOSE ON BIRD
SCREECHER leaps onto the archaeopteryx's back and snuggles into the saddle. HAWK flies up into the saddle and gives the reins a
few shakes.
WIDER ON BIRD, SCREECHER, HAWK
The bird takes off and follows the EAGLE who is now disappearing
o.s. beyond the horizon, out of shot. ARCHY has claws on its wings, teeth in its beak and more scales than feathers. It looks like a green, flying dragon of sorts with a horned crest on its pointy head. It's the same size and an equal match to the EAGLE.
CUT TO:

The sky chase begins. The Archy pursues and catches up to the EAGLE. EAGLE gains speed with ARCHY on its tail.

CLOSE ON ARCY

HAWK

Faster than a hawk could ever fly,

with dragon fire and bog mire.

HAWK points the way and steers the Archy.

WIDE on EAGLE

with ARCHY pursuing close behind. HAWK stretches out his fingers and zaps the eagle with a lightning bolt.

The bolt just misses PICKLES. He jumps out of his seat and

begins to fall toward the ground. The ground comes up very fast as he tumbles earthward. EAGLE takes a dive as FLEDGLING holds onto his hat and swoops under PICKLES as PICKLES is scooped back into

his saddle seat.

EAGLE

Whew! That was a close one.

PICKLES

A cool, blue eagle sure beats the

stress of doing my own flying in

this traffic.

CLOSE ON FLEDGLING

FLEDGLING whips out of his pocket his bird-attracting bracelet and buzzes the gold button. A parrot-shaped beak springs up from the bracelet shaped like a microphone. FLEDGLING speaks into the beak. Then he places the beak by his ear to receive a message. A parrot's voice squawks.

FLEDGLING

Calling all birds. Calling all birds.

PARROT (O.S.)

Awk! We've picked up a bogey

over the Parrotberry bush.

Send us a vector and we're

headed home.

FLEDGLING pushes a blue button on his bracelet. A light flashes.

WIDER ON BIRDS

Suddenly a travelling mound of black CROWS and toucans approach from the east. From the west a mountain of HAWKS approach the battle from the west, each aimed at a head-on collision with HAWK's flying dinosaur bird.

These two humongous clouds of BIRDS both speed into shot at the same time with GARGAMEL caught in the middle as the two giant flocks of birds are headed for collision.

PICKLES

Look! Up in the sky.

It's every bird in the land.

PICKLES points to the tornado of birds, now turned into a cycloning whirlwind of two different flocks. Then that becomes four flocks, eight flocks. The entire sky fills with flocks of all different types of BIRDS.

CLOSER ON HAWK

He's still riding the ARCHY like it was some dragon horse with SCREECHER sitting on his shoulder.

HAWK grabs out of his saddle a lattice device with a spring. This is an expandable device (like a forceps) that reaches across the clouds long enough to latch onto the tail of the EAGLE

flying fast just ahead of him.

WIDE ON EAGLE, PICKLES AND PAPA YELLOW NAPE

This expandable lattice-like device catches the EAGLE in mid-air. The jarring shakes PICKLES and PAPA YELLOW NAPE loose from the EAGLE'S back. PICKLES and PAPA YELLOW NAPE begin to fall again, plummeting almost to the Amazon Parrot Village below.

CLOSER ON THICK FLOCK OF GREEN PARROTS FORMING A MAGIC CARPET

WITH THEIR UNDULATING, FLAPPING FEATHERS

Just before they hit the tops of the trees a thick flock of TOUCANS suddenly rise from the Parrotberry Treetops and berry bushes and rise up to the occasion forming a thick crazy-quilt of colored, feather carpet that allows PICKLES and PAPA YELLOW NAPE to float on this magical carpet of TOUCAN'S wings. The TOUCANS carry Parrotberries in their beaks as they head for home.

WIDER ON PICKLES and FLEDGLING

as they ride the carpet of toucans slowly floating to land in front of their own home.

CLOSER ON PICKLES, FLEDGLING, and PAPA YELLOW NAPE

PICKLES

We must help Eagle and her Eaglets.

FLEDGLING

Looks what's happening to Hawk.

The TOUCANS look skyward. PICKLES and FLEDGLING also look up to the clouds as the two armies of birds enclose HAWK in a tornado of a dark cloud of BIRDS.

The hawks begin to force apart the expandable lattice forceps and EAGLE flaps her wings and breaks free of the pinch.

PARETTE comes running from o.s. (off-screen) into shot.

PARETTE

Hi! Everybody. Look.

WIDER ON EAGLE

PARETTE points up at the sky.

PARETTE

The EAGLE is getting away.

Use the bird finder bracelet on Hawk's bird.

PICKLES presses the red button the bracelet and it attracts all the birds toward the Amazon village and away from the EAGLE.

But the bracelet also attracts the bird HAWK's riding, the ARCHY.

CLOSER ON EAGLE

EAGLE has gotten out of the grips of the lattice-forceps expandable device and is gaining speed. All of a sudden the EAGLE turns and is attracted toward the AMAZON VILLAGE.

WIDE ON TWO ARMIES OF BIRDS

as the two armies of birds DO A DOUBLE TAKE and ATTACK one another. The HAWKS are now attacking the TOUCANS. The attacking birds DESERT HAWK. HAWK is now freed from the tornado of birds and is taking a nosedive straight for the Parrot's Amazon village.

FLEDGLING

You pressed the wrong button. We don't want all those birds to land here and fight one another. Try the blue button.

CLOSE ON PARETTE

PARETTE presses the bracelet's blue button as she aims at the ARCHY. Suddenly There is a beam of blue light filled with dancing rainbow colored soap bubbles.

WIDE ON BIRDS

As the beam reaches all the birds it fans out. Suddenly the birds go peaceful and chirp merrily. The have smiles on their beaks and a very mellow expression of peace and contentment on their faces.

The HAWKS fly to the east. The TOUCANS take to the west. The ARCHY is mellowed.

PULL BACK WIDER ON ARCHY

The mellow dinosaur-bird flaps its wings merrily and flies off back to HAWK'S castle.

DISSOLVE TO:

CLOSE ON HAWK

as he rides atop his mellow, happy ARCHY. The bird now sings the Parrot Song. The ARCHY flies in lazy circles over HAWK'S castle.

ARCHY

(sings his familiar song)

HAWK himself now has a large toucan's beak growing from his former smaller Hawk's beak.

HAWK

What's this?

HAWK pulls at his new beak. Suddenly toucan's black and orange feathers sprout from HAWK'S clothes.

HAWK

SCREECHER, get these feathers off of me.

HAWK pulls at his feathers as his pet iguana on his shoulder arches his back and growls at the bird feathers.

SCREECHER

Rowrrr.

CUT TO:

WIDE ON PARETTE AND PICKLES

PARETTE, FLEDGLING, PAPA YELLOW NAPE, and PICKLES are riding on top of the EAGLE's back. They arrive at HAWK'S castle and confront him.

CLOSE ON HAWK

HAWK has now changed into a TOUCAN. He walks up to PARETTE.

HAWK

Change me back and I'll promise anything.

PARETTE

Will you stop sending those toucans to
eat our Parrotberries?

HAWK

Yes. Yes. I'll do anything you want
only change me back.

I don't want to be Toco the toucan.
PARETTE
Here, have a Parrotberry pie.
PARETTE tosses the pie in his face.
HAWK has a temper tantrum as he wipes the pie from his face.
HAWK
Oh, you naughty Yellow Nape Amazon Parrot.
I'll have parrot pie for dessert tonight instead
of parrotberry turnover.
Suddenly he gets some pie in his mouth with his fingers and calms down fast.
HAWK
Hey, this pie is delicious.
SCREECHER
Magnificent!
PICKLES
So you see if you let our parrotberries grow,
you can eat pie this good all the time.
HAWK
Heh, heh, those toucans sure loved to eat
the special coating I sprayed on your
parrotberry crop. Actually toucans hate
parrotberries. Now change me back.
PICKLES
I'll change you back if you give me the formula
for removing your coating from our parrotberries.
HAWK grabs PARETTE and pulls the bracelet away. He clicks it on himself and turns back into his usual form.
HAWK locks PARETTE in the cuckoo clock on his fireplace mantel. A wooden cuckoo bird pops out of a small window on top of the clock and does its cuckoo whistle, then returns. The Cuckoo door closes. PARETTE bangs on the locked wooden door of the cuckoo clock yelling for help.
SCREECHER leaps onto the ledge of the mantelpiece and menacingly sniffs at the PARROT behind the locked cuckoo's door.
PARETTE
(muffled)
Help! Help!

The EAGLE charges into HAWK. But HAWK hits the pink button on the bracelet and the EAGLE is transformed into a tiny eaglet that peeps loudly for help.

EAGLET

Peep. Peep. Peep.

PICKLES sweeps up the eaglet and tosses her into his pocket as he runs for his life. HAWK chases after him. HAWK points and motions to SCREECHER. The iguana runs to hunt down PICKLES. HAWK rubs his wings in circles and paces in anticipation.

HAWK

Screecher! How about parrot and eaglet

over a bed of noodles?

(rubbing his beak and wings in circles)

Hmmm…I can already hear the sizzle before

I've seen the steak.

CLOSE ON SHADOWS OF SCREECHER AND PICKLES

SCREECHER makes a leap from a tall fireplace mantel to pounce on PICK-LES below who is now corned against a wall. We see the elongated dark shadow of SCREECHER in slow motion in the act of pouncing on PICK-LES who stands against the wall. CAMERA SHOT on the two shadows.

While in midair, quickly PICKLES pulls out of his trousers pocket his MAGICAL SALT SHAKER (which he used before to sprinkle on the Parrot-berries) to chase away the parrots. Now he tosses a sprinkle of golden salt into SCREECHER'S face and a black cloud of awful smelling smoke engulfs and twines about SCREECHER as HAWK comes into the shot from o.s. to come to SCREECHER'S aid.

The cloud kicks up a big stink around SCREECHER. A white stripe forms and runs down the center of SCREECHER's blackening reptile body so that SCREECHER looks just like a skunk. SCREECHER growls and draws back with his tail between his legs, in embarrassment at how stinky he smells.

PICKLES

Now that's what I call smelling salts.

HAWK reacts to the awful stink cloud surrounding SCREECHER. He holds his nose and winces.

HAWK

Peeeuuuu! You smell like a skunk.

WIDER ON PICKLES and HAWK

PICKLES laughs at his own joke as HAWK grabs him in his fist by his feet dangling upside down as HAWK walks to his kitchen.

PICKLES

Help. Put me down.

SCREECHER tries to jump into HAWK'S arms while he's dangling PICKLES. But HAWK shoos him away, holding his nose.

HAWK

Go take a bath, Screecher!

CUT TO:

SCREECHER runs off and jumps in a washtub of water. Clothes that were soaking in the washtub go flying through the air.

CUT TO:

WIDE ON HAWK'S KITCHEN

HAWK carries PICKLES upside down into his kitchen. He sits him down on a serving plate on his table and begins to arrange mushrooms around the platter with PICKLES sitting up in the middle.

CLOSE ON PICKLES AND HAWK IN THE KITCHEN

HAWK

It's parrot pie for dinner,

my friend, stuffed with mushrooms

a la King and cloves. (CACKLE)

HAWK stuffs a clove into a mushroom and then stuffs it into PICKLES's mouth.

With his hands free, PICKLES tosses some golden granules from his magical saltshaker into HAWK'S face.

PICKLES

It's the seasoning to be jolly.

La, la la la la, la la la la.

HAWK RUBS HIS EYES AND SNEEZES.

Suddenly HAWK becomes mellow and peaceful. A silly smile appears on his face as he changes into a giant mushroom stuffed with cloves sitting on an "island" wedge of pie crust.

WIDER ON PICKLES

PICKLES climbs down the table leg and runs along the kitchen floor past SCREECHER who's still splashing in the washtub of water with the wet clothes laying all around the tub on the floor.

PICKLES passes SCREECHER and bravely calls to him as PICKLES continues walking out of shot.

CLOSER ON PICKLES

PICKLES

That should keep him mushroomed on an island
until dinner time.

CLOSE ON PARETTE AND PICKLES

PICKLES climbs up the curtain sash weight and drapery cords until he
reaches the top OF THE MANTELPIECE\FIREPLACE. He breaks open the
cuckoo clock wooden door with a pencil lying in front of him and out rides
PARETTE sitting astride the wooden cuckoo yellow bird as the clock
chimes. CUCKOO, CUCKOO, CUCKOO. She jumps off the cuckoo bird
as the bird goes back inside the clock and the door closes.

PARETTE

What happened?

PICKLES

You remember that special salt shaker
that didn't stop the toucans from
eating our fruit?

PARETTE

Don't tell me it stopped Hawk.

PICKLES

It has the odor of success.

ANGLE ON PICKLES AND PARETTE

PICKLES and PARETTE climb down the drapery cords and sash weight to
the floor.

PARETTE whips out her magical bracelet.

PARETTE

The Eagle!

PARETETE clicks the blue button and the eaglet in PICKLES' pocket peeps
twice, swells and bursts through his pocket, it's muscles growing until it
reaches full size standing on the floor.

CLOSE ON EAGLE

EAGLE

C'mon, let's get out of here!

WIDER ON PICKLES, PARETTE, EAGLE AND SCREECHER

PICKLES and PARETTE leap onto the EAGLE's back just as SCREECHER
runs into the room and leaps does a double take when he sees how large and
ferocious the eagle looks.

EAGLE

Stay back, Screecher, unless you
want to star in my iguana pie.
EAGLE flaps her wings and flies out breaking through the wooden shutters
on the windows. Wood pieces fly over the heads of PICKLES and PARETTE
as they duck. SCREECHER recoils in his tracks, coming to a screeching
halt. He watches them take off.
PICKLES turns around as they soar, yelling back through his cupped hands
to SCREECHER.
PICKLES
Don't worry about Hawk. He'll
be back to his old self by dinner.
So don't eat that old stuffed mushroom
sitting in the kitchen.
DISSOLVE TO:
EXT.—A BRIGHT, LEAFY DAY—AMAZON VILLAGE
WIDE on FLEDGLING, GRANDPA MACAW, NESTLING, EAGLE,
PICKLES, PARETTE, and PAPA YELLOW NAPE.
GRANDPA MACAW
Welcome back, my parrots.
You've saved our tasty
berries from the toucans.
CLOSE ON EAGLE
EAGLE
And look what I have here.
EAGLE pulls out from under its wing a vial of formula.
ANGLE ON NESTLING, PICKLES, and EAGLE
NESTLING sniffs the vial of liquid.
NESTLING
Why, it's Hawk's secret formula
for distracting toucans from our Parrotberries.
PICKLES
What is it?
EAGLE
(laughing)
Oil of eagle.
ANGLE ON PAPA YELLOW NAPE, PARETTE, PICKLES, and
HATCHLING
PARETTE

It was so simple.
The scent of big birds always
frightens away the smaller birds.
PICKLES
Then we don't need those
magical salts that make our
fruit bitter.
PICKLES takes out his salt shaker and gives it to PAPA YELLOW NAPE.
PARETTE takes out her magical bracelet.
PARETTE
And we don't need this bracelet
to attract any more toucans.
PARETTE bends down and hands it to HATCHLING who's crawling into the shot from o.s. HATCHLING takes the bracelet in his mouth and PEEPS.

HATCHLING
Peep. Google. Burble.
HATCHLING puts the bracelet on his own wrist and crawls away into GRANDPA MACAW'S arms. GRANDPA MACAW lifts HATCHLING onto his shoulder.
CLOSE ON FLEDGLING.
as he takes the two eaglets out from under his wing and hands them to EAGLE.
FLEDGLING
I've got my parrotlings and now here's
your eaglets, safe, sound, and well-fed.
ANGLE ON EAGLE, PAPA YELLOW NAPE, and FLEDGLING
EAGLE takes her two eaglets and kisses them, hugging them warmly. A rainbow of colors light up the blue sky and white clouds.
PAPA YELLOW NAPE
Before you go, would you like to see
the birdfeeder in our own garden?
EAGLE
(smiling)
No, I've got to get my eaglets back
to the nest. But I don't know how to
thank you for saving my eaglets.

PAPA YELLOW NAPE
And I don't know how to thank you
for saving Hatchling.
EAGLE
Well, there's one gift I can give you.
FLEDGLING
What's that?
CLOSE ON EAGLE AND PICKLES
EAGLE takes out a Parrotberry pie from his knapsack and hands it to PICK-
LES.
EAGLE
I managed to salvage your last Parrotberry
pie from Hawk's oven.
WIDER ON EAGLE and PICKLES
PICKLES
Beakadoodle. Thanks.
EAGLE
And there's one more present,
for Hyacinth.
HYACINTH hurries into the shot from o.s.
ANGLE ON HYACINTH
HYACINTH
That pie is the last
unless I replace all those
Parrotberry trees and bushes
the toucans ate down to the roots.

EAGLE
Don't worry.
EAGLE takes two draw string purses from his knapsack on his back.
ANGLE ON EAGLE and HYACINTH
EAGLE (CONT'D)
Here's Hawk's last bag of
seeds, one for the trees, and the other
for the bushes.
HYACINTH
I'll be able to replant for the spring.
I don't know how to thank you either.

HYACINTH hugs EAGLE and gives him a kiss on the beak.
EAGLE
So long, Yellow Napes and Macaws.
EAGLE shakes wings with HYACINTH. EAGLE flaps her wings and soars.
She circles low once, swooping down to echo one more message as she hovers in midair.
EAGLE (CONT'D)
Just keep the hunters off of the
top of Bald Eagle Mountain.
ANGLE ON PICKLES
PICKLES
(waving to Eagle)
Sure thing. Everybody knows
eagles taste awful.
WIDER ON EAGLE IN SKY
EAGLE soars again until the bird becomes a black dot on top of the mountain's peak.
FADE OUT TO THE END.

◆   ◆   ◆

Writing Premises for Cartoon Animation & Children's Books

(Premises, springboards, treatments, and synopses or outlines can be written with similar techniques and planning for *comic books, cartoon animation, and children's books*.)

Premises—3 pages
Springboards—5 pages
Treatments—10 pages
Outlines (Varying pages planning your story or script 1–20 pages)
Synopses—One page
Pitches—One sentence or a one-sentence paragraph. (One-line that describes what your story is about is your pitch.) An example of a pitch that's popular in Hollywood circles is, "Star Trek is Wagon Train in space." This one-line pitch is also referred to as part of "high-concept."

Video Podcast Premises for Children's Animation or Video Story Books

The Hatchlings' World History Adventures:

Stories for Children's Books or Animation Script Premises

Story 1
Anne Hart

Premise

Pickles and Macaw Meet the Bog Bird in the Medieval Philippines

Ancient Saluag (later became Philippines), in the year 1000 A.D. was a group of 7,000 islands ruled by the bog-king, Cebuano. The AMAZON HATCHLINGS arrive on the steamy island of Saluag and walk along the shore searching for their BIRD OF PREY REPELLENT which has been washed up in a bottle.

PICKLES crashes into King Cebuano by accident. And his snappy personality insults the enormously obese king who shows him the monster he's captured that awaits PICKLES.

The monster is the bog BIRD OF PREY that was wished away from the tentacles of a love-lorn Dragon lady from the neighboring island of Y'Ami to the king's island bog by the evil magician, HAWK.

Instead of PICKLES, the BOG BIRD captures FLEDGLING when he lags behind the other AMAZON HATCHLINGS as they walk a tight rope over a raging waterfall.

PICKLES begins to tell a tale a night for a hundred nights to the BOG BIRD to keep him from being so lonely so far from his own bog in Australia. The BOG BIRD keeps FLEDGLING imprisoned in a grotto beneath his bog. BOG BIRD tells him he'll go free if FLEDGLING can find the magic words to send him back to his own time and place.

FLEDGLING entertains the BOG BIRD so well by his insight and his reservoir of fantastic stories, his playing of a musical instrument, like an ancient saxophone, that the BOG BIRD doesn't want to harm him.

FLEDGLING promises the BOG BIRD that King Cebuano has a long life stone just like the AMAZON HATCHLING'S one back home, and that if he frees him, FLEDGLING will put on a musical TALKING PARROT show and get one quick wish on the stone as a prize.

FLEDGLING teases the king and gets the AMAZON HATCHLINGS in trouble. But when they search the bog for the great sea snake that bores through the center of the earth, FLEDGLING finds him for the king.

The islanders and the HATCHLINGS go for a ride to the center of the earth and put on a musical adventure at the earth's core.

The BOG BIRD shows himself to the king and frightens the whole village when FLEDGLING escapes after his 101 nights of story telling. The HATCHLINGS now must escape the wrath of the evil HAWK through the cone of an undersea volcano to get back to the island where their MAGICAL BIRD OF PREY REPELLENT DISC is hiding in a parrot's nest.

FLEDGLING is sent to fetch birds' nests for soup for a foreign ambassador. He just misses seeing his scroll which is taken with a bird's nest by PARETTE and turned into a soup crouton.

The king finds the REPELLENT DISC when a dish of bird's nest soup is presented to him by PARETTE who cooks the soup. (She's made to work in the king's kitchen.)

The sea snake gives the king's stone of long life to the BOG BIRD who thinks it's the HATCHLING'S MAGIC DISC. But it doesn't work so well. The HATCHLINGS rid the island of the sea snake that falls in love with BOG BIRD and follows him. They are rewarded by a Philippine stick dance festival in which PARETTE gets her CLAWS slapped by the sticks she has to jump through in the dance as it becomes faster and faster. Restoring the cooked DISC from the birds nest soup, the HATCHLINGS get to leave by bog boat as the king waves "sal-himot" in Tagalog.

Story 2
Anne Hart

Premise

"The Yellow Nape in Antarctica"

The HATCHLINGS land on the uninhabited (by people) Bird Island, near the South Pole in ancient Antarctica. They are swept into the vortex of a fierce blizzard and find themselves surrounded by a crowd of penguins in the middle of an aerial attack by an army of albatrosses that bring the song scroll to their nest on top of a glacier.

Below, on the shore, the ice has frozen the penguin's eggs into a glacier and PICKLES is forced by the henpecking penguins to dig out their eggs before they freeze.

MACAW builds a crude shelter from rocks on the frozen shore. The MACAW'S LOUD CACKLE-SCREECH causes an avalanche and the HATCHLINGS enter an ice cave to escape the winds. There they find a treasure chest from a sunken pirate's ship a thousand years old washed up on Antarctica's lonely shore frozen inside a glacier. They find three seemingly useless objects inside this metal chest, but they have no tools to dig it out.

The MACAW can imitate enough sounds to break up ice. So he utters a high-pitched whistle that cleaves the glacier into calves of ice, thereby releasing the treasure chest.

Inside the chest are three items that they will need to survive in the bitter cold, if they figure out how to use the seemingly unusable items. These provide a ready-made job for PICKLES. While trying to keep warm (without fire) in the ice cave, and no wood to burn, nothing but rock and snow, the HATCHLINGS try to survive at all odds to get them out of this ice prison where only birds and fish come to eat and play.

They try to trek through the blizzard, but realize that inside the treasure chest are three things that will get them out of there, if they only can figure out how to use the three "stupid" objects.

The MACAW uses his imitative sounds to call the albatrosses and arrange them into a flock that provide a type of plane for them. He reaches the summit and retrieves the BIRDS OF PREY REPELLENT DISC, but the summit is frozen all rolled up and won't unfold. The three treasures are 1) a spool of thread. 2) A clay bowl and 3) a wooden wand. How will they use these to survive and get out of the frozen desert of the South Pole?

PICKLES makes a fishing pole from the thread and wand. FLEDGLING uses the spool as a wheel to move a huge rock that opens into a tunnel. PARETTE uses the bowl as a boat and gets stuck in an ice-bound sea.

PARETTE gets the HATCHLINGS in deep trouble until the MACAW grabs the wooden wand in his mouth, and when one parrot wants to break it in two to rub together to build a fire, the MACAW won't let her because he finds out it's magical. The MACAW has to make the right imitative sound to let PARETTE know his secret.

Grandpa MACAW has to undo PARETTE'S mess when she tries to thaw out the scroll and it breaks into tiny pieces. It's up to the MACAW to make the magic wand repair the damage and get them out of the icy desert at the South Pole.

Story 3
By: Anne Hart

Premise

Pickles, the Parrot Meets the Cossacks

Scene opens in 17th century Russia on the banks of the Volga. Cossacks on horseback chase the AMAZON HATCHLINGS as they land in the middle of a Kasatchka dance performed by Cossacks around a campfire ring. The Cossack horsemen chase the HATCHLINGS through the snowy village aoul.

FLEDGLING is watching NESTLING as he repairs and rebuilds PICKLES THE PARROT'S FAVORITE, Australian-accented, ROBOT COCKATOO to help him with the chore of brewing HAWK-REPELLENT. He puts the hawk-repellent powder inside Robot Cockatoo for safekeeping. But NESTLING plays with ROBOT COCKATOO and puts the HAWK REPELLENT POWDER CAPSULE under his bracelet band. NESTLING is soon snatched up by one of the wild Cossack horseman running through the village and kidnapped. NESTLING is brought to the Tsar's palace as replacement for the Tsar and Tsarina's own pet baby bird who, many years before was taken by gypsies.

The HATCHLINGS set out from the village to sail down the Volga in order to find NESTLING whom the Cossacks sold to the Tsar. But they run into the real Tsar's baby pet Myna Bird who wants to help the AMAZON HATCHLINGS.

Warriors are overrunning 17th-century Russia. And the frost created a failure of the wheat crops. The people are hungry.

By returning the evil Tsar's pet bird to him and his queen, the Tsarina, (a witch that puts MACAW inside a frame to hang as a portrait on her walls) the Tsar returns NESTLING but keeps the magic hawk repellent on the condition that PICKLES build the Tsar an army of FLYING BIRD ROBOTS so he can defeat the Caspian Seafaring armies with Russian robots.

PICKLES must enlist the help of the Tsar's son, to defeat his own evil parents, retrieve the MAGIC BIRD OF PREY REPELLENT, get NESTLING, and free MACAW.

Soon the fierce winter returns and the HATCHLINGS must take shelter from the cold as the bears and wolves bite at their heels.

They begin to chop down trees to build a shelter when they are stopped from taking the tsar's firewood by warriors who tell them that as foreign merchants without anything valuable to sell, they must labor all day building the Tsar's new baby a palace full of toys. PICKLES says he'll show the Tsar how he made ROBOT COCKATOOS, if the Tsar will help him search for NESTLING. Only then can they wait on a long line at the wheat "bank" for a small ration of food. They agree to work all day and are given permission to build a toy village for Tsar-baby outside the slave's quarters.

A large military convoy of soldiers flanked by their Siberian bears is moving slowly down the road in the middle of the Valley of the Don, headed toward the bear-faced Tsar's palace. We see the palace in the distance standing alone in the middle of the snow, its entrance guarded by a giant Byzantine spirals, a monument to the bear-Tsar, HAWKOV, and his pet FALCON, Falconovitch.

Two troikas, and two horsemen dressed in ancient Caucasus Mts. costume play balalaikas and descend on the Russian city of Petrograd. The only thing blocking the warrior's path are the freezing AMAZON HATCHLINGS, who are building their village of toys for the Tsar's new rare pet bird (which is really the kidnapped NESTLING).

The troikas RUMBLE PAST CAMERA, followed by an an ancient-looking bear all decked up to look like a red-bearded king of old Russia.

The soldiers have just finished defeating the Tsar's men and pushing them into Poland. The magic troika is covered by a bristling, crackling carpet of eerie energy; this wagon, which is the center of the convoy's attention, is followed by two more Tatar troikas, two more massive giant statues that look just like ROBOT COCKATOO being pulled along on ropes as their monuments they hope to put up in place of the monument to the Tsar of all the 'Russias.'

The warriors put ropes around the monument of the Tsar-bear and pull it down with a loud thud. Then they hoist up their own statue of ROBOT COCK-ATOO. FLEDGLING realizes that ROBOT COCKATOO looks exactly like the monument of the invading army.

There is a definite air of TENSION to this entire scene.

The AMAZON HATCHLINGS are blocking the path of the invading soldiers.

Suddenly, the HATCHLINGS are singled out as foreign spies and captured as field-plowing allies of the Tsar and his Cossacks. One of the soldier's iron swords accidentally topples off a table when the soldier is drunk and rowdy and accidentally lands in PICKLES'S knapsack. The drowsy soldier mistakenly gives PICK-

LES an iron skillet and asks him to cook him some barley cakes, thinking PICKLES is the midget servant in the soldier's tent.

PICKLES cooks him some barley cakes and serves them, putting the frying pan in his knapsack when he's yelled at for stumbling and tripping, making a mess, and sending the pancakes flying on the soldier's head.

The HATCHLINGS are soon allowed to leave if they promise to be double agents and are sent to spy on the Tsar and set him up for a dawn attack by the · invading warriors. When the HATCHLINGS arrive at the Tsar's palace with their toys made by MACAW, they tell the Tsar that the warriors will soon wage war on them and will win because the have ROBOT COCKATOO.

They also show the Tsar gunpowder brought from trade with China which PICKLES has filled inside the hollow of ROBOT COCKATOO.

PICKLES bargains for his life with ROBOT COCKATOO and tells the Tsar that the Cossacks have stolen NESTLING and sold him to the Tsar.

GRANDPA MACAW wanders into the Tsarina's chambers where Tsarina Babutchka, an ugly witch, snatches Macaw to create a masterpiece to hang on her wall because she likes the color green. He paints everything blue and she goes crazy.

The tsarina doesn't know the HATCHLINGS have found NESTLING, and frames MACAW to star in his own portrait. She hangs him on the wall in a picture frame, and he can't escape her witchcraft that turns him into an oil painting of himself. When she discovers her NESTLING is missing, she has to let MACAW go.

With the help of the HATCHLINGS, the Tsar and Tsarina win their kingdom back from the invaders with ROBOT COCKATOO, who is then returned to his own castle far away.

PICKLES tells the Tsar he saw iron frying pans rust in water when he was at their campsite. When he tells the king that his new iron swords will also eventually rust in the snow, PICKLES throws in everything in sight into the melting pot and comes out with diversity, a metal stronger than anything else smelted together.

The HATCHLINGS are given their freedom as the Tsar and Tsarina-witch gives each of them a key to all the Russias and NESTLING back if PICKLES builds them a FLYING ROBOT COCKATOO of their own, which he does. But they ask the king to help them with their adventures map.

The finest translators in Petrograd try to read their ancient secret map, but all they can do is assemble it to look like the Russian alphabet, and it becomes even more jumbled and unreadable to Grandpa MACAW. Thus, the AMAZON

HATCHLINGS are doomed to more travel adventures under the spell of the secret wanderer's map in search for a new Amazon paradise, since all their trees have been cut down in the original Amazon forest from where they started their magic journey of wanderers in search of an eternal parrot forest paradise.

◆   ◆   ◆

How to Write Children's Video 'Books' for Podcasting from Animated Cartoon Scripts and Premises

Before you produce a video featuring animation for podcasting and upload it to a Web site or save it on a DVD, you need to write the animation script including all the camera angles. You also can make a video animation book or include a DVD inside an envelope pasted inside the back of a children's book. Cartoon animation scripts can be turned into both animated video for podcasting or children's books by emphasizing repetition, rhythm, dialogue, and illustration of settings.

To create animation, you need software that makes avatars, human-like figures, or cartoon characters you create yourself. Also you'll use the same writing techniques of dialogue-action-illustration when writing a story book for children aged 4 to eight as you'd use to write the outline or premise for an animation script destined for video podcasting.

Children's books can be adapted or turned into animation scripts by emphasizing dialogue and action. The practice writing springboards, premises, and several drafts polishes your ability to present the highlights of a life story with cartoon animated characters in your computer or online, on disk, or on video. All you have to do is substitute the real person or real personality for the cartoon character, avatar, or robot online, on video, and on disk.

Currently, many animated cartoons are designed overseas, but someone somewhere still has to write the scripts. Here's how to begin. You can write your life story or personal history as an animated cartoon, design animated computer games, including writing the scripts, or think creatively "outside the box." Back in the 1990s, writing a life story sometimes featured 'avatars' or computer-generated persona 'robots' online.

Hypertext fiction and life stories flummoxed many in the mid-nineties, but opened new channels of creative expression online. What other media can you use for your life story time capsules? Feature the highlights of significant events in your own life or rites of passage. Keepsakes include your personal journal, video clips and photos, along with DNA-driven genealogy-for-ancestry reports.

How to Write Life Stories as "Saturday-Morning-Type" Cartoons & How to Write Cartoon Animation Scripts for Multimedia Markets

Begin writing cartoon scripts by watching cartoons all morning several days a week. Animation also can be life story animation scripts on personal history themes. When learning to write cartoon scripts that you also can adapt to children's books, begin by writing animation scripts for four-year olds.

Keep in mind that you can write animation scripts, puppet theater plays, or adapt poems to story also for grown-ups. Writing for adults may emphasize the personal history, memoirs, and autobiography markets that focus on events, experiences, and highlights of any person's life story.

Writing animation for children is tougher than writing live-action or dialogue in first person diary novels. You want to put stretch marks on your wallet? Then call every shot in an animation script. You have up to two lines of dialogue before you have to change the shot, the frame, that is. Shot changed already? Then start describing the scene all over again along with what action is happening.

There's no director in animation that will put in the camera angles on your script or other directions. No one will stage your action other than you. Here's your chance to play master of your universe and do everything as the writer in 37–59 pages for a half-hour script that actually runs only 22 minutes.

An animation script takes twice as much writing as a live action screen play. You write two pages of animation for each screen minute. Saturday morning cartoons are the ultimate in teaching tools when transferred to personal history or life stories and to other educational and training materials. Many writers in animation entered the field decades ago by first writing half-hour television commercials for toys and related educational devices.

Record Cartoons for Study and Analysis

Instead of merely watching cartoons on your TV, record them to tape or DVD. If you're working with tape, stop your VCR machine and freeze a frame. Now write down all the action occurring in that freeze-frame. It should have a beginning, middle, and end—same as in a short story. Put in one line of dialogue. Practice until you become familiar with finding the beginning, middle, and end—the "short story" theme in each freeze-frame. Do you understand what you're looking for—the story line, the action in each frame of animation?

Watch tapes as often as three times a day until the action in each frame becomes familiar as a story with a beginning, middle, and end. There is gold in animation festivals, whether you're writing animation to entertain or writing personal histories in animation format as a way to use your creative expression or as the cliché goes "think outside the box."

Cartoon writers of the eighties and nineties lived in a hypercubed universe where thinking was done in three dimensions. Today it's action, effects, and visual writing. Only it goes beyond thinking in three dimensions. You have to think inside out. Write in sound effects and write visually. Animation writing is an exercise in highly technical visual thinking. You form a team with the skilled computer artist-animator-designer and the computer engineer.

Learn from TV Toy Ads

Saturday morning cartoons are there to sell toys to children (and parents) who must be persuaded either by their children or by the cartoon ad itself. Watch for the commercials. Sponsors pay for them. Writers can work at the educational materials end of the animation market, write ad copy and dialogue with action for the sponsors, or write the animation for entertainment.

There's another inroad—writing personal life stories and histories, even corporate histories, as animation scripts and illustrated novels. Camera angle directions work together showcasing the highlights of a person's life at any age. Another specialty is writing case histories and corporate success stories. Use cartoons for visualizing and animating stories and to sell advertising and jingles, learning materials, or products.

Foreign Animation

In the eighties, when animation began to be sent overseas to be designed, script writers often turned to computer game design and computer game script writing as one alternative. Today many universities have impacted graphic design majors in schools of new media. Computer animation in a variety of countries is shown on TV everywhere. Have you seen the last computer animation from Japan, for example?

What about the 'anime' field and independent producers of animation stories? You could offer animation online and on disk portraying children's life stories for birthday gifts and rites of passage ceremonies. There are so many applications to writing life stories as animation scripts. Only you need a computer animator to be on your team, someone to design the animation art and do the computer editing.

To study animation script writing, hunt for the old cartoon scripts of the thirties and forties. They're rare vintages. Keep a tape or DVD library of dozens of old-time radio programs. Join old-time radio and video clubs online where you can exchange or rent these old cartoons on DVDs or CDs.

Listen to old-time radio shows such as Captain Midnight and The Shadow. Can you write a radio play of someone's life story or personal history in that format—old time radio with special sound effects? If so, put it on a DVD or CD and up on a streaming Web site. That's one way to create a time capsule, keepsake album, or personal and corporate history.

Watch cartoon animation from other lands. Look at the World War II cartoons shown in local theaters in the forties. They are now on DVDs and on VHS tapes. When the tapes deteriorate with time, they are transferred to higher quality DVDs and whatever comes next. Look at the WW 2 themes in the cartoon animation, such as Donald Duck fighting Nazis.

For a personal historian, looking at cartoons from other countries at different times can help you learn how propaganda cartoons were used because people thought them to be patriotic. At different periods in history, foreign governments paid for propaganda cartoons that often turn up in archives and libraries. Look at your own country's cartoons from years ago. Was the theme patriotic? List the ways. What did the themes emphasize here, teamwork, for example.

You can make a hobby or research project out of studying the world of animation script writing during various wars, in time, or in geographic space around the world. The themes go beyond the design of animation or the script writing. There are patterns and values in some of these cartoons. What stories do they tell? What values and virtues? Do they have a purpose, mission, crusade, slogan, proverb, or other message? How do the cartoons impact people, and how do people impact cartoon animation and script writing?

How to Enter the Field of Cartoon Animation Script Writing or Animation of Life Stories and Personal Histories

You can start by either researching the needs of animation design companies or advertising agencies that sponsor the Saturday morning cartoons. Many writers were spiraled into animation script writing from spin-offs of advertising agency electronic ad copywriting and/or graphic illustration jobs.

Some entered animation script writing as former comic-book artists or writers. Others were live-action scriptwriters. Some also are computer game designers. You have the animation artist-designer who turns to script writing. And you have the computer engineer interested in game design.

The animation script writer needs the soul of an illustrator even if you don't do visual art work. You can paint pictures with visual writing. The pictures would emphasize action and dialogue. The best way to train is to study paintings in art galleries and museums and watch cartoon animation for exercising the visual side.

On the writing side, you look at cartoon animation scripts and analyze them for story, length, action, dialogue, and appeal to the audience and age level. You also find out whether the script will sell toys or other educational materials and products advertised between the cartoons.

Toy Marketing

Life stories and corporate histories can be marketed as toys, board games, or computer games. Know what age level you'll be targeting. You can even write story books using the lives of your clients who could be children if the parents give information and specify what kind of life story book or cartoon they want with the 'avatar' or "robot image" or photograph of their child.

You work out with the parent what kind of educational life story approach you want to take with animation and script with the family. It makes a fascinating birthday party presentation and gift. From lives to grand openings of stores, you are marketing a toy or a life story with animation script and design.

Between 1984 and 1986 a flood of animation began being turned out for syndication. Through the advertising agency route, animation writers trained on the job to sell toys and women's products. They wrote copy for advertisements and animation scripts. Animation writers marketed toys to children and skin care products primarily to women. The animated script had to sell shampoo, detergents, and bake mixes.

Artists became writers, and writers trained in animation design. Add that group of creative people to a farrago of Hollywood script writers seeking more work or alternatives. Many script writers with degrees in screenwriting turned to the Saturday morning cartoons to make a living. College campuses began to offer courses in animation and later, new media animation such as desktop video animation and new media writing.

The Boom and the Bust

A tremendous amount of animation flooded the markets around 1986. By 1987, the boom turned to bust, leaving many writers by 1988 vying for what assignments and contracts came their way by the time the Internet brought new hope to the nineties and beyond.

The good news is that those who had been writing animation scripts leaped into writing live-action screen plays or went into multimedia educational design and writing. Others went into Web design and online digital journalism. Still others sought out print-on-demand publishing venues.

Breaking into cartoon animation can take one to five years. Collaboration is common. Often you find work through the multimedia and other computer-related markets. I found work as an independent contractor writing success stories and case histories for a software manufacturer at the end of the nineties. There is a bright side.

Animation Writing Agents

Since writing animation pays no residuals, newcomers are given a second chance if they get the go-ahead to write a sample script. Prime-time TV won't touch you without an agent. So without an agent, you need to pitch a few seconds in writing to a story editor at your chosen animation studio.

You first phone the various studios and independent producers and ask for the name of the story editor. Then you talk to the story editor or pitch in writing. It's the story editor who has the power to work with you and is your first link to the industry. First you have to pitch a story, and most often the story line is related to the cartoon show's 'bible.' The 'bible' is a reference and resource book of what the characters are like and what they do in a particular cartoon show on TV.

If you live out of town from where the studio is located, tell the story editor that you have a computer and can send the script electronically. It can go by email. Most studios have bulletin boards to which you can download or upload all types of pitches, springboards, treatments, stories, and scripts.

Telecommuting

The computer bulletin board for animation writers in the 1980s was called "The Algonquin Board." Its private number and mailing address appealed to members because the only way to become a member was to have someone in the industry · recommend you. You were in a position that sometimes the only way in was to accept an assignment on speculation and then ask your story editor to recommend you as a member. Otherwise, you were left to introduce yourself at professional meetings by volunteering for such types of organizations.

Today, you can check out the many associations and unions for animation writers that are listed online. Network with the many associations listed as links at: The Electronic Media and Film major Web site of Towson University, Electronic Media & Film Department, 8000 York Rd. Towson, MD 21252-0001 The Web site is at: http://www.towson.edu/emf/links.htm.

Networking Online With People in the Industry

What you want to look for on bulletin and message boards or email lists of related associations are job information, marketing ideas, and professional resources. Join associations and volunteer to interview people. Write articles for the association's newsletter or other publications. Mailing lists and bulletin boards online may have job information and valuable resources. Meet people and find out whether they want to spread the news about what they are doing in the field. Write success stories.

Meet other writers and story editors at trade and professional associations in the field of writing for animation. Back in the eighties, there was a bulletin board that served live-action screenwriters called the Wicked Scherzo Board, but back then, the only way to get phone numbers of members was to ask a member in the industry to recommend you.

In those days, you need not have sold a script to network with writers in the industry. Today, most networking is done in various universities departments of electronic media and film with industry internships and professional associations as members volunteer to work on newsletters and at conventions and conferences to 'network.'

Instead of meeting only writers, try to network with musicians, artists, engineers, special effects designers, and technicians who work in the computer animation industry. It's all about teamwork, and every artist needs a script to animate. Check out the advertising agencies, educational publishers and producers, trainers, corporate industrial film producers, and comic book publishers for their writing needs.

There also are the radio scripts for Internet broadcast, podcast, content with RSS feeds of text and audio, streaming video online, DVD, or multicast. Elementary school teachers can use plays for puppet shows as well as the producers of the puppet shows for schools. Everyone works with some kind of script presenting to students or at weddings and other celebrations, and scripts have themes or niche markets. Also try the ethnic and religious markets.

Working with Nets

One way to meet people in the animation and script writing industries is to join the International Animated Film Association (ASIFA). The Web site is at: http://

www.swcp.com/animate/. Email address is: asifa@asifa.org. There are national and international chapters.

The Los Angeles headquarters of ASIFA can help you reach people employed at the various studios in the vicinity of Hollywood. Call the studios directly and speak to the story editors. Check the *Encyclopedia of Associations* in your public library for a long list of animation associations worldwide or look on the Web at www.google.com or other search engines for more associations. Some offer workshops with networking. Stay in communication with the various studios in Los Angeles.

Call the story editors each month, and ask them to send you animation scripts. You can write to them and enclose self-addressed stamped envelopes. Never pester them or call too frequently. Bring to the story editors your related stories and your unique scripts. To prepare, read the animation scripts. Analyze the scripts. Study the scripts to see what was emphasized and find out why those scripts were accepted and satisfactory. Those topics give you factual material to discuss with the story editors.

As story editors to send you the 'bibles' of various animation characters you select. This 'bible' is a book several inches thick that tells everything you need to know about the cartoon character. If you write life stories as cartoon animation, then you'll need to make such a 'scrap book' or 'bible' on the person about whose life you are writing.

Learn all you can about the cartoon character and his henchmen from the cartoon bible. Make yourself valuable to studio officials. Ask them what already has been pitched. Ask what titles have sold the quickest. Ask kids what makes them laugh.

Ask older adults what makes them laugh. Ask kids what they want to see on television cartoons. Ask people of all ages what they would like to see of their own life stories on TV cartoons, even if the TV set is from their own DVD disk of their life story or other significant event.

Story editors will provide a guidebook or 'bible' revealing what are the taboos. The bible and sample scripts will let you know in general, but if you miss a point, ask. There are several types of cartoon shows on TV, the hard and the soft.

Hard and Soft Video Podcasting and TV Animation Shows

There are soft and hard cartoon animation shows on TV. Soft shows don't have too much action adventure. Write sample scripts of each type. The hard shows have the "hit 'em hard" characters that enjoy things that people can't do legally. Do you really enjoy your characters torching toy stores as in the cartoon, *Rob-*

ocop? Or would you prefer to go inward into your imagination and write a zoo story? Look at scripts from the soft animation shows produced fifteen or twenty years ago such as the 1980s Jim Henson's *Muppet Babies*.

You might want to watch the old cartoons and compare the action on screen with the written script. The scripts often are available from the story editors, animation writers' associations, and also from stores in Hollywood that sell old scripts. In the eighties when I was writing sample animation scripts, the story editors from the various studios sent me their 'bible' and sample scripts for various shows.

Chances are no one will buy your sample scripts. You might want to focus writing life story scripts to be later put into computer animation with a variety of animation software. Sample scripts for particular shows that no one buys are not a total waste. They are used as part of your resume. You show a story editor your sample script along with your resume. These samples show the story editors that you know the format. You learn to format a story, and you learn to structure a story. It's one way to showcase your 'handle' on credible cartoon dialogue.

Pitching

Introduce yourself by phone to the story editor. Find out whether they also take email queries. It's more personal by phone if not in person. Tell the story editor that you have a sample script to send. Give your verbal pitch in 20 seconds. Then tell the story editor that you'll send the required written pitch. Find out whether they want the pitch emailed or sent by regular mail.

The story editor will probably say your idea has been pitched. However, if your story line has a fresh angle, you'll me asked to mail it in. Here's your chance to be creative and still stick to the 'bible' or script requirements for a particular show.

Springboard

You first send the story editor a half-page, double-spaced bare-bones summary called a springboard. Every story can be pared to a half-page bare bones summary. Look at it as if it were the marketing material that goes on the back cover of your story. Think of the springboard as the back-cover marketing description of your novel designed to hook the reader. It is there to make the story editor want to open your book or actually read more of your script. You will not be paid to write a springboard.

After you have written this half-page double-spaced springboard containing the bare bones of your script or story, you will be asked to write a premise. So, if the editor likes your springboard and assigns you a premise to write, you will be paid for the premise.

Premise

A premise is a two-page, double-spaced, expanded springboard. Make your premise a story with a beginning, middle, and end. Every frame and sequence of your story needs a beginning, middle, and end. Your premise needs to contain the hook that the story editor will use to sell your idea to the networks or to clients. Cartoons have paid advertising sponsors. They are aired to sell the sponsor's toys. The most important point that can sell your episode for a Saturday morning cartoon is its title.

Work on your title to make it salable. If you're writing a life story as an animation script for use on DVDs or computers, keep the title pertinent and short. Often familiar titles sell. Titles that resemble popular, ageless songs also sell. Talk to your story editor about what is expected or taboo in the title. Look at the best hundred titles that have sold cartoons. What does the story editor or clients like about those titles?

Outline

Once the network or client approves your premise, you will be paid to write an outline. Be specific. Break the action down frame by frame and scene by scene. Use hardly any dialogue at all. Your outline runs between eight and 12 pages in length if you are writing for a half-hour show (which actually is only 22 minutes of screen time).

First Draft

When the story editor approves your outline, you move to the first draft of your script. There's always the first draft followed by the revisions. There may be one or two writers assigned to the script. One writer may be credited with the story and one or two more with the script.

Bumped Off

Before you agree to write any material for pay, you'll be handed a "work for hire" agreement to sign. At any stage, you may be "bumped off." That means being cut off with no more pay or credits. Once you are cut off by the studio it can give your premise or outline to any other writer or shelve your work permanently.

You could be paid for your premise and then cut off. Or this could happen as you hand in your outline, in which case you'll be paid for the outline.

How Much?

Payments vary with each studio. Some pay 40 percent of the script fee if you're cut off at outline. The minimum fee for a half-hour script at several studios started at slightly more than $3,000. For network shows, payment could range from $4,000 to $6,000 or more, depending upon your experience.

What Are You Worth?

Make yourself valuable to studio officials. Ask them what has been pitched in the past. Ask what titles sold the quickest. Talk to children. Ask kids what makes them laugh. Send studios a collection or database of children's reactions to cartoons when you are asking for work. A child's creativity has not been discouraged by rejection. Children don't have writer's block. Comic strip writers, filmmakers, teachers, and anthropologists also can be resources.

Research Comic Books

Many former writers of comic book stories and similar novels have become animation script writers. Talk to the people who write and draw the comic books and their publishers and editors. Many cartoon shows are based on comic-book or comic-strip heroes and heroines. Some scripts are spin-offs of live-action TV programs. The eighties saw Robocop and Star Trek take off in a variety of media from novels to cartoons. Animation writing is a collaborative effort. Firms that publish comic books also may have animation studios on the opposite coast.

Animation Scripts Use Comic-Book Style Dialogue and Descriptive Language

The same descriptive language used in comic strips is written into animation scripts. For example, you'll see the heavy use of sound effects (SFX) in most lines of description and dialogue in adventure-action cartoons. Animation scripting is mostly description of action and hardly any dialogue at all.

Comic Conventions

Attend the comic conventions in your sit, and sit on the "writing for animation" panel. Create your own panel at conferences and conventions for people in similar industries. Phone and write to experts you will be researching or interviewing for articles you may write in a newsletter of one of the trade or professional associations. Ask the experts to come and join you on a panel at a convention or conference or a class or group meeting. An example would be a writer's club or a film society. The topic could be on how to write for the animation industry.

Comic Books

Life stories can be presented as comic books. That's one alternative. Another is writing for the animation industry or speaking about that industry by researching comic books. Talk to people who work at home with computer and Internet connection writing cartoon scripts. Ask these experts to be on your panel at conferences such as comic book publishers' conventions or seminars on writing for the new media.

Timing Is Important

Most cartoon shows are picked up by studios in February. Call various studios during the month when they are pitching network shows. Exceptions to the February pickup rule included the old 1980s shows such as *The Smurfs* (Hanna-Barbera) and *Fraggle Rock* or the *Muppet Babies* (Marvel) which had early pick-ups. *Alf* was produced at Disney Studios in Burbank, California. There were a wide variety of shows such as Pee Wee's Playhouse.

The persons in charge of development as well as the producers are listed in the credits that roll at the end of each cartoon show. Record the cartoons for your personal research and find out who is the appropriate person to query regarding writing springboards or other materials. Sometimes a producer needs public relations material written. That's another side door into the industry, through public relations work on the cartoon shows or with the sponsors. Multimedia animation studies are another door that may offer internships.

The mid-eighties was one of the "golden ages" of Saturday morning cartoon shows on TV when freelance script writers had the chance to walk in and present their writing to story editors or to telephone from anywhere. You didn't necessarily have had to live in Los Angeles to be a cartoon script writer. Today with Internet multimedia, you can produce life stories or corporate histories yourself and present them as animated cartoon shows or other types of multimedia presentations such as time capsules.

What you need to search for is the 'downtime' at the studios of your choice. That downtime is a good time to talk to story editors about writing sample scripts, obtaining 'bibles' and other materials you'll need to begin your springboard for a particular show. Your one best sample script can be used to sell many shows at several studios.

◆   ◆   ◆

Turning Poems, Proverbs, or Humor and Folklore into Children's Video Podcasts and Video Books

We begin with a long, rhythmic poem the size of an average children's book for ages 4–8. The poem to begin with may have words more grown-up that can be adapted in the actual story book to a child's reading level. Use rhythm and repetition of beats in the actual story book that may come from the poem. Pare down the words to fit the reading level of the age group of your intended readers.

Use the original words or the easy-reading words you adapt from the grown-up words to write the lyrics for a song. Then you can contact a musician to set your song to music. Your end product would be one story book for children ages 4–8, your original poem story, possible lyrics for a song, and material for an animation script, children's play, interactive DVD or CD, and a possible puppet theater script.

Here's a sample poem to analyze. Note the rhythm or beat of the syllables. As an exercise, feel free to turn this poem into an illustrated children's book. Any grown-up words should be written for the general comprehension of children in the age 4 to 8 year old reading level.

For the four-year olds, parents would read the story. For eight-year olds, illustrations that take up most of the page would be in a one or two-page spread. In the bottom quarter or third of the page, large print words would tell the story at the rate of about one paragraph per page.

Keep sentences short, under ten words, and rhythmic. Develop a beat in the story so as it is read orally, it sounds rhythmic as it rhymes in hexameter. Key the rhythm to the child's ear to draw in the child's attention to the illustration and the sound of the words when read aloud. Read popular children's books meant for readers of age four to eight. Look at the rhyme, if any, in the books and the beat or rhythm of the syllables.

Animation destined for video podcasting format can be similar to what you see on the TV morning cartoons, or it can rhyme like some children's books. It's easier to write a script that does not contain rhyme as it can become distracting to the story line. Note the rhythm, beat, and rhyme in the poem.

Proverbs also can be fleshed out for a children's story script written for video podcast distribution or syndication. You can set your story to music as song lyrics or use your original song lyrics to create a story as in Country Western style.

Write your story treatment first before you expand any poem or song. To expand a poem into a script for video, you expand the detail and use the theme. The technique is similar to adapting a play or cinematic script to a novel, by adding and expanding detail culled from the theme, message, and outcome of the poem.

To expand a poem into a children's video novel, use appropriate vocabulary levels for the intended age-group of your audience. Most cartoon animation is written to the vocabulary and visual levels of four-year olds. Themes and settings can be expanded in a video podcast to reach children five through eight years of age. Ask children what makes them laugh, and ask their parents what they want their children to see and learn in a video podcast.

Use words in the age group's vocabulary that you select. Compare the vocabulary of published books for readers aged four to eight with the vocabulary that you will use to adapt your poems or stories to a video podcast or video book for various age levels with access to video podcasts. Perhaps you'd want to write for college students using animation to explain concepts in science. Make a vocabulary list of the images and words you will use, and look at the list as you write.

◆　　　◆　　　◆

ADDITIONAL INFORMATION

The Animation Podcast
http://www.animationpodcast.com/archives/2005/06/20/nik-ranieri-part-one/

Animation Podcast (Discussion about the craft of animation)
http://www.idiotvox.com/Movies/
PodCast_Review_Animation_Podcast__10944.html

20

Censored News Video Podcasting

DESCRIPTION OF BUSINESS:

Covering the News Yourself: How Censored News Cuts Media Expenses

Let your video podcast online cover the news that didn't make the news, exposing corporate, institutional, or government corruption through your investigative video reporting. Your video could carry the news that didn't make the newspapers because of censors.

Make a video of underground news. Be an investigative video reporter and expose corruption. Be a video muckraker and raise hell. To understand muckraking video, you need to know a little about what it's like in print.

Read Jessica Mitford's introduction to <u>Poison Penmanship: The Gentle Art of Muckraking</u>. Mitford's investigative writing led to social change by inspiring and motivating the public. In 1963, she exposed the funeral industry in her book, <u>The American Way of Death</u>. Beneficial changes resulted. Therefore, your video surely can find subjects to explore, muckrake, and expose.

INCOME POTENTIAL:

Since fewer than 20 corporations now control most of the United State's mass media, your income potential as an independent is unlimited as long as you cover the subject of information control and how it exploits our minds. Any video on mind manipulation is sure to earn an income for you depending on repetition.

To make a successful video, you must use continuous and lasting propaganda. You must not leave any gaps. If your video lasts a long time, you can expect to gross between $20 and $40 on each video.

Expensive videos usually sell through direct mail order for $39.95. Popular mail order DVDs are priced around $19.95 to $29.95. There are low-cost documentaries and DVD movies for sale online for less—for $5 or $7, plus shipping. You can offer a video mail order distributor a commission to sell your video at their own prices. Make sure that whatever you price your video at that you make a profit and at the same time the video is cheap enough to attract enough customers who think it's a fair price and affordable.

Do a test mailing first to find out your viewer's opinion of the price in relation to the content. Is it really affordable by the majority of your potential market?

The rule is the lower priced the tape, the more copies it will sell. Video stores will only take it if it's priced low enough to have high turnover, and if they can get their cut of your profit.

You could be better off with your own mail order flyer going to a list of club members interested in the subject of your video. If you charge anywhere from $19.95 to $30 to the public by direct mail order, you can expect some income from clubs, workshops, seminars, and association meetings, as well as video-of-the-month clubs. Sell your tapes at a discount during meetings and conventions.

Getting your video into stores usually means it would have to air first—either in front of a national convention of video software dealers, or on the local or public broadcast news—or run as a documentary on one of the news magazine shows on television or on cable television. Create visibility by airing your video at conventions of people interested in the subject matter of your tape.

The tape can make the national meeting rounds. Usually every month there's a convention or conference in different cities of local chapters of various associations, clubs, or organizations interested in the subject matter of your tape. Call public speakers who travel around the country giving presentations at conventions and ask them to show your tape during the meeting or pass flyers out to the captured convention audience.

BEST LOCALE TO OPERATE THE BUSINESS:

You can run your muckraking video production company from any location where there is censored news to be exposed to the public. It's not necessary to live in any special city, but you'll need to have rapport with the underground video and alternate media/broadcast industry as well as the standard media old boys' network.

Being in Washington, DC will help if it is a government or a military service you plan to expose in your videos. It's better to be near the large broadcast media firms in New York, but you have to be on the road all over to tape your investigative reports.

TRAINING REQUIRED:

If you already know how to run your industrial quality camcorder, the next subject to learn is investigative reporting. You can get in touch with the Investigative Journalism Project (Fund for Constitutional Government), 122 Maryland Ave NE, Suite 300, Washington, DC 20002 (202) 546-3732, or join IRE (Investigative Reporters and Editors), 100 Neff Hall, University of Missouri, School of Journalism, Columbia, MO 65211. This organization puts out enough publications to train you at home to be a great investigative reporter if only from reading what they publish—journals, newsletters, books, etc.

Read about Media Watch, Media Alliance, or the Media Institute (addresses are in the appendices at the back of this book). There are enough publications published by the media organizations (listed in the back of this book) to help make you an investigative reporter using video as your medium of expression. You also can connect to the Internet on your personal computer and exchange information with people all over the country and abroad.

GENERAL APTITUDE OR EXPERIENCE:

Good interviewing skills are essential. You need to be a bit of a private investigator, have a willingness to expose corruption, and have an interest in finding out what's happening that affects most people's lives in a universal way. A journalism writing aptitude helps, or a partner who does the writing while you do the technical video work.

Muckraking videos really do dig up the dirt and expose it to the public in order to have beneficial changes made. Generally, you should really want to save the world in a small way with your video camera and have a nose for news.

EQUIPMENT NEEDED:

You'll need your broadcast quality field camera, tape, batteries, sound, lighting, and editing equipment, mobility, and a readiness to travel anywhere to videotape the news or expose corruption. Some taping will be in the homes of people you'll be interviewing.

OPERATING YOUR BUSINESS:

Making underground videos out of news that usually is censored each year has to be one of the most exciting ways to earn money with your video camera. To begin, first you spot important, but overlooked news in the back pages of your local newspaper—or the newspaper in some small town.

Perhaps it's news of ecological disaster. Or you want to make a video on why 12 million children go hungry in this country each day because you saw an alarming report issued by the United Nations Children's Fund.

Perhaps you consulted the Tyndall Report, which monitors evening network news, and wondered why some reports don't make the top ten list of news subjects on the networks during any month. Maybe you disagree and feel that your video is an important way of making sure the censored news gets to the public. Subscribing to a news clipping service or keeping news clippings on your own personal computer database helps to find subjects video worthy.

Perhaps you choose to monitor what's happening in the sparsely-populated desert areas, finding that the military has quietly resumed biowarfare testing. For example on January 27, 1973, the Salt Lake Tribune reported such headlines as: "Army Resumes Biological Agent Test ad Dugway (Utah) After 10-Year Cessation;" and "Dugway to test disease-causing agents at remote lab" (Author: Jim Woolf). There were the headlines of September 21, 1993, "Dugway Base Cited for 22 Waste Violations," (author: Laurie Sullivan). In the High Country News, the title appeared on September 8, 1993, "Biowarfare is Back," (author Jon Christensen). On September 15, 1993, the High Desert Advocate ran an article with the title, "Utah biowarfare oversight group wants to do its work behind closed doors."

If you kept news clippings of what was happening then in Dugway, Utah, you could have found funds from one of the video investigative reporting support groups, perhaps, or used your own low-budget to travel to the high desert area of Dugway, Utah with your video camera and talked to the people interested or involved in the matter.

Your investigative news angle would be: the U.S. Army has brought biological warfare testing back to the Dugway Proving Ground in the same western Utah location that ten years ago it claimed was not safe. The news angle is that military scientists are testing "the Biological Integrated Detection System" at the same facility the military says is now renovated. Is it? Your video would tell the news from an investigative reporting point of view, designed to expose corruption, if any exists, by interviewing experts and scientists.

The defensive weapon is supposed to detect the presence of biological agents. Your video would be about whether it works—whether it gives soldiers enough time to put on biohazard suits. The tests involved anthrax, botulism, and the plague.

To make your video, for an example, you'd have to interview Dugway representatives who would let you know in what liquid the germs were carried because the people of the town were afraid of the germs getting into the air. Doing some local history, you'd find out that the Dugway facility first closed in 1983 because of a fear that if there was an air leak in the sealed chamber, deadly germs would get into the air.

As your video progressed, you'd be able to show the viewers in exactly what ways the facility was renovated, and whether the safety precautions that exist now are enough to prevent a leak. Only experts and scientists interviewed on the video, and an up-close shot on the safety measure, could convince the public that safety was really that secure. Or is it? Would the military let you tape the renovation changes?

This is how you make your investigative videos of the news that normally doesn't get into the big city papers. An excellent resource of the stories that could make great videos can be found in the book, <u>Censored</u>, The News That Didn't Make the News and Why, Carl Jensen & Project Censored, published in 1994 by Four Walls Eight Windows, 39 West 14th St., #503, New York, NY 10011.

This excellent book contains chapters on raking muck and raising hell, U.S. censorship, and a lot of censored news that never made the news but should have. These include the biohazard story, and other news that would make excellent muckraking videos.

You even can send Project Censored interesting news you spot hidden in the back pages of your newspaper. Send your clippings to: Nomination, Project Censored, Sonoma State University, Rohnert Park, CA 94928. Their annual deadline is October 15th.

To make muckraking videos, you'll have to look in small-circulation magazines and or small-town rural newspapers as well as in your local big-city news, if you live in the big town. What you're looking for are stories you think should have received

more coverage. Your video's purpose is to give those stories the coverage they deserve.

The video you make will be designed to show the public what's happening and why. The story should be timely and of national or global importance. If the story is significant, it's worthy of being made into a videocassette that you can offer to a variety of audiences, including the big-time media as well as the locals.

Stories you put on tape need not have appeared in the news. It could have appeared in a trade journal. Or it could have come from a local paper, or even a tabloid—if it's factual. It could have briefly been covered on television or overheard in a radio talk show interview.

Once you have written permission from where ever you saw it first to dig deeper into the story, find out whether it received any follow-up. If the lack of exposure is bothering the people in the news, offer to interview them on tape. Then dig deeper and interview others.

Get shots of where it happened, and ask the usual, what, who, when, where, how, and why questions. Show rather than tell on the tape. Avoid "talking head" shots that go on for minutes. Instead, cut to other scenes and do voice-overs to show movement and action.

What you're selling in this kind of video is simply the censored news, the news that most newspapers and magazines refuse to print. You're satisfying the public's right to know and make beneficial changes.

TARGET MARKET:

Muckraking videos that emphasize the news stories that the media usually censors primarily appeal to mail-order catalog customers. You can offer your video, if it fits the 23 or 53 minute news slots, to half-hour or full-hour news programs, or to producers of specials on network television.

Your advertising usually will be in specialty magazines that appeal to readers interested in a particular subject related to your expose video. You can offer your video to nonprofit organizations related to the subject of your tape, to the government, and to schools. Or you can give seminars on the subject of your expose and sell your tape at conventions or through bookstores, club meetings, and correspondence courses.

RELATED VIDEO OPPORTUNITIES:

Expose hoaxes on video. Making videos that expose corruption is related to alternative media public relations. Any government can hire a videographer to make a propaganda film or video. The question is on whose side are you on? Pick an industry you want to expose. Medicine? Meat packing? The funeral industry? Ecological disasters related to environmental terrorists? Cover-ups?

Related video opportunities exist with the alternative broadcast media producers and organizations. Look at the variety of video direct mail order catalogs.

You can make a social issues expose video of the self-enhancement industry. Find out what corruption hasn't been exposed yet.

Your goal is to empower the public. Show your readers or viewers why experts can be trusted. Have these experts offer solutions to common ground problems.

Expose government cover-ups with air-tight cases that even the tightest skeptics can't disprove. Have facts that can be checked and validated by experts and scientists who have reputations for being credible. Viewers will pay what they can afford to see information they can use to make important decisions—information that may never air on the network news.

ADDITIONAL INFORMATION:

Associations of Interest to Consumer Economics Communications Experts, Nutrition Journalists, Nutritionists, Dieticians, and Health Care Professionals:

American Dietetic Association
http://www.eatright.org

American Obesity Association
http://www.obesity.org

American Society for Nutritional Sciences
http://www.asns.org/

American Society for Clinical Nutrition
http://www.ascn.org/

The Annapolis Center for Science-Based Public Policy
http://www.annapoliscenter.org

Association of Food & Drug Officials
http://www.afdo.org

American Diabetes Association
http://www.diabetes.org

American Farm Bureau Federation
http://www.fb.com

American Heart Association
http://www.americanheart.org

Botanical Center for Age-Related Diseases
http://nccam.nih.gov/news/2005/040705.htm

Calorie Control Council
http://www.caloriecontrol.org

Center for Health Promotion
http://pan.ilsi.org

Consumer Healthcare Products Association
http://www.caloriecontrol.org

CropLife America
http://www.croplifeamerica.org

Egg Nutrition Center
http://www.enc-online.org

Food Marketing Institute
http://www.fmi.org

Food Allergy Research and Resource Program
http://www.farrp.org

Grocery Manufacturers of America
http://www.gmabrands.com

International Association for Food Protection
http://www.foodprotection.org

National Dairy Council/Dairy Management
http://www.dairyinfo.com

National Policy and Resource Center on Nutrition and Aging
http://www.fiu.edu/~nutreldr

North American Agricultural Journalists
http://naaj.tamu.edu/

Society for Nutrition Education
http://www.sne.org

World Sugar Research Organization
http://www.wsro.org

Government-Related Agencies

Centers for Disease Control and Prevention
http://www.cdc.gov

Center for Food Safety and Applied Nutrition
http://www.crfsan.fda.gov

Fight BAC ™
http://www.fightbck.org

Food and Drug Administration: Consumer Inquiries
http://www.fda.gov

Joint Institute for Food Safety and Applied Nutrition
http://www.jifsan.umd.edu

National Cancer Institute: Press Office
http://www.nci.nih.gov

National Digestive Disease Information Clearinghouse
http://www.niddk.nih.gov

National Diabetes Information Clearinghouse
http://www.niddk.ninh.gov

National Health Information Center
http://health.gov/NHIC

National Institutes of Health
http://www.nih.gov

National Marine Fisheries Service
http://www.nmfs.noaa.gov

President's Council on Physical Fitness and Sports
http://fitness.gov

US Dept. of Agriculture
http://www.usda.gov

USDA/Food, Nutrition, and Consumer Services
http://www.fns.usda.gov/fncs

USDA/ Food Safety and Inspection Service Information
http://www.fsis.usda.gov

USDA/Meat and Poultry Hotline
Phone 1-800-535-4555

USDA/Animal and Plant Health Inspection Service
http://www.aphis.usda.gov

USDA/Foreign Agricultural Service
http://www.fas.usda.gov

USDA/National Agricultural Library
http://www.nalusda.gov

USDA/National Agriculture Statistics Service
http://www.fas.usda.gov

US Department of Health and Human Services
http://www.hhs.gov

Foodborne Illness Education Information Center
http://www.nalusda.gov/foodborne/index.html

US Department of Health and Human Services
http://www.hhs.gov

US Environmental Protection Agency
http://www.epa.gov

US Federal Trade Commission
http://www.ftc.gov

◆   ◆   ◆

Associations of Interest to Medical or Science Journalists

American Medical Writers Association
40 West Gude Drive, Suite 101
Rockville, MD 20850-1192
http://www.amwa.org/default.asp?ID=1

American Society of Indexers (for indexing careers)
10200 West 44th Avenue, Suite 304,
Wheat Ridge, CO 80033
http://www.asindexing.org/site/index.html

American Society of Journalists and Authors
1501 Broadway, Suite 302
New York, NY 10036
http://www.asja.org

Association of Health Care Journalists (AHCJ)
Center for Excellence in Health Care Journalism
Missouri School of Journalism
10 Neff Hall
Columbia, MO 62511
http://www.ahcj.umn.edu/

Association of Professional Writing Consultants
http://www.consultingsuccess.org/index.htm

Council of Biology Editors
http://www.monroecc.edu/depts/library/cbe.htm

Council of the Advancement of Science Writing
P.O. Box 910
Hedgesville, WV 25427
http://www.casw.org/

Careers in Science Writing:
http://www.casw.org/careers.htm

Education Writers Association
2122 P Street, NW Suite 201
Washington, DC 20037
http://www.ewa.org/

International Food, Wine & Travel Writers Association (IFW&TWA)
1142 South Diamond Bar Boulevard #177
Diamond Bar, CA 91765-2203
http://www.ifwtwa.org/index.html

Journalism.org—Researches, Resources & Ideas to Improve Journalism
http://www.journalism.org/

National Association of
Science Writers, Inc.
P.O. Box 890, Hedgesville, WV 25427
http://www.nasw.org/

North American Agricultural Journalists
http://naaj.tamu.edu/

Society of Professional Journalists
Eugene S. Pulliam National Journalism Center
3909 N. Meridian St., Indianapolis, IN 46208
http://www.spj.org/

Society for Technical Communication
http://www.stc.org/

Text and Academic Authors Association
TAA
P.O. Box 76477
St. Petersburg, FL
http://www.taaonline.net/

World Association of Medical Editors
http://www.wame.org/
http://www.wame.org/index.htm

Diversified Media Associations of Interest to all Communicators

American Business Press
http://www.americanbusinesspress.com/

American Society of Business Press Editors
http://www.asbpe.org/

Associated Business Writers of America
http://www.poewar.com/articles/associations.htm

Associazioni ed Enti Professionali-America
http://www.alice.it/writers/grp.wri/wgrpame.htm
Contains a list of South American, Canadian, and US writers'
organizations, including language translation firms.

American Marketing Association
http://www.marketingpower.com/content1539.php

Association of Professional Communications Consultants
http://www.consultingsuccess.org/index.htm

Writer's Encyclopedia A-Z List
WritersMarket.com
http://www.writersmarket.com/encyc/azlist.asp

Editorial Freelancers Association
http://www.the-efa.org/

Editor's Guild
http://www.edsguild.org/become.htm
The current online Yellow Pages, published annually since 1997 includes listings by skills as well as a specialties index. This association published the hardcopy, Yellow Pages, a listing of Association members who wished to advertise their skills and specialties, between 1989 and 1999.
http://www.tiac.net/users/freelanc/YP.html

International Women's Writing Guild
http://www.iwwg.com/index.php, Or: http://www.iwwg.com
The International Women's Writing Guild, headquartered in New York and founded in 1976, is a network for the personal and professional empowerment of women through writing.

Video Software Dealers Association
http://www.vsda.org/Resource.phx/vsda/index.htx

Public Relations Society of America
http://www.prsa.org/

Deep Dish TV
http://www.deepdishtv.org/pages/catalogue13.htm

Video History Project
http://www.experimentaltvcenter.org/history/groups/gtext.php3?id=37

Advertising Research Foundation
http://www.arfsite.org/

The Mail Preference Service
http://www.dmaconsumers.org/offmailinglist.html

Advertising Associations Directory
http://paintedcows.com/associations.html

Mailing Fulfillment Service Association
http://www.mfsanet.org/pages/index.cfm?pageid=1

Television Bureau of Advertising
http://www.tvb.org/nav/build_frameset.asp?url=/docs/homepage.asp

Home Improvement Research Institute
http://www.hiri.org/abouthiri.htm

Writers-Editors Network
http://www.writers-editors.com/

Professional and Technical Consultants Association
http://www.patca.org/html/articles/ratesurvey/ratesurvey1.htm

Association of Independent Commercial Producers
http://www.aicp.com/splash-noswf.html

National Cable & Telecommunications Association
http://www.ncta.com/

International Association of Women in Radio and Television
http://www.iawrt.org/

National Communication Association
http://www.natcom.org/nca/Template2.asp

The Association for Women in Communications
http://www.womcom.org/

Society of Telecommunications Consultants
http://www.stcconsultants.org/

European Training Media Association
http://www.etma.org/

Advertising Research Foundation
641 Lexington Avenue • New York, NY 10022
http://www.arfsite.org/

International Women's Media Foundation
http://www.iwmf.org/training/womensmedia.php

Independent Publishers Group
http://www.ipgbook.com/index.cfm?userid=36155756

American Society of Media Photographers
150 North Second Street, Philadelphia, PA 19106
(Electronic imaging and digital technology)
http://www.asmp.org/

International Interactive Communications Society
http://users.rcn.com/sfiics/

International Multimedia Association
http://www.emmac.org/

National Cable Television Association
http://www.museum.tv/archives/etv/N/htmlN/nationalcabl/
nationalcabl.htm

Information Technology Association of America
http://www.itaa.org/eweb/StartPage.aspx

Personal and Oral History Associations

Association of Personal Historians
http://www.personalhistorians.org/index.html

Oral History Association
http://omega.dickinson.edu/organizations/oha/about.html

International Oral History Association
http://www.ioha.fgv.br/ioha/english/index.html

Texas Oral History Association
http://www.baylor.edu/TOHA/

Southwest Oral History Association
http://soha.fullerton.edu/

New England Association for Oral History
http://www.ucc.uconn.edu/~cohadm01/neaoh.html

Michigan Oral History Association
http://www.umich.edu/pres/history/oral.html

UCLA Oral History Program
http://www.library.ucla.edu/libraries/special/ohp/ohpindex.htm

"California As I Saw It," First Person Narratives of California's Early Years:
1849-1900. The Library of Congress.
http://memory.loc.gov/ammem/cbhtml/cbhome.html

◆   ◆   ◆

Nutrition and Health-Related Associations, Research Institutes, Corporations, Academies, and University Programs

American Academy of Family Physicians: http://www.aafp.org/

American Association of Family and Consumer Sciences: http://www.aafcs.org/

American Dietetic Association: http://www.eatright.org/

American Heart Association: http://www.americanheart.org/

American Institute for Cancer Research: http://www.aicr.org/

American Public Health Association: http://www.apha.org/

American Society of Clinical Nutrition: http://www.ascn.org/

Center for Science in the Public Interest: http://www.cspinet.org/

Chocolate Manufacturers Association: http://www.chocolateusa.org/

Consumer Federation of America: http://www.consumerfed.org/

Consumer Healthcare Products Association: http://www.chpa-info.org/

Council for Responsible Nutrition: http://www.crnusa.org/

Egg Nutrition Center: http://www.enc-online.org/

Federal Trade Commission: http://www.ftc.gov/

Food and Nutrition Board, Institute of Medicine:
http://www.iom.edu/board.asp?id=3788

Foundation for American Communications: http://www.facsnet.org/

Asian Food Information Center: http://www.afic.org/Press%20Centre.htm

Institute of Food Technologists: http://www.ift.org/cms/

International Dairy Foods Association: http://www.idfa.org/

International Life Sciences Institute: http://www.ilsi.org/

Kleinfeld Kaplan & Becker:
http://www.fda.gov/ohrms/dockets/dailys/00/Aug00/082400/cp0001.pdf

Lehigh University, Department of Journalism and Communication:
http://www.lehigh.edu/~injrl/sciwrit/

National Cancer Institute, US National Institutes of Health:
http://www.cancer.gov/

National Cooperative Business Association: http://www.ncba.coop/

National Food Processors Association:
http://www.worldfooddayusa.org/CMS/2951/8939.aspx

National Potato Promotion Board: http://www.uspotatoes.com/

Office of Dietary Supplements, National Institutes of Health:
http://ods.od.nih.gov/

The Popcorn Board: http://www.popcorn.org/index.cfm

Purdue University, National Institutes of Health Botanicals Center for Age-Related
Diseases: http://www.purdue.edu/UNS/html4ever/000920.Weaver.nihcenter.html

Purdue University, Department of Foods and Nutrition: http://www.cfs.purdue.edu/

Rutgers University, Nutraceuticals Institute: http://foodsci.rutgers.edu/nci/

Soyfoods Association of North America: http://www.soyfoods.org/

Saint Joseph's University, Erivan K. Haub School of Business: http://www.sju.edu/

Tufts School of Medicine and Nutrition:
http://www.tufts.edu/med/nutrition-infection/

Tufts University Health and Nutrition Letter: http://healthletter.tufts.edu/

United Soybean Board: http://www.unitedsoybean.org/

United States Department of Agriculture, Agricultural Research Service:
http://www.ars.usda.gov/main/main.htm

United States Food and Drug Administration, Center for Food Safety and
Applied Nutrition: http://www.cfsan.fda.gov/list.html

University of California, Davis: http://www.ucdavis.edu/index.html

University of California, Davis, California Institute of Food and Agricultural Research: http://aic.ucdavis.edu/

University of California, Davis, Robert Mondavi Institute for Wine and Food Science: http://www.news.ucdavis.edu/mondavi/iwfs_facts.html

University of Illinois, Department of Food Science and Human Nutrition: http://www.fshn.uiuc.edu/

University of Illinois, Functional Foods for Health Program: http://www.ag.uiuc.edu/~ffh/ffh.html

University of Massachusetts, Department of Food Science: http://www.umass.edu/foodsci/

University of Missouri, Columbia, Department of Food Science and Human Nutrition: http://outreach.missouri.edu/hes/food.htm

University of Missouri, Columbia, Missouri School of Journalism: http://journalism.missouri.edu/

University of Southern California, School of Pharmacy: http://www.usc.edu/schools/pharmacy/

Virginia Tech Center for Food and Nutrition Policy: http://www.vt.edu/

Food Safety Research Information Office: http://www.nal.usda.gov/fsrio/acad.htm

21

DESCRIPTION OF BUSINESS

Grocery Shopping, Cooking, or Nutrition Bargains with Video Podcasts

Help People to Shop for Nutrition, Lower the Costs of Foods and Groceries with Podcasts on Cutting Expenses, Finding Better Quality, and Getting More for Less

What do you think it costs per month for nutritious, healthy food to feed one person, and what do you think it costs per month for food for a family of four? To find out look at **Dr. Matt's Guide to Nutritious Survival Foods** Web site at: http://www.mysteriesofthemind.com/dr-matt.htm. Interestingly, the Web site advises, "Get a high quality sprouter, Sonic Bloom, and a decent cache of seeds. That will be your best bet for long-term survival if everything goes to the toilet."

What I found helpful on the site is the table noting the cost of buying nutritious and healthy foods for a family or for an individual. What's helpful about the site is that it states, "There are two costs listed for every food item. The first is cost per ounce, which will usually be listed in the upper left-hand corner of the tag on the grocery shelf."

Note that the detail of the Web site is very important to making a budget or plan. A short excerpt reads, "The first is cost per ounce, which will usually be listed in the upper left-hand corner of the tag on the grocery shelf."

According to *Dr. Matt's Guide to Nutritious Survival Foods* Web site, "buying larger cans is not always cheaper." The site lists the most relevant cost that you won't find easily elsewhere. It's the cost per hundred calories. In your budget and plan, list the calories you want to eat per meal. Then look up the most important information, which is the cost per hundred calories.

INCOME POTENTIAL

Charge people a flat fee for creating a customized grocery budget depending upon their income, location, number of people in the family, and special food needs. You can use comparative rates based on what bookkeepers, accountants, and financial planners charge to create a working budget for their clients. For example, you might charge $25, $35, $50, or $100 per budget. Or use a sliding scale. You might even try to get social services agencies to contract with you or even grocery chains to create printed budgets for foods depending upon family size.

More of interest to families interested in organic foods or special diets is a grocery budget or grocery buying plan with the latest prices printed on your customized budget. Sell the budgets online or distribute them to grocery chains.

GENERAL APTITUDE OR EXPERIENCE

You should enjoy developing budgets, looking at food comparatively, researching and packaging information as well as publishing or disseminating information. This business helps people cut expenses by customizing food budgets and telling people where to buy the food or grow it themselves. Survivalists also would be interested in food and grocery buying habits, research, demographics, and budgets.

EQUIPMENT NEEDED

You need to be able to print out the budgets on your computer printer. Budget-creating software or list-generating software is necessary unless you plan to write out a budget in fancy calligraphy, like a restaurant menu, with graphics. The quickest and cheapest way to go is by printing out monthly grocery budgets and offering them to supermarkets, food manufacturers, and social service agencies as well as to individual consumers.

You can create a database online or work through the regular mails or have your budgets sent by email to consumers who subscribe to your grocery budgeting service. Your goal is to help people cut food expenses and get more nutrition as well as higher quality nutrients from the foods available. Add cooking tips.

OPERATING YOUR BUSINESS

First gather any grocery pricing and buying habits information you'll need to develop your budget from marketing research firms. See **Dr. Matt's Guide to Nutritious Survival Foods** Web site at: http://www.mysteriesofthemind.com/

dr-matt.htm. Look at the tables on the Web site and decide whether the Web site's "Sample 30-day 'Bare-Bones' Grocery List for a Single Person" is what you need. With a little more than 20 dollars each week, the 30-day grand total grocery list for one person sums up to only **$82.64.**

Then look at the site's "Sample 90-Day Grocery List for a Family of Four." The Web site's sample 90-day grocery list grand total adds up to **$1421.19.**

How do these figures fit in your budget and plan for food expenses? Bookmark the Web site and study those totals. Compare them to your actual expenses and read Dr. Matt's excellent advice. How do your food expenses compare?

Note that food costs change with each passing year. Print out Dr. Matt's Guide to Nutritious Survival Foods and put it in a place where you'll see it daily, like on the side of your refrigerator and in the file where you keep your monthly food expenses budget. *Dr. Matt's Guide to Nutritious Survival Foods* contains recent food prices. The copyright year is 2004. Compare the prices you pay for your food with the cost of the foods listed in the guide.

Are you eating healthy, nutritious foods? How do survival foods compare with comfort foods? Are the same? Should they be? Do you grow your own vegetables? What's your soil like?

Is it free from toxic wastes such as decades-old dumped rocket fuel or other poisons? Think about how much you will spend on food costs. What type of budget and food list, guide, or table can give you more choices?

Now make a budget listing other expenses of living. What's the most important and powerful lesson you've learned from living?

RELATED OPPORTUNITIES

Talk to bookkeepers, financial planners, accountants, grocery store buyers for various food departments, food wholesalers, social service agencies, and people who grow their own food. Go to survivalists conventions and talk to vendors and supplies of natural food products.

Talk to buyers of produce and wholesalers supplying supermarkets. Bring together two different projects—budgeting and cutting expenses in food buying. Then talk to nutritionists to see what foods are required for health. Put all these loose ends together into one business.

You'll find a whole new entity—or business about survival foods and budgeting. You can give seminars or publish information on how to cut food expenses and get higher quality nutrition.

Start clubs for food buying research and making or growing food in nontraditional settings, such as what apartment dwellers can do without the ability to grow food in a backyard (community gardens, for example for whole neighborhoods).

ADDITIONAL INFORMATION

Food Certification Program (American Heart Association)
http://www.americanheart.org/presenter.jhtml?identifier=2115

Organic Consumers Association
http://www.organicconsumers.org/organic/usatoday31005.cfm

American Pregnancy Association
http://www.americanpregnancy.org/duringpregnancy/week6.htm

Guide to Gourmet Clubs
http://www.gourmetfoods101.com/search.aspx?keywords=Wine%20Clubs

Chef to Chef Marketplace (Food Clubs)
http://foodservice.chef2chef.net/classifieds/food-drink/month-clubs.htm

Clinical Medical Science (After School Food Clubs)
http://www.ncl.ac.uk/medi/research/nutrition/research_activity/past/food_clubs.htm

French Wine Explorers (Tours)
http://www.wine-tours-france.com/winetourspro.htm

Grocery Shop Online—While You Can (About Web site with search directories)
http://pcworld.about.com/news/Jan102001id37031.htm

22

DESCRIPTION OF BUSINESS

Demonstration Video Podcast Production

(Producing Video Podcast Demonstrations of Products, Appliances, and/or of Video And Film Scripts For Actors, Producers, Or Writers)

How does a producer know whether a script is worth shooting on expensive film? How does the director know the script dialogue makes an impact on an audience? The answer is to test the script first by taping it on a less costly videocassette.

For a fee, you produce a demonstration video tape called a demo tape using live actors and special effects on a low budget—for any scriptwriter or producer who wonders what a particular script would look like on the more expensive film. The producer or scriptwriter pays you the fee in advance.

You work within your budget to produce the "movie" or "documentary" on relatively lower cost video tape. Actors usually are students or willing to work for low-pay or school credit to get acting experience on tape. Special effects are kept to a minimum or students in multimedia courses are employed for college credit or lower pay to create minimal special effects. You can also create video dramatizations of romance novels or serialized stories adapted to script format.

Taping a script for a producer or writer usually means someone wants to see how the script looks on tape before they commit to expensive film. Or the tape is intended to be sold by mail order to specialized readers, such as those who buy romance novels through mail order.

Readers of romance, religious romance, or suspense novels, or serialized magazine stories may want to see their favorite stories turned into scripts and dramatized on tape by live actors. The readers can play the tapes at home after they've finished reading the books.

Mailing lists can come from markets where readers order books by mail. Niche markets include Christian romances, science fiction, children's stories, short stories appealing to certain audiences, mystery and suspense, and time travel or metaphysical novels as well as stories about current issues in the news.

INCOME POTENTIAL:

You set the fee you will charge someone to produce a-feature-length or docudrama length script on videotape instead of film. It should net you a profit above the cost of the post-production tape editing, actors, props, special effects, taping crew, tape, and sound equipment fees.

Whereas filming an ultra low budget "guerrilla film" of a 90-minute script could cost you anywhere from $12,000 to $180,000 and up, videotaping could cut your fees in half or more using broadcast quality tape. You'll have to estimate projected cable television broadcast grosses if you take a cut of the production fee instead of a flat fee for expensing in taping and editing. It's easier just to ask for a flat fee for expenses plus a 15 percent royalty if the tape is copied and sold to home video viewers.

If you sell dramatized videos of books in print, you should know that Western priced its <u>Golden Books</u> video line very cheap. Such videos sold at $8.95 to $9.95 each in the mid eighties. More than two million videos of its first eight titles were shipped to about 30,000 video and book stores.

If you send your video tapes to book stores, be aware that low-priced cassettes sell. Keep your videocassette prices under $15. Most videos are priced in categories of $24.95, $19.95, $14.95, or less. The less sells more.

BEST LOCALE TO OPERATE THE BUSINESS:

Mail order tapes can sell from any location. However, Hollywood, San Francisco, San Diego, San Jose (Silicon Valley), Chicago, Atlanta and New York are centers where the entertainment industry flourishes and where actors and special effects people are easily found.

Operate anyplace where you can find an abundance of actors, scripts, taping facilities, props, and special effects people working with videotape and/or interactive multimedia.

Los Angeles area and southern California or San Francisco are the most popular as is New York and Atlanta. You can network with the hub of the cable television industry and the information superhighway of multimedia centered in Silicon Valley (San Jose).

The telephone, computer, and video industries are uniting over networks such as Internet for computers and the cable television industry for broadcast. Contact bookstores if you make videos from books already in print or toy stores if you focus on children's scripts.

TRAINING REQUIRED:

A course in financing video production is helpful. Read the books: <u>Home Video: Producing for the Home Market</u>, <u>Film and Video Budgets</u>, and <u>The Independent Film and Videomakers Guide</u>, by Michael Wiese, published by Michael Wiese Film/Video, PO Box 406, Westport, CT 06881 or take an extension or adult education course in home video production, financing, and distribution.

GENERAL APTITUDE OR EXPERIENCE:

Being organized is necessary to stay inside your budget. So is finding and paying for the best studio location and getting your client to pay all expenses on time. Producing a home video of someone else's script is almost the same as making a feature film on a smaller scale at a lower cost.

Getting along with people as well as working within your budget is wise. It helps if you like to read or write scripts yourself or have had acting and directing experience.

EQUIPMENT NEEDED:

You'll need your video camera, tape, sound equipment, post-production editing equipment, special effects, a director, actors, make up artists, studio location rentals, props, and reservations and permits for the location of taping. Don't forget liability insurance for yourself as well as for the crew and actors, catered food while taping, and enough in the budget to hire security.

OPERATING YOUR BUSINESS:

How about producing video podcasts of movie scripts as a demonstration before actual funding is put into a theatrical production? Or on a smaller scale, produce how-to video podcasts demonstrating a product, such as how to operate an appliance or gadget? Let's go back to what had been advertised in flyers back in the early 1990s to give you an idea or inspiration of the possibilities of what can be demonstrated by video—from tapes of the past decades to online Web-based "push technology" by 1996, to streaming video of 2000 to current video podcasts downloaded to varieties of mobile video players, video compression software for Web-based video, and video books on DVDs.

Back in the early 1990s, a flyer arrived in my mail from one video production company specializing in production, acting, camera, makeup, studio location, and special effects. The W.A.V.E. The company's direct mail piece read back then, "We provide custom videos for the action/adventure and horror enthusiast! Bring your characters to life!

The flyer mailed to me unsolicited in 1991 advertised then that for $75 "we will tape a scene from your script for your approval." The firm offered a sampler tape of their own for $12 (1991 price) that included footage from previous productions that showcased their special effects, action, costuming, and makeup.

A coupon inside asked the reader to certify you're an adult over 21. No phone number was listed on the early 1990s flyer. W.A.V.E. produced screenplays on videotape from finished scripts. Before a producer films a script or screenplay on 16mm or 35mm film, he or she could see it first on videotape. The person submitting the script paid for the production.

Fast now forward to current times. It' wonderful to be able to view and critique a screenplay already produced on videotape to see how it would look on film. Your video podcasting show could offer a video recording service for a niche industry (such as scriptwriters) tailored for the times and situations today in the world of iPods, Web sites, and small, mobile players. In addition, a trailer can be created by editing the most impressive scenes from the videotape to form the trailer. The outcome would look like a preview of coming attractions.

Nowadays, a writer can hire a similar video production company to produce the entire low-budget screenplay on DVD or saved to a computer's hard disk drive or on videotape instead of expensive film. One of the reasons for having actors and producers create an inexpensive videotape of a screenplay is to show prospective producers whether it's worth shooting on film.

Another reason for creating a video first before filming is to test dialogue for impact. Every word of dialogue must present a problem, reveal a character, advance the plot, or provide a set up for coming action. A videotape allows a writer to cut out too much exposition or excess words.

The videotaped screenplay could be used to analyze what works and what doesn't without wasting many takes on expensive film. Copies of the videotape could be sent to producers along with the written script as a marketing tool.

A reader may scan a script quickly and decide there's too much written exposition. Only when it's viewed on video tape, can such a decision be made where to cut. Too many times decisions made about what looks good on paper didn't look good on video tape.

TARGET MARKET:

You want to market to scriptwriters testing dialogue for impact and low-budget film producers. You can also target actors and special effects independents who want a demo tape of their talents to use as a portfolio when applying for work.

RELATED VIDEO OPPORTUNITIES:

Approach novelists to ask if you can be a catalyst and bring the novelist and a budding screenwriter together to put that published or unpublished romance or children's novel or story on video tape and make the characters come alive for the home viewing audience. Also, you can work with animators to create children's programming on tape. Capture children's picture books through special effects and computer animation on videotape and market through mail order to teachers and parents.

Contact publishers producing specialized videocassettes, libraries stocking videos, and mail order houses such as Publishers Central Bureau. The Videotape Catalog and Sallyforth Video offer catalogs containing the videos of the very small as well as the large video producers.

If you're going to use animation in your demo tapes, hire a freelance animator to teach you the ropes while the person creates a minimum number of animated special effects. Or join a computer animation club. Pick up a local computer club magazine found in computer supply stores and in adult education classes.

There are always animation software users groups with people ready to teach you or tutor you in animation. Or hungry animators may offer to put their experimental animation on tape for you. If you can afford to hire someone for pay, it's all the better. That way you learn by watching what they're doing combining computer special effects with video imagery.

First find your specialty. Then begin to network within that specialty with video makers and computer animation specialists. Meetings of animation software and video user's clubs usually are held on weekends or evenings at some of the stores that sell computer animation software. Video animation is created on a computer through simulations and graphic designs. Then it's transferred to video tape.

Also query Lieberman Enterprises and Handelman Company. These companies place videos with discount and mass merchant chains. Attend the video and comics annual conventions.

If you are or know storytellers, you can put stories on tape. Take a look at the wonderful National Storytelling Catalog of recorded stories offered by the National Storytelling Network at: http://www.storynet.org/.

ADDITIONAL INFORMATION:

StoryNet
National Storytelling Network
132 Boone Street
Suite 5
Jonesborough, TN 37659
http://www.storynet.org/
E-Mail: nsn@storynet.org

Ethnic Storytelling and Folklore
Click on the Web links at StoryNet's Links List at:
http://www.storynet.org/resources/links.htm#Ethnic
These links include:

19th-Century German Stories
http://www.vcu.edu/hasweb/for/menu.html

Australian Storytelling
http://www.AustralianStorytelling.org.au
The Web page of Australian storytelling features Australian storytellers, stories, guilds, events, and links.

Bodhran Brothers
http://www.bodhranbrothers.com
Irish Music and Stories

California Indian Storytelling Association
http://www.cistory.org

Celtic Folklore—original Celtic Folklore, Legends and Lore
http://www.belinus.co.uk/folklore/Homeextra.htm

Family Folklore Discovery
http://www.educate.si.edu/migrations/seek2/family.html

Folk Tales
http://www.pitt.edu/%7Edash/folktexts.html
Collection of folk tales

Folktales and Legends from Britain
http://www.mysteriousbritain.co.uk/index.html

Folktales from Many Lands, Collected by Peace Corps Volunteers
http://www.peacecorps.gov/wws/students/folktales

Hasidic Stories by Sterna Citron
http://www.613.org/hasid.html
This page is a collection of Hasidic stories read aloud.

Jaliyaa Storytelling
http://www.wovenweb.org
Site examines the ancient West African Bardic tradition known as Jaliyaa;

Joy of Storytelling
http://www.joyofstorytelling.com
Storycards for Passover and Hanukkah using narrative, Bibliodrama, personal story and questions as story prompts.

Kashmiri Folktales
http://www.ikashmir.org/Folk/index.html

Korean Folktales
http://www.csun.edu/~hcedu004/

Nature Story
http://www.naturestory.com

Old Japanese Tales
http://www.dl.ulis.ac.jp/oldtales/

Powerful Symbols
http://www.powersource.com/gallery/objects/
This page contains Native American animal stories and information.

Rabbi's Daughter
http://www.rabbisdaughter.com
Ozzie Nogg writes and tells personal stories based on her life growing up as a rabbi's daughter.

Story Socks
http://pages.zdnet.com/storysocks
This site is the home base for STORY SOCKS. It's the website of Dale Pepin a retired Northern Ontario

StoryBag
http://storybag.net/
Folktales using puppets, magic and story theater. Jewish, African, Earth Friendly, Character Education folktales are my specialties. Storytelling Workshops

Taos Storytelling Festival
www.somostaos.org
5th annual Taos Storytelling Festival. Oct. 15th and 16th, 2004. Taos, New Mexico.

Texas Scrapbook
http://www.texancultures.utsa.edu/publications/scrapbook/index.htm
Click on "Storytelling" in this _Texas Scrapbook_ for a discussion of the development, uses, and meaning of storytelling along with three "pretests"

Wisdom and Spiritual Tales
http://www.wisdomtales.com
Offers a wisdom story every other month from various spiritual and cultural traditions

World Mythology
http://www.artsmia.org/mythology/
Minneapolis Institute of Art World Mythology

WAVE Productions
http://groups.northwestern.edu/wave/
WAVE Productions is a self-supporting, not-for-profit student theatre company operating primarily on Northwestern University's Evanston Campus. WAVE Productions exists to share the stories of the past and present in order to open the door to a better future.

Digital Wave Productions
http://www.wavepro.com/index2.html

Alternative Media
http://www.pathtofreedom.com/links/altmedia/alternativemedia.shtml

Independent Media Center
News Resources Links
http://www.aloha.net/~davidht/koloa/cenews.htm

Video Databank
Video Data Bank is the leading resource in the United States for videotapes by and about contemporary artists.
http://www.vdb.org/

The Video Project: Films and Videos For a Safe and Sustainable World
Post Office Box 411376
San Francisco, CA 94141-1376
http://videoproject.com/

Paper Tiger TV/Deep Dish
http://www.papertiger.org/index.php?name=faq
http://www.papertiger.org/index.php?name=about
http://web.mit.edu/course/21/21f.853/africa-film/0509.html

Point of View
http://www.pointofview.org/aboutus.html

National Federation of Community Broadcasters
http://www.nfcb.org/index.jsp

National Youth in Radio Training Project
http://www.nfcb.org/projects/nyrtp/index.jsp

Empowerment Project
http://www.empowermentproject.org/
8218 Farrington Mill Rd.
Chapel Hill NC 27517

GlobalVision
575 Eighth Avenue, Suite 2200
New York, NY 10018
http://www.globalvision.org/

23

DESCRIPTION OF BUSINESS:

Employee Screening Service Video Podcast (Personnel Interviewing or Job and Image Coaching)

You create video podcast personnel profiles and screen job applicants for employers. Personnel profiling and employee screening services protect an employer's identity and save the cost of the time and labor usually spent on interviewing dozens of job applicants for a single job opening.

You will screen and evaluate job seekers using your video camera. Each video profile will be accompanied by a typed 500- to 750-word profile from in-person interviews on video tape.

The employer generally will spend only sixty seconds viewing the brief video interview or skimming the profile which takes the place of an old fashioned resume. Therefore, the video should emphasize first impression, immediate impact. Keep the videos short, but complete. The average recommended length is under seven minutes.

INCOME POTENTIAL:

You can charge employers $2O to $75 per hour for in-person interviews and $50 to $100 to generate a video tape accompanied by two-to-three-page typed profile reports. You can also charge low rates to job applicants and work from high volume.

For example, charging only $25 to put a video resume on tape for a job applicant will result in a higher volume of business than trying to get an employer to pay a $100 fee for a screening service to save the employer's time. There usually are more job applicants than there are employers who ask for video interviews from independent personnel screeners.

A recommended beginner's strategy is to start by offering-low-cost video profiles to job applicants for a wide variety of occupations and then obtain a secondary market by offering to save employer's interviewing time by pre-screening applicants on video for special hard-to-find job categories.

BEST LOCALE TO OPERATE THE BUSINESS:

A personnel profiling video service operates best in large cities where there is a high turnover of personnel and quality jobs exist. For example, video interviews go over well in cities where the high tech (computer) industry seeks well-qualified specialists, such as San Jose and San Francisco—or in Los Angeles, Las Vegas, New York, Chicago, Houston, Orlando, Miami, and Atlanta, where the entertainment industry seeks creative people, entertainers, media people, and performers in specialized categories. One example is the hiring of corporate animators by advertising agencies where their special effects are wanted on video as part of a portfolio.

Video personnel screening can also be used to track old age job discrimination and race or ethnic discrimination by editing on a separate tape all rejected employees with the same amount of training to see if they fall into a certain age or ethnic group. It's important not to put the highly experienced on the same tape with those who need training and have no experience in the occupation for which they're being interviewed.

TRAINING REQUIRED:

You could read books on the subject of interviewing personnel and screening, or take an extended studies course in human resource management or interviewing. A working knowledge of your video camera and editing equipment is necessary.

Ask how does the person you're taping feel about job security? There will be a different attitude coming from the job applicant depending on whether that person is applying for a more scarce permanent job or more numerous temporary jobs offered to contingency professionals and independents on two-year work contracts.

You'll have to learn to work with downwardly mobile middle-aged professionals on camera trying to make a good impression without revealing their hidden feelings about being downsized at their peak performance, discriminated against because of their aging appearance, and probably angry at the younger competition who insists they make themselves look younger.

On video, image is everything. Part of your training will have to be to make these insecure people feel at ease so the employer viewing the tape won't feel their grief over losing a job some of them held for more than 25 years.

For many workers, a job has become the only family they have. When it's lost, that feeling of separation and emptiness makes an impact on video that employers use to reject the applicant. The video profiler's job is to create a charismatic, positive image of energy behind the applicant, portraying the interviewee in the best light while remaining authentic and loyal to the employer.

Question yourself: Are you working for the potential employee or the employer? When you decide whose side you're on, train yourself to serve the needs of your client.

Find out by talking with recruiters and other profilers how they interview and what they look for. Your best training source is to interview employers on videotape to see what they want in a prospective employee—what their preferred employee should be like. Find out what kind of experience the employer seeks or whether training is available on the job.

GENERAL APTITUDE OR EXPERIENCE:

You need an interest in talking to people and making them feel at ease in your presence. Experience taping people on video is helpful. You should be able to make a list of questions you want to ask at the interview. Ask the employer what questions would be most helpful.

The employer knows the subject matter about the job skills, so it's up to the person hiring you to either create the questions for you or give you enough background on the job tasks and skills or personality requirements to ask the right questions.

You need tact enough to find out whether the employer wants to pay for an applicant's long experience. Or is the employer seeking someone with less experience in the hope that the applicant will accept lower pay in exchange for on-the-job training?

EQUIPMENT NEEDED:

You need a video camera and editing equipment to take out redundant information or images you don't want to present to viewers. A personal computer and printer are helpful.

If you're on a shoestring budget, an old typewriter will do. However, you're expected to keep a database of client's profiles on disk or on file that any employee may access electronically, so it's wisest to buy a computer when you buy your video camera, as the two really work in tandem to create money for you by presenting profiles of job applicants to employers. You will also need a telephone.

The estimated cost is $2,000 to $5,500. If you're on a really tight budget, you could start with only your interviews on tape and use the client's own resume or portfolio. It's best to provide your own summarized resume on your business letterhead, along with a video tape of many employees interviewed briefly. That way, the employer can scan several people at one brief sitting categorized under one umbrella heading according to occupation or skills.

Besides your video camera and editing equipment (to insert and cut out unwanted images), if you choose to go on disk and get a computer to help you market your videos, you'll need word processing software, blank disks, paper supplies with letterheads, business cards, and other personalized stationery for advertising.

A box of ten computer disks costs about $10. The estimated cost for software is $200 to $400 for one word processing program (like Microsoft Word for Windows) and one spreadsheet or data base program (like Excel) to keep your records.

You'll need video recording media to produce video podcasts about 30 minutes in length to hold your interviews. Don't email employers sites for downloading podcasts that are longer than 30 minutes. Most interviews take only five to seven minutes.

Why some employers recommend that each interview be kept under seven minutes long is because the average viewer's attention span is approximately seven minutes or less per scene. In television, commercials are inserted every ten minutes.

Most scenes on video run a few minutes before there is a cutaway to something else. To avoid talking heads, do quick cuts to other parts of the person being interviewed, such as a portfolio of creative work, image of a college degree or close up of transcripts or financial reports of sales success, or any other achievement that can be shown on video.

OPERATING YOUR BUSINESS:

Personnel profiles on videotape are not resumes. They are personal evaluations of job applicants recorded by an independent interviewer and submitted to the employer. Profiles are used when employers do not wish to make public their search for job applicants. They put the interviewing and screening in the hands of an independent third party who creates personnel profiles of candidates and recommends certain applicants after a thorough screening and checking of references.

In a profile, which is not seen by the job applicant, the third party evaluates the applicant and presents the applicant's qualifications. The profile contains comments and recommendations about the applicant's appearance, qualifications, personality, and image.

In short, the purpose of a personnel screening profile video is to create an independent and objective judgment. The employer buys such a video in order to be informed of what qualities an employer seeks in an employee, such as skills, experience, personality, enthusiasm, charisma to draw customers, sales, financial, or creative ability, and image.

The profile of each applicant will be videotaped during an interview—either an employment interview or a stress interview. Accompanying the videotape will be a brief profile entered on your word processing program and printed as a report after the video screening.

Besides a video, there always should be something in writing or on disk that an employer can file with the tape to refer to quickly without having to fast forward through all the interviews.

The videocassette and brief report is sent electronically or by regular mail to the employer. And you can also offer company video profiles to job seekers wishing to evaluate a prospective employer.

TARGET MARKET:

Markets that would benefit by a personnel video profiling service are those that don't maintain a personnel department with interviewers. These include the professional offices of attorneys, physicians, architects, engineers, advertising agencies, restaurants, and most "glamour" jobs that need specialized evaluation.

RELATED VIDEO OPPORTUNITIES:

Human relations departments, business travelers, and image coaches could be significant audiences for visual demonstrations of interviewing experiences via mobile video podcast. In a visual experience such as employee screening, you're video recording and podcasting people competing against one another for the scarce resources available. Use your video camera to train job applicants in how to have an interview in adult education classes, working closely with career counselors and school consultants.

You can specialize in working with specialized populations such as new graduates, seniors, the disabled, special ethnic or new immigrant groups, displaced homemakers, middle-aged executives, or any population you target.

Or work solely with employers to screen the thousands of applicants who apply for certain types of jobs that bring long waiting lines. Or you can tape people who must interview for a variety of situations, such as becoming a new citizen, seeking a job overseas, or trying to enter certain professions or schools that screen out the majority of applicants.

Use your industrial-quality camcorder to screen out people or for selecting only a few qualified applicants for certain types of jobs such as casting for theatrical products or video and films, law enforcement, military, professional, scholarship applicants, dating, or contest applicants. You can videotape competitive interviews for any contest in many categories—from scholarship to athletics.

ADDITIONAL INFORMATION:

Society for Human Resource Management
606 North Washington St.
Alexandria, VA 22314

International Personnel Management Association
1617 Duke St.
Alexandria, VA 22314

Association for Human Resource System Professionals
PO Box 801646
Dallas, TX 75380-1646

Institute for International Human Resources
606 N. Washington St.
Alexandria, VA 22314
(same address and phone as Society for Human Resource Management)

24

DESCRIPTION OF BUSINESS:

Low Cost Digital Talent Management by Video Podcast

Focus your video podcasts on showing people how to decide and make choices by comparing pros and cons against personal likes and dislikes. It can be any subject enhanced by talent and celebrity endorsement from cutting expenses to turning doll houses into pet palaces. Present tips offered by talent.

Find the talent by opening your own video and software talent agency. Concentrate on providing models, announcers, broadcast journalists, public speakers, actors, comedians, musicians, entertainers, dancers, scriptwriters, artists, camera operators, and technicians for television and radio commercials, fashion shows, and film productions to other video producers and directors.

Provide public relations services for the video, music, television, theater, fashion, corporate, education, nonprofit, healthcare, government, science, high-tech, and film industries. Focus your talent search on topics related to cutting expenses and/or financial planning or budgeting, tips for cleaning, or nutrition and shopping.

BEST LOCALE TO OPERATE THE BUSINESS:

Video talent agents need to locate where there is a high demand for video work—big cities such as Los Angeles, New York, San Francisco, and Chicago. Software talent agents can choose to combine their scouting, marketing, or 'agenting' with video talent agents because of the marriage of video and computer software as the information superhighway develops the interactive multimedia field.

Software talent agents will find the Silicon Valley, San Jose, CA and San Francisco area in heavy demand of their services to seek out video as well as software talent and develop it for entertainment, learning, business, education/training, or industrial uses.

TRAINING REQUIRED:

To be a video talent agent, you need to learn how to locate and sell other people's talents in the video field as producers, designers, directors, writers, "casting agents," prop designers, and distributors. To be a software talent agent, you need to know how to recruit and sell software designers and their ideas to video and multimedia pointurers and the video game industry.

Learn about video and multimedia in any community college or subscribe to the multimedia and video trade magazines, but to recruit and market other people's ideas and videos, you need to have sales training or sales experience, or at least be interested in marketing and sales and human resource development within the video industry.

A good place to start is to get in touch with the Video Software Dealer's Association, the Association of Independent Commercial Producers, the Media Research Directors Association, the next decade spin-off of the 1990s Videotex Industry Association, National Cable Television Association, and Women in Cable, International Simulation and Gaming Association, North American Simulation and Games Association, Association of Talent Agents, the National Conference of Personal Managers, and the Society of Photographers and Artists. Their addresses are listed at the end of this section.

To train yourself without formal school coursework in sales, volunteer your services and help to any or all of these professional associations, work on teams at conventions, volunteer for panels and to write for association newsletters or publications. Help to recruit other people whose talents you must sell to other producers, directors, and corporations or for contingent and temporary work at video events.

GENERAL APTITUDE OR EXPERIENCE:

You need a knack for sales. Your job as a video software talent manager is to market talent—video and/or software talent to producers and directors and corporate video departments. In the case of software talent, you'll be dealing with software designers who create video and computer games.

Contact vendors and suppliers at conventions. Instead of using your industrial-quality camcorder directly, you'll be selling, recruiting, publicizing, and marketing video talent to those who hire such talent.

EQUIPMENT NEEDED:

A video camera is required to create, produce, and sell your client's talent portfolio. You'll need the standard video editing equipment and a VCR as well as a computer. You can combine video software talent management with managing photographers and artists or writers as well as music video specialists and special effects talent.

You need a video camera and editing equipment, phones, fax machines, modems, and a personal computer with a printer. The estimated cost of minimum equipment is about $4,000 if you're starting to run the business from a spare room in your home.

Besides your video camera, you need a word-processing program, such as Microsoft Word for Windows or the equivalent for the Mac, a data-base manager, computer discs for writing, paper supplies, and standard forms for contracts. The estimated cost of a word-processing program is $100–$250. You'll need a database program such as Excel, which comes with Microsoft Office software. Video equipment is equally as important as a computer if you're planning to run a video and software talent management business on a shoestring budget from your home.

OPERATING YOUR BUSINESS:

You can open a video software talent management agency that presents various kinds of video, photographic, animation, software game design, and artistic talent to video, film, infomercial, computer game, and commercial producers, television and radio stations, advertising agencies, and department stores for video fashion shows. You can handle MTV musicians for bookings, public speakers, and other performers for conventions, from artists and actors to television voice-over narrators and announcers.

Do a mass mailing of press kits and brochures to everyone you want for a client. This mailing will include producers, fashion-show coordinators, and advertising-agency executives.

Any client who can use your referrals of video software talent may fill out a form that will give you data on their talent needs. Ask your respondents to send you promotional material on their talent needs and a description of what they are selling.

Expect only a one to five percent return on your survey. You can enter the correct information regarding video and software talent needs into your computer. This information will appear later in your software search as you scroll through your talent bank or video talent job hotline to see who's available to match the needs of clients. Keep a video talent manager's job bank in your database or file.

Once you take down a request for talent, you can operate like a home-based temporary employment service for video talent. Your clients will be from all areas of business, education, and entertainment. You'll enter a request for particular talent, process the request, and pull out of your file the best talent for each new video-related job.

You can charge for portfolio preparation services such as video auditions and video screen tests, photos, press releases, and software package design or even resume writing.

Your job is to use your camera to tape other talent and create an image so that you can sell your client's talent to other clients who will hire them for particular video and/or video software or photographic work.

You can charge a percentage of earnings for placement in a permanent job or charge the party hiring your talent in a temporary job—like an employment service. When dealing with video writers, charge a commission on each script you sell for them to producers.

You're a video sales agent managing talent rather than a producer yourself, although you will produce video tapes of your talent and create their portfolios for a fee.

You can also offer publicity to producers, MTV directors, actors, and other talent or artists and writers. You can generate video press releases, transfer photos to video tape, DVD, CD, or to your computer's hard disk drives. Create video resumes on CDs or DVDs or PowerPoint slide shows of portfolios and features to publicize your client and the talent you refer to employers. Save the portfolios to discs or to the Web.

For a fee you can do a software search of videos to obtain a certain type of video for a client, much like a video librarian. In summarized point, you can maintain a video library or database of video titles in your computer or files.

Perform software talent searches for special people in the video field, such as prop or stunt people animators, or special effects designers. Your job is to market video people as well as entertainers, models, public speakers, actors, and any other specialist who works in the video industry.

INCOME POTENTIAL:

Charge a 10- to 35-percent commission on all earnings from your job referrals. An agent finds jobs or assignments, usually temporary, for video producers. The average commission is 20 percent. You can charge a flat fee of $100 to $250 for photography and resume-writing services to create a portfolio for each client for presentation to producers. You can expect to earn an hourly fee of $25 for entertainment public relations.

TARGET MARKET:

Focus on video talent, photographers, artists, music television specialists, performers, models, software designers, animators, writers, artists, producers, directors, and narrators as well as any voice-over and acting talent, video editors, and distributors.

RELATED VIDEO OPPORTUNITIES:

Photographer's agents and software talent managers are related in preparation, to the video software talent agent's career. You can be a video talent agent managing casting directors for video productions.

Act as an agent for video writers. Represent digital and video artists or music video producers if you can apprentice with or become a student intern or extern with upstart music video production companies.

Sample Video Podcast Resume

Software Talent Agent or Manager

Name

Address

Career Goal: Video Software Talent Agent Staff Position

Video Software Experience

-Wrote book on video software talent agent practices for public relations agency owners, published by West & West. Marketing Promotions Press, London. England, 1988.

-Weekly national newspaper columnist for The Talent Agent's News (for owners of software talent agencies).

Video Software Agenting Experience

-1980-Present: Account Executive, Dynamic Software Talent Agency Inc., Eugene, OR.

Ten years' experience operating a vide software talent agency for absentee owner with over 150 clients. Specialist in marketing and promoting patented and copyrighted videos and software for independent video producers, software video and computer game designers, interactive multimedia producers, corporate animators, and consultants.

Abilities

-Find software designers for leading manufacturers.

-Package software created by independent contractors.

-Recruit software talent for software firms.

-Copyright and patent software for designers.

-Refer software designers and engineers to jobs.

-Consult and counsel software talent seeking markets.

-Create promotions, publicity, ad campaigns, marketing programs, videos with own camera, and press kits for software designers, producers, artists, or manufacturers.

-Train video producers and software designers in packaging, distributing, marketing, and selling their videos or software for the entertainment, educational, and game markets. Recruit and place writers and video talent.

-Track software audiences for market research.

-Research talent markets and create mailing lists.

-Locate publishers and producers for software writers, multimedia or video artists, and software designers.

EDUCATION

Master of Arts in English (Writing emphasis)

University of _____City_____State__ Year____

References on Request

◆   ◆   ◆

ADDITIONAL INFORMATION:

Video Software Dealers Association
303 Harper Dr.
Morristown, NJ 08057-3229

Association of Talent Agents
9255 Sunset Blvd.
Los Angeles, CA 90069

National Conference of Personal Managers
210 E. 51st St.
New York, NY 10022

Society of Photographers and Artists
Representatives (Agents)
1123 Broadway, #914
New York, NY 10010

Videon/International Association of Video
1440 N St., NW, Ste. 601
Washington, DC 20005

International Television Association
6311 North O'Connor Rd. DB51
Irving, TX 75039

Training Media Association
198 Thomas Johnson Dr.
Folk, MD 21702

Software Publishers Association
1703 M St. NW, Ste. 700
Washington, DC 20036

American Telemarketing Association
5000 Van Nuys Blvd., #300
Sherman Oaks, CA 91403

Multimedia Publishers Group
Advanced Strategies
60 Cutter Mill Rd., Ste. 502
Great Neck, NY 11021

Optical Publishing Association
PO Box 21268
Columbus, OH 43221

Institute for International Human Resources
606 N. Washington St.
Alexandria, VA 22314

Electronic Artists Group
PO Box 580783
Memphis, MN 55458

25

DESCRIPTION OF BUSINESS:

Digital Dating Service via Video Podcast

Busy people have difficulty finding a mate because it is so hard to make the right love connection. Let your video tape do the matching. You cannot guarantee marriage will result, but you can mail your clients a profile sheet of their prospective match if they are subscribing members of your digital, video or combination video/digital/audio and computer dating service.

INCOME POTENTIAL:

Single persons may subscribe to your video podcast and computerized dating service for $200 to $400 per year. This fee will guarantee that they receive at least one or more video tapes with names and telephone numbers per week to call for dates.

If you plan to use your video camera to run a marriage brokerage service rather than a video dating service, there will be fewer matches and more in-depth video interviews of prospective marriage matches with the appropriate background check on video accompanied by a signed letter of permission from the client to approve the background check using the methods of a private detective for credibility on video.

If you want to make big money, you can run an exclusive video matchmaking service and charge a $100,000 fee for romantically matching the superrich with marriage in mind. Your video clients may come from the ranks of foreign royalty, wealthy industrialists from around the world, American professionals and business owners, actors, politicians, TV and film producers, and anyone with little time and lots of money to find exactly the right mate by video screen test.

BEST LOCALE TO OPERATE THE BUSINESS:

Your best bet is to operate your business where there are an abundance of singles. Check the number of singles magazines, newspapers, and personal ads appearing in your local media. Find out what cities have the most singles, and where most of the matchmakers are operating successfully—and why.

You can do informational interviews with satisfied clients as well as operators of introduction services to find out why they picked various locations. Visit the singles clubs and find out how many singles in which age groups are in specific cities.

Network with other introduction services owners and study the competition. If you're running an ethnic or religious-based video introduction service, it's more important to find out which cities and neighborhoods attract the particular group you're helping.

Some of the singles, ethnic, religious, women's, men's, behavior- and relationship-oriented magazines have published surveys to find out which cities have the most singles, the cheapest places to live, find a job, (or retire to) and who is most likely to use a video dating or matrimonial introduction service.

You might even get by opening a video dating service for such specialized populations as those people who have specific needs, earn high incomes, or those with certain time requirements, such as night shift workers. People in certain professions may want to date others in similar occupations. Or match by personality preferences and other similar traits.

TRAINING REQUIRED:

You'll probably want to learn how to operate your video camera, editing equipment, and VCR, your computer for matching people and mailing letters, and books on how to run a small business from home or office.

As far as matching people, read books on how to become a marriage broker or on how to run a dating service. Interview owners of video dating services and join their professional associations. Subscribe to publications of business associations for marriage brokers and dating service owners, and speak to a lot of singles about what they want in a video dating service.

Study the personal ads in newspapers where singles advertise for dating and meeting a marriage-minded significant other for a deep and meaning relationship. Visit singles clubs, singles groups and seminars, and interview members.

You can specialize in certain religious or ethnic groups, in young professionals, or senior citizens, or in any niche single market you choose—such as single pet lovers, vegetarians, orthodox Jews, college educated, travel-oriented, or book readers. Know your market and make it as niche-oriented or as wide and general as you wish.

GENERAL APTITUDE OR EXPERIENCE:

A video matchmaker must love to interview people and bring people together to form loving relationships. You must have the courage of a private detective to check on people's backgrounds, and understand how to bring out the best qualities in people on videotape. After all, you're selling people as potential dates or mates in an infomercial video through non-broadcast television. Most of the tapes will go to people's homes or be viewed by singles clubs. For anyone appearing on video tape, you need a signed letter of permission that the person on tape knows where the video will be mailed.

EQUIPMENT NEEDED:

You need a video camera and editing equipment, a personal computer and word processor, a printer, and a telephone. The estimated cost is $1,500 for the computer and $700 for the printer.

You should have blank disks, report paper, mailing-list software, and a merge program, available for almost any computer or word processor. The estimated cost of software is $200 to $500 for mailing-list and merge programs. You will need a list of single people, and you need to know their ages. You can purchase this list from a list broker for less than $100, or you can create your own from research and advertisements in singles publications.

OPERATING YOUR BUSINESS:

A video dating or marital matching service utilizes a video camera, VCR, editing equipment, and a personal computer word processor by using mailing lists and video interviews to pair off clients. Your video subscribers will describe to you the kind of person they are looking for. The file in your word processor searches until it sorts out by age, status, income, and other information an appropriate date. Interview and check your candidates before you put their names into your file. Ask about the following characteristics.

1) Race, including Caucasian, Black, Oriental, Latin, or Other (specify).

2) Age.

3) Height.

4) Sex.

5) Dependents: none; one or more.

6) Marital status: divorced or separated; widowed; never married.

7) Religion (specify).

8) Smoking habits: None; if any, then describe.

9) Average cost of evening out: less than five dollars; five to ten dollars; ten to twenty dollars; more than twenty dollars.

10) Education: grade school; high school; some college; degree (specify).

11) Occupation and interests, including hobbies or volunteer work.

12) Personality: introvert; extrovert; dominant; submissive; moody; warm; temperamental; carefree; generous; shy; reserved; self-assured; serious.

13) Disposition: independent; cheerful; sociable; talkative; fearful; quiet; passive; nervous; energetic; easily discouraged; neat.

14) Politics; ultraconservative; conservative; middle-of-the-road; liberal; ultraliberal.

15) Income level: wealthy; over $40,000; over $25,000; over $12,000; under $12,000.

16) Where do you like to go on a date: movies; dances; lunch; dinner; driving; bars; concerts; plays; group activities; weekend trips; sports events; friends' homes; outdoor activities.

17) Which activity do you enjoy most: reading; driving; card playing; housework; dancing; talking; camping; working; loafing; gardening; thinking; watching television

18) Language spoken usually. (Specify foreign language or English.)

This profile data is put on video tape along with a five-minute video interview of your client. The same information is fed into your computer, and you then arrange a date. When the client agrees that you have made an acceptable match, your fee is paid.

Always agree in writing as to what an acceptable match means to your client. It may take you several introductions to satisfy your clients.

TARGET MARKET:

Clients will be unmarried men and women in almost every age range. You may have clients from all occupations and from a wide variety of educational back grounds or focus on niche markets—the very rich, all income levels, certain ethnicities or religions, selected professions, or different age groups.

RELATED VIDEO OPPORTUNITIES:

Match business partners on videotape. Why limit yourself to singles? How about matching pen pals, the incarcerated, home-based seniors, hobby groups, similar interests associations, or personality types, couples who merely want friends for conversation or travel, children or teenagers who want video friends around the globe, or recruiters seeking job applicants digitally and on disc, Web, or on videotape?

ADDITIONAL INFORMATION:

International Society of Introduction Services
PO Box 31408
San Francisco, CA 94131

National Association of Single People
4256 N. Brown Ave., Suite H
Scottsdale, AZ 85251

National Association of Christian Singles
1933 W. Wisconsin Ave.
Milwaukee, WI 53233

Association for Couples in Marriage Enrichment
PO Box 10596
Winston-Salem, NC 27108

Wives of Older Men
1029 Sycamore Ave.
Tinton Falls, NJ 07724

26

DESCRIPTION OF BUSINESS

Special Interest Training Video Podcasts

Produce or Sell Special Interest Training Video Podcasts Showing Individuals or Corporations How to Cut Expenses or Making the Most of What You Have

Did you ever think of writing letters to 2,000 famous people asking them, "What is the most important lesson they learned from life?" What if enough celebrities, physicians, millionaires, scientists, or famous authors replied with common sense advice, such as, "Make the most of what you have?"

What if you produced a video, wrote a short book, formed a national association, sold a franchise, or gave a seminar on how to cut expenses and get higher quality for less money? You could compile all the lessons a lot of famous people learned from life on a videotape and sell it to the self-enhancement video distributors or distribute the tape yourself as a special interest self-enhancement tape.

Although making money with a video camera is part of a $17 billion industry, special interest videos, according to a recent issue of <u>Entrepreneur</u> magazine, are ready to advance. It's the instructional video boom, the how-to video, that industry experts believe will dwarf the gross sales figures of feature film rentals.

A special interest training video tells the viewer how to do something, how to do something better. Or it fills a special interest request for new and timely summarized information by which the viewer can make more informed choices.

The how-to video trains you in skills. The selling point of the video is that it will show you how to make money or have fun doing something you love to do or want to learn.

The video is always instructional. It fills a niche market interest to improve your life by doing something new.

Special interest videos supplement books. They don't replace them. They are for hands-on and visually-oriented people who find reading abstract, dry. They are for viewers who want to make learning entertaining and fun.

The living room becomes the center of learning and entertainment. The next step for special interest videos are interactive multimedia using videos with personal computers to interact with an instructional video.

INCOME POTENTIAL:

You could market your tapes to the chains of how-to special interest video stores springing up nationally in shopping malls. Or through self-distribution, you can receive more income than if you accepted a small royalty of 15 to 20 percent of your distributor's gross. Some distributors will offer you a percentage of their net, which will cut your income greatly.

The downside of self distribution is that you will spend a lot of money on advertising and promotional expenses as well as duplication and packaging. You'll also have freight expenses. With some distributors, you can expect to earn a percentage of net sales on each video. Distributors usually want to own home video rights.

In the mid-eighties, the number of video stores began to fall, and video rental stores reached its plateau. This cutback gave video wholesalers more territory and power. There's only one secret of success, and that's know your market.

Your income will depend on how well your video is produced, marketed, promoted, backed by experts such as medical colleges giving it credibility (or another credible organization), and how well the market is targeted. Income depends on how well your tape is cross-promoted. Amortize your costs.

Use well-known people in your tape or to promote it. Know your packaging budget and legal fees, how much you'll pay for accounting and postage. Study your competition. Talk to successful self-distributors.

Income is affected by the lack of strong product on small wholesalers. The result is that non-theatrical special interest videos are arousing attention. When wholesalers can't get feature films on video, they turn to special interest videos. However, the video stores still want "A" (first class) movie titles.

What you earn will depend on the popularity of your tape. It's a good idea to charge as little as you can for sales. A $19.95 tape will sell better than a $39.95 tape. A midline price is $29.95. Most people prefer to pay $20 for a one or two hour instructional tape rather than $40.

Keep your prices below $29.95. If you're producing children's tapes, prices generally are under $29.95. Sometimes the really cheap kids tapes sell poorly.

When Lorimar priced children's specialty tapes around $10–$15, the tapes didn't sell well because there was too little margin for the seller.

BEST LOCALE TO OPERATE THE BUSINESS:

You can operate your business anywhere. Your business is national, advertised through national television or in national trade and specialty magazines, through special interest associations, or through conventions, seminars, courses, and their related special interest publications.

Where you distribute your tapes are more important than where you tape the instructional subject. Many instructional tapes are made indoors for demonstration of equipment. Sports videos often are made outdoors or in a gym. Sometimes the best place for a Yoga tape is in an instructor's studio, decorated with backlighting and a brilliant use of decoration to promote the mood and meditation in the environment.

TRAINING REQUIRED:

You'll need to ask your local video supplies store when they have classes to train you how to use your video equipment—camera, editing, special effects, sound equipment. However, your real training comes in picking how-to subjects to tape.

If you can teach people how to do something or offer a training tape, you can make full use of the lighting and camera equipment. In addition, you'll need to read a book or take a short course in marketing and distribution of the specialty video market. Such marketing and distribution courses are always offered by video industry trade associations. Get on their mailing lists, or talk to your video supplies store instructor.

GENERAL APTITUDE OR EXPERIENCE:

You'll need the entrepreneur's autonomy and desire to be your own employer. Teaching skills are important. You want to make the complex simpler. It's important to make instructions concrete, clear, and easy to understand. The viewer probably bought your tape because he couldn't understand the complicated manual.

Show hands-on demonstrations. You're dealing with visual learners. Viewers need to see and hear how to do something while using the equipment, making the point, or making the moves.

The average attention span per scene is under seven minutes—before the mind drifts. Your most important attitude is patience with the learner with lots of praise to build the viewer's confidence.

Use praise to make the viewer feel important and good. Develop confidence that practice makes better. Good teaching skills help make a great video.

If you have the industrial skill, but are a lousy teacher, hire a narrator who comes across as friendly, outgoing, and easy to understand to work with your video script. If you have trouble expressing yourself in writing, or in trying to explain how you do something, hire a scriptwriter to communicate effectively and a narrator to speak the words in front of the camera while you perform the skill, hands-on.

If you're the writer or narrator who wants to make a how-to video but don't have any hands-on skill to show, hire the skilled expert to demonstrate on camera. Do the voice over or write the script after interviewing and taping the expert off-camera first to get the procedures in sequence. Then you can make a voice-over with the narrator reading your script, the expert demonstrating hands-on in front of the camera, and you operating your video camera.

EQUIPMENT NEEDED:

You need a video camera, editing and tape duplicating equipment, and a way of distributing your tapes. You'll need a marketing program to advertise to consumers, business owners, schools, libraries, professional associations, and event planners.

By offering to operate a video camera at conventions, you can network with potential consumers when you create your own tapes on related or specialty subjects of interest to event planners and convention attendees, or members of professional/business associations, and business owners. You'll need circulars, order forms, and newsletters to mail out to potential customers—and a plan to distribute your promotional material.

You'll need enough video equipment to fill all areas of instruction and demonstration, which can be different for each tape. Your video supply store can give you a production equipment list individualized and customized to your needs with each different video.

OPERATING YOUR BUSINESS:

Business owners, schools, libraries, professional associations, home parties, event planners, specialty shops, and video clubs can help you sell your special interest tape. You can send out your own catalog from a purchased mailing list.

Have other video producers share your mailing expenses by advertising their tapes in your mail order catalog. More retail outlets carry specialty videos. Try in-store posters, stand-ups, and special offers or display racks of specialty market videos in stores.

Hardware stores, pharmacy chains, gardening outlets, maternity shops, gift stores, bookstores, and health food stores could carry your specialty video. Approach the specialty stores whose theme is similar to yours.

Videocassette sales to video stores on one title usually last only six weeks. You'll have to use alternative markets. Every six weeks video stores move to market a new, fresh product. Your specialty video should have a one-year life, unless it's a software instructional video, where new software keeps coming on the market. Keep your tape updated and timely.

Try the video clubs, such as CBS, Time-Life, Reader's Digest, and National Geographic as well as the small specialty video clubs and distributors in specialty magazines. For example, alternative health, lifestyle, inspirational, paranormal, or new age-related videos are sold through niche magazine advertisements, specialized gift shops, catalogues, online, and through events and conventions globally.

Belly-dancing videos are marketed to belly-dance teachers, costume designers, events, conventions, and through advertisements in belly-dance magazines and newsletters and local chapters of national belly-dance organizations. The same rule applies to all other special interest groups and their videos.

To operate your business, you'll need a marketing program that includes mail order catalogs, promotional videos about your videos, circulars, ads, and television commercials.

TARGET MARKET:

You can sell your video at home parties or by wholesaling to retailers. Use the theme and title of your video to locate retailers and home parties that cater to the kind of audience interest you're seeking.

If you're making a tape on how to use a particular computer software program, you're not going to sell your video to the owner of a maternity garment store. However, if you're selling a videotape on infant massage and preschool exercise, that maternity store, toy store, children's clothing chain, and sports store would definitely be a target market for your tape.

Specialty tapes are sold by video and rental stores, mass merchants, bookstores, toy stores, convenience stores, sports stores, through infomercials and direct response television, and through direct mail order catalogs sent to a targeted audience from a purchased mailing list. You could market your instructional tapes to the Peace Corps or VISTA, or to the government.

Your audience mailing list should be designated as having an interest in your subject matter. Frequently these mailing lists are composed of specialty magazine subscribers or buyers of equipment related to the special interest.

A feature film video tape usually ships 250,000 rental titles. Specialty tapes differ according to the niche market appeal of the tape. Retailers demand that video suppliers commit to television advertising. You'll have to advertise either on television or through direct mail order catalog.

Television pulls people into rental and video stores. However, your tape may have such a small audience that only through direct mail order catalog or advertisements in trade journals and specialty magazines can you reach your niche audience. Target markets for educational tapes include schools, libraries, and book publishers as well as supply shops.

If you don't want to produce video tapes yourself, hard-to-find specialty video tapes are sold below wholesale prices. You can buy up these low-priced video tapes that other producers have made and sell them yourself through mail order or at home parties and events, or even through door-to-door sales calling on stores.

Or if you don't want to spend a lot of money to buy or handle other producer's instructional videos yourself, only find customers, you could work for a company that distributes and sells videos at wholesale or below wholesale prices. Such firms may stock the videos and make the choice for you whether the videos are in demand.

Working as an independent contractor for a video sales and distribution company, you don't have to buy up video tape inventory yourself. The company will drop-ship to your customers, so you don't even have to handle the videos. Or you can ask them to drop ship to your home.

What you do, is find the customers. It's really sales. You visit stores, events, ask friends, have sales parties, and approach vendors, suppliers, and leave flyers at trade show booths. You ask anyone you think will be a customer. You stamp your address on the franchiser's catalog, and people order from you. You buy a membership kit from sales and distribution companies. The way you make money is by sales, finding your own customers for the companies that drop-ships videos, DVDs, audio books, or printed material either to your customers or to your home. You don't produce your own video.

RELATED VIDEO OPPORTUNITIES:

Variety in specialty videos is what the market is about. With nine out of people in the United States owning a VCR, informative videos could be on any subject related to cashing in on some skill or information.

Be a documentarian, and record how-to subjects, travel, or educational themes on audio or video discs. Make documentaries on sports, travel, home, health, cooking, fitness, dance, music, hobbies, crafts, business, arts, creativity, writing, science, children's programming, animation, folklore, ethnomusicology, history, or relationships.

The point is that people buy specialty tapes to improve their lives or skills, or to learn something new. Information allows people to make choices and decisions based on current or historic facts and realities. Don't overlook the gift market and gift shops or online gift sellers or book sellers for self-enhancement discs or tapes and the corporate market to train employees. Include corporate success stories.

Information can vary from supplying people with information such as the least costly cities to live in to statistics on neighborhoods of different cities for people relocating. You can help newcomers to a neighborhood or city by referring them to services or housing, shopping, and schools. Being a local travel agent in reverse, catering to visitors and newcomers or locating rooms in private homes for business travelers all focus on niche markets and consumer demand.

ADDITIONAL INFORMATION:

Association for Independent Video & Filmmakers
625 Broadway, 9th fl.
New York, NY 10012

Educational Broadcasting Corporation
356 W. 58th St.
New York, NY 10019

Media Network
39 W. 14th St., Suite 403
New York, NY 10011

Forbes Media Guide
1400 route 206 N
PO Box 89
Bedminster, NJ 07921

Video Direct Corporation
Dept. D9
400 Morris Ave
Long Branch, NJ 07740
(a company that distributes and sells videos)

27

DESCRIPTION OF BUSINESS:

Apartment/House Rental Agency and Roommate Locator & Screener Video Podcasts

Locate by video podcasts the least costly places to live—cities to live, including rooms, apartments, homes, or hotels and inns. Or focus on finding living quarters, vacation homes, or relocation for the rich and famous. Welcome newcomers by video podcasts updated regularly. Or the safest—or where they are most likely to find a job in their special fields. Your personal video or audio, book, report, or seminar, can be used to create a niche market non-broadcast video rental agency.

Help single parents and children find less costly and safer housing, or assisted living for seniors at a rate they can afford. Give seminars for seniors on how to get help with living expenses or meals deliveries, or low-cost rides to their medical appointments.

Provide screening for referrals to help seniors stay independent in their homes with non-medical home-care or personal shopping services. Your focus would be on cutting expenses and finding quality products or services, including the safest, cheapest, and most economical cities to live in for different age groups and requirements.

Locate and screen roommates or older adults to share houses, condominiums, and apartments, and you can locate vacant houses and apartments for individuals or families and even keep an updated video library of international houses for vacation exchange and time-share rentals.

Help seniors or students or people in similar occupations to find adequate housing or houses to share in order to cut living expenses. Find housing for seniors located walking distance from supermarkets, community centers, and any other type of shopping or cultural programs.

INCOME POTENTIAL:

Charge landlords a fee of one month's rent to screen either tenants or property or both on video and show the videos to the landlords and to videotape their properties. If the landlords have no time to screen the videos of the tenants being interviewed, then screen them yourself on or off video for a fee. Select the best tenants according to what the landlord wants. Check credit and employment. Abide by antidiscrimination laws, and select the best matched tenant for the property.

If the landlord only wants the property videotaped and shown to prospective tenants, then charge the landlords one month's rental fee to screen and place selected tenants in their vacant properties. You would not charge any fee to the tenant if the landlord is paying a fee to put properties on videotape.

BEST LOCALE TO OPERATE THE BUSINESS:

Tourist and resort areas or areas where large numbers of people are moving in are ideal. Boom towns, large cities, glamour job cities, all attract young professionals seeking rentals. Retirees are excellent to approach in Sunbelt cities, especially those who seek retirement community apartments, condominiums, and homes in resort areas.

Travel agents can be helpful to network with when trying to rent vacation homes and condominiums by the week or month in resort areas such as Hawaii, Europe, The Riviera, Mexico, San Diego, San Francisco, the Caribbean, Orlando, Florida, or anywhere else that is popular for vacationers. Ask travel agencies whether they'd like to carry a display rack of your vacation home rental videos in their store windows, especially if they are in high foot traffic malls or near colleges at vacation times. You'll have to be your own video distributor, since your tapes are updated daily or weekly.

TRAINING REQUIRED:

You can train yourself by talking to real estate rental and management agencies that still use computers to generate lists of rentals available or roommates seeking to share apartments or homes. Join organizations of property managers or apartment owners and sit in on their seminars and annual conferences. You don't need a real estate license to make real estate videos or to rent apartments, but it helps to take a course in how to lease apartments or in how to select tenants.

Familiarize yourself with leasing agreements and contracts. Best of all is a night course in property management and renting along with a course in how to operate your video camera. Practice videotaping the interior of your own dwelling and make a mockup promotional tape presenting your house to make believe tenants.

Ask viewers to critique your tape to see how well you presented your house on tape to renters. If you want to screen and match roommates on tape, make a few demonstration tapes of your friends to see how they come across on video as prospective roommates.

Network and connect with landlords at your local Apartment Owners Association meetings. Ask them how you can best be of service with your video tape to help them locate and screen prospective tenants. Artfully present their property on tape to help fill vacancies.

You can start by matching roommates and then expand into apartments, homes, time-share condominiums, and expensive vacation homes overseas for rent. Some videotapes specialize in bartering or trading vacation homes without money changing hands.

For example, a couple in Switzerland will rent their home for the summer to an American couple if they can have the American couple's spacious New York or San Francisco home or apartment for that summer. Your videos can specialize in vacation home exchanges for executives of a corporation, for professional associations, or other purposes. In such cases, you'd be paid a fee for showing video tapes taken overseas by each party of their own homes and for making a suitable match. Your fee would come from each party when the match is agreed upon.

GENERAL APTITUDE OR EXPERIENCE:

You need an uncanny ability to observe and make judgments about people, much like a private investigator and psychologist rolled into one. You should enjoy checking details on people and property and getting contracts legally in writing. It's important to find out about insurance, liability, and responsibility from both parties you deal with in case something goes wrong.

EQUIPMENT NEEDED:

You'll need a video camera to tape the interior of the house or apartment or to interview and screen the roommates. Editing equipment is helpful to take out and insert scenes. You'll need backlighting and video lighting equipment to make the interior of a house appear inviting.

You don't need industrial or broadcast quality cameras if your apartments or roommates have a frequent and high turnover rate so that you're constantly erasing tape and putting new people on camera. A super 8 camera is fine. You'll be going to people's homes to do your taping. So portability of camera, sound, and lighting is important.

In addition to your video camera, you'll find a personal computer with a database program helpful to maintain your updated lists. Back in the nineties, Software *Property Listings Comparables* was an excellent software program for the IBM PC. The program maintained real-estate listings and comparable sold properties and includes screening capability for selecting properties. Property information is easily entered and updated by filling in a form on the screen.

The program listed properties in the file by minimum and maximum price, number of bedrooms, units, and city and zone—and required 128Kb of memory. The program was available from Realty Software Company, 1926 South Pacific Coast Highway, Number 229, Redondo Beach, CA 90277.

Another great 1990s software came out called UNIVAIR PROPERTY MANAGEMENT SYSTEM. It was designed for managers of residential rental properties. Rental agencies can use this program if management is done for owners of properties rented.

The software managed duplexes, apartments, and condominiums. It allowed the user to keep an exact cost accounting on each separate building within a complex or project as well as on individual lease or rental units within each building itself. It required at least a DOS 2.0 operating systems. Research the type of software for property management that is on the market today, more than a decade later.

Hard disk was recommended. The minimum memory required was 128Kb. A 132-column printer was necessary. An interface was provided as a link to word processing, DBMS, and telecommunications software. It was available from Umvair, 9024 St. Charles Rock Road, St. Louis, MO 63114. Your homework is to find the last versions of similar software, now that a decade has passed.

OPERATING YOUR BUSINESS:

Before you buy or rent a house, look at it on videotape first from thousands of miles away. Match a tenant to a vacant apartment, house, condominium, mobile home, international vacation house rental, time share condominium, yacht, recreational living quarters, trailer, mobile home, recreational vehicle, or house-boat on your videotape—to rent, to buy, or to rent with option to buy.

Match roommates on video based on a questionnaire. Let prospective roommates view the videos. Many will think you're operating like a dating service. It's a lot like looking at a videotape of a new work facility before you choose to transfer up there. Only you'll have to include personality preferences material.

Your roommate service can match people who are seeking to share apartments or homes. Use your videos to locate vacant houses to share living expenses, for individuals or families.

It's becoming more popular for several senior citizens to share a home with a home health aide five people chip in to pay for then to move to a nursing home because one person living alone can't pay for hired household help.

How do you select a home, apartment or a roommate? The answer is by looking at several video tapes before selecting the right match. Roommate matching videos emphasize responsibility and dependability. You're being relied upon to make decisions about people and property from videotaped interviews that could have legal ramifications.

To start a video rental agency, first obtain listings of apartments and houses with vacancies from organizations such as The Apartment Owners Association in your community. Contact landlords and list them for one month's rental fee on your video. Or list the landlords for a small fee and charge the tenants a small fee.

It's easier to get landlords with vacancies they can't fill to pay you a month's rental fee to be included in your video than to try to get a fee from poor tenants who will be stuck with two months rent and a security deposit to put down before they can move in, once they find a place.

Clip classified advertisements, and telephone landlords asking permission to include their vacancy in your computer listing. Apartments and houses are rented quickly. Your video information should be updated daily.

This is why vacancies clipped from several daily newspapers in your city and some weekly papers should keep you updated. Place your fliers on college, military, senior-citizen, church, realty, and company bulletin boards. Always phone ahead for an appointment to make sure the vacancy still exists before sending a tenant to inspect a house.

If the house is still occupied, you can make an appointment to send over a prospective renter at the tenant's convenience. You can provide a video of rentals available to tenants and screen them before you send anyone to see a landlord. All credit information, identification, financial data, and previous addresses as well as the number of people who will be living in a household should be put into your computer and made available to landlords.

Tenants will want you to provide them with a video that includes the cost of rent, the size of the apartment or house, security features, the landlord's attitude toward children, and access to public schools, houses of worship, shopping centers, parking facilities, and public transportation.

Videotape the entire neighborhood, schools nearby, and shopping malls as well as the interior and exterior of the house. Some prospective tenants wish a video would include what the neighbors and daily foot traffic going past the house act like.

It's friendly to have the neighbors put out a welcome wagon atmosphere on your promotional tape, if you can talk them into doing it. Your video should focus on selling the apartment or house as well as the neighborhood and its conveniences or view with all its best features.

Landlords use home, apartment, timeshare, and commercial real estate videos as sales tools. Commercial real estate videos target the business buyer, including buyers, sellers, and business brokers of shopping malls and medical office building renters who are health professionals. You can specialize in making videos catering to the medical office renter's market, for example, near hospitals, and also help them locate a nearby home rental, for interns or physicians new to an area.

TARGET MARKET:

Landlords, property managers, real-estate brokers, students, recent graduates, military families, senior citizens, families with small children, recently transferred employees, newcomers, professionals and traveling executives in relocation, and the newly single are most likely to use the services of a video rental and roommate agency or service. Advertise in military newspapers, college newspapers, the daily papers, weekly newspapers, singles newspapers, and publications of apartment owners associations.

RELATED VIDEO OPPORTUNITIES:

You can create video tapes that locate almost anything for a prospective buyer—from finding venture capital investors to putting inventors on videotape to hawk their wares to venture capitalists, bankers, investors, scientific foundations, or the public. You can also specialize in catering to a certain type of relocation business: finding homes for newly transferred executives, for example, or finding new careers for their uprooted spouses.

A video rental service serves as a catalyst in bringing people together or matching people with property or potential new business. Related video opportunities could consist of making videotapes for real estate or business appraisers, or for banks, lenders, and investment brokers.

Videos are used to screen customers and to view or appraise property and businesses for a variety of clients. Find loans for home or business buyers by interviewing the lenders or owners on videotape. Or help tax shelter wholesalers promote their tax shelters to the government. In summarized point, the government is one of the biggest buyers of videotaped information.

The tax shelter wholesaler sells to the National Association of Securities Dealers brokers, marketing organizations, and financial planners, who then retail those tax shelter investments to the public. You could videotape energy-related investment companies who sponsor investments as multiple tax write-off private placement programs.

Videotape sponsors of energy-related investment programs, marketing firms, limited partnerships, securities dealers, stock brokerage houses, and venture capital corporations. If you're interested in this niche market, write to the National Association of Securities Dealers, 1735 K St. NW, Washington, DC 20006, or the Public Securities Association (PSA). The association's Web site is at: http://www.investopedia.com/terms/p/psa.asp.

If you'd like to offer videotaped information to the Federal Government, write to the U.S. Government Printing House, Washington, DC, for a catalog of government publications and videos available related to your area of interest. Real estate, business, and industrial producers may re-edit videos to use as clips or stock footage in other videos.

ADDITIONAL INFORMATION:

Property Management Association of America
8811 Colesville Rd., Suite 225
Silver Spring, MD 20910

National Association of Realtors
Department of Education
155 East Superior St.
Chicago, IL 60611

Institute of Financial Education
111 East Wacker Drive
Chicago, IL 60601

Association for Corporate Growth
5940 West Touhy Ave, Suite 300
Chicago IL 60648

**International Association of Merger
and Acquisition Consultants**
11258 Goodnight Lane
Dallas, TX 75229

Institute of Business Appraisers
PO Box 1447
Boynton Beach, FL 33435

28

DESCRIPTION OF BUSINESS:

Personal History/Videobiography Podcasts

Videobiographers interview people who want to put a variety of life stories, events, or corporate histories on videotape. Your non-corporate client may make a videobiography to clarify life purposes or values, record family history, or document events for historical preservation. Your corporate client may wish to make a video record of the history of a family business or company, documenting several generations of business history, including annual and financial reports, mergers and acquisitions, or expansion starting with the founding family members.

Videobiographies also may contain an oral history, documentation of events affecting a person's life, a legal deposition, local history, autobiography, life events and rites of passage, corporate history, poetry, love letters, messages to children and future descendants, fiction, Reader's Theatre, war stories, holocaust survival documentation, life validation, confessions to family members, apologies, psychohistory, or biographies of celebrities on video tape for collectors, museums, libraries, genealogy archives, and family records.

Other people who may wish to make a videobiography to give to friends are those in hospices whose time is short. Religious leaders may want sermons combined with slices of life experience stories or anecdotes put on tape.

Videobiographies may contain images of persons reading their love letters and poetry to loved ones. Prisoners, may want to make a videobiography to send to their relatives or their victims, Prisoners on death row may want a tape to send to relatives who live too far away to visit regularly, and the relatives may wish to chip in to have such a tape produced. Some prisoners use such a tape to make confessions, to apologize to their victims or relatives, or to get onto broadcast television to appeal their cases.

Videobiographies are requested by the elderly home based, the disabled, psychotherapists, hypnotists, and counselors, people with confessions to make on video to send to someone, entertainers, or entrepreneurs seeking the one-on-one personal approach with customers. There is a popular market for hypnosis tapes, and some hypnotherapists may hire a video producer to make tapes for special clients or to sell to the public.

Why stop at video? Put your videos and still images on virtual reality CD-ROM, compact disk, read only memory on your computer to be played with a CD-ROM player. Create interactive photo shoots and combine them with biographical videos. Make an impact by combining high quality video images with regular video tapes on CD-ROM, or edited back onto your video tape.

Snap your favorite pictures and save them to your computer's hard disk. Then transfer them to video tape. Use your computer controls to direct the people or items in your photos to a variety of poses. Pick your own multiple camera angles or close-ups.

Practice your video and photography skills on your personal computer and edit your best shots back onto your videotape. Create a CD-ROM game using your videos and still shots. Your videotapes can be transferred onto computer disks to create virtual reality imagery or video. Or work exclusively in video to produce exquisite videobiographies.

INCOME POTENTIAL:

Charge $100 to $175 an hour to individuals for taping, directing, editing, and producing a videobiography, genealogy, or autobiography on tape and a $200 per minute fee to corporations to record and edit a corporate history. You can charge a discount to other family members for separate tapes that include clips of a relative's tape.

Decide whether you will charge special rates for ministers and officials of religious organizations. Video podcasts can document the life stories of members of their congregations. They may be able to give you a continuing list of referrals. Most videographers who monitor people in the news charge approximately $175 an hour for monitoring events on tape. Updates can be made and edited to an original tape, or older tape can be edited to new tape to preserve it.

You can videotape profiles and portfolios of actors, performers, or speakers. Interview people at their homes and social centers or in your home or studio. What types of personal history projects would you like to emphasize? If you interview people on camera for other journalists, charge $175–$200 an hour for a taping using the journalist's questions rather than your own. You can interview people for television stations and news programs for a fee to save the studio money or when the person interviewed can't come out to the studio.

You can also travel on cruise ships or in flight and interview people on vacation to make vacation videobiographies for them to document their vacations. Charge $100 to $175 per hour to videotape vacationers, travelers, or people on cruise ships. Keep a copy of the tape for your library and get a letter of permission from them in writing if you plan to use clips of your clients in your own future videos.

Many people who travel for business or tourism would love to have a professionally edited 60-minute tape of their vacation or honeymoon. For a flat fee, usually $200 if you're traveling along with them, plus expenses, you can go anywhere in the world to capture honeymooners, vacationers, business travelers, or business deals being made on tape.

Edit special life events onto videobiogaphies, like documented surgical operations or daring sports events, musical performances, or a client's photographs and illustrations. You can charge a special fee to tape parachute or bungee jumps, car races, ski jumps, ice skating, tennis matches, or any other sports event. If the client wants you to go up in a plane and videotape them sky diving, then charge expenses plus your usual fee.

Although video monitoring fees range around $175–$200 an hour plus expenses, producing a 10 or 20-minute corporate history or training film has a different fee scale at $200 PER MINUTE for scriptwriting it, plus $200 an hour for taping it—only for the videography or camera work. Editing is extra, especially if you send the video out to a post production editing studio. Learn to edit the tape yourself and make extra money.

You can add expenses to that for props, lighting, studio rental, hiring the narrator, and other expenses when you make up your first budget. A straight taping of someone telling his or her life story runs about $175 an hour, plus editing expenses.

BEST LOCALE TO OPERATE THE BUSINESS:

Videobiographies may be produced from any location. Or you could travel around the world or work on cruise ships. Corporate histories are videotaped from office locations (or even the golf course) anywhere in the world and may be edited for global videoconferences by satellite. Approach businesses or community centers where people want to put their experiences on tape.

Compile video books by asking many people one provocative question. Then put their response on tape as well as in an accompanying booklet. Choose universal questions that apply to all people's lives. Or ask controversial questions. Another approach is to make unauthorized celebrity biographies by talking to friends and acquaintances of the person in the biography.

Ask the children of famous parents or parents with extremist views to talk about how they feel. Most of your videobiography business will be from older people who want to preserve their memories, confessions, messages, love letters, and life experiences on tape for their grandchildren to pass on to future generations.

Design a workbook and audio tapes to accompany the videobiography, especially if it's going to schools, libraries, and museums or is to be used for instructional or historical research purposes.

TRAINING REQUIRED:

The best way to learn about creating biographies is to read brief biographies and view as many videobiographies as you can—the 30 and 60 minute tapes. Visit your museum libraries and view oral histories on videotape, including the libraries and archives of the videobiographies of war, disaster, and holocaust survivors of the past half century. Look at biographies on film as well as on videocassette.

In addition to studying the technique of creating a videobiography, learn to use your video camera to create interviews. Read a few books (you'll find in college bookstores) on how to take oral histories on tape and how to interview people from any beginning course in journalism, interviewing, or producing interviews on tape in a news video course at a local community college.

Attend video conventions. Take seminars and workshops offered by video associations such as local chapters of the International Documentary Association, videographer organizations or clubs, and video suppliers that focus on creating videobiographies. Join the International Documentary Association or a local chapter of a documentary video group, sometimes listed in video trade magazines. Consult the <u>Encyclopedia of Associations</u> to find new national video organizations. Read the publications of associations and the usual video trade magazines (trade journals) and newsletters.

GENERAL APTITUDE OR EXPERIENCE:

You'll need a knack for interviewing people and putting them at ease in front of your camera. It helps to practice interviewing people in video. Sometimes adult education courses offer workshops on how to interview for a job. They tape the student job applicants to help them feel more at ease in front of a camera and during a job interview. It may be helpful to sit in such a course.

You can always get in touch with an actor's support group and inquire whether anyone will volunteer to be interviewed in front of your camera in a mock biography. In summarized point, the actors may want to keep the tape after you study or copy it to be edited for their video portfolios.

The best aptitude is a nose for news or a flair for video journalism, experience making interviews easy for someone to tell their life story on tape, and practice in composing a list of questions.

EQUIPMENT NEEDED:

You'll need a video camera, tripod, tape, editing and dubbing equipment, and sound props. You may want to use some props and special effects in your studio or interview setting, which may be outdoors showing the person walking, in which case, you'll need to hold the camera or pan in a vehicle. You may want to cut in scenes of the person's wedding, bar mitzvah or confirmation, a relative's funeral, childbirth, or any life event your clients want cut to tape.

Avoid talking heads by using many cuts and montages or outdoor scenes of the person in action, working, gardening, cooking, walking along the waterside, bicycling, driving, working, or in some kind of constant motion or action doing a variety of tasks.

If you make videbiographies of scientists or doctors, you'll have to set up studio in a laboratory, operating room, hospital, or medical office, and may need special micro-video recording equipment supplied by the scientist for videotaping what's seen through an electronic microscope.

If you videotape the biographies of astronauts, you'll have to get clips and stills of their missions in space from NASA, the government, or private archives and edit the stock footage onto your videotape. Obtain written permission for anything that's not public domain.

OPERATING YOUR BUSINESS:

Decide what kind of videobiographies you'll specialize in. They could be executive's corporate histories, autobiographies, senior citizen's life experiences, children interviewed every seven years to document them from early childhood into adulthood, public history, celebrity interviews, scientist's videobiographies, inventors, artists and writers interviewed on tape for schools, genealogy/family history documentation and memoirs, life stories, legal depositions, an individual's war, disaster, and holocaust recollections to document and preserve history for future generations, or anyone's life story on videotape.

You'll have to compose a list of questions for the interview. Ask your client what questions should be asked in order to compose the list while you do a preliminary interview on tape to gather information.

Set up your props in the person's home, senior center, or studio, and vary the scenes by showing the person at work, outside, in play, travel, driving, swimming, community service, or whatever they want to do in order to create a variety of scene changes and cutaways. Use backlighting to create a less harsh image of the person's face under bright lights. Use some television makeup on your client to create a matte rather than a shiny face, as people tend to sweat on their face during a video interview.

In the usual video interview, you sit next to your client and ask a variety of questions while someone else turns the video camera mounted on a tripod to catch interviewer and interviewee having a dialogue. As your client talks about specific life events, you can edit in scenes of the person performing some activity. The effect is the client's voice-over, while clips of your client in action outdoors or at a variety of settings shows the person in action, moving from one place to another, or actual footage of stock video or film on video scenes (such as war documentation) are cut in.

The result is your client's voice over speaking about the experience and answering your questions, while the viewer sees cuts and flashbacks to the particular events, war scenes, or news events. You can rent or buy the video/film stock footage from video and film libraries and archives.

Videobiographies, like instructional videos, are inspirational or motivational and end on an upbeat, optimistic note. Autobiographies of senior citizens are people's final comments on their own life purposes, experiences, relationships, and values. So train yourself to ask pertinent questions to help your clients put on tape their life purpose clarifications by asking the following questions of your clients:

1. What do you love to do?
2. What do you enjoy?
3. What do you do well?
4. What, in your own opinion, are your 10 greatest successes?
5. What do you feel enthusiastic or passionate about?
6. What are the 10 most important lessons you've learned in life?
7. What issues keep coming back?
8. What do you daydream about doing?
9. What do you want to be remembered for?
10. What would you do if you knew you could never fail?

Train yourself to help your client look beyond self-imposed limitations by focusing on asking your client to speak only in the client's own opinion, not in the opinion of friends, relatives, employers, co-workers, or criticizers, on the client's life successes. Attend video store or studio workshops given by traveling lecturers who are professional videographers, and view their videos. Producers may re-edit a corporate history videobiography.

Anything you edit to your videotape can also be cut into a computer disk or CD-ROM so the client can access the video clip or scene on a computer or watch it on video tape. Video footage combined with computer text and music sounds are useful if you're planning to create interactive software for students and market your videobiographies to schools.

Videotapes can also be marketed, either as interactive or plain videos. If you plan to cut segments of your video on software, there are many options available.

You can use the latest computer software to create fascinating biographical videos. In summarized point, you can not only create videobiographies and corporate histories on videotape, you can put the video tape on CD-ROM, computer disk, or laser disk. Adobe Systems, Inc. provides an update for Adobe Premier, a video editing software program for Windows.

Create multimedia biographical, genealogical, corporate, educational, or historical graphic presentations in video or on CD-ROM computer disk. Put your autobiography on videotape and then cut segments of it onto computer disks to combine your talking, live action, family photos, film and home movies, or corporate histories.

Adobe Premier software captures video-at-large. Select a version that supports direct video capture using Adobe Video Capture software. It's included in the package, which also has sample video, audio, and still images on CD-ROM.

You use a video capture board and the capture program. You can digitize analog video and audio signals directly from your VCR, video camera, or laser disc player. Specify options for capture type, frame rate (how many frames you want captured per second), image size, video format, and audio format. Customize your videos by controlling the output data rate for optimizing your CD-ROM playback. To keep your colors consistent throughout your video, there's a color palette.

Also, you can import still images onto your video as a single video clip. For information, call Adobe Systems at (415) 961-4400 or 1(800) 833-6687. Put your videobiographies on CD-ROM so they can be played on a computer as videos or as videotape segments or "movies" combined with text, pictures, animation, illustration, still photos, music, and other sounds.

TARGET MARKET:

You want to reach anyone interested in putting an interview, oral history, or life story on videotape. Videobiographies are becoming popular among corporate executives who want to document corporate history or a family business on videotape. Many senior citizens centers offer courses in how to create videobiographies with your video camera.

Older people want to find ways to put life stories and messages or even confessions on video to give to their grandchildren to preserve their memories for future generations. You can even market your videobiographies to parents of young children and approach parenting classes. Many parents would like a videobiography of their child at different stages of life.

Some people want to create a tape every seven years to mark the rites of passage or stages of life. A tape should be made of everyone at birth, at age seven, 14, 21, 28, 35, 42,49, 56, 63, 70 and every decade after to mark all the stages of life. We all change every seven years, physically and in many other ways. Send out flyers to mailing lists of people at various ages seven years apart from birth to a hundred announcing your videobiographies to document them and their memoirs every seven years.

You can buy mailing lists of people at the various ages or stages of life spaced seven years apart. You can also advertise their age number and explain why a tape is made to document and celebrate a rite of passage marking change and growth every seven years of a person's life span. Documenting life passages on tape creates a library of tradition and change to be preserved by every future generation, hopefully, in a family time capsule.

RELATED VIDEO OPPORTUNITIES:

Teach senior citizens at adult education centers and senior centers how to create beautiful and professional-looking videobiographies. Offer your services as a video consultant in the schools. You don't need a credential or degree to offer your videotape to schools or approach teachers with your flyer.

You can volunteer to show children how to use the school's camcorders or other video cameras to create their life stories on tape or to document their growth, activities, and childhood creativity. Apply to the state government for a paid grant to be a visiting video artist in residence in the schools for a year.

Teach teenagers in neighborhood community centers how to make a teen video magazine or run their own video news and events video production team to discuss events with their peers or other generations for a meeting of the minds.

You can start your own videobiography workshops in the YMCA or YWCA, in adult education classes, at community centers, or schools and senior centers or in children's hospitals or work with disabled teens or adults showing them how to put their biographies on videotape.

Volunteer to work with gifted high school students or community college students showing them how to compile biographies of celebrities or famous people in science or their vocational field of choice by putting together stock video footage or interviewing people on the job in their chosen occupations.

ADDITIONAL INFORMATION:

The Association of Music Podcasting
http://www.musicpodcasting.org/

Digital Video Professionals Association
28 East Jackson Bldg #10-D572
Chicago, IL, USA 60604
http://www.dvpa.com/default.aspx

INFO Links (List of Video-Related Associations)
http://www.nonlinear4.com/info.htm

International Documentary Association
1551 S. Robertson Blvd. Suite 201
Los Angeles, CA 90035
http://www.documentary.org/

The Internet Movie Database (Movie-Related Urls)
http://www.imdb.com/links

National Association of PhotoShop Professionals
http://www.photoshopuser.com/

NYC Podcasting Association
http://podcasting.meetup.com/33/

Podcasting News
http://www.podcastingnews.com/

The Hawaii Association of Podcasters
http://www.hawaiipodcasting.com/page/2/

29

DESCRIPTION OF BUSINESS:

Domestic Violence Prevention Video Podcasts

Medico-legal Documentation Videos

Does the family that produces podcasts together communicate in new ways that help solve problems, share meaning, or tackle issues at each stage of life? Produce video podcasts on the prevention of and getting help for issues surrounding gender violence, domestic violence, and elderly abuse.

Gender violence prevention video podcasts would include discussing dating violence issues. There's also the field of child abuse prevention and elderly abuse prevention and solutions. The domestic violence safe houses usually are crowded or full, and abuse survivors need to know where to go for help and how to ask for it as well as alternatives to the safe houses when there is no room.

Video podcasts that can be turned into videos on DVD for public access or satellite TV stations also target the educational market. Network television and the public schools show videos (many are interviews) on how to prevent domestic and dating violence. In Los Angeles, one woman is battered every nine minutes, usually by a spouse, lover, or male relative. Battered men are often not portrayed in videos. Male batterers in counseling are not frequently shown on video. Also, the home schooling market should be researched regarding consumer demand for family violence prevention podcasts.

More than 1.4 million domestic violence-related calls were reported by law enforcement agencies to the State Department of Justice since domestic violence was made a separate crime from other assault crimes in 1986. The figure includes all calls, not only those in which an attacker was arrested.

The U.S. Department of Justice conducted 400,000 individual interviews between 1987 and 1991 that revealed friends and relatives were responsible for

33 percent of single offender attacks on females. Domestic violence accounted for only five percent of all assaults against males.

The hour-long news magazines frequently air programs on spouse battering, overcrowded shelters, women who have killed their husbands, same sex partners domestic violence, and teenage date rape or dating violence based on a need to control the partner.

The newspapers report that more than half of all women have experienced being hit, shoved, or beaten by a lover or spouse. Considering all the new research studies being compiled daily, creating videos on domestic violence prevention—showing people the warning signals to look for before committing to a relationship—is in demand by schools, nonprofit agencies, consumers, the government, and the news media.

Make a video following the ombudsman in family violence prevention programs and safe houses who acts as a spokesperson for the battered partner in legal matters. You can interview the director of a battered spouses' shelter or child care counselors in receiving homes designed to meet the needs of abused children.

Show on video tape what the director of a battered women's shelter or safe house does—how new arrivals are processed, counseling, arranging employment or training interviews to help residents make the transition from the temporary living quarters of a safe house or shelter to a halfway house where job training and employment counseling are performed.

Your video can show how the residents are guided to take the last step towards independent living and financial self-sufficiency or why they return home to the batterer when they can't make it on their own. Keep the video realistic, but positive enough to be of value if shown to an audience of battered women or men with low self esteem trying to find a way to be self-supporting.

INCOME POTENTIAL:

You could sell your tapes at a reasonable fee—$20 to $40 or $70 for a series of three tapes to therapists, law enforcement agencies, the government, schools, hospitals, social workers, or counselors. You can ask the government to assign you as an independent contractor to make tapes on specific issues in domestic or gender violence prevention.

Contact the teenage counseling and rehabilitation services, substance abuse counseling services and hospitals, and other workers in the helping professions. Your workbook to accompany the tapes could be self-published or sold to educational producers, or sold separately for a fee, averaging about $10 for the workbook and $20 for the videotape. Or produce a series videotapes for counselors and therapists on gender violence prevention, such as three tapes for $69.95. Audio tapes can accompany the videos and booklet or workbook.

Your income from tape producing can vary with the funding of the agency involved, if you're assigned to produce a video for a government task force. Income varies geographically. You could apply for a grant to make a social service film nationally or to record/report on domestic violence overseas.

BEST LOCALE TO OPERATE THE BUSINESS:

Operate your video production business near the center of any large city, possibly near community centers, law enforcement agencies, the appropriate court house, law offices, or battered spouse's shelters. You may be adding other legal video services, such as deposition taking, compiling evidence photography and forensic video, or preparing videos for court presentations.

Apply at battered women's shelters and safe houses, nonprofit and social agencies, community service foundations, the YWCA/YMCA, women's organizations and hospitals to find out whether training films are needed on the subject of how to recognize and deal with domestic violence cases.

TRAINING REQUIRED:

Volunteer to work on your local battered women's shelter hotline, answering crisis telephone calls. Your videos really provide direction for parents and children in crisis. Read books and articles on domestic violence prevention. Visit battered women's shelters (and if you can, visit the few shelters for battered husbands). Visit safe houses, battered women's shelters, men's support groups, and assisted living support groups, such as those for the older woman and those for women with infants and small children, or religious-affiliated shelters. Talk to counselors and therapists who counsel the battered and the batterer.

After you've done your research homework, learn how to operate your camera and how to interview people. See the section on how to make videobiographies. Edit interviews. Ask counselors and group therapists to give you permission to tape their anonymous participants who volunteer to be on the video, in writing.

Make sure their identities are disguised. You can have them wear masks and disguise their voices on the tape. If you're taping inside a prison, for example, making a video of women who have killed their batterers, ask whether they want anonymity or not. Some may want the videos to air in order to get publicity in their appeals to have their sentences reduced under new laws.

GENERAL APTITUDE OR EXPERIENCE:

Empathy, the ability to figuratively stand in the other person's shoes is the best qualification. Make a few simple interview-based videos before you go out to tape in front of a therapist, a group of people in counseling, or an individual talking under stress. Familiarize yourself with domestic violence laws in your area.

EQUIPMENT NEEDED:

Use video podcasting software and hardware for your broadcasts. For excellent quality suitable for DVDs marketed to consumers, you'll need an industrial or broadcast quality camera, editing and dubbing equipment, a tripod, tapes and DVDs, a rented field video camera for outside tapings, sound equipment, special effects and title making attachments, and someone to hold the camera while you interview. You'll also need computer drives that record to DVDs so your results can be played not only on computers and iPod-like devices, but also on DVD players and viewed on TV screens.

It helps if you can use your computer in tandem with your camera to produce titles and special effects with appropriate title-creating software. You'll need a device to link your computer with your VCR or camcorder—such as a video cable. (I use a Fire Wire 1394 cable with four pins that connect to my camera and 6 pins at the other end to connect to my computer's Fire Wire slot.)

Some video cameras record directly onto DVDs, but the technology may not be excellent enough to allow editing in the camera. Try out different types of camcorders before you buy any type of video recording devices, including digital video Internet cameras. Your best bet is an educational or broadcast-quality camcorder that can be plugged into your computer.

Software's available that lets you use your camera with your computer and the Internet. My camera is an older Sony digital high 8 camcorder hooked to my PC with a FireWire cable. I use Windows MovieMaker to edit my tapes and save them on my hard drive and then saved the edited files to a DVD.

Inquire at your video supply store outfitters for specific equipment besides your camera that you'll need for a particular videobiography. If you're a beginner, keep everything simple by making a first video based on interviews with a variety of people edited together. Sometimes you'll get only on chance to tape because people won't be able to repeat with the same impact a second time.

OPERATING YOUR BUSINESS:

Produce specific targeted audience videos on preventing domestic violence or create your original ideas based on community need. Include national phone numbers to call or crisis hotlines where someone can inquire about finding local number referrals.

Write the script yourself based on research and interviews with experts and professional counselors, law enforcement personnel, and community agency workers. If writing the script yourself from your research is impossible, work with a scriptwriting partner to produce domestic violence videos on the following subjects:

1. Preventing teenage dating violence and date rape.
2. Preventing elderly abuse.
3. Gender violence: the issues and prevention.
4. Child abuse and domestic violence issues.
5. Warning signals to look for before you marry.
6. Control, jealousy, stalking, and obsession.
7. The battered spouse syndrome: how it's used in court for lawyers and therapists.
8. Preventing international child abduction.
9. How to interview children for court or witness: techniques on video.
10. Battering by same sex partners.
12. Counseling male or female batterers.
13. How to leave if you're a battered spouse with small children and no job.
14. Verbal abuse in marriage or the effects of verbal abuse on children's behavior.
15. Why so many battered women can't leave, or agoraphobia, loss, and the battered spouse.
16. How to create a new identity in another state: for the battered spouse being stalked by a life-threatening mate.
17. Preventing workplace violence.
18. When domestic violence follows a partner into the workplace.
19. Counseling co-workers after workplace violence experiences.
20. Preventing traffic and public transportation fights and other stress-related random violence, including carjackings and road-rage incidents. (When you see the car in front of you as an extension of your own personality and feel hostile enough to physically punish the other driver for cutting in front of you.)

21. How to get away from and/or stop stalkers, peeping Toms, and others obsessed with you. How to gather evidence, prosecute, navigate legal avenues, or relocate with a new identity.

22. When you're threatened or are in a witness protection program, what to expect: an informative video.

23. Dealing with difficult people.

24. Assertiveness training videos.

25. Dealing with Obsession or Jealousy:

26. Explain what is meant by the "battered women's syndrome" and how such a defense is used in court: a video for attorneys, therapists, social workers, survivors of spousal abuse, and batterers in counseling.

Other topics for related-subject videos include, living with or leaving an angry or controlling spouse or dealing with an angry, controlling, dangerous, or abusive adult child trying to return to your home.

Or produce tapes on persons who are emotionally or financially dependent on the domestic partners or relatives who abuse them. Your video should make viewers aware of why it's so hard for the battered spouse to walk out.

A battered partner who returns to the home of the batterer may be suffering emotionally from "the battered spouse syndrome." Additionally, there may be financial woes, child care problems, age, emotional dependency and fear of change, low-self esteem, fear of never being able to hold a job over a long period of time, fear of being stalked and killed, or fear of leaving the house because of panic attacks.

You can focus on any of these issues to build up a video on why so many women return to the men who batter them, only to eventually be killed by their lovers or spouses, or in the cases of teens, controlling dating partners. If you want to tap the tabloid video market, produce a video on celebrity battered spouses and their batterers, an authorized or unauthorized expose of domestic or gender violence among the rich and famous.

Create a historical video of domestic violence for schools and public broadcasting. Use clips and quotes of famous scholars and preachers who were batterers, or battered women who set themselves free. (Use well-known historical figures with validated documentation.) Pepper your video with famous quotes on domestic or gender violence from books of famous quotations. You could even make a video on words about women. (See Jane Mill's Womanwords, a Dictionary of Words About Women, The Free Press, a division of Macmillan, Inc., NY, 1989.)

These are only a few suggestions for creating gender violence prevention videos accompanied by workbooks and/or audio tapes. Your video could consist of interviewing experts, therapists, law enforcement personnel or attorneys, doctors in emergency rooms who care for battered spouses, formerly battered spouses, companions, or dating partners, and people who have battered or who are obsessed and controlling.

After you have collected enough interviews of experts and survivors of domestic violence as well as the batterers, find a transition point to tie in under one umbrella all the interviews. Then edit the interviews in sequence to show still photos of the battered person's injuries, the re-enactment of events, perhaps with actors, and interviews with relatives or employers.

Find out from community and nonprofit groups, law enforcement agencies, the government, schools, social work agencies, hospitals, psychologists and counselors as well as from local law schools, universities, family services, and training centers, and the media (network and non-broadcast television) whether training or expose videos would find a niche market in your community.

Your market survey would ask schools and agencies whether they had the budget for buying or renting your videos on domestic violence prevention. Write to the director of the nation's hundreds of battered women's shelters, including some of the religious-oriented shelters as well as the public ones. Contact churches and the clergy and pastoral counselors as well as domestic violence counselors and therapists. Court-ordered counseling could include the viewing of tapes if you find out what kind of tapes the court would approve of before you begin to produce them.

TARGET MARKET:

As a documentarian or educational materials producer, your videos are best targeted to schools, hospitals, law enforcement agencies, attorneys, social workers, therapists, counselors, the government, nonprofit organizations, and other helping professionals. Or target extended study college courses for continuing education of nurses, psychologists, and social workers.

Make videos directed towards children's markets. One example is a video on what to do if one or both of your parents are being battered, or what a child can do if abused or if witnessing abuse of the frail elderly in the home. What should a child do if a parent is housebound with agoraphobia and panic disorder?

Also, focus on the teenage market with videos of preventing teenage dating violence or teenage pregnancy and other problems specific to various age groups. Make a video on how to prevent domestic violence by knowing ahead of time what warning signals to watch for—before getting further involved in a controlling, obsessive relationship.

RELATED VIDEO OPPORTUNITIES:

Produce video podcasts and short documentaries for DVD distribution on domestic violence prevention or elder abuse issues for the government or protective agencies. Videotape a variety of themes and causes for fundraising purposes. Help to cut expenses and at the same time raise money for battered spouse's shelters. Become an ombudsman or spokesperson for hospitalized patients by videotaping them during interviews concerning their rights and needs.

Collect news clippings on related subjects and make a video following the progression of the news or contemporary and controversial issues in the news on the subject of domestic or gender violence. Call radio and television talk show hosts and interview as many as you can for your video.

Interview a variety of trainers and teachers. Ask about their experiences with children's exposure to violence at home. Work with controversial themes. Record people speaking about what it felt like as a child to witness their mothers or fathers getting beaten by a spouse. Or interview parents how it felt for their children to beat or control them with threats and violence.

Make videos for children's classes to alert them how to act if approached by strangers—videos for the child's protection or-self-defense. Or focus on making videos for attorneys to be used in courtroom presentations, to take depositions, or to include forensic evidence for trials. Make a video on your own experience with domestic violence and compare it with those of your neighbors.

Producing videos on controversial issues sell well with students. Include in your video package a booklet and workbook so teachers can use your video in their lesson plans and give assignments on your video from your workbook. Make sure your video emphasizes plenty of alternative ways to solve family problems without using violence.

Or focus on workplace violence. Often, domestic violence ends with the batterer coming into the ex-partner's workplace. Finally, bring in what happens when domestic violence spills over into workplace. Include clips on harassment, stalking, and show how new stalking laws are helping.

Show by inserting video clips with interviews why violence escalates when someone tries to leave a relationship. Show why leaving is the time most often when the batterer kills the person trying to leave.

A marketable video should do more than ask questions or give summarized information. Offer the equivalent of newspaper quotes, so the video won't be like a flat piece of writing.

Show a charismatic expert giving active solutions to problems in an interview instead of answering the interviewer's questions with more questions.

Have the narrator end with an upbeat comment or point in the direction of a solution, if only as a starting point and guide. Use your video as a map or navigation tool to arrive at a conclusion rather than only state needs.

ADDITIONAL INFORMATION:

National Coalition Against Domestic Violence
PO Box 34103
Washington, DC 20043-4103

Illusion Theatre-Domestic Violence
528 Hennepin Ave
Suite 704
Minneapolis, MN 55403

Task Force on the Study of Domestic Violence
Justice Department
Constitution Ave between 9th and 10th Streets
Washington, DC 20530
or

Emergency Housing Division
of the Urbanization and Development Division
of the Association for City Government (individual cities).

30

DESCRIPTION OF BUSINESS

Video Podcasting Monitoring of Media Tours for Authors and Speakers

According to the American Marketing Association's Dictionary of Marketing Terms, a video news release is defined as "a publicity device designed to look (and sound like) a television news story. The publicist prepares a 60- to 90-second news release on videotape, which can then be used by television stations as is or after further editing. It is more sophisticated than a news clip."

You have a choice of monitoring video news releases or writing and producing them yourself as video podcasts, news segments, CDs, and DVDs to give authors and speakers publicity before they begin their media tour of speaking engagements and/or book signings. Combine your podcasts, industrial-quality camcorder, DVD-player/recorder and video monitoring dubbing equipment with a network of other freelance video monitors and recorders to follow authors on national book tours, celebrities, public speakers (or spokespersons), and all types of media personalities on every step of a promotional media tour.

Track VNRs (video news releases), new product announcements, breaking news stories, and press releases in more than 100 markets for a specified period of the month. The most important job of a media tour monitor is to create a video library and database on tape and on disk for computer each time the person on a media tour appears on television or radio.

INCOME POTENTIAL:

For media tour monitoring current rate charge is around $400 plus notification fees. For frequency reports (time, date, station, city), charge around $15 per notification. Charge about $25 per printed schedule notification. For a synopsis (time, date, station, city, summary), charge about $20 per telephone notification and about $30 per printed schedule notification. A frequency synopsis of broadcast appearances or product announcements on television contains the time, date, station, city, and a summary (your synopsis of what went on the air).

Track television and radio coverage for major media events and client tours. For news monitoring services videocassettes charge about $100 for each videocassette up to five minutes.

From 5–10 minutes charge about $110–$140 per videocassette. From 10–30 minutes, charge from about $145–175 per videocassette. From 30–60 minutes, charge about $175–$210 per videocassette. From 60–90 minutes, charge about $250–$285. And from 90–120 minutes, charge from $300–$335 for videocassettes in 1/2 inch or 3/4 inch formats.

You charge ask for at least one hour advance notice to monitor and record anything. If the segment doesn't air, you should charge about $85 for your search, handling, and recording charge.

For radio segments, charge about $35–$85 up to five minutes, $45–$95, up to ten minutes, $60–$110 for a ten to thirty minute radio segment recording. For 30 to 60 minutes, charge $85–$135 for radio or audio monitoring and recording.

For TV and radio transcripts, charge about $40–$50 for the first 100 lines in a one-hundred line minute. For each additional line you can charge about 40 to 50 cents. Charge about $5 per fax per transcript for local transmission and about $8 for out-of-town transmission. Mail hard copy.

For your monitoring reports that reveal how many times a client's product or presence appeared in a broadcast: Charge about $400 plus notification fees for frequency reports for each airing or broadcast that contains the time, date, station, and city. Charge $15 for each phone notification, and charge $25 for each print notification.

BEST LOCALE TO OPERATE THE BUSINESS:

You can open monitoring service offices anywhere in the nation, or work from your spare room. With television, satellite, and short wave radio, you can live almost anywhere or cater to local markets. For national markets taped from a local area that are not syndicated nationwide or on a network, one alternative is to have branch offices open in a variety of locations. Have people running your franchised monitoring business from their own homes or studios and take a commission.

TRAINING REQUIRED:

Training can be learned by becoming involved with professional associations and their workshop offerings as well as through video monitoring equipment suppliers, advertising agencies, and doing informational interviews video monitoring services and occasionally, their clients.

Practice monitoring and dubbing television and radio broadcasts at home with dubbing equipment. Practice editing dubbed tape. Look for irregularities and conflicts. Compare competitors advertising similar products. Tape any references to competitors mentioning one another's product names. Tape radio segments on audio cassette.

Low-cost or free courses in television and video dubbing and editing are available from adult education or regional occupational programs in television monitoring. Call your local Regional Occupational Program or adult education department.

Join business associations for video monitoring service proprietors and suppliers, and take their seminars and workshops. Attend television products conventions. Volunteer to monitor broadcasts at presentations, lectures, seminars, and conferences.

Ask your dubbing equipment supplier to refer you to local classes or how-to books on operating the equipment. The best training is to intern with a video monitoring service and learn hands-on, the ropes. Also do informational interviews and talk to clients who frequently use the services of video monitors.

Volunteer to work in a radio or television news library. Or donate your services to public affairs libraries. Create logging reports, audio tapes, or transcripts from television and radio stations. You're dealing in preserving information broadcast on television or radio. You can also volunteer to cover media tours for local authors and keep a video record of their presentations or media appearances.

Ask authors or performers for their permission to record them. Have them sign a release form giving you publishing rights. You can specialize in only covering local media tours on video recordings with your industrial-quality camcorder.

GENERAL APTITUDE OR EXPERIENCE:

You'll need a good public relations sense and an eye for picking out conflict or irregularities in television and/or radio commercials. The best experience is to get some practice recording information from your television for local advertising agencies, authors on book tours, or news services.

EQUIPMENT NEEDED:

You'll need a variety of dubbing and editing equipment and a video camera. Study your competition wisely to make sure you are not undercapitalized. Start on a very small scale at home with a video camera, VCRs, half inch and three quarter formats, television sets, radios with tape recorders, and a computer to provide you with a database of videos and clients or potential markets. Make sure you can make laser printer color copies of visuals when your client asks for hard copy on paper.

OPERATING YOUR BUSINESS:

Monitor all types of media tours for spokespersons. Travel with authors, media personality figures, politicians, sports figures, scientists, business executives, and celebrities on a media tour. Videotape them as they speak before the public in libraries, schools, auditoriums, at conventions, or in bookstore signings and author's receptions. Or tape them while you stay at home and they appear on syndicated or network television or radio on national or global tours.

Look for conflicts and irregularities or monitor competing products being advertised on television and radio. Let your video monitoring equipment and camera play receiver/recorder as you follow a schedule of cities, stations, dates, and times. Set up special monitoring for a variety of markets focusing on events that few others record.

Keep a library of more than 100 markets. Retrieve air checks for your clients. You will be able to track down and retrieve air checks up to a month after they have been broadcast.

Track video news releases, new product announcements, breaking news stories, talk shows, client phone-ins and appearances, interviews, and press releases. You'll be able to reach more than 100 markets for a period of one month after a broadcast segment. Keep your own video archives available for two months for retrieval for clients.

To keep an organized file or record of what video or audio segments you have recorded for your clients, ask your client to provide as many identifying keywords as possible. These keywords go into your personal computer database. They are for your personal video library, archives, or database search.

Right after you monitor/videotape a media tour or any other markets, phone your clients immediately (or the next morning) and let your clients know that you've monitored their markets. Charge a telephone notification fee or a fee for printed information within a few days after your airdate.

You can add an all-market monitoring service to your media tour monitoring service. Include new product announcements, news stories, press releases and video news releases (VNRs).

Keep a keyword database in your personal computer so you can tap into your computerized keyword system like an index of video segments that's organized. Your client wants you to find video segments as fast as possible.

Do a computer search. Keep a monitor database. Ask the client to provide you with key words about their broadcast or video. Notify the client each time a story about the client appears in the news or on television, video, or radio.

Keep everything about the client in confidence. To use keywords, let the client know they can be product names, people, events, topics, places, or subjects. Keywords can stand by themselves as one word—as in "Students." They can also be linked—as in "Teenage" (in conjunction with) "mothers." The more keywords your client gives you, the better you'll be able to search for a reference each time a story appears in the news or on the air about your client.

Send your client a schedule of broadcast activity that lists the name of the program followed by date, station, city, and time on your monitoring report. Also send your client a transcript of what was announced or read on the particular network news station. The single spaced, usually half-page report as read on the news, should also contain the date, time, station, location, and name of the program.

You'll be sending videocassettes to your client in any format asked for. The videocassettes should be made available to your client up to 31 days from the air date. Audiocassettes should be made available to your client for 14 days from air date.

If you want to give away some free service, keep it a printout service, such as free local and network news notification. Your media tour tracking and recording service should also work well with a news monitoring service. So read the section in this book on running a news monitoring service.

Monitor any news as soon as it is broadcast. Notify your client the same day if the broadcast is in the daytime. If the broadcast airs at night, notify your client the next morning. Your client will frequently insist that news segment tapes and transcripts be produced for same day delivery.

TARGET MARKET:

You want to target anyone on a media tour to follow your spokesperson on every inch of a media tour around the country or around the world. You'll be recording all the stations in all the cities, being aware of all dates and times of broadcast or preliminary taping. You'll focus on special markets to monitor, those not normally recorded. Keep a video library of as many markets as you can locate—at least 135, so you'll be able to retrieve air checks up to a month after they've been broadcast.

RELATED VIDEO OPPORTUNITIES:

You can produce VNRs or video news releases with your video camera for clients. Your video camera can be used for recording from the air or from your VCR, or you can purchase dubbing and editing equipment if you are monitoring your television screen more frequently than you're recording with your camera.

Offer services such as TV commercial retrieval, radio commercial retrieval, laser boards (produce space-age photo boards by computerized conversion methods). Capture images from videotape and print out visuals using your color laser computer printer. Customize your monitoring. Monitor competing commercials from network, cable, or local test markets.

Report on diskette activities on products. Verify advertisement (commercial or infomercial) schedules for network, spot, cut-ins, black-outs, regional and syndication. Flag specific problems and irregularities for clients.

Record product conflicts and technical difficulties in television or radio product commercials. Provide your clients with video and audio cassettes of commercials in local test markets as well as on any broadcast, network, syndication, or radio airing. See the article on video news releases from the Source Watch, a project of the Center for Media and Democracy at: http://www.sourcewatch.org/index.php?title=Video_news_releases. Also see the article on How VNRs are Produced and Distributed at: http://www.sourcewatch.org/index.php?title=Video_news_releases#How_VNRs_are_produced_and_distributed. Also recommended is reading the article by Robert B. Charles, *"Video News Releases: News or advertising?"* See the Web site at: http://www.worldandi.com/public/1994/september/ci11.cf, *WorldandI.com*, Volume 9, September 1994.

Also check out the article titled, *Do's and don'ts of VNRs*, Public Relations Tactics, Volume 5, Number 6, June 1998, page 19. A fascinating article to read is titled, *Falling for Fake News,* by Scott M. Libin. The article is posted at: http://www.poynter.org/column.asp?id=34&aid=79766, PoynterOnline, March 15, 2005.

ADDITIONAL INFORMATION:

PR Newswire (United Business Media)
http://media.prnewswire.com/

The Video-Documentary Clearinghouse Archives
Harbor Square, Suite 2201
700 Richards St.
Honolulu, HI 96813-4631

The Broadcast Advertising Bureau
(Radio Advertising Bureau)
304 Park Ave South
New York, NY 10010

Association of Independent Commercial Producers
http://www.aicp.com/home.html

American Society of Media Photographers
419 Park Ave. South
New York, NY 10016
http://www.chimwasmp.org/

Public Relations Society of America
33 Irving Place
New York, NY
http://www.mnprsa.com/

Video Monitoring Services of America, Inc.
http://www.vmsinfo.com/

Resources for Pet-Related News

International Cat Writers' Association
http://www.catwriters.org

The Dog Writers Association of America Inc.
http://www.dwaa.org/

31

DESCRIPTION OF BUSINESS:

News Monitoring Service

Use your video podcasts to create video news clippings from all types of other news releases given to the media to use with permission and with all credits given to the news release organization, writers and researchers. Similar to the media tour monitor is the entrepreneur who creates video news clippings from video news releases (VNRs) and other types of news, drama, and product advertising broadcasts. Some news monitors will be asked to compare news broadcasts and look for discrepancies, conflicts, and other irregularities.

As mentioned in Chapter 30, According to the American Marketing Association's Dictionary of Marketing Terms, a video news release is defined as "a publicity device designed to look and sound like a television news story. The publicist prepares a 60- to 90-second news release on videotape, which can then be used by television stations as is or after further editing. It is more sophisticated than a news clip."

Video podcasts might emphasize how competing businesses compare products broadcasted for test markets. You also might compare how the competition advertises a variety of similar products in your podcast. You'll be asked to check to see whether ads are broadcasted at specific times and whether there are problems, conflicts or products, or other irregularities.

Review advertisements and infomercials for ad agencies in your podcasts and do more than monitor broadcasts and send reports back to the sponsors as to the quality and consistency of the TV program or advertisement you're asked to monitor. Video podcasts also can act like news clipping services for video segments rather than print articles clipped from newspapers or magazines. Audio podcasts can monitor and comment on or review radio shows and advertising.

Specialize in news or in advertising or combine monitoring services across the board. Monitor and record television broadcast news. Pick up news from all over with use of a satellite dish. News monitors specialize mainly in taping and comparing a variety of news broadcasts, sometimes on the same subject. You're a video librarian, news clipping bureau, comparison checker, and researcher rolled into one monitoring service.

Air-checking also is a specialization. It's defined as monitoring and recording television commercials, infomercials, and other broadcasts. Your goal is to create a news, segment, and commercial advertisement clipping business using video and/or other electronic media. It's the electronic side of operating a newspaper, coupon, and magazine clipping service bureau.

Publicists who send out press releases frequently want the news clipped to send back to their clients. Some public relations agents, book publicists, and advertising media buyers send electronic press releases and want to know if and when they moved their client into the media. Or publicists and their clients want videotapes of their clients appearing on television talk shows or broadcast news interviews.

INCOME POTENTIAL:

Charge about $175 an hour to sit at home or in your own studio with your satellite dish and pick up the news around the world, recording the news and any commercials or infomercials or special broadcasts. If you work for other monitoring companies or air checkers, they will pay you a small hourly fee or a small fee per each broadcast you tape.

It's better to work for yourself doing television news monitoring than to sit at home and wait for someone to hire you to record at home. However, if you can't afford video recording equipment yet, working for a video monitoring service is one way to learn hands-on and acquire experience and training.

You'll find several classified or small display advertisements asking for people to record on videotape at home in entrepreneurial type magazines on your news or book store magazine display racks.

For example, more than a decade ago, in the summer 1994 edition of <u>Small Business Opportunities</u> magazine, a small display advertisement appeared on page 74 entitled, "Record Videotapes At Home For Profit." The advertisement stated that there…are no copyright violation or pornography involved and stated some of the details of recording videotapes at home for profit, including how much profit is possible.

Write to advertisers, advertising agencies, and marketing firms for information on how you can record commercials or other videotapes at home. Each of us has different business and income requirements. Learn as much as you can.

Remember, that recording videotapes at home is different from *monitoring* live or taped news broadcasts, commercials, infomercials or talk show segments. Other opportunities exist such as recording cable channel and pay television feature film broadcasts. Check with your client and the broadcaster to make sure you are not recording copyrighted material without written permission to record it.

BEST LOCALE TO OPERATE THE BUSINESS:

With a satellite dish, you can pick up hundreds of television stations around the world. You need to subscribe to the cable stations or purchase the type of satellite where you get everything out there, around the world or at least around the nation. The more stations you can receive, the better your chances are of finding clients who will pay you to monitor the news or commercials.

TRAINING REQUIRED:

It has been said that all you need to know to get started is how to sit at home in front of your television set, record, dub, and edit on your VCR and other television monitoring equipment what you are told to monitor on your television screen. However, you need to know how to tune in your satellite dish, dub a television program on your VCR or other monitoring equipment, and make video news clippings on a videotape.

Ask at your local video supplies store what you'll need to get set up at industrial quality to compete with local news monitoring services. Your video camera capabilities need to be at industrial quality. Any news clippings on video are played so many times that anything less than industrial quality camera and tape will wear out fast.

You could get training from a video supply store or take an adult education class in how to do news monitoring or "air checking" (recording television commercials). Sometimes seminars are offered in air checking or news monitoring by local chapters of national video associations, advertising organizations, and groups of media professionals. Inquire at your local community college or university's department of broadcasting and television, or join a business association for people in the video business.

GENERAL APTITUDE OR EXPERIENCE:

News monitoring and air checking are for people who really enjoy sitting home all day recording television news, commercials, infomercials, and other broadcasts for clients. If you rent a studio and fill it with equipment, you'll need room for your satellite dish so you can pick up all the stations. You also can record radio broadcasts on audio tape.

You'll need patience with people. It helps to have an aptitude for getting along with a variety of clients, including advertising agency executives, demanding media/broadcast people in a hurry, and video news clipping bureau competitors who insist on perfection on tape. You don't have to stay up all night anymore to record commercials or news if you program your VCR and recording equipment in other formats to turn on and off at certain times.

EQUIPMENT NEEDED:

Eventually, you will be asked by different clients to record in all formats. A satellite dish is necessary to pick up all the television stations around the nation and/ or around the world. You'll need to get all the cable or satellite stations. An industrial quality video camcorder, VCR and DVD equipment is required for recording at industrial quality, dubbing or editing equipment for clipping the tapes at the right moment, and video tape of the client-specified length.

If you work at home, you'll need a backyard to put your satellite dish. Check to see whether your home is zoned for satellite dishes in case your neighbors complain. If you rent a recording studio, it should have enough space to put your satellite dish and recording equipment.

Find out whether your clients want broadcast quality or industrial quality videocassettes. That determines whether your camera will be broadcast or industrial quality, what kind of tape and editing or dubbing equipment you'll use, or what kind of packaging is preferred.

Industrial quality video can be copied many times without losing resolution. Broadcast quality video is more expensive and better, because it will stand up to more copying without losing quality. It's generally is used for network television broadcasting. It's what you see on the local TV news station.

Industrial quality tape or DVDs are used for non-broadcast television training purposes and to make industrial videos that will appear on corporate training videos rather than be broadcast nationally or locally to the public on television stations. Choose your format according to where your client wants to broadcast. Communication channels could be industrial, on national network television, or cable TV, non-broadcast media, via phone lines, Internet, or by satellite video-conferencing.

How many copies will be made from the tape or how much will it be played? Choose the best quality for your client, and bill accordingly.

Check with your video supplies store and the competition to see what they are using. You'll have to record in all formats. Look in video and television newsletters coming from local chapters of the International Television Association to see what the most popular formats are, and what supplies you'll need.

Talk to video equipment suppliers, especially at the booths during video and electronic trade conventions. Attend as many video-related industrial equipment conventions as you can because you learn the most by chatting with video outfitters who are not in competition with you.

Check what equipment your more silent competition has by networking at local chapter meetings of podcasting, television, and broadcast-related trade associations. Go on tours of the competition's businesses which are often sponsored by these professional broadcast industry associations, local chapters.

Study your local markets. Check out businesses that will buy your services, not the average person in the street.

OPERATING YOUR BUSINESS:

What you'll be offering to clients primarily is television news monitoring. You'll be recording from all formats. You'll record from film to tape. You'll edit videos, dub videos, and do video production.

Join the trade organizations for networking and mutual support. There are several national organizations with local chapters also who publish newsletters, such as the International Television Association or NATAS. Some of their ads are for television news monitoring companies. Call these businesses and chat with the owners.

Clients will ask you to monitor news broadcasts and tape or record to DVD, the entire program or certain segments, such as the commercials. You may be asked to tape educational or cultural broadcasts, public television presentations, or special cable television cultural broadcasts. What you are running is a news clipping service, and instead of clipping articles from newspapers, you are monitoring and recording the news, special broadcasts, commercials, and infomercials.

Sometimes you'll find clients appearing on television talk shows frequently, such as authors on book tours, speakers for special causes or associations, or celebrities, who want you to record all the shows on which your clients appear.

You'll send the client the requested video news clippings and keep a copy for yourself for your videobrary (video library). If the client's tape is destroyed, you can always copy from your original tape and send another to your client in the future.

Monitoring the news on videotape also can be made into computer software. Using multimedia software, you can transfer the entire videotape or edited scenes to computer disk, or use it in a videophone conference (or televised videoconference) on non-broadcast television by satellite around the globe.

If you transfer your video taped news or commercial segment to computer disk, you can add text, music or other sounds, and illustrations, animation, or other graphic images along with the text, video, and music. You can even make the disk interactive. So you have a choice of monitoring the news in the following ways on:

1. Video or audio tape.

2. Computer disk as a multimedia presentation

3. Text only in a computer database or, the old fashioned way, as a photocopied news clipping cut from a publication.

4. Interactive multimedia, as on an interactive cable television shopping channel, or in a video computer game.

5. Interactive laser disk to be played on a special laser-disk player, for example Philip's "Imagination Machine" for family entertainment and learning, making the living room the learning room and entertainment center of the house.

How Do You Package A Video News Clipping Or Air Check?

When you package an air check of a broadcast television commercial or infomercial (28-minute cable informational television commercial), or a video clipping of a monitored news broadcast—the name of the show, the date, time, names of persons appearing, and any other pertinent information must be included on your labels. Send a sheet stating all information requested in addition to what appears on your labels, and keep your information in your database or files.

Advertisements in a variety of entrepreneurial magazines include selling videos for profit or learning VCR repair. Some ads offer information about little known home businesses and include audio cassettes and booklets. Use these ads as inspiration for you to consider making videos on related themes.

You can even make a video about how to earn money monitoring the news and commercials. Accompany the video by your own 50-page how-to booklet. Sell your video package to readers of home-based business and entrepreneurial magazines for a fee that includes all your expenses with enough of a margin left for at least a 15 percent profit.

A lot of people watch the news and would love to become involved in some way with the media. Monitoring the news gives anyone the chance to expand their knowledge of current events and issues.

TARGET MARKET:

Advertising agencies, television stations, publicists and public relations agencies, clients who advertise on television, cable television companies, persons in the news, celebrities, authors, researchers, talk show hosts, talk show guests, the government, corporations, hospitals, educational foundations, nonprofit agencies, schools, and broadcasters are all potential clients.

Anyone who ever appears on television or in the broadcast news would probably like to be monitored on videotape and sent a copy of the tape. Clients and business owners who pay for advertising want to know whether their ads were aired at certain times of the night or day.

Your target audience eventually may reach the point where you want national assignments from businesses. The chances of getting national assignments are based on your visibility, publicity, and advertising in a variety of broadcast industry trade journals.

Include yourself in direct marketing mail inserts. Expose your qualifications to businesses that use video monitoring services by advertising in the newsletters of professional associations, trade journals, and business newspapers read by your potential clients.

Advertise on video, including cable television, non-broadcast television, videophone, videoconference ads, on shopping channels, and on radio. Share the costs of television spot advertising and trade show/convention non-broadcast television demonstration screen ads with other advertisers. Your clients are broadcast viewers themselves. That's where you're likely to reach them.

If you decide to make a video about how to earn money at home recording video tapes, news broadcasts, or commercials, be aware that many broadcast news monitors enjoy working alone in home-based studios. Your market would include readers of entrepreneurial publications.

RELATED VIDEO OPPORTUNITIES:

Offer a news clipping bureau on video. Monitor news and commercials. You do production, film to tape, editing, dubbing, cable, and satellite recording. What else can you offer? Clip newspaper and magazine articles, stories, ads, announcements, coupons, notices, photos, and other material and offer them to clients as news clippings or put them on tape or on computer disk.

Specialize in doing attorney's legal presentations for the courtroom, including forensic evidence recording, or medical video for attorneys, for the courtroom, or for hospital training or technical presentations. Or you can specialize in monitoring/recording those 28 1/2 minute infomercials broadcasted late at night on the cable television stations.

You can even make money on the side videotaping weddings. If you're mechanical, you can learn by correspondence courses to repair VCRs at home.

ADDITIONAL INFORMATION:

Video Monitoring Services of America, Inc.
http://www.vmsinfo.com/

EIN News-World News Media Monitoring (a news service, not an association)
http://www.einnews.com/?afid=73

Broadcast Education Association
http://www.beaweb.org/96news/itva.html

International Television Association
http://itvadc.org/itvadc/index.cfm/fuseaction/about

National Academy of Television Arts and Sciences
http://www.natasdc.org/

Association of Independent Video and Film Makers
http://www.aivf.org/

Public Relations Society of America
http://www.prsa.org/

American Marketing Association's "Dictionary of Marketing Terms."
http://www.marketingpower.com/mg-dictionary.php?Searched=1&SearchFor=video%20news%20release

32

DESCRIPTION OF BUSINESS

Customize Auto Travel/Auto-Trip Planning with Video Podcasting Segments

Create international home exchange video podcasts. For inspiration, look at the Web site at: Home Exchange International, http://www.singleshomeexchange.com/. Also use your video podcasts to help parents plan long vacation or moving and relocation auto trips.

Include suggestions how to use video podcasts to entertain children in the back seat of a car or while traveling by public transportation. Help plan and organize executive relocation moving and job transfer or newcomer information. Vary your video podcasts from newcomer's welcome wagons in neighborhoods to helping the spouse of an executive newly transferred to another city find jobs or social clubs, housing or other adjustments.

Cut expenses while planning auto-trips and share this information with others planning auto trips. Contact auto clubs and travel agencies. Auto clubs cannot really customize their auto-trip planning services, but for your clients you can with your camcorder. Video podcasts can be used to help people making cross-country auto trips or to plan family travel abroad.

Use video podcasts to show housing environments for travelers who exchange houses for months at a time in different countries. Help with finding housing exchange clients and in screening people as well as housing and environments—yards, shopping, schools, recreation, socializing, and business. Or help people locate transportation, rooms, entertainment, or city tours during business travel or while attending conventions.

Compile auto trip plans, giving your clients detailed and personalized information. The video accompanied by a brief report can contain the best (or cheapest, yet clean and safe) motels, the most comfortable or shortest routes, mileage, cost, time, and prices for trips ranging from one-day excursions or week-ends to motorized vacations for retirees or families traveling with small children.

INCOME POTENTIAL:

You can charge a flat fee of $100 to $300 for planning a client's auto trip and producing a video on it before the person makes the long drive. Or make your videos first and then charge from $20 to $30 for a customized auto trip planning video.

Charge a flat fee of $200 to $1,000 for planning trips on video for small trucking-company fleets. Expect to earn a commission from travel agencies, motels, auto clubs, gas stations, and other businesses that service the automobile-travel, motor-home or recreational vehicle industry.

BEST LOCALE TO OPERATE THE BUSINESS:

Locate your auto trip planning videos in areas frequenting by tourists. Focus on resorts, theme parks, and family vacation spots as well as business travel centers. Call upon wedding consultants to recommend or market your honeymooners customized video on auto travel.

TRAINING REQUIRED:

You can benefit from knowledge of how to use your video camera combined with a course in running a travel agency usually found in extended study classes of community colleges. It pays to read up on automobile clubs and auto trip planning services and to join your local visitors and conventions bureau or chamber of commerce.

GENERAL APTITUDE OR EXPERIENCE:

You'll need a good knowledge of driving. If you're a former trucker, it's great. If not, study up on roads taken and not taken, auto travel, travel agency planning, and budgeting. You want to learn as much as possible about travel by auto for all types of people. Pay a trip to Traveler's Aid in your area.

You'll need patience, an eye for detail, and an aptitude for sales. The best experience is driving cross country and using your video camera.

EQUIPMENT NEEDED:

You'll need a video camera and editing equipment. A personal computer is helpful when you're generating pamphlets, reports, or print out sheets to accompany your video.

In your report and in your video customize for your individual customer's car trip or make enough videos to cover every major highway and back road in the United States and Canada. Use your computer software to calculate fuel consumption and costs per week.

OPERATING YOUR BUSINESS:

You can customize auto trips for individuals and possibly write a booklet to accompany your video or even write a syndicated newspaper or magazine column answering readers' questions regarding planning auto trips. Your computer software will compute miles, gallons, and so on, and uses graphics to plot trends for visual analysis. It can be used for several vehicles.

Put all this information on videotape by using computer to videotape transfer devices. Use computer software that shows which vehicle is most economical to use and helps budget travel and fuel costs. You can write to the software manufacturer at DMLK Enterprises, P.O. Box 2022, Lynnwood, WA 98036 for further information on auto trip planning and customizing software.

Most auto trip planning software is inexpensive and can be purchased at any software store. Use these programs to help you put your video together and customize it to either individual or universal auto travel planning needs for individual, family, or group auto trips.

Videographed auto trips may include trips in vans or motor homes, trips in small cars or station wagons, and trips under special circumstances. Auto trips need to be planned for paraplegics, for families with infants or small children, and for retirees. It is best to associate yourself with travel agencies and offer a service to their customers to customize motor trips.

To plan a trip for a client you need to take into account the age of the travelers, their health, travel time, motel preferences, camping expenses, and food. Variables such as weather, season, distance, and driving time all must be keyed into the computer to customize a trip.

Sit down with a client and find out about the traveler's personality and driving stamina, the condition of the car, how many people are sharing the driving, and whether the driver is sleeping in the vehicle and is traveling alone or in a fleet with other motorists. You can customize the plan so persons with special needs can plan safe and stress-free auto trips.

In addition to family travel planning, small trucking companies may ask you to computerize their fleet of trucks and work out plans for getting the trucks from one point to another within a budget and time limit. Transfer your summarized points to videotape once your computer software prints out all the variables, figures, costs, distances, and probabilities.

TARGET MARKET:

Members of automobile clubs, travel agency clients, and individual families may use your auto planning video. Small trucking firms may retain you for customizing their fleets. You can find clients and viewers by advertising in automobile club magazines, travel publications, and travel agency fliers. Contact motels for permission to place your flier or your entire library of auto trip videos in each room.

Make a video podcast for every major route or highway and the back roads or off the beaten paths. Focus on the United States, Canada, Mexico, or driving in Europe for cruise and airline passengers. Or emphasize a special area you know well.

RELATED VIDEO OPPORTUNITIES:

You can become a video wedding consultant, a travel agent, a visual travel planner, or a videographer to anthropologists on treks and world-wide trips. You can be a tour guide who also advises people how to make great travel and driving trip videos or teach video production to tourists and persons planning to travel—at travel agencies or senior centers.

ADDITIONAL INFORMATION:

American Automobile Association
1000 AAA Drive
Heathrow, FL 32746-5063
http://www.csaa.com/home/

American Society of Travel Agents
1101 King St.
Alexandria, VA 22314
http://www.astanet.com/

International Home Exchange
http://www.4homex.com/why.htm

Vacation Homes Unlimited-Exchange Homes.Com
http://exchangehomes.com/

Holi-Swaps.Com
http://www.holi-swaps.com/Home.asp

The Vacation Exchange
http://www.thevacationexchange.com/

Home Exchange International
http://www.singleshomeexchange.com/

33

DESCRIPTION OF BUSINESS

Political Campaign Management

Video podcasts can be used to manage campaigns for politicians and also for any type of public relations clientele—people, services, or products. You promote both the people and the products the people offer by showing viewers step-by-step how the products and the people solve problems.

Use video podcasts to showcase and promote campaigning politicians. Point out to politicians (and other viewers) how to cut unnecessary expenses and get higher quality services and items for less money. Use your camcorder, digital camera, and audio recording equipment to manage political campaigns for candidates. Perform public opinion polling, do direct-mail solicitation, media buying, candidate scheduling, and financial reporting in compliance with government guidelines.

INCOME POTENTIAL:

You can charge an hourly fee of $200 to $300 to manage a candidate's political campaign or a flat fee of $500 or more to manage a campaign from inception to election. Your videotaping fee can be approximately $175 an hour for straight taping or monitoring and $200 a minute to write a short video script, usually 10 to 12 minutes in length. The price rises with the level of campaign.

For designing campaigns for candidates who must travel throughout the year, charge a monthly retainer of $50 or more. Use a sliding scale, charging more to candidates for higher offices.

BEST LOCALE TO OPERATE THE BUSINESS:

Operate a video political campaign management business in Washington, DC or in major city offices, in state capitals, and close to seats of government in the states. You can begin in almost any city running video campaigns for minor political offices and school board candidates, city clerk, or other elected offices.

Volunteer to work for your favorite candidates and bring your video camera along every time you talk to them. Collect video clips of your candidate in different cities. If you can, travel with your candidates and combine political videos with travel videos, if you're part time in each arena. Offer campaign management services, including flyers and media releases, video recordings, photos, Web radio, speech archives, and ads.

TRAINING REQUIRED:

The best training is in video camera techniques and political volunteerism as well as a course in publicity and campaign management. You can find training hands-on by volunteering for your political candidates, helping in fundraising, sending press releases, and making videos as a freelancer for your local television news stations.

GENERAL APTITUDE OR EXPERIENCE:

You should be able to carry a camera wherever you go, be good in writing press releases, and take pictures—both still and video of your candidates. The best aptitude is to be a natural revealer of news with a flair for video production and design. You're an image maker with your video camera.

EQUIPMENT NEEDED:

You'll need a video camera and editing equipment, a tripod, tapes, and a personal computer to keep track of your records, videos, and video scripts. You can also benefit by owning an automatic telephone dialer. You'll need a VCR and dubbing equipment so you can monitor, record, and create a library of video clippings on your candidates. The equipment is similar to what a video news monitor needs to keep tabs on a candidate on video for the purposes of fundraising and image-making in the public eye.

After you've bought your industrial-quality or broadcast-quality camcorder, buy a word-processing program such as Microsoft Word for Windows and a desktop publishing software program for your personal computer, blank disks, paper supplies, and envelopes. The estimated cost of computer software is $400 to $500. Make sure you have Internet access.

A decade or more ago, CAMPAIGN MANAGER software designed and managed political or corporate campaigns. The software program automatically performed opinion polling, direct mail solicitation, media buying, candidate scheduling, and financial reporting. Today, you have an excellent choice of software for managing campaigns. Check the Web for reviews and consumer ratings of campaign management software as there is an excellent variety at a variety of prices. Press releases are generated automatically.

The program you select should prepare position papers, speeches, and sends thank you letters to donors—or ask for money. Buy software that has a password protector to prevent unauthorized access. The program that was popular for managing political campaigns more than a decade ago came from Aristotle Industries, 3 Outer Road, South Norwalk, CT 06854. You'll probably want to send videos asking benevolent people for money (contributions to the political campaign), and then follow up the direct mail marketing fundraising videos with computer-generated letters asking for money.

OPERATING YOUR BUSINESS:

The first step in managing a political campaign for a candidate is to prepare press releases for newspaper deadlines and press release videos for the broadcast media (television producers and public broadcasting specials). You can use your personal computer's word processor to generate releases.

The next step is to compose position papers, write speeches, put all this on videotape, and electronically send thank-you letters to volunteers and donors. You may be asked to perform opinion polling.

Your software program can do this automatically. You will have to solicit voters and donors by direct mail. Again, the software generates this for you. You fill in the names with mail-merge software.

Campaign managers need to buy media for a candidate. When you buy media, it usually means purchasing advertising and obtaining free publicity or news coverage. Use your campaign management software to guide you in media buying and placing paid ads in appropriate publications. The candidate must be scheduled to speak in different neighborhoods, cities, states. Send videos where the candidate cannot visit.

Financial reporting is required by state and federal governments. The software program can generate all necessary reports in the correct formats. Position papers are both speeches and published documents. You can create these on your word processor by interviewing the client on his position, recording all speeches or comments, and writing the speech on your word processor and reading it back into your tape recorder for timing and emphasis.

Listen for the meaning between the lines. Read it to your candidate. As soon as it is authorized, approved, and signed, key it into your computer and put everything you can on videotape. When donors and volunteers respond, your computer program will generate thank-you letters. Opinion polling is the biggest task your computer can be asked to do.

Your computer will have to handle a large amount of data, but the results can be analyzed and studied on the computer. You're using your video camera to show your favorite candidates in the best light, in family settings, shaking hands, making speeches, and discussing the issues. You'll do a lot of videotaping of speeches while you travel. If you can't travel, you can monitor the speeches on television and record them as video news clippings for the candidate's publicist.

TARGET MARKET:

Political candidates at all levels may rent your video-oriented campaign-management services. Beginners may find success with candidates running for neighborhood and community elections, for offices like city manager, assemblyperson, school-board representative, district representative, later working up to the offices of mayor, congressperson, governor, senator.

Other target markets for utilizing your video camera include fundraising, videotaping fundraising dinners and parties, planning events and taping them, and finding ways to create an image, credibility, and visibility for your favorite candidates. You can target volunteers and make videos of how people pull together to work for the candidates.

RELATED VIDEO OPPORTUNITIES:

You can create an image with your camcorder for just about anyone who can afford to pay you. You can create video press kits and video releases or clips (video and sound bites), or produce fundraising videos for charities, hospitals, the government, speakers, other types of candidates seeking offices, products, schools, or corporations. In short, you're using your video camera to create images, illusions of credibility, and validation—to sell the sizzle—the emotion behind the face or product. It's public relations applied to campaign management.

Your goal is to move, motivate, and inspire viewers to take action and make changes or donate money to a worthy cause. Let personal ethics be your guide.

ADDITIONAL INFORMATION:

American Society of Media Photographers
419 Park Ave. South
New York, NY 10016

Public Relations Society of America
33 Irving Place
New York, NY

Association of Independent Commercial Producers
http://www.aicp.com/

National Cable TV Association
1724 Massachusetts Ave. NW
Washington, DC 20036

International Teleconferencing Association
1150 Connecticut Ave. NW, Suite 1050
Washington, DC 20036

International Television Association
6311 North O'Connor Rd. DB51
Irving, TX 75039

National Communications Association
7 Park Ave., Suite 14-3
New York, NY 10016

Direct Marketing Computer Association
60 East 42nd St.
New York, NY 10165

Information Industry Association
316 Pennsylvania Ave SE
Washington, DC 20003

Society of Telecommunications Consultants
One Rockefeller Plaza, Room 1410
New York, NY 10020

Advertising Research Foundation
3 East 54th St.
New York, NY 10022

Training Media Association
198 Thomas Johnson Dr.
Folk, MD 21702

34

DESCRIPTION OF BUSINESS

Music Video Podcasts

Your video podcasts can help video music producers to cut expenses by research-ing hidden markets for the suppliers, vendors, and people who sell to the video music production firms. It costs $50,000 to $100,000 and up to produce one MTV music video that will air on the cable television stations or be sold as a home video. The MTV market is primarily adult pop rock consumers now, fans in the 20–38 age group, teenage rock concert attendees, preteen and teenage rap fans, adult country music lovers, and adult music business professionals.

MTV became so popular in the eighties that Time magazine featured music videos as a cover story in 1983—when it was still possible and popular to produce a music video for $30,000. Some people who enter MTV production come from the ranks of advertising commercial producers.

By 1984, MTV slumped. Record companies cut back MTV production up to 25 percent. By the mid nineties, MTV production is up again, booming, by selecting niches that appeal to specialized audiences and special genres of music. MTV has climbed in ratings also with the European and Australian markets.

More than one hundred music video programs are broadcast across the nation covering network shows and cable systems. Some cable stations air MTV all night. In addition to heavy metal, MTV includes niche and special program-ming. The most popular fields include adult-oriented rock, country music, and rap.

Music videos are full of subgenres appealing to different buyers. Success in musical video production depends on information such as producing the right compilations of old music video clips. Vintage music video is a subgenre with its own niche market and direct television response customers.

You're dealing with non narrative as well as narrative music videos. There are music movies and long-form animation videos with music competing with short form music videos. Success could depend on whether you're working inside or outside the record companies when a time-sensitive music video is produced.

If you produce corporate musical videos that will not be broadcast on cable or network television stations or sold in retail stores, you'll need an industrial quality video camera rather than a broadcast quality format. Corporate musical video production is not limited to cities where the television stations or record companies are located. You'll still need to rent your equipment.

As a non-broadcast television producer or director, you'll be dealing in-house with corporate executives or you'll be hired as an independent contractor. Most corporations that don't have their own in-house video production and advertising department hire an advertising agency to handle their account and their production. The advertising agency hires the independent production team. Branch offices of advertising agencies are found in major cities. Most have headquarters in New York or Los Angeles. Ad agencies, like producers, are often one-person independent firms. As a musical video producer, director, videographer, technical specialist, distributor, salesperson, or post-production manager, you are a specialist in a genre that has a variety of subgenres full of niche markets.

INCOME POTENTIAL:

Unless you have a superstar on national tour, with a major hit on the charts and frequent airings to produce on your first music video, it's going to be difficult to sell more than 10,000 videocassettes as an independent. You'll be selling your videos for an average price of between $9.95 and $19.95. Prices are falling with the competition and approaching the same price as CD albums.

The lower your price, the more videos you'll sell in the music business, especially to the very young, who may have trouble gaining access to their parent's VCRs. (Some teenagers do have their own VCRs in their rooms.) Lowering prices way down didn't increase the sales of some children's videos.

Since popular music is a time-sensitive industry, you'll have to compete with the free MTVs on television stations. You'll stand a better chance working with the record companies. Develop dramatic programs for music superstars.

Compare major hits regarding pricing at twenty-year intervals. Major hits *of the eighties* included <u>Making Michael Jackson's Thriller</u>, (Vestron Video), which sold more than one million copies, Prince's <u>Purple Rain</u> (Warner Home Video), a feature film priced to sell at $29. <u>We Are The World</u> (RCA/Columbia), was a hit of the eighties that sold for $14.95.

Other hits that sold thousands of videocassette units were <u>Lionel Ritchie</u> (RCA/Columbia), $14.95; <u>BandAid</u> (Vestron Video), $9.95, and <u>Rolling Stones Video Rewind</u>, (Vestron Video), $29.95. These top six sellers of the eighties accounted for 67 percent of sales and 64 percent of wholesale income. Remember, these sales are all competing with the TV music video freebies.

Prices are high even for teens with their own VCRs. Major performing stars are best-sellers. Videos are released too often when the star or the music has faded out with passing time. Music is so time-sensitive, that this flash fad grounded in the immediate moment and in the senses has affected retail sales. If your video and a CD are released at the same time, it could do well if the cross-promotion is there.

By working with the record companies, with their own video labels, you can get a foot in the door. As an independent producer, you can also earn an income by developing special music videos for certain stars if you catch talent at the right time and focus your musical video on having the star acting rather than only singing, playing an instrument, or dancing.

Major artists have sold more than 25,000 videocassette units each. Retail outlets may not be the best place to sell your videos if the major recording artists have averaged sales of only 1.4 cassettes per retail outlet. Record stores and video retailers are afraid of taking on new unknown videos if the stars have fared this way in retail outlets.

It's the time-sensitive aspect of music video that's responsible. You could focus on children's music videos combined with animation, or making musical videos for the corporate world or TV advertising commercials.

Study Sony Video Software's music titles (which usually are four short videos that sold well in the mid-eighties for $16.95). They released about 50 of 80 titles in the eighties that were in this format. Compare the past with the present regarding production types and sales figures.

Your income will be from royalties, and you may get no or little advances. So pick artists you think will be in demand for a long time. Forget the flash-in-the-pan fad music acts. Long-term profit is your goal.

Record companies release their own videos that are made with promotion in mind for the CDs, DVDs, streaming Internet audio/video or audio CDs and tapes. Records are history and CDs, laser-disk players, and quickly-fading audio tapes are being replaced by DVDs and smaller, newer technology for music listening, or music combined with video and special effects, including Internet · streaming for purchase and downloading or subscriptions.

For the record companies, income from music video sales still remains promotional. Sales of musical videos from record companies recoup their production and promotion costs. The psychology of the music, video, computer, and financial markets can be as important as any alternative or underlying reality. Market psychology ties together the music, video, computer, and financial markets.

If you are looking for that all-encompassing umbrella, container, or common thread, in the video business, it's always market psychology that deals with appearances as if appearances were reality. In the music video market, appearances cause reality to change quickly.

Psychology is music video's theme. Production financing is based on the faith that your video can deliver the profit it promises.

BEST LOCALE TO OPERATE THE BUSINESS:

Stay near the record companies, the cable or network television stations, the video equipment rental companies, the major advertising agencies, and the mobile production units. This usually means Los Angeles, New York, and San Francisco.

The majority of record companies are in Los Angeles with New York offices. Major ad agency headquarters are in New York City. Check out record company and agency branch offices, cable television stations, and smaller video rental and mobile production unit equipment firms for the corporate musical video market in a variety of cities.

Some corporate headquarters have in-house advertising and promotional video studios. Some production companies may be relocating to Atlanta, Chicago, San Diego, San Jose, or other cities. Also try the Canadian markets. The record companies tend to be headquartered in Los Angeles and New York.

Companies making a promotional video for a corporation in a certain city may hire independent producers on location rather than bring someone from across the country. Others may ask a video equipment rental firm to send a producer along with a complete crew to run the cameras, set up the lighting, and do other technical tasks. Research the Canadian, Australian, British, and other markets.

TRAINING REQUIRED:

Take a course in streaming Internet video, sound mixing, operating the latest digital video equipment and specialize in one or more specialties such as videography or lighting, being a recording professional, or digital music production. If you want quick training, try working for the video equipment rental firms as an intern or freelancer. You might want to combine the works of a documentarian with the art and craft of a producer of MTV recordings for a fresh angle or trend.

Learn all you can about producing from workshops or a community college course, or from extended studies courses given in music video production at local universities. If you compose music already, or are trained as a musician desiring to get into producing musical videos, then learn how to use the types of broadcast and industrial quality cameras and formats. Keep learning by volunteering for internships.

GENERAL APTITUDE OR EXPERIENCE:

You'll need a love of music, drama, and technical special effects. Experience working with the equipment helps. Volunteer for that internship or take that workshop so you can get hands-on experience. If you analyze, freeze frame, and study music videos carefully, you can learn a lot from them.

Study any animation, corporate musical video presentations, and TV commercials and compare them with entertainment musical videos and musical films. Learn to mix music, sounds, and lighting on your own video camera, and visit the equipment rental places to learn what the professionals use.

EQUIPMENT NEEDED:

Besides your broadcast quality video camera, you'll need lighting, crew, and post production equipment. Therefore, it pays to consult a video equipment rental company or a mobile production unit to find out specifically what you'll need to rent to customize a particular musical production. Every production will require different types of equipment depending upon location, talent, crew, and needs of the script.

OPERATING YOUR BUSINESS:

Star-quality MTVs can earn a lot of money. You don't have to do a rap music video or country pop. You can put classical music together with animation and do a children's fantasy adventure MTV.

Use your video camera to make an MTV, if you can find enough investors to chip in a bare bones minimum of $50,000—perhaps ten investors putting in $10,000 each. Use the MTV as a stepping stone in building your career up from music video into producing musical television commercials and then into making feature films for the home video market.

Start by quizzing advertising agencies at informational interviews. Learn the ropes by interning with advertising agencies that make musical commercials. More commercials are based on quick-cut music. You'll have to clear music rights.

Once you have produced an MTV or music video, you will be quickly contacted by advertising agencies to produce commercials. Get a music video background first, if you want to expand into making commercials for ad agencies or into production of feature films.

You can transfer any video skills you have between music videos and making advertising commercials for television, which are produced by advertising agencies. You can also direct music videos if you can't afford to produce them.

One opportunity for someone who wants to work with MTVs is to set up as an independent music video director. Print up business cards, intern with the small independent producers, take some courses in directing music videos at your local college, and read all the books you can on how to direct and produce MTVs.

Join the professional associations for music video directors. You don't have to invest in a production to create a team or join one with you as the director or even the director's assistant to start.

Apply to the corporate world at first, rather than only targeting the entertainment industry where competition is stiff. In the corporate world, music video is used by executives when they make presentations—at meetings, seminars, conventions, conferences, and while trying to pitch a sale or make a speech presentation before clients or potential customers with audio visual presentations and demonstrations of products or new ideas.

Trade shows make big business for budding music video directors or producers. Show corporate executives at trade shows how to deliver their sales pitches set to musical videos. Show sales managers how exciting business presentations are when set to music video. The alternative usually is a slow-moving slide presentation or hard-to-see flip chart lecture.

Corporate videos increasingly are music videos. They use the same quick cuts that MTVs use. Corporate videos use the same computer animation, star filters, and pulsating rock.

The corporate video's background uses the same MTV flickering light rolls, fog, dancers, and musicians in flashy costumes. The goal of the corporate music video is to attract attention, to make an impact, to send shock waves through the broadcast. This is purposely emphasized to contrast to the navy blue and gray corporate image (dress for success) suits of the corporate viewers watching in the audience—and watching one another's reaction to the corporate music video.

A new market invites the independent producer and director of musical videos. Apply to the on-air promotions department of an MTV cable or network television station for an informational interview to begin your preparation to make money with your video camera in musical video.

Learn how to design graphics or find someone to work with who does this. Volunteer to work show openings. Learn about how animation goes in between videos or top-of-the-hour station identifications at television studios.

Talk to video jockeys and how they do their segments. Talk to music video producers. Videos usually are produced by record companies. Visit the record companies and conduct informational interviews with the producers and directors. Pass your business card along and ask to intern for a summer at a record company.

Most people start working at cable and network musical television stations as interns. Sign up for a course in doing an internship or write to the station directly and ask to be let on as an unpaid or paid intern. Apply both to record companies and musical television stations for internships.

After your internship is completed, ask to come back as a freelance production assistant for either the TV station or the record company. If you can hack an unpaid internship during your summer vacation, you could have a good chance of being hired as a paid production assistant because people have gotten to know how you work under pressure.

Freelance production assistants are on call. The next promotion up the ladder is to associate producer and then to producers. Most MTV promotions come from the inside track. If you're really independent, you can set yourself up as an independent musical video director or producer and start your own company with your own crew—working with graduate students in music and television production or directing.

The most independent way to start with your video camera is to come in as a freelancer. Sometimes producers are brought into an MTV station as an independent producer/researcher, scriptwriter, intern or assistant to do special projects.

Take the reigns by opening your own music business by contacting musicians and selling their music to the movie industry and to independent producers of dramatic, industrial/corporate, educational/training, trade/marketing, documentary, special/tailored, medical marketing, and infomercial productions.

If the station likes you, you'll get more assignments on a variety of projects. From then on, you can move up to staff producer or director. Most freelance music video producers prefer to remain independent so they can take on only the projects that interest them.

After you've finished an internship in MTV at a station or as a freelancer, move into the record companies as an intern or freelancer. Another way to start out operating your business as an independent music video producer is to work for the video equipment rental houses and mobile music video production units.

It's probably less glamorous, and therefore, easier to approach a video equipment rental supplier and ask to do an internship, for freelance work, or for a job after you do an informational interview without asking to be hired—even as an independent. Do the same at a mobile production unit.

Most videotape producers rent their equipment as they use it for specific projects. If you work for the video rental house, you'll have constant contact with producers who can use you as a freelancer.

Rental facilities deliver cameras, lighting packages, and a variety of video equipment to music video producers, television producers, record companies, stations, news teams, musicians, at to production crews at events and concerts, trade shows, exhibits, conventions, ad agencies, and to a variety of other media teams.

The very first approach to entering the music video business should be through the video equipment rental firms and mobile production units that are always renting MTV equipment to the record companies. This is the place where you learn on the job, hands-on how to produce music videos—not as a file clerk working for a cable station or record company.

Learn to use the equipment daily at the video equipment rental firms and the mobile production units. It's you, the rental person, who will show the producer how you use the equipment. You'll work the equipment as part of the crew when the producer rents equipment. It's a way to begin and move up, to get in on the inside from being an outside independent. There's no better way to learn how to produce music videos hands-on, on the job.

You'll be in demand in the MTV business as a videographer, lighting technician, recording engineer, or other help—either freelance or as a temporary or permanent videographer with the rental or mobile company. The video rentals come in big packages.

You'll operate the equipment at each production location, working on a variety of projects. And you'll get continuous training as new technology is purchased by the rental firm or mobile unit.

Begin by offering to set up the lights or operate the recording equipment so you can become part of the crew, as a temporary, freelancer, or intern at a rental agency or mobile unit. You can even go into business by operating your own rental agency or mobile unit.

Video rental agencies and mobile production units visit theatres, events, courtrooms, hotels, record studios, television stations, and are found on location during the production of feature films. If you can't afford even a video camera, but want to become a music video producer, the cheapest way to start—that-doesn't cost you anything—is to work for a video rental agency operating the equipment at a variety of production sights when producers ask for a rental.

Mobile units have a need for freelancers, staff employees, and temporary workers to operate complete production facilities on wheels. You can find work with postproduction editing there also. They have mobile one-inch videotape switches, recorders, Two decades ago, students used Ultimattes, Chyrons, and all types of video cameras, sound, and lighting equipment to practice recording video for broadcast within one building or through community access TV. Today, most equipment is digital.

All this rental equipment drives up in a vehicle to a variety of sites when a producer wants to make a musical or any other kind of video. You'll work out of a truck that also is a completely equipped studio.

There is a need for operators of digital and audio equipment as well as lighting, cameras, and recording equipment. For postproduction, editors are in demand, as are the people who make the video titles with a Chyron (or the next level of technology), and do the special effects by computer, which are then transferred to video tape.

There are opportunities to do character generation, graphics design, digital effects, slow motion, wipes, zooms, swirls, and create patterns to blend with the music sounds. You can approach music video production from the point of view of the musician working with digital sounds and synthesizers, or from the visual producer and videographer, working with visual special effects and video scripts, or as a writer, or a specialist in interactive multimedia writing, directing, programming, engineering, illustrating, or producing.

Specialize only in postproduction or quick-cut video editing, or distribution. Another alternative is the design and construction of mobile video production equipment units. Mobile unit design and construction is a big business in itself—supplying the video supplier. Building a musical video or commercial from the ground up is a collaborative, team effort. What's big in music video is computer graphics.

The booming postproduction industry alone has a need for independent salespersons, artists, technicians, engineers, computer operators, designers, on-and-off-line editors, videotape production managers, supervisors, financial administrators, and managers as well as interns. The best way to get a foot in the door is to network through businesses that advertise in postproduction publications, look at classified ads or place your own projects-wanted or job-wanted advertisement.

Join business associations, Volunteer to help out on their publications. Ask to speak or find speakers for conference panels. Attend trade-related conventions and sign up for workshops or seminars given at conferences. Workshops also are offered by advertisers in the trade publications.

To get an idea of what you and your camcorder can accomplish by trying to break into the video postproduction industry, read the postproduction industry magazine, <u>Post, The Magazine for Animation, Audio, Film & Video Professionals</u>, (25 Willowdale Ave, Port Washington, NY 11050) Opportunities to earn money in video spring up in direct relation to the advancement of technology.

There are even opportunities to earn money writing about video. Everyone is interested in reading articles and books on how to keep costs down. If you and your video camera still want to make money producing musical videos, you'll have to get the rights to the music, deal with the big egos of the talent, markets are expanding just as teenagers now own a lot of their own VCRs in their own rooms.

Stay close to the music publishers and record companies. Learn how to deal with those who hold the rights to what you want to put on your video. Do informational interviews with the home video program distributors before you start your research. Also, don't forget that the federal government and government agencies produce videos with music, on more than 200 subjects annually in a variety of media.

TARGET MARKET:

Your clients will be producers of music videos for record companies and television stations. However, you can contact mobile production units, video rental equipment agencies, computer graphics companies and professional associations, postproduction firms, and advertising agencies as well as in-house production departments of large corporations.

Also contact the federal government. The federal agencies provide videotapes on every subject from deafness research to defense. Even the U.S. Secret Service, Department of the Treasury has a Visual Information Branch that provides videotapes.

RELATED VIDEO OPPORTUNITIES:

Attend the video festivals to see what others are doing to earn money in video. See the book, <u>AVIF Guide to International Film & Video</u> Festivals, (FIVF—Foundation for Independent Video & Film), 625 Broadway, 9th floor, New York, NY 10012, 1988.

You could be a producer, director, stylist, video game show designer, postproduction salesperson, distributor, multimedia computer game producer, instructional video designer, recording engineer, lighting technician, or writer of music video scripts—for corporations, recording companies, cable or network televi-sion, or children's programming. Specifically, you could do the following:

1. Produce or direct TV commercials or sell air time.

2. Produce or direct corporate music videos at trade shows.

3. Produce and distribute your own MTVs for entertainment broadcast and home video nationally and overseas.

4. Specialize in post production special effects.

5. Sell music videos, video equipment, or postproduction services. Or export/import musical videos.

6. Design mobile video production units

7. Own a video equipment rental firm.

8. Open a music video talent agency.

9. Be a music video casting director.

10. Write music video scripts or work as a script supervisor on production or as a music video script reader/analyst.

11. Open a public relations agency specializing in music video production.

12. Design record jackets and music video packages.

13. Illustrate musical videos with computer graphics and animation.

14. Create digital music and special effects with computers.

15. Work as a sound mixer for a video equipment rental firm or mobile production unit, or in the postproduction industry.

16. Be a freelance lighting specialist.

17. Work as an independent musical videographer and provide short video clips and cut-ins of unusual music and effects to music video producers.

18. Be an independent producer for a record company.

19. Run a temporary employment agency for musical video personnel, including distributor's assistants.

20. Work for a home video program distributor or become one. Study the techniques of self-distribution by linking up with the distribution industry through their networks, journals, associations, trade shows, and conventions.

21. Produce government musical audiovisual programs as an independent contractor, freelancer, or on staff.

22. Produce video game shows for teachers and children and sell to the school and preschool/daycare market, or produce the usual type of game shows for the cable television and interactive multimedia markets.

23. Become a music video talent agent.

24. Combine music videos with instructional computer software.

25. Dub music videos from other languages into English or acquire rights on foreign music videos. Or use visual anthropology to create new music videos from other cultures—such as New Guinea dances and costumes set to original or pop rock music, featuring a popular singer.

ADDITIONAL INFORMATION:

ASSOCIATIONS

Computer Musician Coalition
1024 W. Wilcox Ave.
Peoria, IL 61604

International MIDI Association
5316 W. 57th St.
Los Angeles, CA., 90056

Multimedia Electronic Music And Audio Periodicals/Resources
Post, The Magazine for Animation, Audio, Film & Video Professionals,
25 Willowdale Ave.
Port Washington, NY 11050
(a magazine for the postproduction industry)

Film/Tape Production Source Book
Television Radio Age (publisher)
1270 Ave. of the Americas
New York, NY 10019
Electronic Musician

Act III
P.O. Box 41094
Nashville, TN 37204

Keyboard
Miller Freeman, Inc.
Box 58528
Boulder, CO 80322-8528

Recording Engineer/Producer
Intertec Publishing Corp.
9221 Quivira Road, P.O. Box 12901
Overland Park, KS 66212

Directory of US Government and Audiovisual Personnel
or Media Resources Catalog
National Archives and Records Administration—or,
National Audiovisual Center
8700 Edgeworth Drive
Capitol Heights, MD 20743-3701

New York Public Library for the Performing Arts-
Rogers and Hammerstein Archives of Recorded Sound
40 Lincoln Center Plaza
New York, NY 10023

Multimedia Publishers Group
Advanced Strategies
60 Cutter Mill Rd., Suite 502
Great Neck, NY 11021

American Society of Media Photographers
419 Park Ave. South
New York, NY 10016

Electronic Artists Group
PO Box 580783
Memphis, MN 55458

International Interactive Communications Society
PO Box 1862
Lake Oswego, OR 97035

International Multimedia Association
3 Church Circle, Suite 800
Annapolis, MD 20401

National Cable Television Association
1724 Massachusetts Ave. NW
Washington, DC 20036

National Academy of Cable Programming
1724 Massachusetts Ave NW
Washington, DC 20036

35

DESCRIPTION OF BUSINESS

New Age Video Podcasts: Mind-Body-Spirit Businesses

Numerology Video Podcasts and Games for Entertainment

Numerologists interpret the numbers that determine life cycles and believe success is attracted to certain combinations of numbers. When you produce a numerology instructional video podcast, give clients readings by video podcast. Make sure that only the client can access the podcast on a Web site and download the reading. The podcast would only remain posted until the client has saved it.

As a numerologist, you give clients a reading based on how the client's first, middle, and last names influence their chances of success in finance, employment, marriage, or overall happiness. For entertainment purposes only, readings by numerologists, astrologists, or other practitioners work well with personal video podcasts that can be saved on iPods, mobile players, or in computers. The videos can be saved to DVDs or CDs using compression software.

Numerologists believe that you can change the way people react to you by changing your name, thereby influencing your chances for success.

EQUIPMENT NEEDED

You'll need your video podcasting software, a personal computer, video camcorder or digital video Web camera, DVD and CD recording drives, and disks. The estimated costs are about $1,000 worth of computer equipment and about $1,000–$3,000 for an industrial quality camcorder. Of course, you can use your digital high 8 camcorder, but the broadcast quality for professional-quality DVDs would be better with an industrial broadcast quality camcorder. For enter-

377

tainment purposes, any digital video Web camera or amateur home video camcorder will record a reading.

Numerology software will be helpful. There is plenty of free numerology software on the Web for you to download. Some Web sites include: Decoz®Numerology—Free Numerology Software—Free Numerology Readings at: http://www.decoz.com/ and Numerology Software to purchase called Professional Numerologist at: http://www.wideninghorizons.com/. There is a free evaluation copy of numerology software to test before you buy. It's on the Web site at: http://www. wideninghorizons.com/download.shtml. A free Numerology Analysis Tool software is at: http://www.aboriginemundi.com/numerology.html. Search under "Numerology Software" as key words in your search engine online and find all types of numerology software, either free ware, evaluation copies, or software to purchase.

OPERATING YOUR NEW AGE NUMEROLOGY VIDEO PODCAST BUSINESS

To give a numerological reading, begin by obtaining the first, middle, and last name of your client and your client's birthdate. In most interpretations of numerology each letter of the alphabet is assigned a number. These numbers are attributed with descriptions of personality. The numbers correspond to the following designations of the alphabet.

A B C D E F G H I J K L M N O P Q R S T U V W X Y Z
1 2 3 4 5 6 7 8 9 1 2 3 4 5 6 7 8 9 1 2 3 4 5 6 7 8

Number   1) leadership

2) artistic ability

3) humor

4) logical thinking

5) communications ability

6) domesticity

7) analytical and intellectual skills

8) business ethicality

9) entertainment

Some systems of numerology attribute personality quality to numbers. Number 9 in some systems is negative. By changing your name you avoid the repelling quality of your number.

In order to forecast with a numerological reading, you must add up the day, month, and year of a person's birth date and then add that figure to the sum arrived at from adding the letters of the first, middle, and last name. Then you take that sum and add the figures until you arrive at a number of 9 or less. For example, if you arrive at the number 22, each figure must be added until you get 4. The number 10 is 1 plus 0 or 1.

A person's reading consists of reducing all the numbers to between 1 and 9. One example is your client with the name "Anne Joan." These names are represented by the numbers 1555 and 1615. Add the numbers in the first name and the sum is 16. Add the two figures, and the sum is 7.

The next name adds up to 13. Then, 1 plus 3 equals 4. Take the 7 and 4 and add them to get 11. Add the 1 plus 1, and get a 2. Now take the number 2 and add it to the sum of the person's birth date. For example, if the person was born on November 18, 1941, it would be done this way: 1941 plus 11 plus 18. The sum total is 1970. Add each figure and get 17. Add these two figures to get one figure.

You end up with 8. Now add the number 2 from the name to 8 and get 10. Since one plus 0 is 1, your client is a number 1. In numerology number 1 means strong leadership ability. You could then advise your client to study for careers in which the leadership qualities would be used.

In addition to names, numerologists predict success is attracted to certain combinations of numbers in street addresses, telephone numbers, and other number sequences found in the life cycle that are believed to be predestined. Some numerologists predict stock market swings by observing recurring number cycles and ten-year patterns. Full instruction can be obtained by studying several good books on numerology and the instructions accompanying numerology software.

When you have learned the techniques, it's time to practice making private video podcasts of numerology readings for your clients. Your video podcasts also can be used to offer instruction and courses in numerology or related fields. In . addition to numerology there are other noetic areas to explore such as astrology or other types of readings. Video podcasts work well when giving instruction in how to do numerology as most readings for clients are private and more suitable for saving on a CD or DVD. You wouldn't post private readings for clients on public Web sites, but you might put up a video for a client to download from a private site or send the client a CD or DVD with the video reading. The video podcast also may be produced in interview format.

TARGET MARKET

Convention attendees, party entertainment planners, public access TV panels, creative salons, interviewers, radio talk show hosts, community centers, senior centers, astrology and numerology clubs, and subscribers to numerology and/or astrology publications, students of numerology courses or subscribers related new-age, intuitive, and mind-body-spirit publications are all potential audiences. You can also write for niche newspapers and magazines, or attend new age fairs.

Other people in the mind-body-spirit arena include spiritualists, ministers of new age-related churches, mystic and noetic science course instructors, members of parapsychology clubs, and groups or publications interested in forecasting and insight may be interested. Even some nightclub acts may feature numerologists and mentalists.

INCOME POTENTIAL

For entertainment purposes, most numerologists on radio talk show are not paid. To give individual readings, a top-notch numerologist who is asked to speak on numerous radio or TV shows can ask for approximately $200 to answer a question or give a reading. Your purpose would be to help people figuratively balance.

Lesser known numerologists can ask anywhere from $15 to $25 or even $50 for a numerology reading. The more time you spend analyzing a client's numbers, the more you can ask. Readings also can be done online, by phone, or through video or audio podcasts. In video podcasting, the client can actually see how the numbers are grouped and interpreted if you have charts, Power point slide shows, or excellent quality video close-ups showing how you work with the numbers. How can podcasts work for you?

Don't forget other new age and health-related video podcast markets for exercises and workouts or touch and healing arts such as tai chi, qi gong, Reiki, and Yoga instruction and discussion. Research what 'Lightworkers' actually do. Can they be featured on video podcasts? Combine numerology with other venues. Also check out the Web site for the Awakening Center at: http://www.theawakeningcenter.com/. Their site states, "OFALFO.org—a project of The Awakening Center, reaching out on the web and in the community, in Audio/Video/Text chats, community portal site and distance learning with a group of volunteers who give of their time and heart to assist others to find their 'center.' Continuing to grow and CO-create the essences for communicating in more vibrant methods to assist in reaching as many as we can."

◆   ◆   ◆

Epilogue: What Aptitudes and Skills Do You Need to Succeed in Video Podcasting?

Help people get what they pay for, make improved choices, and solve problems by watching your informative video podcasts. Find higher quality for less money from hidden, niche, and wholesaler's markets. Your video podcasting business can be run at minimum cost online and at home.

The purpose of your business is to show people step-by-step how to transform their lives, grow, build, gain skills, solve problems, achieve results, and obtain at lower cost higher quality food, clothing, shelter, healthcare, education, and career opportunities. While doing all this, you can showcase your talent as a communicator or video podcasting artist, writer, producer, or engineer.

Your goal would be to broadcast your news or opinion, sermon or course online or get more items and services of higher quality for less money. In showing others these techniques and strategies, you are training them to share what they know with others.

Your business would have the potential to turn into a franchise-like group of trained seminar leaders starting their own classes or groups. Begin a publishing and production service to provide training materials to share with others how to make money from the frugal lifestyle. At the same time, you can spin-off business that have a commitment to simple, natural ingredients and the do-it-yourself attitude.

To start a business showing people how to cut expenses you begin by interviewing and recording many different and/or competing businesses on the step-by-step methods business owners use to cut expenses and get higher quality items as well as how they avoid the pitfalls.

You learn how to cut expenses by interviewing people who have cut expenses in the area and products in which they work. Then you organize the ways they cut expenses on files, on cards, and in your computer. Your goal is to find the hidden markets and show others how to do the same.

Compile and analyze how people cut expenses and list the ways. Then list the ways they avoid pitfalls. When you have this information in front of you, it becomes part of your repertoire that you present to others showing your audience how to cut expenses and get more for their money by focusing on higher quality, hidden markets, shelf-pulls, overstocked items, and wholesale prices.

People pay for information they can use to make choices and decisions, especially information so new the media hasn't made it available to the public yet. These fresh angles on universal items or new applications become ancillaries. You can make a business by showing others how to spend less and get more because you get what you pay for.

Make use of proverbs and universal 'sayings' that are true. Make a business out of showing people how to get more quality for less money and still 'get' what they pay for in the lifetime of the product and its ability not to break down quickly. If you don't do public speaking, put your information on other media, such as on DVDs, CDs, or broadcast/pod-cast in MP3 audio files on the Internet and on disks.

You can also make pamphlets and booklets, or create Web sites. Another avenue would be to start a national association and franchise chapters in various cities whereby other people take a course you compile and qualify to start groups showing others how to open businesses showing people how to cut expenses and get higher quality rather than how to "live on less."

Show people not only how to live the frugal lifestyle, but how to live better, get better nutrition or health products, cleaning compounds, or pet care by doing it yourself is a business that helps people cut expenses to set up their own businesses. Here's how to start your home-based online business showing others how to cut expenses.

Where are the best and yet least costly cities to live? Show people who are relocating for specific reasons the most appropriate place for them to move. Research a variety of studies and reports, including Web sites that list the best and cheapest areas to live. Find out why the city had been recommended by reputable magazines and sites. Where did the research originate? Are the facts current and reliable?

When you've checked the facts, then you can let people know this valuable information and develop a budget for your clients about to relocate. To open a business showing others how to cut expenses, you need to be a listener and observer of current, credible research. Think of yourself as a mini-think tank. Your own budget can be minimal, and you can operate at home and online. What you're compiling and marketing is information so current that the media may not have seen it yet.

If you can find information for one client, you can do the same for a corporation that has decided to relocate. Keep your eye on the goal—showing others how to cut expenses and still get what they pay for—quality. Everyone wants more for less money. Your job is to reveal to clients and/or the public those places where people can find what they need at an affordable price.

If the item is a product, find out through customers who have used the product about how long it will last before the item wears out. You're business is about searching for durability as well as quality and less expenditure. Planning budgets for clients also is part of the picture of showing others how to cut expenses.

If you're helping people relocate to inexpensive-to-live cities, consider what your client wants. The Web site called "Cheap Stingy Bastard.Com at: http://cheap.typepad.com/cheapster/2004/09/cheapest_cities.html offers a link to the Forbes' Magazine site where the 60 cheapest cities to live are listed in that Forbes magazine research piece dated 2004. There are categories of individual needs to consider.

The "*Cheap Stingy Bastard.Com*" Web site notes that Forbes magazine divides communities into the following categories: "Porch-Swing, Happy Hootervilles, IQ Campuses, Steroid Cities, Bohemian Bargains, or Telecommuting Heavens." The *Forbes* magazine link is at: http://www.forbes.com/home/bestplaces/2004/08/09/life2land.html. You'll have to consider individual needs when customizing information on the cheapest cities to live in for your particular client.

The cheapest cities to live in reports update annually, and the cities change. Also see the 2005 CNN Money site that notes a new report from Salary.com looks at the relationship between salaries and cost of living in 188 large, metropolitan areas in the USA. See the Salary.com site at: http://www.salary.com. Whether you choose Tulsa, Oklahoma, or Huntsville, Alabama, or another city, you can find the cheapest city to live in for one year, but what happens when the various reports on the cheapest city to live in changes the following year?

Note that addresses and Web sites listed in this book may change over time and/or change frequently. To keep updated, check your Internet's search engine for new mailing addresses and Web site changes. The companies may have recently moved or changed their names and addresses. Check the Web before you write to anyone listed to see whether their address has changed. Also, see my Web site at http://www.newswriting.net for articles and various links.

What You Need to Get Started

The person who can share cutting expenses and getting more with higher quality develops the following abilities:

1. Sees patterns in everything.

2. Makes connections between two unrelated subjects and brings them together creating a whole new third subject or object.

3. Sees symbols in nature and makes them concrete and easy to grasp. Takes the abstract and applies it to what is of universal interest to all people. Makes the hard-to-understand symbols clear, useful, and practical.

4. Uses intuition (imagination based on experience and judgment) plus feeling to move the video forward. The forward action creates a measurable range of change from beginning to end known as growth.

5. Knows how to communicate, inspire, persuade, and motivate with video clips that reach people at their feeling/gut/emotional level while appealing to and respecting the viewer's logic/intellect.

6. Knows how to fill a void/need in the community with material that has universal appeal, even in a niche or specialty video.

7. Caters to the majority of pragmatic, down-to-earth viewers who want timely, useful information to make important life decisions, do something better, or improve themselves.

8. Presents learning as entertainment. Shows viewers how to have more fun with escape while learning new skills at the same time.

9. Shows the viewer without preaching how to reach his/her maximum potential or how to grow from the inside out. Works for a cause. Shows the viewer why and how to become involved.

10. Improves the quality of the viewer's lives while making the audience feel important and respected. The video leaves the viewer feeling good/positive at the end.

To integrate seeing patterns in everything with carrying out the concrete details of camera angles, it's highly recommended to work with a partner or team member who uses extroverted sensing well either as a dominant or auxiliary part of the personality.

Two people may be able to improve on each other's Web video or videobiography designs if one is an extroverted intuitive and the other is an extroverted sensor, either in dominant or auxiliary personality. The intuitive may write the first draft of a script, and the sensor may flesh out the concrete details in the second draft.

The same works in reverse with camera angles or storyboards. The personality that focuses on concrete details draws sketches from the personality that emphasizes abstract and intuitive designs.

The detail-and-reality-oriented person brings in the finer details of texture, colors, and script that the abstract person visualizes so that little is overlooked in photo-reality. Imagery as a big picture recombines with detailed photo-reality so that the viewer sees both the impression of the entire forest and the detail in each tree.

How do you open a business showing people how to live on less? Begin by interviewing competing businesses on how they cut expenses and still find higher quality items. Record step-by-step instruction or other information. Use plain language that your readers or listeners can follow.

This book has offered numerous video podcasting business possibilities that you can start that show people how to accomplish a project step-by-step. These steps should be clear and simple so that others can follow each step. Choose an enterprise that fits in with your specialties or areas of interest.

The purpose of the video podcast would be to make it possible for people without any previous training to follow each step in order to solve problems and get results along with benefits. Your purpose in making each video podcast would be to help people make more informed choices.

Write down what you have learned from former mistakes. How can your video podcast help others to do at least one kindness each day? Ask whether your informative video podcast can help others to be healthier, happier, or improve the quality of lives?

Appendix A

List of Writing Web Links for Video Podcasters

The Business of Writing for the Digital and Print Media

The business of writing for beginners, intermediate, and advanced freelancers and those seeking staff jobs reaches the print media through the digital media. You get to the print media through the digital, the online media.

Here's how you begin launching and jumpstarting your writing career by positioning to gain media visibility long before you publish. The business of writing also means learning to promote and sell your writing through the writing markets and many other industries.

Web Links

Training Beginners in the Business of Writing and the Writing of Business

Alexander Communications, Business Writing Seminars
Provides on-site, customized seminars in business writing skills. The seminars are practical and tailored especially for employee needs. Yvonne Alexander founded Alexander Communications, a San Francisco-based company, in 1986 to help her clients increase profits and persuasiveness by developing effective writing skills. Trainers will travel to your training site.
http://www.alexcommunications.com/

The Business Writing Center
Online, Instructor-Led Business Writing Courses Business Writing Workshops at Company Sites. Currently, over 400 students from 158 companies in 12 countries taking 15 online business writing courses to enhance their work performance and success
http://www.writingtrainers.com/

Business Writing Workshop Catalog
The Basic Grammar for Business Writing workshop is for people who have a good command of the English language, but need to make their sentences and paragraphs clearer, or who show a small number of consistent errors in grammar, syntax, punctuation, and spelling. It is suitable for non-native speakers of English as well as people who are native speakers.
http://www.writingtrainers.com/workshop/workcat.htm

Salary Wizard
Thousands of jobs are listed with free salary information as well as compensation packages, stock options, and bonus information. Select the Media designation.
http://www.salary.com

Copywriter.com
This is a Web site where words get results. Site is created by Al Bredenberg Creative Services.
http://www.copywriter.com

American Reporter
This magazine is the online cooperative "reporter's newspaper."
http://www.compumedia.com/~albowh/.

Executive Speech and Business Writing Internet And Marketing Strategies For Writers
Practical advice books on how to use the Internet to further your writing career and market your writing.
http://www.speechwriter.net/

Instructional Solutions: Instructional Solutions Online is a leader in online business writing training. Writing services and training materials at this training site for business writing. All of their training is instructor-led, providing personalized coaching and evaluation of writing tasks.

The training offered measures and improves skill gaps, tracks progress, and boasts a 96% completion rate across programs. Instructional Solutions is very proud to have been chosen by FedEx University and Liberty Mutual Insurance Company to provide online business writing training to their employees worldwide, including clients from 11 nations.
http://www.instructionalsolutions.com/

Internet Strategies for Writers
Moira Allen's book, ***Writing.com: Creative Internet Strategies to Advance Your Writing Career*** offers practical advice with chapters on finding markets online. Also included is information about electronic rights, netiquette, joining online discussions, Web site construction, and online publishing. At the end of each chapter are resources online for writers.
http://www.amazon.com/gp/product/1581150296/103-3227987-1607033?v=glance&n=283155

Rules of Punctuation for Business Writing
The rules are excerpted from "The Perfect Letter" published by Scott Foresman, with a link to the book.
http://www.smartbiz.com/sbs/arts/tpl4.htm

Writing Successful Business Proposals
Skills are taught at this site to prepare successful business proposals for potential customers or clients, structure of a business proposal as a series of slots into which you put persuasive information. The training also teaches methods of persuasion and effective, clear, correct writing. Grant writing is also taught at the Business Writing Center as is public relations writing and copywriting.
http://www.writingtrainers.com/center/bwc360.htm

Writers Conferences and Seminars

E-book World
Offering conferences, networking, and information on writing and publishing as well as all other business aspects of the e-book marketplace.
http://www.e-book-world.com/ebook-fr.shtml.

Newspaper Association of America
Conferences, marketing resources, circulation data, surveys, and events.
http://www.naa.org

Finding Paying Markets for Freelance Writers

Finding Writing Markets Online:
Online sources for finding the latest print markets: electronic newsstands, publication Web sites and guideline databases. Electronic newsstands help you find e-markets for writing.

http://www.NewsDirectory.com.

Writers Guideline Databases.
Online listing of writing markets and databases on marketing your writing.
www.Marketlist.com

Writers Guideline Publications
These may link you to guidelines on a publication's Web site.
www.writersdigest.com

Media Directories

To send review copies of books and freelance article queries to publications listed in media directories.

General Major Media Directories for Freelance Writers

Gebbie Press

The All-in-One Media Directory

PR Media Directory: Newspapers Radio TV Magazines:Press releases,

Faxes, e-mail, publicity, and freelance. Media directory includes TV and radio stations, daily and weekly newspapers, and consumer and trade magazines.

http://www.gebbieinc.com/

http://www.gebbieinc.com/presto1.htm

Gebbie Press:

Magazine Publishers on the Internet

An alphabetical listing of leading publishers in the United States, and links to their web sites.

http://www.gebbieinc.com/publish.htm

Electronic Media Directories

Press Flash

Distribute your Web firm's press releases to media outlets throughout the world using the services and resources provided by Press Flash. Press release writing services are also provided.

http://www.pressflash.com/

E-zine directories

E-Publications Directors Resource List

If you want to write for electronic publications, see these e-publications directories. At this site you can find out information on writing for electronic markets.

http://www.zinebook.com.

E-Zine Advice Publications Online

Contentious

This publication is the e-zine that advises and offers information for people who write or publish content on the Web. Find out where to write for other electronic magazines. Offers online options for frustrated journalists.

http://www.contentious.com/.

Ethnic Media Directories

American Minorities Media
American Minorities Media is a subsidiary of Market Place Media, the leading media placement company reaching specialized markets.
http://www.marketmedia.com/amm

Specialized Markets

MarketMedia.com
Media and promotions solutions for reaching specialized markets such as senior citizens, minorities, military, students, and others. Also media analysis is offered.
http://www.marketmedia.com/

Freelance Editorial Association
(Includes desktop publishers)
The current online *Yellow Pages,* published annually since 1997, includes listings by skills as well as a specialties index. This association published the hardcopy, *Yellow Pages*, a listing of Association members who wished to advertise their skills and specialties, between 1989 and 1999.

http://www.tiac.net/users/freelanc/YP.html

International

International Journalists' Network
If you write about overseas subjects or travel, you'll find the International Center for Journalists' online source full of training information and media directories.
http://www.ijnet.org

SAJA: South Asian Journalists Association
Writers interested in South Asian features, covering the people, businesses, and processes that impact South Asia will find excellent resources in this association and its publications.
http://www.saja.org/job.html

International Women's Writing Guild
The International Women's Writing Guild, headquartered in New York and founded in 1976, is a network for the personal and professional empowerment of women through writing.
http://www.iwwg.com

Pressbox-UK
Pressbox is the UK online press center offering press release and copywriting services providing a professional resource for news, press releases, and postings to carefully targeted audiences.
http://www.pressbox.co.uk

Associazioni ed Enti Professionali-America
List of South American, Canadian, and US writers' organizations. This site contains a fine list of writers' associations and language translation firms.
http://www.alice.it/writers/grp.wri/wgrpame.htm

Rural Press Interactive
Rural Press Interactive outlines opportunities to target specific markets throughout Australia, includes metro, regional and rural. The association brings press and Internet together with a network of publications and sites.
http://www.rpinteractive.com.au

Electronic Pages and E-Marketing for Writers

The development journal of the International Informatics Institute is called Electronic Pages. It offers at the site, articles, forums, and announcements of conferences as well as great advice on writing for the electronic market http://www.electric-pages.com/.

Tailwind.com
Responsible e-mail marketing, help for small businesses, help for the small business owner such as freelance writers.
http://www.tailwind.com/db/y.asp?hid=90&nid=1

Marketing Strategies and Techniques for Writers

101 Marketing Tips for Writers.
This site offers a list of 101 marketing tips, Cassell Success Guide, and some links for writers, such as if you "want to break into advertising, go to church." Published by Cassell Network of Writers, Cassell Communications, Inc.
http://www.bitcave.com/101tips.htm

Elaine's Marketing Suggestions for Writers.
Writers Information Network (WIN). Christian writers information network and advice. Excellent site for writers interested in writing for the Christian markets and quality Christian writing.
http://www.bluejaypub.com/win/ElaineTips.htm.

Associations

American Business Press
The American Business Press is the industry association for business-to-business information providers, including producers of magazines, CD-ROMS, Web sites, trade shows and products that build upon the printed product. The association has a staff of specialists in government affairs, marketing, communications, promotion · and finance. http://www.salesdoctors.com/directory/dircos/3103a03.htm

American Society of Business Press Editors
(ASBPE) is the professional association for full-time and freelance editors and writers employed in the business, trade, and specialty press.
http://www.asbpe.org/

American Society of Journalists and Authors.
Links on how electronic publishing allows a writer to create a parallel product line to profitably meet more needs in a different way. This site contains links and resources for the organization called American Society of Journalists and Authors and features books by members and speakers. ASJA Writer Referral Service is at (212) 398-1934 or writers@asja.org.
http://www.asja.org/index9.php

American Copy Editors Society
The society focuses on improving the quality of journalism. Writerly resources include editorial advice, job openings, discussion boards and conference updates.
http://www.copydesk.org/

The American Society of Composers, Authors and Publishers (ASCAP)
More than 80,000 composers, songwriters, lyricists and music publishers belong to this society. ASCAP protects the rights of its members by licensing and paying royalties for copyrighted works. The job board and Resource Guide to the Music Business are excellent resources for writers interested in the business of writing lyrics or song and music publishing. http://www.ascap.com/ascap.html

American Society of Journalists and Authors
This organization for professional freelance nonfiction writers whose career focus is writing offers online job resources.
http://www.asja.org

American Jewish Press Association
Founded nearly 50 years ago as an association for the English-language Jewish press in North America, today more than 150 newspapers, publications and individual journalists are members. Excellent job bank. Publishes a directory of members.
http://www.ajpa.org/

Academy Of American Poets
Provides information, events, publications, education, and professional services to people writing poetry as a profession. The Academy of American Poets offers poetry exhibits online and biographies, photographs, and selected poems.
http://www.poets.org/LIT/poet/kkochfst.htm

Writers Guild of America
Association of screenwriters and animation scriptwriters who work for union wages for the film and TV production industry. You may register scripts here, find a list of agents, WGA news, online mentor service, and research links.
http://www.wga.org/

Society for Professional Journalists
This society offers local chapters, a code of ethics in journalism, and professional membership events, contests, and awards as well as meetings covering the business of journalism to any working journalist, freelance or staff.
Maintains local and student chapters nationwide. The society offers ethics news, publications, job referrals, and continuing education seminars for journalists and grants scholarships in journalism. SPJ publishes Quill magazine, a trade journal for journalists. Maintains a site called The Electronic Journalist for online writers.
http://spj.org/

National Writers Association
Foundation partnerships, courses, publications, services for writers. Excellent site for contract reading, critiques, and help for all types of writers. National Writers Press, a leader in self-publishing of books.
http://www.nationalwriters.com/

American Society of Media Photographers,
Offers an online gallery of work done by members of this professional association for photographers. The links of this national organization includes a directory and links to members' Web pages. Useful for writers seeking a media photographer to work with them on an article or book that needs media photography work.
http://www.asmp.org/

Society of Children's Book Writers and Illustrators (SCBWI)
SCBWI is dedicated to serving those who write, illustrate, or share an interest in children's literature. The site offers conferences, regional newsletters, a bimonthly bulletin, writing and publishing links and tips, including other informational publications.
http://www.scbwi.org/

Writersclub.com
Links to clubs, socials, and partying in different cities at the Writersclub.com site.
Party weekends at the Club Media Ventures site with links to Writersclub.com.
http://www.writers.club.com/

California Writers Clubs
List of writers clubs and resources with links to seminars, training, magazines,
groups, conferences, career centers, area writers organizations, book cafes, and
directories of newspapers.
http://pw1.netcom.com/~mcrowe1/cwcsbb/resource.htm

Society for Professional Journalists
Their New Way Journalism Page is excellent.
http://www.journalism.sfsu.edu/

Society of American Business Editors and Writers
Members of the Society of American Business Editors and Writers have joined
together in the common pursuit of the highest standards of economic journalism,
through both individual and collective efforts.
http://www.sabew.org/sabew.nsf/home?OpenPage

Technical Writers Associations

Society for Technical Communication
STC is the largest professional organization serving the technical communication
profession.
http://www.stc.org/

Society for Technical Communicators
Technical writing information, grants, salary surveys, loans, and book listings.
http://www.stc-va.org

HTML Writers Guild
International association of Web Authors, tips on good Web writing, design
information and technology resources for writers of html.
http://www.hwg.org

Hypertext Writers Guild
If you write content in hypertext or want to learn, you can benefit from the resources, tips, and networks at the Hypertext Writers Guild.
http://www.mindspring.com/guild/

Computer Press Association
The Computer Press Association (CPA) was established to promote excellence in the field of computer journalism. Members include working editors, writers, producers, and freelancers who cover issues related to computers and technology.
http://www.computerpress.org/

Associations for Business or Marketing Journalists and Copywriters

American Business Press
Non-profit, global association for business-to-business information
Providers, including databases, conventions, and other media.
http://www.americanbusinesspress.com/

American Society of Business Press Editors
(ASBPE) is the professional association for full-time and freelance editors and writers employed in the business, trade, and specialty press.
http://www.asbpe.org/

Associated Business Writers of America
This site contains an excellent list of writers' associations.
http://www.poewar.com/articles/associations.htm

Association of Professional Communication Consultants
APCC creates a "professional community where communication consultants increase their knowledge, grow their businesses, and achieve high standards of professional practice." APCC's mission is to "support members as they help clients reach their goals through better communication."
http://www.apcc-online.org/

Freelance Editorial Association
Freelance Editorial Association
(Includes desktop publishers)
The current online *Yellow Pages,* published annually since 1997, includes listings by skills as well as a specialties index. This association published the hard-

copy, **Yellow Pages**, a listing of Association members who wished to advertise their skills and specialties, between 1989 and 1999.
http://www.tiac.net/users/freelanc/YP.html

Selected List Of Multimedia Publishers/Producers/Distributors
Kay E. Vandergrift has compiled an excellent list in order to facilitate easy access to contact media publishers, producers and distributors.
http://www.scils.rutgers.edu/special/kay/mediacatalog.html

Society of American Business Editors and Writers
Members of the Society of American Business Editors and Writers have joined together in the common pursuit of the highest standards of economic journalism, through both individual and collective efforts.
http://www.sabew.org/sabew.nsf/home?OpenPage

Software Publishers Association
Are you a multimedia developer or publisher? Or do you own multimedia content that you want to license? See The Software Publishers Association **Legal Guide to Multimedia**. It's a guide to the legal issues of developing, protecting, and distributing multimedia products.
http://www.awl-he.com/titles/0201409313.html

Women In Scholarly Publishing
Women in Scholarly Publishing (WiSP) is a professional organization serving the educational and professional advancement of its members. WiSP is committed to achieving equal opportunity and compensation for all those employed in the field of scholarly publishing.
http://www.wispnet.org/about.html

Writers Guild of America
Association of screenwriters and animation script writers who work for union wages for the film and TV production industry. You may register scripts here, find a list of agents, WGA news, online mentor service, and research links.
http://www.wga.org/

Truck Writers of North America
This site lists a glossary of trucking terms for writers and a list of freelance writing jobs available for writers specializing in writing about trucking and the truck

industry. Excellent freelance writing job postings listed in their job bank. TWNA is an organization of professionals who are involved in gathering, writing and reporting news and information about trucks, trucking and the trucking industry.

http://www.twna.org/job_postings.htm

Advertising/Multimedia
Association of Independent Commercial Producers
Kaufman Astoria Studios
This association specializes in photo-real visual effects. It's a job bank on site for programmers, artists, and other creative people interested in working on photorealistic projects.

http://www.telefilm-south.com/index.html

International Chain of Industrial and Technical Advertising Agencies
http://www.thevines.com

National Writers Association (NWA)
Foundation partnerships, courses, publications, services for writers. Excellent site for contract reading, critiques, and help for all types of writers. National Writers Press, a leader in self-publishing of books.

http://www.nationalwriters.com/

Academy Of Television Arts And Sciences
News, activities, committee events, publications, and awards related to the TV production, marketing, and scriptwriting industry.

http://www.emmys.tv/

Advertising Club Of New York
Strives to elevate the understanding of marketing and advertising communications by providing a common forum.

http://www.adclubny.org/index_home.shtml

Advertising Production Club of New York (APC)
Has products, manufacturers, and associations database and information at site.

http://www.arcat.com/arcatcos/cos36/arc36681.cfm

Advertising Women of New York
Holds events and has mentoring program. AWNY'S mission is to provide a forum for personal and professional growth; to serve as a catalyst for the advancement of women in the communications field; to promote and support philanthropic endeavors through the AWNY Foundation.
http://www.awny.org/

Science Writers Associations

American Medical Writers Association
For freelance and staff writers focusing on medical issues in the news, pharmaceutical copywriting, healthcare articles, health and nutrition, and related medical writing. Also see American Medical Writers Association Job Market for freelancers and full-time staff, for members.
http://www.amwa.org/about/about.html

National Association of Science Writers.
For writing, marketing, publishing, job information, and legal issues discussion of writers and journalists in all of the sciences such as pharmaceutical, life sciences, physical sciences, social sciences, and archaeology/anthropology.
http://nasw.org/

Aviation/Space Writers Association (AWA)
This professional association has publications, events, and tips for freelance and staff writers or journalists who cover the space and aviation industries.
http://brad.net/aero_outlook/other_resources/orgs.html#awa

Council of Biology Editors
Council of Biology Editors offers documentation. The 1994 CBE (Council of Biology Editors) manual, Scientific Style and Format, describes two systems of documentation in the handbook they offer in this association for editors working on biological documentation.
www.wisc.edu/writing/Handbook/DocCBE6.html

D.C. Science Writers Association
Washington, DC area science writers group for local science writers in Washington and surrounding states.
http://www.nasw.org/dcswa/

Georgia Area Science Writers Association—GASWA:
Local science writers group in the state of Georgia, USA.
http://www.nasw.org/users/GASWA/

New England Science Writers Association:
Science writers in the New England states have this organization.
http://www.umass.edu/pubaffs/nesw/

Canadian Science Writers Association
For science writers in Canada, an association offering networking and education
in science writing as well as writing tips.
http://www.interlog.com/~cswa/

Canadian Farm Writers' Federation
Founded in 1955, The Canadian Farm Writers' Federation (CFWF) serves the
common interests of agricultural journalists, editors and broadcasters as well as
those in business and government whose primary responsibility is agricultural
communications.
http://www.uoguelph.ca/Research/cfwf/

Penn State Association of Science Writers
An association for science writers in Pennsylvania.
http://nasw.org/users/cpnasw/cpnasw.htm

Society of Environmental Journalists.
The world's largest organization of journalists, students, and teachers who write
about the environment and are interested in the business of writing and selling
writing covering the environment.
http://www.sej.org/.

Indexers, Editors, Proofreaders, and Copywriters Associations

American Society of Indexers
ASI is a nonprofit educational and charitable organization, serving and dedicated
to the advancement of indexers, librarians, abstractors, editors, publishers, database producers, data searchers, product developers, technical writers, academic
professionals, researchers and readers, and others concerned with indexing of
books and periodicals.
http://www.asindexing.org/goals.shtml

The Editorial Freelancers Association

The professional resource for editorial freelancers, EFA, is a national, non-profit, professional organization of self-employed workers in publishing and communications. The Freelance Editorial Association merged with the Editorial Freelancers Association in June 2000 and is now known as EFA.

The association offers jobs listings, marketing, setting fees information, a Yellow Pages of freelancers, skills listing, and the e-publication, Freelance Editorial Association News.

http://www.the-efa.org/ or http://www.tiac.net/users/freelanc/index.html or the newsletter http://www.tiac.net/users/freelanc/Newsletter.html

Writing Help Resources with Links

Children's Book Council
Resource site for children's books with a guide to children's writing and material on forthcoming books.
http://www.cbcbooks.org

Associated Writing Programs
Offers lists of university writing programs, conferences, and resources. Publishes *The Writers Chronicle*.
http://www.awpwriter.org

Absolute Write
Writing links offered on how to write or publish novels, nonfiction, plays, poetry, and scripts.
http://www.absolutewrite.com

Writers Toolbox
Resources for fiction and nonfiction writers, screenwriters, journalists, and technical writers. Excellent resource for writing help.
http://www.geocities.com/Athens/6346

Proofreaders
List of names and addresses of freelance proofreaders, from the Editorial Freelancers Association (EFA).
http://www.tiac.net/users/freelanc/YP/proofreaders.htm

Biology Editors, Rates and Payment, Editing and Proofreading
Biology editors and proofreaders charge upwards of $35 an hour. Biology Editors Company has an excellent Web site discussing how much to charge for technical writing or proofreading and editing scientific material, or proposal development and technical writing.
http://www.biologyeditors.com/rates_and_payment.html

Marketing Associations Writers Use for Resources

Writers Market Online
Writers Market book listing publishers and their needs is now online if you subscribe to the updated market information.
http://www.writersmarket.com

Fiction Writer Online
Answers to questions about writing fiction from novelists, agent, and editor.
http://www.fictionwritermag.com

American Marketing Association
The American Marketing Association is an organization for those interested in marketing. Network with marketing professionals to get timely and factual information for business articles or read marketing research publications.
http://www.ama.org/.

Artslynx: International Writing Resources
If you want more listings of writers' associations with links, including information for poets, these are excellent resources.
http://www.artslynx.org/

Hollywood Creative Directory
Job board for the entertainment industry, directories, and places to contact.
http://www.hcdonline.com

Publishers Marketing Association
For writers thinking of self-publishing, the Publishers Marketing Association (PMA) is the largest non-profit trade association representing independent publishers of books, audio, video and CDs. Their mission is to advance independent publishing through professional development, creative marketing, and global affiliation.
http://www.pma-online.org/

The Market Research Industry
Information on what the Market Research Industry is doing, special interest for writers seeking trends and marketing behavior. Market Research. A full-service market research and consulting firm.
http://www.asiresearch.com/mri/mri.htm

Market Research Organizations
Market research conference schedules and links to other market research sites. Study the latest market trends.
http://www.wsa.com/wsa/directories/membership/MarketTrend/info.html

Center For Research In Marketing
Bridging the gap between Marketing theory and practice through rigorous and relevant research.
http://www.csom.umn.edu/CSOM/MktgCenter/MktgCenter.html

Content Exchange LLC
Content creators online list their resumes and job opportunities are listed as well. Mailing list also.
http://www.content-exchange.com

PubList.com
Reference of more than 150,000 publications and contacts for writers or those who need permissions.
http://www.publist.com

Book Marketing Update
Self-published authors may subscribe to access independent book publishers, booksellers, and self-publishing feedback.
http://www.bookmarket.com/index.html

The Slot
Style points not in most stylebooks for copy editors or those who want to be freelance copy editors.
http://www.theslot.com

Software Publishing Association
Find any software or computer book publisher or games. A good resource for writers looking for publishers.
http://www.shopforacomputer.com/software/
software_publishing_association.html

Software and Information Industry Council
Many press release articles, news and conferences on trends shaping digital content and the educational technology market. Excellent link to keep current on news and resource material, especially about protecting privacy during the evolution of the digital economy.
http://www.siia.net/

Copyright, ISBN Number, and Library of Congress Registration Information for Self-Publishing Writers and Publishers

U.S. Copyright Office.
All the information you need to know in order to learn how to copyright your writing before you market your work. A link also features information on registration of copyright procedures and instruction.
http://www.loc.gov/copyright/
http://www.loc.gov/copyright/circs/circ1.html#rp

Library of Congress
Learn how to get a Library of Congress registration number for your self-published book, pamphlet, or booklet and other services to publishers and self-publishers
http://lcweb.loc.gov/loc/infopub/

International ISBN Agency.
How to Get an ISBN Number. Does your self-published book need an ISBN number? Find out how to receive an ISBN number at this Web site.
www.isbn.spk-berlin.de/html/howtoget.htm

International Standard Book Numbers (ISBN)
The International standard numbering system for the information industry is administered by R.R. Bowker. The U.S. Agency for ISBN assignment can be contacted at: 121 Chanlon Road, New Providence, NJ 07974, Tel: 908-665-6770—Fax: 908-665-2895.
http://www.bowker.com/standards/home/

International Standard Serial Numbers

Do you write and self-publish serials or would like to publish serials written by other authors? Perhaps you need an International Standard Serials number. Serials are print or non-print publications issued in parts, usually bearing issue numbers and/or dates.

A serial is expected to continue indefinitely. Serials include magazines, newspapers, annuals (such as reports, yearbooks, and directories), journals, memoirs, proceedings, transactions of societies, and monographic series.
http://lcweb.loc.gov/issn/ and http://lcweb.loc.gov/issn/issnbro.html

Resources for Business, Technical, and Humanities Writers

Internet Resources for Business and Technical Writers
This site provides excellent resources for the business writer. Links to resources for business writers. Internet Technical Writing Course Guide and career links.
http://www.english.uiuc.edu/cws/wworkshop/ww_tech.html.

Hypertext Writer's Guide and the Research and Documentation Online List of Style Manuals and Glossary of Internet and Library Terms
Helpful resources for business writers and others who want to learn about how to write in hypertext.
http://hildegard.engl.uvic.ca/writers/resources.htm
http://www.bedfordstmartins.com/hacker/resdoc/.

Researching Humanities Links
The humanities links are useful to the writer learning the business of writing from any genre of writing business, science, art, nutrition, or your own specialty.
http://www.bedfordstmartins.com/hacker/resdoc/humanities/overview.htm

Finding Writing Jobs Online

Techwriters.com
Technical writers will find Techwriters.com the best place to look for a technical writing job, other than through membership in technical writer's organizations.
http://www.techwriters.com/.

Technical Writing Jobs
Find current technical writing jobs here, including both staff and contract job listings. Excellent site for technical writing and similar communications media jobs.
http://www.techwriters.com/placement/writer_nationwide_jobs.asp

JournalismJobs.com
This the job board for finding jobs if you're a media person. Post your resume, look at recent job listings, or receive job notification by email at:
http://www.journalismjobs.com/.

Journalism Jobs Page
The Journalism Jobs site lists current journalism jobs around the nation. It has links to other journalism job listing sites.
http://www.towson.edu/~bhalle/jjobs.html.

Sun Oasis Jobs
Good site for freelance writers, also staff journalism and tech writing jobs offered. Search by location. Updated frequently. Contains classified ads from editors.
http://www.sunoasis.com

Truck Writers of North America
  This site lists a glossary of trucking terms for writers and a list of freelance writing jobs available for writers specializing in writing about trucking and the truck industry. Excellent freelance writing job postings listed in their job bank.
  TWNA is an organization of professionals who are involved in gathering, writing and reporting news and information about trucks, trucking and the trucking industry.
http://www.twna.org/job_postings.htm

All Freelance
Links to resources, articles, and job listings for freelance writers, illustrators, designers, programmers, and other independent contractors.
http://www.allfreelance.com/

Hire Minds
Job postings, e-newsletter, message board, and gatherings in New York City for media, publishing, or creative people.
http://www.hireminds.com/

Net Read
Publishing jobs listed along with content on publishing industry employment.
www.netread.com/jobs/jobs/

Monique's Newsjobs
Monique's Newsjobs is a comprehensive list of jobs for journalists. Working journalists highly recommended this site. It's recommended by Writer's Digest as the best list for journalists around to date.
http://www.news.jobs.net

Creative Freelancers
Submit your resume and samples, or look at the help-wanted area offering freelance writing, editing, or proofreading employment.
http://www.freelancers.com

Writing Employment Center
You'll find a daily updated listing of jobs here for writers and related editorial workers.
http://poewar.com/jobs/htm

Creative Nonfiction
Creative Nonfiction is a magazine of essays and literary nonfiction that offers job opportunities on the magazine from time to time. The publication is dedicated solely to the creative nonfiction genre. It offers different themes with each publication such as diversity, what men think, what men write, and emerging women writers.
http://www.creativenonfiction.org/thejournal/opportunities.htm

Broadcast-Related Links:
Finding Radio, TV, and Film or Film School Jobs, Airchecks, and Talent

TVand radio Jobs.Com lists timely jobs and talent, including radio, TV, and film school, as well as links to real audio airchecks, available talent, and you can post an air check. You can find broadcast-related links here.
at http://tvandradiojobs.com/

All Starr Radio
An excellent site sampling what writers write about when they speak on the radio. Includes information on comedy, such as a link where you can list the weird things that happened to you.
http://www.allstarradio.com

TV and RadioJobs.com
TV andRadioJobs.com has 13,000+ Unique Visits a day. Almost half their visitors are radio management types looking for fresh talent. Available for a small fee: post your 6-minute aircheck on their streaming server for 5 months.
http://tvandradiojobs.com/.

Air Newslink Job Link for journalists
Search JobLink ads for journalists. Links to resources, publications, or interact with their search engine. Fill out their online form to narrow your job search in journalism.
http://ajr.newslink.org/joblink.html.

Reference Books/Sites for Writers

Allwords.com
Word definitions, origins, and translations. Look up works in five languages. Some audio pronunciations available, and information for crossword puzzle enthusiasts.
http://www.allwords.com

Guinness World Records
Guinness Book of Records for entertainment.
http://www.guinnessworldrecords.com

Rare Diseases Information
If you're a health or medical writer interested in writing about rare diseases and support groups or need to find more information, try this health site.
http://www.rarediseases.org

Fundraising
If you need to raise funds for a worthy cause, or to publish your own book, look at these tips on how to pan a fundraiser by an excellent Internet fundraising company.
http://www.fundraising.com

Mystery Writers

Sisters in Crime
Sisters in Crime combats discrimination against women in the mystery field, educates publishers, the public, and mystery writers and readers as to the inequalities in the treatment of female authors, and raises the awareness of their contribution to the field.
http://www.netaxs.com/~sincdv/sincnatl.htm

MysteryNet's Mystery Organizations
Mystery Network. Mystery entertainment and information for mystery fans and enthusiasts
http://www.mysterynet.com/organizations

ClueLass
Network with other mystery writers here for news, mystery releases, and look at the resource directory for mystery writers, Deadly Directory.
http://www.cluelass.com

Romance Writers Associations

Romance Writers of America
RWA is a non-profit professional/educational association of 8,400 romance writers and other industry professionals.
http://www.rwanational.com/

eHarlequin.com
Harlequin publishers runs this site for romance readers and writers. Gives writers a picture of what readers expect as it focuses on readers.
http://eharlequin.women.com/harl/

Young Writers

The Writing Corner
Writers under 18 may publish their writing on the site.
http://www.writingcorner.com

The Quill Society
Free writing club for young writers from 12 to 24 with online publishing resources, help, and forums.
http://www.quilll.net/home/index.htm

Templates for Feedback
Flashbase.com
Templates available on site to help writers track reader feedback or responses
from proofreaders or agents and editors.
http://www.flashbase.com

Writers' Unions

National Writers Union

Excellent, timely informational articles on preventing your written work from
being used without your permission electronically. Offers articles on all aspects of
prevention of abuses to writers at work, including independent writers. Job referral listings and other services as union.
http://www.nwu.org/

Communications Workers of America
This is the largest union in America of journalists, printers, publishers, telecommunications workers, broadcast workers, and others involved in communications
from writers to telephone company employees and broadcasters.
http://www3.cwa-union.org/

Articles:

Training in the Business of Writing and the Writing of Business

How to Get Publicity (Buzz Appeal) in the Media for Your Writing
(before or after publication)

Here's how to get buzz appeal, that is, achieve visibility, credibility, and respectability in the media before or after you find a publisher for your work by making
it possible for a popular media person to write about you and discuss what you
write in a feature or news article. Published in the *Internet Writing Journal.*
http://www.writerswrite.com/journal/jul99/hart1.htm

Writing Inspirational Books, Articles, Columns, or Scripts

How to write, promote, market, and publish inspirational material, also religious
and motivational works. Writing for the inspirational markets. Published in the
Internet Writing Journal.
http://www.writerswrite.com/journal/sep99/hart2.htm

What is Creative Nonfiction?

(Audio excerpts) from the magazine, *Creative Nonfiction*
Audio excerpts online on the definition and discussion of what is creative nonfiction for writers interested in writing for this genre.
http://www.creativenonfiction.org/thejournal/whatiscnf.htm

Eastgate Systems, Inc.

"The primary source for serious hypertext,"—Robert Coover, The New York Times Book Review. The role of narrative in the Web experience is a pressing concern throughout the Web world, from entertainment to e-commerce. Subscribe to electronic roundtable newsletter, E-Narrative.
http://www.eNarrative.org/1/news.html

E-Lance Economy Not Happening

Read how and why the decline in self-employment has accelerated since 1997.
http://www.asja.org/newspub/x0101b.php

Hungry Minds, Red Hat, Join to Form Press

Hungry Minds Inc, (Nasdaq: HMIN) (formerly IDG Books Worldwide) and Red Hat Inc. (Nasdaq: RHAT) announced a joint multi-title publishing agreement to produce books around Red Hat's extensive product line, including Red Hat(R) Linux.
http://www.authorlink.com/pubnews.html#redhat

Niche Marketing Via the Web

This article is a case history of interest to journalists working online or those who want to Niche Marketing Via the Web: A Case Study Creating a Parallel Electronic Publishing Line by Gordon Burgett, from the December 2000 issue of the ASJA Newsletter, is an excellent article on electronic publishing by the author of Publishing to Niche Markets, by Gordon Burgett. Find a need and fill it.
http://www.asja.org/newspub/x0012a.php

Grant Proposal Writing Instruction

How to Write a Research Grant

How to get grant guidelines and sample proposals so you can write a research grant proposal.
http://www.ialc.wsu.edu/ialc/faculty_teaching/grants/
WtngGrantProposal.html#research

How to Write an Institutional Grant

Instruction and techniques in writing great institutional grant proposals adapted from Bob Lucas's workshop.
http://www.ialc.wsu.edu/ialc/faculty_teaching/grants/
WtngGrantProposal.html#institutional

The Intensive American Language Center's site on Grant Proposal Writing

How to write proposals for grants. Methods of how to implement your idea. Article and free instruction site offered by the Intensive American Language Center of Washington State University. Excellent article on how to write grant proposals. The Intensive American Language Center's site on Grant Proposal Writing is adapted from a workshop by Bob Lucas.
http://www.ialc.wsu.edu/ialc/faculty_teaching/grants/WtngGrantProposal.html

Creative Nonfiction

This magazine offers excellent articles online or by subscription. See archived articles online specializing in creative nonfiction, including essays.
http://www.creativenonfiction.org/thejournal/articles/issue14/14contents.htm

"Traps," by Lee Martin.
Also issue #14, *Creative Nonfiction*, "What Men Think, What Men Write," contains two articles than can be read online.
http://www.creativenonfiction.org/thejournal/articles/issue14/
14martin_traps.htm

See issue #12, *Creative Nonfiction,* Emerging Women Writers II, "The Old Sort: of Connemaras & Sweet Corn," by Caroline Nesbitt.
http://www.creativenonfiction.org/thejournal/articles/issue12/12nesbitt_theoldsort.htm

Training Beginners in the Business of Writing and the Writing of Business

How to Get Publicity (Buzz Appeal) in the Media for Your Writing (before or after publication)

Here's how to get buzz appeal, that is, achieve visibility, credibility, and respectability in the media before or after you find a publisher for your work by making it possible for a popular media person to write about you and discuss what you write in a feature or news article. Published in the *Internet Writing Journal.*
http://www.writerswrite.com/journal/jul99/hart1.htm

Writing Inspirational Books, Articles, Columns, or Scripts

How to write, promote, market, and publish inspirational material, also religious and motivational works. Writing for the inspirational markets. Published in the *Internet Writing Journal.*
http://www.writerswrite.com/journal/sep99/hart2.htm

Writing Personal History

http://www.newswriting.net

Audio (MP3) and Video Files for Writers and Personal Historians

http://www.newswriting.net/writingvideos.htm

APPENDIX B

435 Video Podcasting Businesses to Start

1. Video therapist technician

2. Video Infomercial production

3. Video inventory checker

4. Video Demo tape production

5. Video international reunion service and satellite videoconferencing/video courier

6. Video public relations service

7. Employee screening service video

8. Video software talent management

9. Video dating service

10. Muckraking and underground (censored news) videos

(Cover the news that didn't make the news, exposing corporate, institutional, or government corruption through your investigative video reporting.)

11. Videotape game or video storyteller

12. Instructional videos and How To Have a Good Life Video: teach sewing, costume design, painting, cooking, remodeling, makeup, self-esteem enhance-

ment, etc. (Produce any how-to instructional or training video on whatever you know how to do really well.)

13. Video close captioning for the deaf. Or video hand sign language interpretation for the deaf.

14. Video UFO research/interviews/abductees/sightings recorded.

15. Public histories on video production.

16. Videobiographies

17. Family identification service

18. Instructional and training videos

19. Surgery and operations on video tape

20. Childbirth on video tape

21. Deathbed, last images, and last will and testament on tape

22. Weddings, parties, anniversaries, bar mitzvahs, confirmations, and life events on tape

23. Conventions and public speakers on tape

24. Trade shows, exhibits, and new technology events

25. Direct mail marketing and sales by video

26. Private Investigator search techniques on tape: how to check up on anybody.

27. Software video instruction on tape (video manuals).

28. Corporate histories and annual marketing or financial reports.

29. Editing other people's videos

30. Financial planning on video

31. Basic skills instruction on video

32. Foreign languages on video or English as a second language

33. Video advertisements

34. Videos on ethics

35. Corporate training on video

36. Healthcare professionals training tapes

37. Personality assessment questionnaire videos

38. Preschool physical exercise and fitness on video

39. Nutrition videos

40. Senior citizens networking and courses on video

41. Courses for home-based students on video

42. Videos for particular disabilities

43. Workability videos for persons entering the workforce

44. Multimedia videos using computers and video cameras

45. Games on video, including animation

46. Hospital videos for patient viewing

47. Cultural diversity videos for businesses or schools.

48. Videos for wild animal viewing (primates in sanctuaries, labs, zoos, and research centers)

49. Legal depositions on video

50. Forensic, (forensic medical videos) and crime lab photography videos for evidence technology (including accident scene diagrams, chronology of events, photos, scale models, charts, graphs, maps, accident scene diagrams, and technical illustration videos).

51. Security and surveillance/mobile surveillance

52. Pet videos or pet training for pet owners

53. Accident reconstruction videos for insurance firms

54. Home healthcare videos and home response taping

55. Corporate animation videos

56 Art show videos

57. Resumes and Non-resume Job Portfolios on video tape

58. Real estate sales videos, commercial or residential

59. Appraisal videos, property or real estate

60. Cartography videos (maps) on video (cross-country or international driving routes and sights videos).

61. Travel videos

62. Visual anthropology tapes, preservation on video of tribal and ethnic cultures around the world, or esoteric languages and customs on tape. Videos on secret, rare religous rites.

63. Cooking for kids videos, video cookbooks. Vegetarian videos.

64. Religious videos of customs and rituals preserved or church sermons, religious services on tape for homebound viewers. View a variety of religions at home. Conventional or other religions.

65. Videopals: Pen pal videos, for people who can't be there in person to chat and exchange conversation or souvenirs.

66. Prisoner-to-family correspondence on video. Also videos for the institutionalized person.

67. Virtual reality video simulation: How your home will look after it's remodeled. Or create medical or architectural models on video using virtual reality technology on video tape.

68. Virtual reality simulation video games or medical virtual reality videos for training allied health personnel.

69. Computer-assisted reporting videos.

70. Videos for foster parents, child daycare workers.

71. Video dating and marriage brokerage service

72. Video business partner matching

73. Family photos on video, genealogy videos, and family histories: video-biographies and autobiographies on tape.

74. Poetry reading on videos.

75. Greeting cards and love letters on video.

76. Close captioning and hand signing for the deaf

77. Distance teaching tapes

78. Bellydancing videos

79. Psychic predictions videos: one each month or quarterly

80. Futurist trend forecasting on video

81. Video magazine for teenagers.

88. Music videos: auditioning new composers and musicians

89. Video software talent agent

90. Mediums and channelers on video

91. University courses by video

92. Writing or art instruction videos

93. Matching services: students with scholarships or schools.

94. Baby sitters and nanny services or household managers screening videos. Choose your nanny from the monthly video of applicants.

95. Toy store video products

96. Children's interests videos

97. Air checker (record television advertisements for ad agencies and product manufacturers and their representatives that advertise on T.V.)

98. Newspaper clipping service on video and T.V. news video clipping. Produce video news releases (VNRs).

99. Video market research and audience tracking

100. Book publicist video service (Interview writers on video for their book publicists and create video book tours).

101. Talk show video library: (Record television talk show interviews for clients appearing on the show and their public relations agencies.)

102. Documentaries

103. Compilations of previously existing material

104. Personalities and Trailers for film and video producers

105. Exercise

106. How-to

107. Children and animation videos

108. Music

109. Book-based videos

110. Romance novels on video

111. Video distribution by mail

112. Video agent

113. Video foster grandparents

114. Video packager, including corporate animation

115. Licensed toy character and celebrity videos

116. Sports videos

117. Video bartending

118. Foreign TV videos

119. Video budget planner

120. Financial, stocks videos

121. Children's videos

122. History on video

123. Children's picture books on videotape.

124. Video questionnaires: Personality, psychological, and aptitude questionnaire videos.

125. Scholastic testing on video of basic or advanced skills and/or oral interview and oral exam testing.

126. Video classified advertisments/ad agency

127. Play production videos, including church and local theatrical play taping and taping pays for playwrights, students, and actors.

128. Publisher's video library

129. Video shopping coupon book

130. corporate animation and children's animation, appealing to the newest toy store video trade...animated dolls and toys.

131. Script supervisor

132. Story editor/ reader for home video scripts/plays.

133. Dramaturg (Literary Manager) with analysis on video

134. Video/Literary Agent

135. Videotherapist or Video therapist technician

136. Electronic Editor

137. Desktop Video Programner

138. Desktop Video Producer

139. Video Magazine or Newsletter

Publisher/Designer

140. Mentalist (non-supernatural), Psychic (supernatural-oriented) or reality-based UFO Investigator. Collect mentalist, remote viewer, or UFO video clips and transfer to tape, or make UFO or 'abductee' witness/speak-out videos.

141. Seminar Planner

142. Event Planner

143. Videoconferencing Designer

144. Convention Recorder

145. Publicist

146. National Organization

Startup Planner

147. Documentation Analyst

148. Electronic Translator

149. Visual Anthropology

Researcher

150. Video Indexer

151. Freelance video editor

152. Public Speaker

153. Electronic Farm Newsletter

Broadcaster

154. Technical Video Editor/Writer Freelance

155. Video script proofreader

156. Children's video book

consultant/buyer or media buyer

157. Collaborator

158. Educational video producer/Mobile Editor

159. Video and Audio Cassette Tape Agent or Software/Video Talent Manager

160. New Age Video Producer/self-enhancement

161. Artist's Event Videographer

162. Art Show Promoter/Art Video producer

163. Cruise-Line Videography Teacher

164. Instructional Video Producer/Technical Editor

165. Trainer

166. Instructional technologist

167. Executive health promotion video producer or speaker

168. Forensic Photographer

169. Photojournalist

170. Distance Teacher

171. Crafts Video

Scriptwriter/Producer (How-To)

172. Autobiography Videographer or Personal Historian/Oral Historian/ Transcriber of Oral History

173. Animator, corporate ad, or children's programming

174. Preschool exercise video producer/instructor/consultant

175. Videobiographer specializing in life story videos for older adults or corporate histories.

176. Oral historian. Videotape holocaust survivors and survivors of various disasters and wars for specialty museum libraries.

177. Video script supervisor

178. Video Greeting Card designer

179. Graphic Novel Writer (video comic books for grownups)

180. Ethnic customs and costumes or world foods Video Consultant

181. Video Food Stylist

182. Video Software designer for writers, artists, special effects

183. Interactive Multimedia Producer, Designer, or Writer for Video and computer video games

184. Video romance novels on tape: producer/writer

185. Videos for deaf, close captioned or signing

186. Adult Education Teacher of video production or video writing

187. Agent's Reader/Screener/Video producer's representative

188. Video and Book Tour Promoter

189. Travel video producer: specialty travel: for students, the disabled, seniors, teens, etc.

190. International Video Scriptwriter's Agent and Video Agent or Video Distributor International Producer's and Publisher's Representative

191. Teen video magazine or specialty news video magazine

192. Information Broker/Competitive Intelligence Researcher to the video industry

193. Software or Video Locator

194. Special effects designer or video titles creator

195. Storefront Video and Video Writer's School Director

196. Correspondence School Instructor

197. Hospital video therapist

198. Video Playwright for Children's Theatre and Schools of Performing Arts

199. Comedy Writer or standup comic video producer, suppliers of video comedy for institutionalized and hospitalized patients or prisoners.

200. Comedy Trainer/ comedy and humor training videos: train the trainer tapes.

201. Story Structure Analyst (to screenwriters/novelists)

202. Writer's Office Designer

203. Kitchen Designer and Cookbook Writer

204. Video columnist: Newspaper/Trade Journal/Specialty Newsletter

205. Video colorist

206. Personnel screener/interview in screening videos for employers.

207. Infomercial Producer/Designer/Writer

208. Autobiographer

209. Electronic (video) Advertising Copywriter

210. Cable Television Media Buyer

211. Market Researcher/Audience Analyst/for consumers of video.

212. Telecommuting Planner (for Government and Corporations) (You set up corporate and government employees to work at home with video cameras and computers linked to the government or corporate central computer

213. Videotext editor

214. Air-Checker (record commercials at home on your TV and/or radio for ad agencies)

215. Visual Anthropological data analyst/visual anthropology video library owner or maintain database clearinghouse on visual anthropology videos, video grants, and participants.

216. Medical video producer physician's television or radio network or health care scriptwriter

217. Personality Assessment Coordinator/Sales Representative and Video Producer

218. Psychological Type and Temperament Video Producer

219. Gambling How-To, game playing: how to beat the odds of gambling, card-playing and other games of chance videos.

220. Self-defense videos.

221. Modern or fad dances, skating, skateboarding, surfing videos

222. Stocks and bonds: investments

223. Psychic predictions for the year or month videos

224. Job search videos

225. Computer aided design video producer

226. Video accident reconstructionist/forensic videographer

227. Time management video producer

228. Political campaign management video producer/publicist

229. Customer support video producer/writer

230. Nurses' training video producer

231. Direct mail video copywriter

232 Exhibit and trade show event video creative director

233. Domestic violence prevention video producer/trainer

234. Video earth satellite technician

235. Video fashion show producer/including music videos.

236. Media Buyer/Audience Research

237. Market Research Video Analyst and Planner

238. Telecommuting planner for government and Corporations (You set up corporate and government employees to work at home with video cameras and personal computers linked to videoconferencing with the government, school or corporate central computers and video players/cameras.)

239. Videotext editor.

240. Air-Checker (record commercials or monitor news)

241. Visual/Video Anthropologist/producer

242. Medical Videographer

243. Physician's video/radio network producer/writer or distributor

244. Personality assessment video coordinator/personality training videos.

245. Trade show display event planner/videographer/publicist/direct mail video copywriter

246. Animation designer or writer/producer or packager and distributor of animation

247. Video and Electronic Greeting Card Designer or salesperson

248. Video apartments producer/Real Estate Advertising Copywriter/videographer

249. Video Software Reviewer/

250. Restaurant/Entertainment video trailer producer or Reviewer 251. Camcorder Buyer's Guide Writer

252. Music video producer/Lyric Song Writer's Agent/Lyric song writer/videos and portfolio videos for auditions of other song writers composing on video or Midi synthesizer video musical television producer.

253. Wedding and family videobiographies

254. Amateur producer's video sales and rental store owner/video sharing and public domain video sales and rentals. (Including mail order amateur and public domain video sales or rentals.)

255. Video mail order catalog producer/Publisher

256. Wholesale video security dealer/for video management of stores, malls, schools, offices, and homes.

257. Video producer's Retreat Owner/Renter

258. How to repair-video producer, director, packager, distributor, or writer: fish out assignments to other

video producers/writers/repair technicians.

259. Medical or legal transcription dictated on video instead of audio cassette. (Dictationist or speech recognition audio liaison. Or transcribe recordings from videoconferencing or videophones.)

260. Computer-generated video special effects and title designer for home videos.

261. Video tape editing service owner.

262. Cultural diversity videos producer

263. Direct mail video and infomercial producer/ Mail Marketing Videos and script writing/copywriting

264. Novelty videos/humor/video gag writer/

265. Gift videos/self-enhancement wholesaler

266. Video Patent Searchers

267. Create videos that develop one's tolerance for ambiguity

268. Import/Export video and interactive multimedia book buyer

269. Specialty video dating service/introduction or matching service for business partners, social dating, or matching compatible people for venture capital raising and business establishment.)

270. Pet matchmaking videos for mating certain lines of dogs, cats, horses, birds, foul, fish, game animals, rare zoo animals, endangered species animals, or a variety of species for land or sea animal theme parks. Or match farm animals for breeding by their DNA lines.

271. Video producer's and writer's independent or freelance Job Information video clearinghouse

272. 900 Video information Telephone Line

273. Testing Service/interactive video response testing

274. Video Production Grants Writer/Government and Technical Contract Bids or Educational video production.

275. Videos for matching students with Scholarships, fellowships, grants and residencies: video locator service

276. Land or financial video locating

277. Video Scriptwriter

278. Interactive Multimedia Scriptwriter or producer

279. Carpet sculpture videos—insert woven logo design into carpet for corporate client and design motto and logo.)

280. Virtual reality entertainment, amusement park, or game video producer

281. Video fund raiser

282. Trade show demonstration exhibit designer/producer

283. Video career/employment counselor/consultant

284. Video production business plan writer for new video businesses applying for financing

285. Video grants proposal writer

286. Toy video producer

287. Gag video producer/writer

288. Idea Generator/Motivator/Inspirational Speaker/Writer video producer

289. Military video producer.

290. Religious producer: sermons on video for home-based religious services or events

291. Ethnic Cookbook videos

292. Playology or Playography and cruise ship or long-term care activity specialist training video producer

293. Animal care videos.

294. Travel videographer

295. Women's studies video producer

296. Video advertising researcher

297. Media buyer

298. Cooking videos or catering instruction

299. Booklet, workbook, and pamphlet publisher to accompany videos.

300. Teen magazine or music video producer

301. Gift videos for special holidays and occasions.

302. Video comparison shopping research

303. Niche video distributor

304. Film festival videos/ video monitor reporter/representative

305. Underwater cave archaeology videos: fossil hunting on tape

306. Professional video finder

307. Selling videos and video-related information from around the world in many languages.

308. Motivational/New Age video and pamphlet production

309. Freelance video advertising copywriter

310. Restaurant review videos

311. Book and software review videos

312. Paid volunteer video trainer

313. Nursing continuing education videos.

314. Mobile nursery school exercise program video designer

315. Poet resident in the city schools with videos.

316. Art as virtual reality on video

317. Video direct mail marketing copywriter

318. Promotional video producer

319. Hypnosis videos, or past life regressions and future life progressions tapes

320. Adult survivor of child abuse therapy videos.

321. Industrial training videos.

322. Corporate training on personality differences in the workplace video productions.

323. American Sign Language Videos for the deaf or to train the hearing to work with deaf employees.

324. Video press and media kit designer

325. Videos to engage latchkey kids in learning as fun activities

326. Science for children or adults

327. True ghost stories recorded in audio, video, or written as a book of collected stories from around the world or nation

328. True confessions on video

329. Video shopping direct mail marketing

330. Video sights and sounds to quiet crying infants

331. Children's bedtime calming stories and music on video

332. Videos for store and exhibit hall product demonstrations

333. Hard to find courses on video.

334. Interior decorating on video, or home remodeling techniques

335. Art instruction videos

336. Wholesaling by video or videoconference

337. Seminar promotion videos

338. Distance teaching

339. Homebirth instruction, preparation and supplies, including LaMaze or similar type birthing instruction and exercises

340. Infant care for new parents or babysitters

341. Nanny training videos

342. First aid and/or home remedies videos

344. Women's opportunity week videos for networking

345. Penpals on video

346. I.Q. Testing

347. Puzzles, riddles, and word games on video.

348. Math quizzes on video

349. Critical thinking videos.

350. Quizzes and aptitude tests on video.

351. Personality testing

352. Metaphysical videos

342. Media Interface Liaison

343. Procedure writer for video producers

344. Instructional technology producer/writer

345. Post Production video editor

346. Virtual reality producer

347. Interactive multimedia videographer

348. Technical video producer/writer

349. Videotape production coordinator

350. Video Informationist or Book Packager/Package Salable Book Proposals for Publishers and Agents

351. Software video interface producer/writer

352. Computer software instruction video producer

353. Micrographics designer

354. Video market trend forecaster

355. Mentoring videos for trainees:Retirees mentoring recent graduates

356. Videopals: penpals via video: children and older people

357. Beautiful images videos: scenes to lower your blood pressure

358. How women express anger and its effect on their health.

359. Aerospace videos

360. Architectural videos.

361. Art performance videos.

362. Assistive technology videos.

363. Automotive and mechanical videos.

364. Biotechnical and biomedicine videos.

365. Business mentorship videos.

366. Computer graphics instruction videos.

367. Conference sponsorship videoconferencing or video.

368. Design prototyping videos.

369. Design visualization or hypnotherapy with design visuals.

370. Educational videos.

371. Entertainment and standup comics.

372. Ice skating or dance on ice videos or instruction.

373. Health and safety or occupational safety videos.

374. Ergonomics and office furniture for health videos.

375. Human summarized pointors videos.

376. Managing anger videos/dealing with anger/research.

377. Gender differences and potential studies.

378. Industrial robotics instructional videos.

379. Marketing and promotions instruction on video.

380. Mechanical techniques on video.

381. Medical videos and family health/home pharmacy information.

382. First aid videos and CPR: Preventing choking on food, etc.

383. Military videos or historical military preservation.

384. Multimedia videos.

385. Museums of the world and museum science.

386. Evolution of homo-sapiens videos: paleoanthropology

387. Self-publishing video: instructional/promotional

388. Virtual reality simulation on home video.

389. Sounds, sights, and music for relaxation.

390. Systems modeling on video.

391. Teleconferencing/videoconferencing for causes.

392. Telepresence on video: all about telepresence/virtual reality.

393. Telerobotics information on video.

394. Corporate training and graphic presentations on video.

395. Visualization for health improvement videos.

396. Funeral eulogies for pets: videos on a variety of species.

397. Film producer's location scout/finder videos.

398. Handwriting analysis on video.

399. Military transition to civilian adjustment/job hunting.

400. Childrens' museums on video.

401. Mail order swap meets on video.

402. Video script breakdown and budget analysis for producers.

403. Video costume design.

404. Child passenger safety videos.

405. Video logo design.

406. Trade and bartering exchange videos.

407. Medical terminology instruction/training transcriptionists.

408. Review for college entrance exams on video.

409. Course outlines on video for college and high-school students.

410. How to write a romance novel instruction on video.

411. Nutrition and food information for specific health problems.

412. Prenuptial agreements on video.

413. Last will and testament and legal documents on video.

414. Preparation for marriage videos.

415. Preparation and going through divorce crisis videos.

416. Furnishing your first apartment videos.

417. Videos to help rebellious teenagers get involved with community service.

418. Weight loss information videos.

419. Poetry and poetry therapy/bibliotherapy on video.

420. How to write the perfect letter/consumer complaint letters, love letters, business letters, or letters for verbal assertiveness. Learn to stand up for yourself by letter.

421. Great female and/or minority doctors/lawyers in history.

422. Great female and/or minority scientists in history.

423. Headline histories on video.

424. Understanding a variety of diseases on video.

425. Locating the best: A video survey of the best companies to work for (for men or women), or the best cities to live in.

426. World religions or philosophies explained on video.

427. American citizenship preparation for immigrants.

428. Consumer's research guides for quality purchases on video.

429. Protecting seniors against fraud and con-artists videos.

430. Choosing the right pet, behavior modification, and/or pet training/pet care, pet massage techniques, and product analysis videos

431. Pod Casting Informational MP3 Audio or Streaming Video Files or Courses Online

432. Show People How to Cut Expenses by Making Their Own Cleaning Products, Safer Pesticides, Home Repair Techniques, Clothing, Shelter, or Foods Online, on disks, or in print

433. Share through your video podcasts, information for consumers on how to buy overstocked items, shelf-pulls, and wholesale items of higher quality for less money than marked-up retail buying

434. Tax Preparation Instructional video podcasts

435. Grant Proposal Writing, Fundraising, and Research video podcasts

Appendix C

List of Published Paperback Books Written by Anne Hart. Click on underlined link to reach publisher's Web site and read each book's description.

1. <u>Predictive Medicine for Rookies: Consumer Watchdogs, Reviews, & Genetics Testing Firms Online</u>

ISBN: 0-595-35146-8

2. <u>Popular Health & Medical Writing for Magazines: How to Turn Current Research & Trends into Salable Feature Articles</u>

ISBN: 0-595-35178-6

3. <u>Writing 45-Minute One-Act Plays, Skits, Monologues, & Animation Scripts for Drama Workshops</u>: Adapting Current Events, Social Issues, Life Stories, News & Histories

ISBN: 0-595-34597-2

4. <u>Cutting Expenses and Getting More for Less</u>: 41+ Ways to Earn an Income from Opportune Living

ISBN: 0-595-34772-X

5. How to Interpret Family History and Ancestry DNA Test Results for Beginners: The Geography and History of Your Relatives

ISBN: 0-595-31684-0

6. Cover Letters, Follow-Ups, and Book Proposals: Samples with Templates

ISBN: 0-595-31663-8

7. Writer's Guide to Book Proposals: Templates, Query Letters, & Free Media Publicity

ISBN: 0-595-31673-5

8. Search Your Middle Eastern and European Genealogy: In the Former Ottoman Empire's Records and Online

ISBN: 0-595-31811-8

9. Ancient and Medieval Teenage Diaries: Writing, Righting, and Riding for Righteousness

ISBN: 0-595-32009-0

10. Is Radical Liberalism or Extreme Conservatism a Character Disorder, Mental Disease, or Publicity Campaign?—A Novel of Intrigue—

ISBN: 0-595-31751-0

11. How to Write Plays, Monologues, and Skits from Life Stories, Social Issues, and Current Events—for all Ages.

ISBN: 0-595-31866-5

12. How to Make Money Organizing Information

ISBN: 0-595-23695-2

13. How To Stop Elderly Abuse: A Prevention Guidebook

ISBN: 0-595-23550-6

14. <u>How to Make Money Teaching Online With Your Camcorder and PC</u>: 25 Practical and Creative How-To Start-Ups To Teach Online

ISBN: 0-595-22123-8

15. <u>A Private Eye Called Mama Africa</u>: What's an Egyptian Jewish Female Psycho-Sleuth Doing Fighting Hate Crimes in California?

ISBN: 0-595-18940-7

16. <u>The Freelance Writer's E-Publishing Guidebook</u>: 25+ E-Publishing Home-based Online Writing Businesses to Start for Freelancers

ISBN: 0-595-18952-0

17. <u>The Courage to Be Jewish and the Wife of an Arab Sheik</u>: What's a Jewish Girl from Brooklyn Doing Living as a Bedouin?

ISBN: 0-595-18790-0

18. <u>The Year My Whole Country Turned Jewish</u>: A Time-Travel Adventure Novel in Medieval Khazaria

ISBN: 0-75967-251-2

19. The Day My Whole Country Turned Jewish: The Silk Road Kids

ISBN: 0-7596-6380-7

20. <u>Four Astronauts and a Kitten</u>: A Mother and Daughter Astronaut Team, the Teen Twin Sons, and Patches, the Kitten: The Intergalactic Friendship Club

ISBN: 0-595-19202-5

21. <u>The Writer's Bible</u>: Digital and Print Media: Skills, Promotion, and Marketing for Novelists, Playwrights, and Script Writers. Writing Entertainment Content for the New and Print Media.

ISBN: 0-595-19305-6

22. New Afghanistan's TV Anchorwoman: A novel of mystery set in the New Afghanistan

ISBN: 0-595-21557-2

23. Tools for Mystery Writers: Writing Suspense Using Hidden Personality Traits

ISBN: 0-595-21747-8

24. The Khazars Will Rise Again!: Mystery Tales of the Khazars

ISBN: 0-595-21830-X

25. Murder in the Women's Studies Department: A Professor Sleuth Novel of Mystery

ISBN: 0-595-21859-8

26. Make Money With Your Camcorder and PC: 25+ Businesses: Make Money With Your Camcorder and Your Personal Computer by Linking Them.

ISBN: 0-595-21864-4

27. Writing What People Buy: 101+ Projects That Get Results

ISBN: 0-595-21936-5

28. Anne Joan Levine, Private Eye: Internal adventure through first-person mystery writer's diary novels

ISBN: 0-595-21860-1

29. Verbal Intercourse: A Darkly Humorous Novel of Interpersonal Couples and Family Communication

ISBN: 0-595-21946-2

30. The Date Who Unleashed Hell: If You Love Me, Why Do You Humiliate Me? "The Date" Mystery Fiction

ISBN: 0-595-21982-9

31. <u>Cleopatra's Daughter</u>: Global Intercourse

ISBN: 0-595-22021-5

32. <u>Cyber Snoop Nation</u>: The Adventures Of Littanie Webster, Sixteen-Year-Old Genius Private Eye On Internet Radio

ISBN: 0-595-22033-9

33. <u>Counseling Anarchists</u>: We All Marry Our Mirrors—Someone Who Reflects How We Feel About Ourselves. Folding Inside Ourselves: A Novel of Mystery

ISBN: 0-595-22054-1

34. <u>Sacramento Latina</u>: When the One Universal We Have In Common Divides Us

ISBN: 0-595-22061-4

35. <u>Astronauts and Their Cats</u>: At night, the space station is cat-shadow dark

ISBN: 0-595-22330-3

36. <u>How Two Yellow Labs</u> Saved the Space Program: When Smart Dogs Shape Shift in Space

ISBN: 0-595-23181-0

37. <u>The DNA Detectives</u>: Working Against Time

ISBN: 0-595-25339-3

38. <u>How to Interpret Your DNA Test Results</u> For Family History & Ancestry: Scientists Speak Out on Genealogy Joining Genetics

ISBN: 0-595-26334-8

39. <u>Roman Justice</u>: SPQR: Too Roman To Handle

ISBN: 0-595-27282-7

40. <u>How to Make Money Selling Facts</u>: to Non-Traditional Markets

ISBN: 0-595-27842-6

41. <u>Tracing Your Jewish DNA</u> For Family History & Ancestry: Merging a Mosaic of Communities

ISBN: 0-595-28127-3

42. <u>The Beginner's Guide</u> to Interpreting Ethnic DNA Origins for Family History: How Ashkenazi, Sephardi, Mizrahi & Europeans Are Related to Everyone Else

ISBN: 0-595-28306-3

43. <u>Nutritional Genomics</u>—A Consumer's Guide to How Your Genes and Ancestry Respond to Food: Tailoring What You Eat to Your DNA

ISBN: 0-595-29067-1

44. <u>How to Safely Tailor Your Food, Medicines, & Cosmetics to Your Genes</u>: A Consumer's Guide to Genetic Testing Kits from Ancestry to Nourishment

ISBN: 0-595-29403-0

45. <u>One Day Some Schlemiel Will Marry Me</u>, Pay the Bills, and Hug Me.: Parents & Children Kvetch on Arab & Jewish Intermarriage

ISBN: 0-595-29826-5

46. <u>Find Your Personal Adam And Eve</u>: Make DNA-Driven Genealogy Time Capsules

ISBN: 0-595-30633-0

47. <u>Creative Genealogy Projects</u>: Writing Salable Life Stories

ISBN: 0-595-31305-1

48. <u>Power Dating Games</u>: What's Important to Know About the Person You'll Marry

ISBN: 0-595-19186-X

49. <u>Dramatizing 17th Century Family History of Deacon Stephen Hart & Other Early New England Settlers</u>: How to Write Historical Plays, Skits, Biographies, Novels, Stories, or Monologues from Genealogy Records, Social Issues, & Current Events for All Ages

ISBN: 0-595-34345-7

50. <u>Problem-Solving and Cat Tales for the Holidays</u>: Historical—Time-Travel—Adventure

ISBN: 0-595-32692-7

51. <u>801 Action Verbs for Communicators:</u> Position Yourself First with Action Verbs for Journalists, Speakers, Educators, Students, Resume-Writers, Editors & Travelers

ISBN: 0-595-31911-4

52. <u>Writing 7-Minute Inspirational Life Experience Vignettes</u>: Create and Link 1,500-Word True Stories

ISBN: 0-595-32237-9

53. <u>Large Print Crossword Puzzles for Memory Enhancement</u> : Neuron-Growing Stimulation for the Age-Wise Brain

ISBN: 0-595-35663-X

54. <u>Tracing Your Baltic</u>, Scandinavian, Eastern European, & Middle Eastern Ancestry Online: Finnish, Swedish, Norwegian, Danish, Icelandic, Estonian, Latvian, Polish, Lithuanian, Greek, Macedonian, Bulgarian, Armenian, Hungarian, Eastern European & Middle Eastern Genealogy (All Faiths)

ISBN: 0-595-35773-3

55. <u>32 Podcasting & Other Businesses to Open Showing People How to Cut Expenses</u>: Get Higher Quality for Less Money

ISBN: 0-595-36083-1

56. <u>Middle Eastern Honor Killings in the USA</u>: (A Thriller)

ISBN: 0-595-36066-1

57. <u>Infant Gender Selection & Personalized Medicine</u>: Consumer's Guide

ISBN: 0-595-36539-6

58. <u>Writing, Financing, & Producing Documentaries</u>: Creating Salable Reality Video

ISBN: 0-595-36633-3

59. <u>How to Turn Poems, Lyrics, & Folklore into Salable Children's Books</u>: Using Humor or Proverbs

ISBN: 0-595-36735-6

60. <u>Job Coach-Life Coach-Executive Coach-Letter & Resume-Writing Service</u>:

ISBN: 0-595-37100-0

61. <u>Diet Fads, Careers, & Controversies in Nutrition Journalism</u>: How to Organize Term Papers, News, or Debates

ISBN: 0-595-37823-4

62. <u>Where to Find Your Arab-American or Jewish Genealogy Records</u>: Also: Mediterranean, Assyrian, Iranian, Greek & Armenian

ISBN: 0-595-37325-9

63. <u>Video Podcasting Careers & Businesses to Start</u>: Step-by-Step Guide for Home-Grown Broadcasters

ISBN-10: 0-595-37882-X

To Order Call 1-800 AUTHORS

About the Author

Anne Hart is the author of 64+ published paperback books, a member of the American Society of Journalists and Authors, Mensa, and the International Documentary Association. She holds a graduate degree and writes independently for numerous national magazines. Hart researches trends that help others share information for wiser choices.

Her Web sites are at:
http://www.newswriting.net
http://www.newswriting.net/id1.htm
http://www.newswriting.net/writingvideos.htm and
http://annehart.tripod.com

Index

W

978-0-595-37882-1
0-595-37882-X